DATE DUE			

Teaching Them to Read

Teaching Them to Read

Fifth Edition

Dolores Durkin

University of Illinois at Urbana-Champaign

Allyn and Bacon

Boston   London   Sydney   Toronto

Series Editor: Sean W. Wakely
Manufacturing Buyer: Bill Alberti
Text Designer: Denise Hoffman, Glenview Studios
Editorial-Production Service: Grace Sheldrick, Wordsworth Associates
Cover Administrator: Linda Dickinson
Cover Designer: Susan Slovinsky

Library of Congress Cataloging-in-Publication Data

Durkin, Dolores.
    Teaching them to read.

    Bibliography: p.
    Includes index.
    1. Reading.   I. Title.
LB1050.D84   1988   372.4'1   88–19259
ISBN 0–205–11706–6

Printed in the United States of America
10 9 8 7 6 5 4 3 2 1   93 92 91 90 89 88

To Gene

Brief Contents

Contents

Preface

The preparation of this fifth edition of *Teaching Them to Read* was affected in obvious ways by our increased understanding of the reading process. As early as the Introduction, which is a highly abbreviated course in how-to-read informational material, the effects are apparent. The effects are equally clear in Chapter 1, in which individuals reading the chapter are encouraged to become consciously involved not only in comprehending but also in analyzing what they do and use in order to comprehend.

Because the intended audience for *Teaching Them to Read*, fifth edition, includes teachers and prospective teachers, Chapter 1 and all the other chapters discuss reading in a nontechnical way that still takes into account recent important research. Many chapters also consider common classroom practices so that they can be examined in light of the comprehension process. With that illumination, some typical uses of the time allocated to reading instruction are questioned. Whenever this seems necessary to do, replacements for what is criticized are described. This pattern is found as early as Chapter 2, in which the all-too-familiar routine known as "round robin reading" is critiqued. Chapter 2 deals with "Silent or Oral Reading?" because this is one of the general questions for which teachers need answers. Other broadly based questions are dealt with in Chapter 3, entitled "Reading Instruction." Together, Chapters 1, 2, and 3 provide a framework for the very specific treatment of instruction that is at the core of subsequent chapters.

The specific content of Chapters 4 and 5 reflects that it is now common to initiate reading instruction in kindergarten, or earlier. Recognizing that success at the beginning is *uniquely* important, the two chapters describe instructional programs that are grounded in the belief that what is done with reading at the start should ease—not push—children into reading in ways that foster not only achievement but also a love of reading. It is within this context that emergent literacy is discussed.

Even though comprehension requires much more than a substantial reading vocabulary, Chapters 6 through 10 deal with ways for helping students learn words. Chapter 6, "Whole Word Methodology," shows how to get reading vocabularies started and, further, what to do to help students with irregularly spelled words, such as *two, eye, aisle,* and *colonel.* The next four chapters reflect the need for students to be able to learn words on their own. Because it is the cueing system of written English that allows for this independence, Chapters 7 through 10 cover instruction for contextual, graphophonic, and structural cues. The chapter about word structure, Chapter 10, also deals with word meanings, because knowledge about prefixes and suffixes helps with the meaning of derived and inflected words. How teachers can expand the number of words whose meanings are known is the sole concern of Chapter 11, "Vocabulary Knowledge."

Although interest in comprehension permeates the whole of *Teaching Them to Read*, fifth edition, Chapter 12 starts a three-chapter coverage of that topic. Chapter 12 concentrates on the nature of comprehension instruction, Chapter 13 on what can be done to help students understand stories, and Chapter 14 on ways to help students learn how to acquire information from expository text. As is true of all other chapters that deal with instruction, Chapters 12, 13, and 14 include sample lessons described in a variety of formats. The same chapters recognize the importance of practice by providing suggestions for all topics covered.

The newer conceptions of what is involved in comprehending have fostered comparisons between the reading and the writing processes. Chapter 15, therefore, deals with the comparison and, in particular, suggests how writing can be used to help with reading.

The two final chapters cover decisions that teachers make about instruction and classroom organization. Chapter 16 deals with "Assessing Instructional Needs," and Chapter 17 concludes *Teaching Them to Read*, fifth edition, with a consideration of "Organizing for Instructional Needs."

Because the vast majority of persons who make decisions in kindergarten and elementary school classrooms are women, feminine pronouns are used in *Teaching Them to Read*, fifth edition, whenever references are made to teachers. The exceptions are cases in which a specific teacher was a man. To avoid ambiguity, masculine pronouns are used to refer to children, again with the exception of times when a specific girl is the referent.

If *Teaching Them to Read*, fifth edition, adds even a little to an understanding of how to teach reading and if, in addition, it does this in a somewhat interesting way, the book's two goals will have been realized.

Dolores Durkin

Introduction _____

Like other textbooks, *Teaching Them to Read*, fifth edition, is made up of *expository* material, since its purpose is to inform. The book's more specific purpose is to provide information about reading instruction from kindergarten through the elementary grades that is sufficiently clear and specific that it will be helpful to anyone who is, or will be, teaching reading.

STUDY GUIDELINES

To make *Teaching Them to Read*, fifth edition, maximally comprehensible, certain procedures were followed in its preparation. To begin, each chapter starts with a Preview and concludes with a Summary, both of which give an overview of the content. When studying a chapter, you are urged to read those parts first, because keeping the big picture in mind will help you not only understand the important details but also retain them longer.

You will also find an outline facing each Preview. Examining the headings and subheadings in the outline—again, before you start a chapter—will identify the parts of the chapter as well as how the parts fit together. Knowing ahead of time the organization or structure of a chapter also facilitates both comprehension and recall.

As is true of the Introduction you are now reading, certain terms in the chapters are in italic print. Use the special type as a signal to make sure you understand the term, which is always directly or indirectly explained. (Based on your reading of this Introduction, the meaning of "expository text" should be clear. If it is not, it is time to reread the very first sentence.) Other parts of chapters meriting careful attention are reproductions of instructional materials, which are generally supplemented with commentary. Take the time to examine both before proceeding with a chapter.

The samples of instructional materials are one means used to produce a book that offers specific help. Other means are numerous descriptions of actual classrooms covering a wide range of grade levels. What teachers and students in these rooms were heard to say or seen to do are used to illustrate or support something said in a chapter. Adding even further to the specificity of the content are descriptions of lessons presented in various formats. Because teachers are always looking for practice that is productive and also sufficiently interesting to maintain students' attention, every chapter that deals with instruction includes descriptions of practice. In some instances, what is offered for practice can be used as written. At other times, a suggestion will have to be changed and adapted for particular students.

Also at the end of every chapter is a Review section in which, with questions and requests, the most important content is highlighted. At times, questions also bring out practical implications of the content. Skimming the Review—again, before a chapter is begun—should keep you from wandering through it aimlessly, not knowing what to attend to or what is important to remember.

SUMMARY

"Learning How to Learn from Expository Text" is one possible title for this Introduction. Guidelines offered for maximizing the information you acquire from *Teaching Them to Read* include the following:

1. Before a chapter is begun, read the Preview and Summary. The purpose of this reading is to get a sense of the overall content.
2. What the parts of the content are, as well as how the parts are interrelated, can be gleaned by examining the outline of a chapter.
3. One further step before starting a chapter is to read the Review section in order to identify some of the most important content.
4. Key terms in a chapter are in italics. Your ability to define these terms, coupled with your ability to summarize the content of each part of a chapter, are signs of adequate comprehension. If the definitions or the summaries do not come readily to mind, remedial action in the form of rereading may be necessary.

A FINAL REMINDER

Even though not all of you have taught reading, all *have* learned to be readers in the settings of a number of classrooms. Therefore, compare what you know based on those experiences with what a chapter says about a given topic. Again, the comparisons should facilitate comprehension and retention, since new learnings are acquired most easily when they relate in some way to what is already known or has been experienced.

All this is to say that successful comprehenders are anything but passive individuals. Instead, they make their way through a piece of text consciously guided by preestablished purposes that become goals to be attained with the reading.

Teaching Them to Read

Part I

Background Information

Each of the three chapters that comprise the first part of Teaching Them to Read *is intended to provide background information for the study of subsequent chapters. Because early information about the nature of the reading process ought to be helpful, that topic is considered in the first chapter. Chapter 1 discusses reading in a nontechnical way that still takes into account recent and important research about this complex, highly useful process.*

Chapter 2 continues the discussion of reading by looking at it in relation to the two modes in which the processing of text can occur: silently and orally. The second chapter, entitled "Silent or Oral Reading?," should clarify not only the circumstances in which each mode is appropriate but also those times when a combination of the two is desirable or, as the case may be, undesirable. Chapter 2 thus shows the need for teachers to be introspective about how they use their time as well as the time of their students.

Having focused on reading itself in Chapters 1 and 2, the book moves on to consider reading instruction. Although such instruction is the concern of the whole of Teaching Them to Read, a separate discussion of the features of instruction that either facilitate or impede the attainment of objectives should be helpful. Chapter 3 discusses these features; other chapters then complement it with descriptions of specific lessons designed to realize the numerous objectives that an instructional program must achieve.

As you now prepare to start Chapter 1, keep in mind the guidelines for learning from expository text that were presented in the Introduction. As a start, use the Preview and Summary to orient yourself to Chapter 1; then examine the outline to see how its pieces fit together.

Chapter 1

The Reading
Process

PREVIEW

Traditionally, the opening chapter in reading methodology textbooks starts with a definition of *reading*. Instead of adhering to tradition, the initial chapter in this book starts with an attempt to get you actively involved with the reading process so you will become more consciously aware of its nature. Afterward, definitions of reading are offered because, by then, they should be meaningful.

Even before you finish Chapter 1, it should be clear that *reading* and *comprehending* are synonymous terms. Before finishing the chapter, you should also understand why it is possible for a student to know all the words on a page and still have problems with comprehension.

As you go through this first chapter, try to keep the following questions in mind:

1. What am I learning about reading that I did not know before?
2. Am I finding any unexpected statements about reading?
3. Based on what I myself have experienced as a reader, do I disagree with anything in the chapter?

Keeping in mind such concerns should minimize the possibility of your reading Chapter 1 without a purpose. It will also permit you to *monitor* your own comprehension, as you can now ask, How am I doing insofar as those questions are concerned? Later, when Chapter 14 deals with content subject textbooks, *comprehension monitoring* will be cited as something teachers need to foster in students' reading habits, especially with expository text. If you now develop the habit of monitoring your own comprehension, helping students do the same will come naturally.

Far removed in time from their own efforts to acquire reading ability, adults are not in the best position to appreciate all that is necessary for comprehending even a simple piece of text. Because reading for such individuals is usually a taken-for-granted, unexamined behavior, most adults are not likely to think very much about what they have to do and know to be a reader. This suggests that anyone who is, or will be, responsible for teaching reading needs to make an effort to become consciously aware of the requirements of comprehension. Such conscious knowledge is important, because it helps identify what has to be done to help students either begin to read or add to the abilities they already possess. Conscious awareness of what is involved in comprehending also helps teachers establish correct priorities for instructional programs.

EXPERIENCING COMPREHENSION

With these comments in the background, it seems entirely fitting to start a textbook whose purpose is to describe reading instruction with an effort to get its readers actively and consciously involved with comprehending. To do that, I am going to ask you to draw a picture (in color) that portrays the content of the following sentence:

> The man is digging a hole for the tree.

Please draw the picture now even if, like me, you lack artistic ability and must use stick figures along with explanations of what it is that you draw. (As an alternative, list everything in the mental image evoked by the sentence.)

On the assumption that you have completed the picture or made your list, let me tell you about my picture.

To begin, I have one man in the picture dressed in work clothes (blue shirt, jeans, and high, heavy shoes). He is in the backyard of a home. The yard is covered with grass and surrounded by a fence. Standing on one foot, the man has his other foot on the top of a spade as he pushes down into the ground to remove dirt in order to make a hole. Since part of the hole has already been dug, a pile of dirt is close to the edge of the hole. Lying on the grass and near the hole, too, is a small tree whose roots are wrapped in burlap. The sun is shining with only a few clouds in the blue sky.

Let me continue by explaining why the one-sentence text suggested the picture just described.

One male figure is present because of the word *man* in the sentence. I have the figure dressed in work clothes not because the text described his clothing but because I know from observation that men who are digging holes do not usually wear a suit and tie, or even good sports clothes. Although the sentence says nothing about a spade, I put one in the man's hands because it is unlikely he is digging with his hands since the hole has to be large enough to accommodate a tree. Admittedly, the man might not be using a spade but, based on my knowledge of the activity described by the words *digging for a tree,* some kind of an instrument or a machine should be in the picture. I have the man actively working on an unfinished hole because of the words *is digging.* Although my picture could have omitted the tree, I included it and placed it close to the hole because, again, experience tells me the man is likely to want the tree to be nearby once the hole is dug. Because I see trees with roots wrapped in burlap whenever I go to a nursery, I added that detail. The setting for the digging could vary, as trees are planted in a wide variety of places. It is possible that I thought of a backyard immediately because trees will soon be planted in my own yard, which has both grass and a fence. Finally, I made the day sunny and dry because my knowledge informs me that the planting of trees does not usually occur on cold or wet days.

REQUIREMENTS FOR COMPREHENDING

In all probability, a comparison of the content of your picture with that in mine will support the following conclusions about the reading process.

1. Comprehending calls for the ability to identify an author's words and to understand their meanings in a given context. In the case of the requested picture, this requirement is verified by the need to identify and understand the words *man, is digging, hole,* and *for the tree.* Knowing those words and understanding them in the order in which they occur results in a *literal comprehension* of the sentence.
2. Comprehending also depends on the ability to go beyond an author's words by inferring what they imply. (Authors imply whereas readers infer.) The ability to use the author's words to add information results in *text-based inferential comprehension.* With the text about the tree, the word *digging* implied that the digger was likely to be wearing a certain type of clothing and, further, that he was using an instrument. The fact that the hole is for a tree (rather than for flower seeds, for example) suggests something about the size of the hole.
3. Commonly, comprehending also requires readers to use what they know that is relevant in order to add more to the message than an author's words communicate (1, 3). The use of relevant information results in *knowledge-based inferential comprehension.* In my picture of the man digging, knowledge-based inferences accounted for such details as the backyard and the burlap on the roots of the tree.

The analysis of as little as the one-sentence text about digging should help you understand why the commercially produced material shown in Figure 1.1 elicited the comments found on the page facing Figure 1.1. (Please read the commentary now.) The analysis of the single sentence about dig-

Figure 1.1 Sources of Answers

The unprecedented number of studies of reading comprehension that began to appear in the 1970s led to widespread interest not only in the comprehension process but also in ways to teach students how to comprehend (2, 4, 5, 6, 7, 8, 9, 10).

Predictably, commercial materials bearing titles related to comprehension soon became available. Although many claimed to describe procedures for teaching students how to become more successful comprehenders, the majority of the suggestions pertained to assessment.

Figure 1.1 reproduces a page from a series of workbooks entitled *Lessons in Reading Comprehension*. The page is from the workbook said to be for grade three. Even though most of the material in this series is for assessing comprehension, the purpose of some pages—for instance, the one displayed in Figure 1.1—is not apparent.

Based on what has been said in Chapter 1 thus far, you should understand why, instead of doing what is on this workbook page, students will profit much more from instruction that clarifies the three sources available to readers for answering questions: (a) an author's words, (b) implications that derive from those words, and (c) implications that derive from the reader's own knowledge that relates to the content of the text (11). Having students draw pictures of mental images evoked by brief samples of text can figure in some of this instruction.

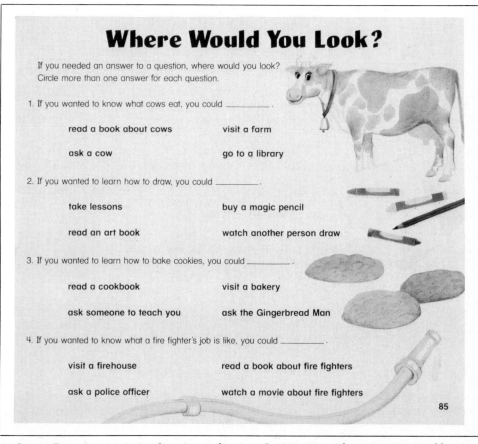

Where Would You Look?

If you needed an answer to a question, where would you look?
Circle more than one answer for each question.

1. If you wanted to know what cows eat, you could _____ .

    read a book about cows   visit a farm

    ask a cow   go to a library

2. If you wanted to learn how to draw, you could _____ .

    take lessons   buy a magic pencil

    read an art book   watch another person draw

3. If you wanted to learn how to bake cookies, you could _____ .

    read a cookbook   visit a bakery

    ask someone to teach you   ask the Gingerbread Man

4. If you wanted to know what a fire fighter's job is like, you could _____ .

    visit a firehouse   read a book about fire fighters

    ask a police officer   watch a movie about fire fighters

85

Source: From *Lessons in Reading Comprehension.* © 1981, Zaner-Bloser, Inc. Reprinted by permission.

ging should also prepare you to understand the following statements about the nature of the reading process.

Nature of the Reading Process

- Written text is a blueprint to which readers add the details.
- Comprehending requires readers to *construct* meaning. This is accomplished by using the direct and indirect meanings of an author's words, plus what the reader knows that is relevant.
- Comprehending is an *interactive* process in which the reader's knowledge of the world interacts with the message conveyed directly and indirectly by the text. The result is fully developed communication between author and reader.

ONE FURTHER EXPERIENCE WITH COMPREHENDING

Thus far, everything that has been said about comprehending highlighted it as being anything but a passive response to print. To keep *you* actively involved now, let me make a second request. This time, please write a paragraph that communicates the content that is both directly stated and indirectly implied in the sentence below:

> Of the three girls, only Bonnie can reach the shelf on which their mother keeps the cookies.

Let me assume you have written your paragraph; it is now time to compare yours with mine, which is shown below under the heading *Internal Text*.

External Text	*Internal Text*
Of the three girls, only Bonnie can reach the shelf on which their mother keeps the cookies.	Bonnie and her two sisters are in the kitchen. Since their mother keeps the cookies in a jar on a high shelf, only Bonnie, the tallest of the girls, can reach the cookies.

As indicated above, the author's words are the *external text*. In contrast, the *internal, mental text* is what a particular reader ends up comprehending. The internal text, then, is composed of the external text plus the reader's text-based and knowledge-based inferences.

The text-based inferences in my internal text are underlined once. Why these are text-based inferences can be explained as follows. The fact that Bonnie and the remaining two girls are sisters is implied by the words *their mother*. The word *reach* prompted the conclusion that the shelf on which the cookies are kept is high enough that only one girl can reach it. That girl, therefore, is the tallest of the sisters.

The knowledge-based inferences in my internal text are underscored with two lines. Presumably, they may be different from yours. The first such inference, which is that the girls are in a kitchen, is suggested by my experiences, specifically by those that point to the fact that the common place for keeping cookies is a kitchen. The second knowledge-based inference (in a jar) was prompted by the knowledge that cookies are usually in some kind of a container.

ADDITIONAL COMMENTS
ABOUT COMPREHENSION

Two further points may now need to be made about reading comprehension. One is that comprehending is *not* a matter of constructing any message that a reader feels like constructing. Instead, the message is always constrained by the author's words. More specifically, if the text about the girls and the cookies had been something like *As the girls walked home from school, they looked forward to a snack. Only Bonnie can reach the shelf on which their mother keeps the cookies*, an internal text that indicates the girls are in a kitchen shows evidence of deficiencies in literal comprehension (*As the girls walked home from school* . . .). The first point, therefore, can be summarized by saying that the content of an internal text embellishes but also reflects the external text. This means that literal comprehension is hardly unimportant even though it is often insufficient.

The second point that may need explicit attention is that comprehending is not always as objective as it is sometimes thought to be. This is the case because, as has been illustrated, knowledge-based inferences often vary from one reader to another simply because the experiences and knowledge of people vary. When you wrote the internal text about the girls and the cookies, for instance, some of you may have explained the mother's motivation for keeping cookies in a somewhat inaccessible place. This addition is most likely to come from individuals whose mothers did their best to keep cookies hidden to avoid spoiling appetites or, perhaps, to make certain that dessert is available for the next meal.

The fact that comprehending may be partially subjective is something teachers need to keep in mind whenever they evaluate students' responses to assessment questions. Even though many such questions have only one right answer, others allow for a variety of responses. Distinctions between the two kinds of questions should be in the minds of teachers and also clarified for students, as many children go through school believing that every question has but one right answer. Teachers can make distinctions among various kinds of questions by pointing out the three different sources of answers. Examples taken from text that students are being asked to read can be used. (Because the three sources of answers are referred to in the commentary about Figure 1.1, please read that page again.)

REACTIONS TO WHAT WAS COMPREHENDED

Figure 1.2 summarizes the analysis of comprehending that made use of the sentence about Bonnie and the cookies. The content of Figure 1.2 also adds another dimension to the picture of comprehension drawn thus far: reader reactions to what they were able to comprehend. As the illustrative reaction listed in Figure 1.2 demonstrates, meaningful responses to text are possible only when the message has been constructed. Admittedly, this may seem like stating the obvious; nonetheless, classroom observations do provide evidence of requests for reactions even when it is clear that the students in question did not, or could not, comprehend what they are supposed to react to. This suggests the need for teachers to keep priorities in mind: Make certain that students have understood what is important to understand before

Text: *Of the three girls, only Bonnie can reach the shelf on which their mother keeps the cookies.*			
Literal Comprehension	**Inferential Comprehension**		**Possible Reaction to What Was Comprehended**
	Text-Based	**Knowledge-Based**	
There are three girls. Mother keeps cookies on a shelf. Bonnie can reach the shelf.	The three girls are sisters. Bonnie is the tallest. Bonnie's sisters are unable to reach the shelf.	The three girls are in a kitchen. The cookies are in a container. Mother keeps cookies on a high shelf to keep them from being eaten before dinner. Mother wants her daughters to have a good appetite for dinner.	If a mother wants to be sure that cookies are not eaten, she should put them where nobody will know where they are.

Figure 1.2 Dimensions of Comprehension

asking questions like, "Do you think Ted was brave or foolish?" and "What did the author of the article tell you about bats that was surprising?"

Text-Based Reactions

Like comprehension itself, some reactions are directed to what is explicitly or implicitly conveyed by the words on a page. This was the case in one first grade when a girl objected to a sentence under a picture in a workbook. Her justified complaint was, "It says the ball is yellow, but it looks orange!"

Another text-based reaction in the form of a complaint was heard during a visit to a third grade in which the class was doing a page in a workbook that went with a new social studies textbook. Although the directions were about a dot-to-dot picture that was supposed to portray something described in the textbook, drawing lines from one number to the next resulted in nothing recognizable. Soon, a letter to the publisher about the error was being composed by the class.

At times, text-based reactions are more personal and subjective than the two just described. A poet's portrayal of a sunset, for example, may be inspirational for one reader while seeming to be nonsense to another.

Knowledge-Based Reactions

Like knowledge-based inferential comprehension, certain reactions to text are limited to readers who have some prior knowledge of the topic about which an author is writing. Often, for example, only knowledgeable readers can discern a writer's failure to distinguish between what is probable and what is certain or between a fact and an opinion. A many-sided issue treated by a writer as if there were but one side is another instance when only readers who have some knowledge about the issue are in a position to be both comprehenders and evaluators. Again, therefore, teachers need to keep priorities in mind: Do not ask students to evaluate an author's treatment of a topic if they know so little about the topic that they can react only to such variables as the clarity and the appeal of the author's treatment.

SOME COMPONENTS
OF COMPREHENSION ABILITY

Now that the process of comprehending has been discussed and at least partially illuminated, it is time to return to the earlier characterization of reading as "unexamined behavior." You will recall that the point being made was that anyone with responsibility for teaching reading needs to become consciously aware of what might be called taken-for-granted prerequisites for comprehending text. A few such prerequisites are listed below. As you read the list, you may be surprised to learn how much you do take for granted.

Some Basic Requirements for Comprehending

- An understanding of what is meant by *word* and of how empty space separates one written word from others.
- An understanding that English words are read in a left-to-right order and that lines of text are read from top to bottom.
- The ability to identify written words automatically and to understand their meaning in a given context.
- The ability to work out the pronunciation of unknown root words with the help of their spelling.
- The ability to work out the pronunciation and meaning of unknown derived and inflected words with the help of their structure.
- The ability to arrive at the identity and meaning of a word with the help of known words that are in the same context.
- The ability to make both text-based and knowledge-based inferences.
- The ability to use the context in which a given set of words is embedded in order to assign to those words either a literal or a figurative meaning.
- The ability to make semantic connections between the parts of a sentence and across separate sentences:

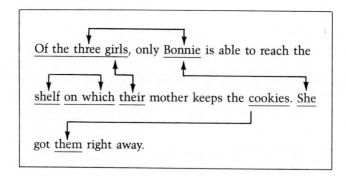

Even the incomplete list of prerequisites just provided is enough to suggest that "teaching reading" covers a very large number of topics, some of which call for attention immediately, others of which require both early *and* constant attention. A brief look now, first, at a few of the most important contributors to the comprehension of text and, second, at the implications of their importance for instruction, brings the chapter to a close.

IMPORTANT CONTRIBUTORS
TO COMPREHENSION:
INSTRUCTIONAL IMPLICATIONS

Anyone who has been reading this chapter should not be surprised to learn that three contributors viewed to be very important are the reader's (a) experiences, (b) oral language, and (c) knowledge of the world. These three interrelated variables are singled out for attention in this first chapter because their significance for comprehension is not universally understood. One consequence is that the significance of the three is not consistently reflected in how instructional time is used in classrooms (5, 7).

An appreciation of the importance of experiences, oral language, and knowledge about the world for comprehending also allows teachers to see that what appears to bear little relationship to reading (e.g., developing an understanding of *float* and *sink* with the help of water experiments) may, in fact, be making a valuable contribution to students' potential for acquiring reading ability. Keeping the same three variables in mind should also clarify for parents and professional educators alike that teaching reading exceeds asking questions and giving assignments—two activities that consume excessively large amounts of time in classrooms (7).

In contrast, the time spent on encouraging students to use what they know or have experienced to help with comprehension is inadequate. This can be illustrated with an incident that occurred during a visit to one fourth grade during social studies. At the time, the following interchange took place before the students started a chapter in their textbook. The book had a sociological orientation, which seemed much too advanced for the observed students:

Teacher: Who can give us an example of a group?
Student 1:   A fight.
Teacher: When we find out the four reasons that make a group, you'll see that a fight isn't a group.
Student 2:   When you're on a bus in Chicago.
Teacher: Once we read about the rules of a group, that will fit.

Evidence of the failure to encourage students to use what has been experienced to help themselves comprehend was also found in a first grade. In this case, the teacher and children were engaged in a postreading discussion:

Teacher: Where were the children going?
Student: To Krannert. [This is the name of an auditorium in the community in which the students live.]
Teacher: The story doesn't say that. It says, "They are going to a play."
Student: But Krannert is where we go to see plays!
Teacher: Let's get back to the story. Who . . . ?

In addition to minimizing the value for reading of what has been experienced, the two teachers just referred to were assigning—at least during the observations—too much importance to individual words and too little to the fact that reading and comprehending are synonymous. More specifically, does it not seem correct to conclude that the first grader who referred to a particular auditorium had successfully comprehended *They are going to a play?* And in the following interchange, is it not equally likely that another

child in a different classroom understood the text *They looked everywhere!*
In this instance, a teacher and a group of second graders were discussing a
story that had just been read:

Teacher: Where did they look for her?
Student: All over.
Teacher: That's not what it said. The story says they looked "everywhere."

Before anyone concludes because of the comments just made that the
philosophy underlying *Teaching Them to Read* is that an author's words
are relatively unimportant, let me be quick to point out that a number of the
chapters in this book are included *because* an author's words *are* critical. All
that is being attempted here is to make the point that the essence of reading
is comprehending. Keeping that equation in mind, effective teachers take
the time to reward successful efforts to comprehend without undermining
the fundamental importance of the text. In the case of the child who used
her experiences in going to plays to respond to a question, the teacher might
have responded as follows: "Well, you really did understand where the children were going. In our city, we do go to Krannert for plays, but Krannert—
let me write it on the board—is not mentioned in the story, is it? Maybe
the person who wrote this story hasn't even heard of Krannert. Maybe that's
why the author only said, "They are going to a play."

Teacher comments like those just suggested correctly reflect the interactive nature of the comprehension process. In no way, therefore, do they
take anything away from the importance of the words on a page; nor do
they overlook the contributions that experiences and knowledge make to
successful comprehension.

SUMMARY

Even though mental processes can hardly be put on display for purposes of
examination and study, Chapter 1 nonetheless tried to make the reading
process "visible." It did this initially by requesting a picture of the content
of a sentence, which was then described and analyzed. The intent of the
analysis was, first, to show the difference between literal and inferential
comprehension. The second goal was to differentiate between text-based
and knowledge-based inferences. The three kinds of comprehension (literal
comprehension, text-based inferential comprehension, and knowledge-
based inferential comprehension) were then brought together in the subsequent comparison of an external text (author's words) and an internal text
(author's words plus inferences based on the words plus inferences based on
the reader's relevant knowledge).

What should have emerged from the discussion is the active role that
students must play if they are to succeed in comprehending. How that role
is performed was implied when reading was defined as an interactive process. What results from that process was alluded to when it was stated that
readers construct meaning.

Sometimes, readers should also interact with the meaning they construct. At times, an interaction will take the form of evaluation; at other times, a response may be more emotive. Either way, reactions are possible only when comprehension has been achieved.

REVIEW

1. With examples, explain the difference between:
    a. literal comprehension and inferential comprehension.
    b. text-based inferential comprehension and knowledge-based inferential comprehension.

2. Toward the end of Chapter 1 in the section called "Some Components of Comprehension Ability," a few of the understandings and abilities required for comprehending are listed. Experiences, oral language, and knowledge of the world are not included on the assumption that their contributions were so obvious by that time as to make their inclusion unnecessary. In case the assumption is *in*correct, explain with a specific example how each of the three does contribute to the comprehension of text.

3. Randomly select something to read. Based on that reading, what else could be added to the list of required understandings and abilities in addition to experiences, oral language, and world knowledge?

4. Having read Chapter 1, you should be able to explain the following statements.
    a. Individuals who are successful comprehenders play an *active* role in the reading process.
    b. That active role accounts for reading being viewed as an *interactive* process.
    c. The active role taken by successful comprehenders also accounts for the contention that readers *construct* meaning.
    d. Comprehension is a *requirement* for reacting to a piece of text.

5. Let's assume you comprehended Chapter 1 and thus are ready to react to its content.
    a. What did you learn about the reading process that you did not know before studying the chapter?
    b. Was any of the content unexpected or surprising?
    c. Do you disagree with any of the content? If so, explain the reason(s) for your disagreement.

REFERENCES

1. Anderson, Richard C. "The Notion of Schemata and the Educational Enterprise." In R. C. Anderson, R. J. Spiro, and W. E. Montague (Eds.), *Schooling and the Acquisition of Knowledge.* Hillsdale, N.J.: Lawrence Erlbaum, 1977.

2. Baumann, James F. "Teaching Third-Grade Students to Comprehend Anaphoric Relationships: The Application of a Direct Instruction Model." *Reading Research Quarterly* 21 (Winter, 1986), 70–90.

3. Bransford, John. "Schema Activation—Schema Acquisition." In R. C. Anderson, J. Osborn, and R. C. Tierney (Eds.), *Learning to Read in American Schools.* Hillsdale, N.J.: Lawrence Erlbaum, 1983.

4. Duffy, Gerald G.; Roehler, Laura R.; and Putnam, Joyce. "Putting the Teacher in Control: Basal Reading Textbooks and Instructional Decision Making." *Elementary School Journal* 87 (January, 1987), 357–366.

5. Durkin, Dolores. "Is There a Match between What Elementary Teachers Do and What Basal Reader Manuals Recommend?" *Reading Teacher* 37 (April, 1984), 734–744.

6. Durkin, Dolores. "Reading Methodology Textbooks: Are They Helping Teachers Teach Comprehension?" *Reading Teacher* 39 (January, 1986), 410–417.

7. Durkin, Dolores. "What Classroom Observations Reveal about Reading Comprehension Instruction." *Reading Research Quarterly* 14 (1978–79, No. 4), 481–533.

8. Nessel, Denise. "The New Face of Comprehension Instruction: A Closer Look at Questions." *Reading Teacher* 40 (March, 1987), 604–606.

9. Palincsar, Annamarie S., and Brown, Ann L. "Reciprocal Teaching of Comprehension-Monitoring Activities." Technical Report No. 269. Urbana: University of Illinois, Center for the Study of Reading, 1983.

10. Pearson, P. David, and Dole, Janice A. "Explicit Comprehension Instruction: A Review of Research and a New Conceptualization of Instruction." *Elementary School Journal* 88 (November, 1987), 151–165.

11. Raphael, Taffy E. "Teaching Question–Answer Relationships." *Reading Teacher* 39 (February, 1986), 516–522.

12. Taylor, Barbara M., and Beach, Richard W. "The Effects of Text Structure on Middle-Grade Students' Comprehension and Production of Expository Text." *Reading Research Quarterly* 19 (Winter, 1984), 134–146.

Chapter 2

Silent or Oral Reading?

PREVIEW

Whether the attainment of an instructional objective calls for silent or oral reading is one of the many questions teachers need to be able to answer. On what bases they should make such a decision is the underlying theme of Chapter 2. In the process of developing that theme, the chapter gives considerable attention to oral reading because the primary concern of all of the other chapters is silent reading.

The first topic Chapter 2 addresses is the role that oral reading plays in instruction. The more specific concern is when comprehension instruction requires oral reading. Then the chapter deals with oral reading from a broader perspective in order to identify more generally the various contributions it can make to instructional programs.

Following the discussion of positive uses of oral reading, the focus shifts to a critique of a highly questionable use: round robin reading. This is the practice of having students take turns reading something aloud while other students are expected to follow the same text silently. The frequency of round robin reading accounts for the comprehensive nature of the critique.

Although it is common to associate round robin reading with the primary grades, classroom-observation research indicates it is unexpectedly frequent at later levels. Used with older students, the poorest readers in a class are likely to be the participants (2, 9). On the other hand, when round robin reading functions in middle and upper grades as a means for covering content in something like a social studies textbook, the whole class will probably be involved (11, 33). You may, in fact, remember this practice as one in which you yourself participated. It will be helpful to keep those experiences in mind as you make your way through Chapter 2.

The question of whether reading should be silent or oral is dealt with early in this book because some teachers, and many parents, still equate "teaching reading" with "listening to children read aloud." Presumably, such an equation will seem indefensible, or at least questionable, by the time you reach the end of Chapter 2.

While studying Chapter 1, you probably equated "reading" with silent reading without giving the matter a second thought. That is a natural association given the fact that reading is typically done silently, except in school. When it is kept in mind that large amounts of classroom time may be spent on oral reading, it is only natural to wonder about the discrepancy. Before examining the most time-consuming use of oral reading (round robin reading), let's first look at oral reading in the framework of its positive contributions to instructional programs.

ORAL READING FOR INSTRUCTION

Because Chapter 1 stressed that reading and comprehending are synonymous, the initial consideration of oral reading is in the context of comprehension instruction.

Oral Reading and Samples of Comprehension Instruction

Even though silent reading is the usual medium for comprehending text, certain instructional objectives having to do with improving comprehension abilities must rely on oral reading for their attainment. Such objectives are the focus now. The ensuing discussion of illustrative instruction covers two topics: (a) typographic signals, and (b) inferences about dialogues in stories.

Typographic Signals. Written English is characterized by physical properties (often referred to as *typographic signals*) that are aids for comprehending. Therefore, teaching students about the functions of such signals (e.g., comma and period) constitutes comprehension instruction.

As the content of Figure 2.1 points out, some instruction for typographic signals requires the use of oral reading whereas other instruction does not. What *is* required depends on the objective. If, to cite one example, commas are receiving attention in order to explain how they set off appositives that add information about the subject of a sentence (e.g., *Andy, the only one in his family to go to college, has the best job*), oral reading is unnecessary. On the other hand, if the reason for a lesson is to explain that commas signal the need for brief pauses that are essential for achieving meaning, then sentences like the one just referred to, as well as others such as *Ann is tall, slender, and very bright,* need to be read aloud so that pauses can be demonstrated and their significance for meaning illustrated.

To cite another example, if the purpose of instruction is to explain that interrogative sentences end with question marks, oral reading is unnecessary because the goal is to provide information. In contrast, if the intent is to make explicit the rise in intonation when certain kinds of questions are posed, oral reading must be used so the change in pitch can be heard. In this

Oral Reading: Not Required	*Oral Reading: Required*
Comma: sets off appositive	*Comma:* need for brief pause
Period: a. signals abbreviation b. signals end of sentence	*Period:* need for longer pause
Question mark: signals question	*Question mark:* possible need for rising intonation at end of sentence
Exclamation mark: signals end of sentence expressing emotion or excitement	*Exclamation mark:* need for reading text with certain emotion (e.g., anger, surprise)
Underlined word(s): may signal title, heading, subheading, or special stress	*Underlined word(s):* possible need for special stress
Quotation marks: may signal title or exact words spoken	
Indented line: may signal new paragraph and, possibly, shift in focus	

Figure 2.1 Typographic Signals: Subject Matter for Comprehension Instruction

case, the oral reading of yes/no questions like *Will you do me a favor?* and of tag questions like *You'll do me a favor, won't you?* is necessary for demonstrating how rising intonation clarifies an author's intended message.

As with other topics, the use of contrasts is often helpful in clarifying the significance of typographic signals for meaning. For example, when students know about the function of commas in setting off (a) the one addressed, and (b) an appositive, identical strings of words like the following are useful.

> Tom, my son is your age.
> Tom, my son, is your age.

Teacher-questions about the meaning of the two sentences, coupled with an appropriate oral reading of each, serve well in highlighting the significance of commas and pauses for constructing meaning.

More contrasts that point up how typographic signals and pauses affect meaning follow:

> For her birthday, they had ice cream, cake, and juice.
> For her birthday, they had ice cream cake and juice.

Other sentences show how typographic signals help readers chunk text into meaningful units—another ability required for comprehending. The same examples further suggest the value of oral reading for highlighting "same words but different message":

> His mother said who will be invited.
> His mother said, "Who will be invited?"
>
> Andria said her brother is not home.
> "Andria," said her brother, "is not home."

How the need to assign special stress to a word is signaled and, even more important, how such stress affects meaning, can be explained with the oral reading of contrasts like those below:

> This is my <u>new</u> coat.   I <u>care</u>.
> This is <u>my</u> new coat.   I <u>care</u>.
>
> I <u>won't</u> go with you.   Keep your <u>feet</u> off that table.
> I won't go with <u>you</u>.   Keep your <u>feet</u> off <u>that</u> table.

Again, teacher-questions are important for specifying differences in meaning. For instance: "In the first sentence, we have to give special stress to *new*. Listen as I read the sentence. . . . What am I especially trying to let you know by the way I read the sentence? . . . Yes, I'm letting you know that the coat I'm referring to is a new one. I'm going to read the very same words again, but this time I'll stress *my*. Listen. . . . What did I do my best to tell you this time? . . . That's right. I wanted to be very certain you were aware that *I* have a new coat. That's why I said, 'This is *my* new coat.'"

Here, an observation made by a linguist, Alfred Hayes, is pertinent as he reminds teachers:

> *Remember that you are* not *teaching children stress and intonation; they already use them naturally when they talk. You are* teaching them to respond to print in a way which helps them understand its meaning. *(21, p. 5)*

What the foregoing discussion should also prompt teachers to remember is the importance of asking themselves, *Why* am I doing what I'm doing? Without the introspection that such a question fosters, it is all too easy to spend time on tasks that make little or even no contribution to students' ability to read.

Inferences about Dialogue. To show another instance when oral reading should enter into efforts to improve comprehension abilities, let's move the focus to stories. We will assume that the students in question know that authors often state directly how a character says something (e.g., "Joel snapped back, . . . " and "Amy pleaded, . . . "). These same students now need to learn that how a character says something may only be implied.

Their teacher thus starts by having them silently read an unfamiliar story for the purpose of identifying both the outstanding traits of the main character and how the author reveals them. (The protagonist, in this case, is a boy named Eddy who loses his temper at the slightest provocation and, in the end, also loses what he wants most because of his quick, uncontrolled temper.)

Once the story is read and discussed, the teacher selects passages containing dialogue spoken by the protagonist when he is experiencing a variety of emotions. (The author does not state directly how the words are spoken.) The teacher's question for each passage is, "Who can read what Eddy is saying in just the way he is likely to be saying it?" This is followed by the very important question, *"Why* did you read that the way you did?"

The instruction just described has students correctly use information from the text to arrive at an inference about how something is said. In contrast, commercially prepared manuals commonly suggest procedures that make expressive oral reading an end in itself. Contrast, if you will, the procedure just referred to with two recommendations in a manual:

Ask how Connie would say that if she was disappointed.
Select children to read the sentence as if they were frightened.

The two manual recommendations reflect an *elocutionary* concept of reading that portrays it as a performance. That is, the recommended procedures would have a teacher name an emotional state (disappointed, frightened) that is to be displayed in oral reading. At such times, saying words with suitable expression is what counts. If that is not only what counts but also what routinely wins a teacher's praise, some students may become confused about the nature and purpose of reading. From the beginning, then, teachers must show that reading is a *cognitive* process that is concerned not with giving a message but with getting or constructing one.

Oral Reading and Other Kinds of Instruction

The fact that oral reading is sometimes helpful when young children are just beginning to be readers must be acknowledged. For instance, the fact that what is said can be written or, to put it differently, the fact that text is not as strange as it may first appear to be, needs to be explained with oral reading. The same holds true for helping young children understand the meaning of instructional language like "word" and "the beginning sound in words."

These and other instructional objectives that are typically necessary for young children are dealt with when kindergarten is the topic of Chapter 5. Now, the present discussion shifts to another contribution oral reading makes: it allows students to share what they have read.

ORAL READING FOR SHARING

As mentioned at the start of this chapter, the reading we ourselves do is mainly silent. Periodically, however, we either need or want to share something we have read. The same is true for children. The following section, therefore, considers requirements for oral reading when the purpose is sharing.

Requirements

When oral reading is done for sharing, teachers should make sure that two requirements are met. The first, which may seem too obvious to mention, is the availability of an audience (big or small) that has a desire, or at least a willingness, to listen. Whether a genuine audience is likely to exist depends on a combination of factors, one of which is the material being read. If it is dull, too familiar, or excessively long, nobody should be surprised if the expected listeners fail to pay attention or become restless. On the other hand, if the material is something like an announcement of a forthcoming surprise, neither lack of attention nor restlessness is likely to be a problem.

A second factor that affects whether an oral reader will have a genuine audience is the quality of the reading. This points to the second requirement for oral reading done to share: preparation. If what is to be read is short and simple, skimming the text is usually sufficient. On the other hand, if the material is difficult or lengthy, adequate preparation might be a complete, careful (and silent) prereading.

Because productive preparation requires knowing what it means to be an effective oral reader, how teachers can both define and promote effectiveness is discussed next.

Fostering Effective Oral Reading

To begin, it is important to keep in mind that some students will never be more than minimally successful oral readers. This is so because how well anyone reads aloud is partially dependent on factors outside the domain of a teacher—for instance, on personality and quality of speech. Fortunately, reading programs have no obligation to produce students who read telephone directories with gusto. Instead, their more modest aim is the acquisition of moderate amounts of skill in oral reading. In some instances, individuals will go far beyond this; in other cases, they will not reach the goal. But that is not a major worry because it is comprehension that is of primary importance.

The fact that comprehension *is* what matters is not always apparent in classroom practices. Here I cannot help but recall a conversation with a third-grade teacher who works with low achievers. Surprisingly, her overwhelming concern was for an effective oral delivery, which she expressed with the complaint, "I can never get these children to read smoothly even when I have them practice reading the same material over and over again." Such a worry suggests that this teacher may hold to an elocutionary concept of reading in which success is equated with expressive oral reading. Yet with her students, who are still struggling to overcome basic problems, such reading is like frosting on a cake—nice but not necessary.

To work on the frosting when this seems appropriate, teachers can allow time for a number of activities that promote effective oral reading. Some are discussed now.

Reading to Children. One assumption of this textbook is that good oral reading is as much caught as it is taught, which suggests one of the many reasons teachers ought to read regularly to their students. Ideally, this reading demonstrates the importance of careful pronunciation and enunciation of words, appropriate volume, and an expression that succeeds in communicating feelings as well as facts. Because children always enjoy being read to— assuming appropriate material is selected and presented effectively—*teachers at all grade levels should allow time for reading to students on a regular basis.**

An article by Sterl Artley (4) reminds everyone how students both remember and enjoy being read to. The article is based on responses from junior and senior education majors when they were asked to recall elementary school experiences that "turned them on or off reading." After describing the bleak picture drawn by the response, Artley shifts to the positive and notes:

> *The greatest number said that teachers reading to the class on any level was the thing they remembered and enjoyed most. In some cases the teacher read the opening chapter of a book or an interesting episode from it as a starter, the pupils then finishing it themselves, in some instances having to wait in turn because of the book's sudden popularity. Other teachers read a book to completion, chapter by chapter. . . . Some students reported that their teachers frequently talked about books they thought some of them might enjoy, and in other cases a teacher told about a book that she was reading for her own information or enjoyment. In this way the pupils saw that reading was important to the teacher. (4, p. 27)*

Choral Reading. Another way to foster effective oral reading is with choral reading (group oral reading). For students whose potential for oral reading is diminished by shyness, choral reading can be especially effective because it reduces fears. The repetition of words commonly found in material suitable for choral reading also allows for word practice that is not tedious.

The most important point to remember about choral reading is that it

---

* Two references at the end of the chapter (27, 40) offer generous help to teachers who want to be as sure as possible that their selections are well received. Summaries of books, age levels likely to enjoy them, and even the amount of time required to read each book aloud (or each chapter) are the types of information provided.

should not be treated as an end in itself. Perfect performances may be a legitimate expectation for the theater, but they hardly are necessary in classrooms. In fact, demands for perfection may become petty, ignoring the real reasons for having choral reading, which are the promotion of ability in oral reading *and* enjoyment. With the twin goals in the foreground, choral reading will be handled with an appropriate amount of seriousness.

Publications are available to help teachers choose material, organize students, and plan the details of a reading (23, 39). For anyone who lacks experience with choral reading, or who wants to use plays from time to time (31), the Benefic Press Oral Readers provide a suitable starting point (see Figures 2.2 and 2.3). These materials offer explicit directions and include text that ranges from a first- to about a third-grade level of difficulty. (Material that is overly difficult for any student involved in the activity should be avoided.) The range in difficulty makes the Benefic Readers useful not only in primary grades but also in middle and upper grades where students with reading deficiencies and those who are more proficient can work together. The same books also include other types of text suitable for oral reading—riddles and tongue twisters, for instance.

Commercial Recordings. Like the oral reading done by teachers, commercial recordings of stories provide models. They have the added advantage of allowing students to analyze why they are excellent, average, or perhaps ineffective. Some students also enjoy comparing a professional recording with their own taped reading of the same material. (Comparisons should be made privately unless a student is fairly skillful.) A comparison can be made systematic with a checklist like the one in Figure 2.4, once a teacher has clarified the criteria listed.

Because this chapter is the only one that considers oral reading done for sharing, descriptions of other ways to give time to that objective bring this section to a close.

Other Times for Oral Reading. Additional ways to allow for reading aloud to an audience are described below. Each suggestion is followed by comments.

> *Prepare written descriptions of objects and scenes. Direct students in an instructional group to draw a picture that corresponds to a description. Later, each will display his drawing and read the description. Others will be asked to listen in order to see whether all the details are in the picture.*

Comment. This suggestion illustrates how one assignment can achieve multiple goals. First, students practice reading aloud to communicate to an audience; they also practice reading silently in order to visualize a picture suggested by text. Notice, too, that the oral reader has a chance to preread the material and that the audience has a definite purpose for listening.

Organize students in pairs. One member of each pair will be responsible, first, for finding material likely to be of interest to a partner (e.g., a short magazine article or a chapter in a library book) and, second, for preparing to read it to the partner on a designated day. Following the reading, the text can be discussed. Why the partner did not like what was read can be part of the discussion—although negative responses should probably not be openly encouraged.

Comment.   Whenever students are unaccustomed to doing something, preparation or even a rehearsal is often required. With the activity described above, a teacher can model what is to be done before the paired reading starts. To do this, she can select a student to be her partner and then demonstrate expectations.

Periodically, have able readers write questions (on a chalkboard or ditto master) about interesting material covering one or more topics currently being studied in social studies or science. The second responsibility is to prepare to read the material aloud to less able classmates whose responsibilities are threefold: (a) read the questions silently, (b) listen to the reader, and (c) answer the questions.

Comment.   This suggestion provides one solution (not to be overdone) for a problem that middle- and upper-grade teachers refer to regularly—the need to cover certain content in textbooks even when a number of students are insufficiently advanced to read it. As time passes and the activity described above is used more than once, able readers can usually direct the postreading discussions without help, thus freeing a teacher to give time to other students.

To foster interest in word meanings and word histories, distribute to members of an instructional group copies of books that tell about words. (Examples of such books are listed in Chapter 11.) Have each student skim a book to find a word with an especially interesting history. Allow time for reading the selection silently before it is read aloud to the group. Prior to each reading, write the word (or have a student do this) so that all students can see what it looks like. Following a reading, encourage discussion.

Comment.   Once more, an assignment is such that it can realize more than a single objective. In addition to providing practice in reading aloud to an audience, this activity can help promote interest in words, provide practice in skimming, and allow for participation in a discussion. Since many words in English are tied to myths, the same activity might kindle an interest in mythology.

To provide motivation for improving oral reading skills, let volunteers take turns reading aloud to younger children—kindergartners and first graders, for instance.

Music with ng Endings

Listen to the word sounds as your teacher reads this poem. Listen for the music of the ng words.

Next read the poem with your teacher. The boys may read the boy's part, the girls may read the girl's part.

The City Things

Boys: Hear them trotting, jumping, running.
            Hear them whizzing down the street!

Girls: Hear them yowling, tooting, humming!
            Hear their wheels or hear their feet!

Boys: Working, playing, racing, chasing,
            Up above or down below;

Girls: Flying, wiggling, rumbling, grumbling,
            City things are on the go!

Lucy Sprague Mitchell

Figure 2.2

Source: Dawson, Mildred A., and Newman, Georgina. *Say and Hear.* Westchester, Ill.: Benefic Press, 1969, p. 27.

Speaking in Refrain

Listen as your teacher reads this poem. As she reads it a second time, say the refrain softly.

Now, as the teacher reads the poem again, whisper the part you will read along with her.

Speak clearly now as you say your part of the poem. Make sure you keep together as a group. After you have practiced saying this poem, try speaking the poem to other classes.

Boys:	'Tis a lesson you should heed,
All:	Try again;
Boys:	If at first you don't succeed,
All:	Try again;
Girls:	Then your courage should appear, For if you will persevere, You will conquer, never fear,
All:	Try again.
Boys:	If you find your task is hard,
All:	Try again;
Boys:	Time will bring you your reward,
All:	Try again;
Girls:	All that other folk can do, Why, with patience, may not you? Only keep this rule in view,
All:	Try again.

T. H. Palmer

32

Figure 2.3

Source: Dawson, Mildred A., and Newman, Georgina. *Loud and Clear.* Westchester, Ill.: Benefic Press, 1969, p. 32.

Oral Reading

When I read aloud, do I: *Yes*   *No*

1. Pronounce all the words correctly?   _____   _____

2. Enunciate each word so that all my words can be
   understood?   _____   _____

3. Read smoothly, not stopping when there is no reason
   to stop?   _____   _____

4. Read loudly enough to be easily heard?   _____   _____

5. Read with an expression that helps my audience under-
   stand and enjoy what I am reading?   _____   _____

Things I do well:

Things I need to work on:

Figure 2.4   Oral Reading: Self-Evaluation Checklist

Comment.   If older students select stories or informational books that are appropriate in content and length (with the help of a teacher or librarian) and their preparations are adequate, they will be amply rewarded with a most appreciative, attentive audience. On the other hand, if the material is inappropriate or the reading poor, they will learn very quickly that they made some mistakes along the way.

> *Using wordless picture books covering a wide variety of topics, have interested students compose anything from brief captions to a well-developed text to go with the pictures.* * *Later, composers can read what they wrote while the teacher or another student displays the illustrations to an audience.*

Comment.   Reading one's own material is another type of oral reading practice. As just described, the material on some occasions can be written in connection with commercial picture books. Another possible stimulus is a student's own artwork. Either way, an audience should be available for the oral reading.

---

* A reference at the end of the chapter lists more than 100 wordless picture books (13).

Teachers' Questions about Oral Reading

To conclude the discussion of oral reading done to share, two questions are considered. The first is, "When students are reading aloud to others and are unable to identify a word, should I tell them what it says?" As with many other queries about teaching, the answer to this one is found in a consideration of purpose and goals. (Remember? *Why* am I doing what I'm doing?) Because, in this case, the reason for the oral reading is communication, the only response that makes sense is to supply the word so the reader can move on.

Consideration of purpose also provides an answer for a second question teachers often ask, namely, "What should I do when the student who is reading aloud misidentifies a word?" If the misidentification distorts or confuses meaning, it should be quickly corrected in a nonpunitive way. Otherwise, a correction is unnecessary.

Should it happen that one or more students frequently require help when they read aloud, insufficient preparation might be indicated. This should be discussed and remedied. It is also possible that the material is excessively difficult, in which case a change to easier text resolves the problem.

ORAL READING FOR DIAGNOSIS

Although the usual purpose for reading aloud is sharing, oral reading is sometimes used in school for diagnosis—that is, to help identify a student's particular abilities and shortcomings. Serving that purpose, oral reading has different—in fact, opposite—requirements from what it does when the intent is communication. For diagnosis, a student should *not* have a chance to prepare, as the purpose is to learn what is done in the act of reading. Because flaws are likely to show up, the oral reading should also be as private as circumstances permit, preferably with only the teacher listening.

These two purposes can be summarized as follows:

Requirements for Oral Reading

To share:	audience
	familiar material
To diagnose:	privacy
	unfamiliar material

Because diagnosis is the concern of Chapter 16, it is not discussed further here. Instead, the focus shifts to the most common form of oral reading, namely, round robin reading. To lay the groundwork for taking a knowledgeable look at this practice of having one student read aloud while classmates are expected to follow the same material silently, significant differences between oral reading and silent reading are identified.

DIFFERENCES BETWEEN ORAL
AND SILENT READING

Oral and silent reading are similar in some ways, dissimilar in others. Because it is the dissimilarities that are pertinent for the forthcoming discussion of round robin reading, three differences that set oral and silent reading apart are discussed.

Vocalization

The most apparent difference between oral and silent reading is that the former is heard whereas the latter is not. The observable pronunciation of words that is the very essence of oral reading is called *vocalization*.

Vocalization contrasts with *subvocalization,* which is commonly present in silent reading. As the name may suggest, subvocalization (also called *inner speech*) is a mental pronunciation of words that is neither heard nor seen.

Whether subvocalizing assists with comprehending is one of the many questions about reading that lacks a carefully documented answer. When Gibson and Levin (15) reviewed existing research, for example, they noted both the difficulties in studying subvocalization and the conflicting findings whenever it was examined. They suggested, nonetheless, that subvocalizing may facilitate the comprehension of difficult material by focusing the reader's attention on meaning.

Frank Smith offers a different hypothesis about why difficult material and increases in subvocalization often go together (36). He believes that "the explanation is more likely to be that reading a difficult passage automatically reduces speed, and we have a habit of articulating individual words when we read at a speed slow enough for individual words to be enunciated" (p. 200).

Until facts about the relationship among subvocalization, difficult material, and comprehension are available, the position taken here is as follows:

1. Probably everyone subvocalizes too much, even with easy material.
2. Subvocalization not only reduces the speed of silent reading but also is "annoying and difficult to turn off" (15).
3. Because the ability to comprehend at a reasonably fast rate is desirable, anything that may foster needless subvocalization should be avoided.
4. It is possible that the daily use of round robin reading increases subvocalization.

More is said about the final point later in this chapter. Now, the discussion of the three differences between oral and silent reading continues.

Eye Movements

How eye movements account for a second difference is explained once the movements themselves are discussed.

Studies of Eye Movements. When researchers first began to study reading, ideas about it were often generated from the method of introspection (24). That is, research subjects were asked to report what was happening within themselves as they read. Based on the reports, hypotheses were formulated, some of which included hunches about eye movements. Among the latter was that people's eyes sweep steadily across each line of print as they read.

Later, this conclusion was replaced by another because newly invented cameras allowed for eye-movement monitoring that was both more objective and more precise.* Although cameras did not figure extensively in research until the 1920s and 1930s, their initial use showed that a reader's eyes stop intermittently as they move rapidly across a line (3, 6). Eye behavior is thus characterized not by a steady sweep but by stop-and-go movements. The active part is called *saccades* (sǝ cādǿ); the periods of inactivity, *fixations.* (To understand eye movements correctly, it is essential to keep in mind that an eye fixation is so brief that its duration has to be measured in milliseconds.) Research also showed that "the leaping eye" (which makes the fastest movement that occurs in a human's body) "is practically blind" (36). Consequently, "the reading of text occurs only during fixations" (30). What seems like visual continuity, then, is provided by the brain, not the eyes.

Another characteristic identified with the more sophisticated research is that a reader's eyes move backward on occasion. This right-to-left movement, referred to as a *regression,* has a variety of causes. In some instances, readers miss one or more words and have to return to pick them up. At other times, a person might be reading something like the following paragraph. To read it is to identify another reason for regressions.

> *The boys' arrows were nearly gone so they sat down on the grass and stopped hunting. Over at the edge of the woods they saw Henry making a bow to a little girl who was coming down the road. She had tears in her dress and also tears in her eyes. She gave Henry a note which he brought over to the group of young hunters. Read to the boys it caused great excitement. After a minute but rapid examination of their weapons they*

---

* Current research using computers verifies the ensuing description of eye movements (29, 30, 39).

ran down the valley. Does were standing at the end of the lake making an
excellent target. (5, p. 87)

The paragraph you just read was written by Guy Buswell for one of his
eye-movement studies. Reading it demonstrates that homographs (identi-
cally spelled words with different pronunciations and meanings) are another
reason for regressions. A different but related cause has to do with expectations. That is, when a text does not conform to what a reader expects to see,
regressive eye movements occur in order to correct what was erroneously
anticipated.

Another reason for eye regressions is linked to the need to move from
the end of one line to the start of the next. (This essential right-to-left movement is called a *return sweep*.) If it happens that the eyes miss what is at
the beginning of the new line, the return sweep is likely to be followed by
one or more regressions.

One further reason for regressions pertains only to oral reading—specifically, to the *eye-voice span*. Before discussing that, let me synthesize this
more general discussion of eye movements with definitions:

Eye fixation. Pause in eye movements at which time print is seen.
    Duration of fixations is so brief it is measured in milliseconds. (One
    msec. = 1/1000 of a second.)

Saccade. Movement of eye from one fixation to the next. "The average
    length of saccades during reading is about 8–10 letter positions. . . .
    This is about the size of the region seen during a fixation" (30, p.
    163).

Eye regression. Backward (right-to-left) movement caused by such fac-
    tors as missed words, homographs, concern or confusion about
    meaning, and incorrect predictions.

Return sweep. The necessary right-to-left eye movement required by
    the start of each new line of text.

Table 2.1, which summarizes data from another of Buswell's studies,
shows that progress in silent reading is characterized by reduced numbers
of fixations, shorter fixations, and fewer regressions. This reference to a developmental pattern, it should be noted, is not suggesting that an individual's eye movements are always the same. Difficulty of material and the purpose for reading it are two factors that account for variation (29). Keith
Stanovich, for example, concluded from a meticulous review of pertinent
studies (37) that "when skilled readers are forced to read material too difficult for them, their eye movement patterns deteriorate and approximate
those usually shown by the less skilled readers" (p. 365).

Eye Movements during Oral and Silent Reading.   The earlier reference to Buswell's data noted that they were collected while subjects read silently. That
was essential to mention because eye-movement records for the same indi-

Grade	Average Number of Fixations per Line	Average Duration of Fixation Pauses	Average Number of Regressive Movements per Line
1	18.6	660 msec	5.1
5	6.9	252 msec	1.3
11	5.5	224 msec	0.7

Table 2.1   Children's Eye Movements during Silent Reading at Different Grade Levels

viduals reading the same material aloud (with the possible exception of the first graders) would yield noticeably different data. You should be able to predict the differences once *eye-voice span* is explained.

With oral reading, it is necessary to pronounce and carefully enunciate every word, which takes much longer than the eye requires to scan the same material. The difference in rate accounts for the *eye-voice span,* which is "the number of words or letter spaces that visual processing is ahead of oral reading" (15, p. 640). Differences in the rate at which the eye and the voice can deal with text cause a conflict. Of necessity, the voice wins out as the eye yields (unconsciously) to the slower pace. While accommodating the voice, the eye is still active; as it waits, it wanders and regresses. Now, regressions "operate to reduce the separation between the eyes and the voice" (3, p. 125). The eye also fixates longer than would be the case were the reading silent.

All these consequences of the eye's accommodation to the voice are verified when eye-movement records of a person reading the same material orally and then silently are compared. Predictably—at least when the reader is past the initial stage of learning to read—eye movements for oral reading show more and longer fixations and more regressions. Stated differently, the findings indicate that eye movements required for oral reading are inefficient for silent reading.

It is relevant to note in this context a conclusion reached by Roberta Golinkoff (17) after she reviewed research on comprehension: "Poor comprehenders' eye movements showed greater correspondence in oral and silent reading than did the good comprehenders' eye movements. Poor comprehenders seemed to continue laborious word-by-word reading even when reading silently" (p. 637).

Functions

A third difference between oral and silent reading lies in their respective functions. The primary purpose of silent reading is to get or construct an author's message. Even though other purposes may exist—for instance, to critique the message—the first concern is to understand it.

With oral reading, the customary function is similar to that of speaking: to communicate to one or more listeners. Although an effective oral presentation often indicates that the reader understands the text, comprehension is not an essential requirement. What *is* required are correct pronunciations and phrasing, suitable volume, and appropriate expression. These can all be present when the oral reader does not understand everything an author wrote.

IMPLICATIONS OF DIFFERENCES
FOR INSTRUCTIONAL PRACTICES

The foregoing sections highlighted three differences between oral and silent reading having to do with vocalization, eye movements, and functions. Implications of the differences for instructional programs are discussed now in the context of round robin reading, because data from classroom-observation research (2, 10, 11, 33) support the following two conclusions:

1. Round robin reading consumes a considerable amount of the time allocated to reading in primary-grade classrooms. At later levels, it continues to be used but less frequently. When it is used with older children, they are usually the poorest readers.
2. Round robin reading in which the entire class participates is common in middle- and upper-grade classrooms during social studies. In this instance, it is viewed as a way to cover the content of textbooks.

In the following sections, round robin reading is scrutinized in a framework defined by the three differences between oral and silent reading discussed earlier.

Round Robin Reading and Subvocalization

Regardless of the position taken on the function of subvocalization, most reading specialists agree that much of the subvocalizing that goes on during silent reading results in little more than needlessly slow rates—plus annoyance. To be taken seriously, therefore, is the likelihood that the habitual practice of having children follow silently what another person is reading aloud is encouraging the silent followers to pronounce mentally the words they hear. Said differently, a regular use of round robin reading is likely to foster purposeless subvocalization.

Round Robin Reading and Eye Movements

The possible connection between round robin reading and excessive subvocalization has not been formally studied, but one researcher did look into the effect of round robin reading on eye movements. Luther Gilbert (16) reported a study, entitled "Effect on Silent Reading of Attempting to Follow Oral Reading," whose findings have been neither supported nor questioned because subsequent research was never done—which is surprising, given the amount of time that round robin reading consumes.

Gilbert studied children in grades 2 through 6 by photographing their eye movements first while they read silently and then while they followed silently what another subject was reading aloud. (Gilbert deliberately chose oral readers with varying abilities.) When the two sets of eye-movement records were compared, predictable differences were found. Eye movements for the silent reading that was accompanied by oral reading showed more fixations and regressions than did the silent reading done independently. Expectedly, too, the fixations were longer. It was also shown that the poorer the quality of the oral reading, the poorer (that is, the less efficient) were the eye movements of the subjects following the material silently. The latter finding prompted Gilbert to write, "The data are unmistakable in condemning the routine practice of requiring silent readers to follow the oral reading of poor and mediocre readers" (16, p. 621). Because observations in classrooms uncover a paucity of excellent oral reading when around-the-group oral reading takes place (1, 10, 11), Gilbert's data are a second reason to question the day-by-day, year-by-year use of round robin reading.

Round Robin Reading in Relation to Function

As mentioned many times, the primary purpose of reading is to comprehend, which is usually accomplished more easily with silent reading. In contrast, the common goal of oral reading is to communicate the content of a piece of text to others. Keeping the two functions in mind, let's take another look at round robin reading when it is preceded by a silent reading of the text and when it is not.

When silent reading does not precede round robin reading, the logical reason for the round robin reading is comprehension. However, why a silent-oral combination is more likely than silent reading to achieve that goal is unclear, especially when it is remembered that the oral reading is likely to be a halting, listlike rendition of a text that bears little relationship to the spoken language with which children are familiar. For that reason, the oral reading commonly heard during round robin reading may obscure rather than elucidate meaning.

Even though the oral reading is usually better when the selection was read silently beforehand, the reason to have oral reading under these circumstances is hardly obvious, except when certain parts of the selection are read aloud for specific purposes. These purposes may include clarifying or verifying a point, identifying a sentence that explains a word's meaning, recalling a vivid mental image, finding examples of what was taught recently (for example, the function of commas in setting off appositives), or pointing out the clue that suggested a particular outcome.

What we have, then, is another reason to question the routine use of round robin reading: It fails to make distinctions between the respective functions of silent and oral reading.

REASONS FOR CONTINUED USE
OF ROUND ROBIN READING

As long ago as 1908 (24) and continuing to the present (1, 8, 10, 22), round robin reading has been criticized for the reasons just discussed. Still another reason has to do with achievement. Reporting findings in a two-year observation study of eleven primary-grade classrooms, John Guthrie notes that

> the amount of time spent in silent reading is significantly correlated with achievement. In contrast, no contribution to achievement was made by traditional oral reading nor by indirect reading, which included story discussion, listening, circling pictures with a common phonetic element, and writing. (20, pp. 766–767)

All the questions that have now been raised about round robin reading prompt another about its persistent presence in classrooms: Why have efforts either to eliminate round robin reading or to reduce the time allotted to it met with failure?

Commonly Cited Reasons
for Round Robin Reading

Without doubt, unexamined habits is one reason for the longevity of round robin reading. Still another is teachers' unexamined dependence on basal reader manuals, which continue not only to encourage round robin reading but also to support an elocutionary concept of reading.* For example, after suggesting that a selection with little content be read orally twice, one first-grade manual states: "The major emphasis during the oral reading period should be placed on reading the text with the voice intonations—emphasis, pauses, and inflections—called for by the situation in the story" (12, p. 24). This point of view explains why it was not surprising in one study to hear a fourth-grade subject say that the most important reason for reading her basal textbook was "to learn to say all the words right and with expression" (43, p. 351). A more recent explanation for the routine use of round robin reading is that teachers view it as a way to control or manage students' behavior (8). This is an interesting explanation, given the fact that visits to classrooms show that round robin reading is a source of, not a cure for, discipline problems.

---

* If it has been a while since you looked at basal reader materials, you are urged to examine one or more basal series as soon as possible because they are referred to in most chapters.

Reasons Cited by Teachers

Teachers have their own explanations for scheduling round robin reading. The most common ones are listed below in a reason–response format.

Reason: If I do not have my students read a selection aloud, how will I know whether they are remembering new words?

Response: Monitoring word identification ability is important; however, learning about any given student's ability can be achieved during round robin reading only when he has a turn to read aloud. Since the oral reading is usually of a brief passage that may include neither new nor troublesome words, reliable conclusions are ruled out. Because teachers do need to know which words are or are not being retained, alternative ways of learning about word identification abilities are considered in a later chapter.

Reason: Expression reveals whether the oral reader is comprehending.

Response: This claim is common but unfounded, since an effective oral delivery may be little more than expressive word calling (14, 22). Not to be forgotten is that teachers' persistent attention to expression can lead children to conclude erroneously that reading is a performing art, not a thought-getting or thought-constructing process. When such a conclusion *is* reached, students might not comprehend even when they read silently because they do not know that that is what they are supposed to do.

Kenneth Goodman offers another thought about expression and comprehension (18). He observes:

There are periods in the development of reading competence when oral reading becomes very awkward. Readers who have recently become rapid, relatively effective silent readers seem to be distracted and disrupted by the necessity of encoding oral output while they are decoding meaning. Ironically, then, poor oral reading performance may reflect a high degree of reading competence rather than a lack of such competence. (p. 489)

Reason: My students like round robin reading. They object when I do not have it.

Response: Some children do seem to like round robin reading but only until they get their turn to read. After that, off-task behavior is common—which, actually, helps minimize problems related to subvocalization and inefficient eye movements. However, the lack of attention generally means that such individuals are attending to other matters and are getting into trouble as a result. Not to be overlooked, either, is the likelihood that some children are intimidated by the need to read aloud, knowing that others will be listening to their mistakes.

Reason: Even though oral reading is not as important as silent reading, I still think children should have a chance to read aloud—especially the young ones. That is why I have round robin reading.

Response: As this reason suggests, many teachers seem to think that round robin reading is the only way to allow for oral reading (19). Yet, as earlier sections in the chapter pointed out, opportunities exist for oral reading that is free of the negative consequences likely to occur when round robin is used day by day and even year after year.

ACCEPTABLE COMBINATIONS OF ORAL AND SILENT READING

With all the criticism that has been directed to round robin reading, you may have concluded that the implication is to eliminate all combinations of oral and silent reading. To correct that erroneous conclusion, descriptions of a few acceptable combinations bring the chapter to a close.

Read-Along Tapes

The use of read-along tapes merits initial attention because these tapes have children follow text that, presumably, was recorded by a proficient oral reader. Comments—which are no more than conjecture—about this combination of silent and oral reading follow.

1. For beginning readers who actually follow the text as it is being read, this activity *may* promote faster and more fluent reading. The oral reader will also be modeling correct phrasing, which is necessary for comprehension.
2. For more advanced readers, this reading-listening activity—if done often—might be detrimental by slowing down the rate at which these students read silently, because even the best oral readers cannot read at a rate that is possible for silent readers.
3. For all children who do not follow the text, hearing an effective reading of an interesting story may add to their desire to become better readers themselves. In addition, hearing expository (informational) text provides an opportunity to acquire knowledge of the world.

Plays

Reading plays is a second acceptable combination of oral and silent reading. In this case, let's assume that certain children need to improve their oral reading; the teacher decides to use a play to help. Because it is oral reading, not a perfect play, that is the concern, the teacher bypasses memorization. Instead, she has members of an instructional group read from a script, which requires one child to read aloud while the others follow the text silently in order to be ready with their own parts. For special occasions, the teacher might combine play reading with puppet making. In that case, speaking parts for the play are taped by the children, which frees them to give full attention to manipulating the puppets while the pretaped dialogue runs smoothly in the background. (A reference at the end of the chapter [42] provides directions for making various kinds of puppets: paper bag, stick, sock, finger, fist, and hand.) The point of significance now is that dramatizations—whether simply or elaborately presented—occur infrequently and thus differ in that respect from the round robin reading that has been questioned.

Additional Combinations of Oral and Silent Reading

You might now be wondering, What about day-to-day practices? Should they ever combine oral and silent reading? Surely, but only in certain ways.

To illustrate, let's say that a teacher is working with nine students. The group has just finished reading a selection silently, which might be material the teacher wrote, a story in a textbook, or, perhaps, a newspaper article. What was read does not matter; what does matter is how the teacher combines silent and oral reading. (It is possible, of course, that oral reading is not used.) In this case, the teacher might decide to discuss the questions that were raised before the silent reading began. If some call for a subjective answer (Which paragraphs include descriptions that make you feel as if you are right at the scene?), the teacher might have individual students read aloud the passages that succeeded in transplanting them right into the scene of the story or article. But, please note, the others just listen while the paragraphs are read.

It could turn out that even factual questions elicit different responses. Should this happen, oral reading again might be required, this time to allow for comparisons and verification. As individual students read aloud, the others listen—critically, it is hoped.

At still other times, a teacher might choose to have parts of a selection read aloud in order to review something taught earlier. More specifically, if italic print is in a selection to indicate the need to stress certain words, individuals might be asked to read aloud sentences that include the italicized words in order to see whether they remember the significance of the special print.

To sum up, certain circumstances do call for combinations of silent and oral reading. Such circumstances are not a daily occurrence, nor are they usually a time to require students to follow silently what another is reading aloud. To hold to such a requirement, which is the case with round robin reading, is to encourage needless subvocalization and inefficient eye movements among the silent followers. In addition, when the followers have already read the text, the oral reader can hardly be said to have a genuine audience.

SUMMARY

Subsequent chapters focus on proficient silent reading; the present one attended for the most part to oral reading. At the start, samples of instructional objectives that require the use of oral reading were described. This was done, first, to point out one contribution of oral reading and, second, to reinforce the need for teachers to habitually ask themselves, "What am I trying to accomplish?" and "What is the best way to accomplish it?"

The importance of these two questions should have remained apparent when the chapter proceeded to identify two additional contributions that oral reading makes to an instructional program. This is so because the two contributions (allows for sharing and diagnosis) have opposite requirements. Specifically, when oral reading functions in allowing students to share the content of a piece of text, preparation and an audience are necessary. On the other hand, when oral reading is the medium for diagnosis, it should be of unfamiliar material that is read under circumstances that permit maximum privacy. This indicates that indiscriminate uses of oral reading do not characterize the instructional programs of knowledgeable, introspective teachers.

Once the three contributions of oral reading were discussed, the silent-oral reading combination known as round robin reading received generous coverage because of the extensive amount of classroom time it consumes. To prepare for a critique of this exceedingly common activity, Chapter 2 discussed differences between oral and silent reading having to do with vocalization, eye movements, and functions. The discussion was intended to show how the habitual use of round robin reading is likely to foster what nobody wants when students read silently: needless subvocalization and inefficient eye movements. The same discussion should have suggested, too, that round robin reading often confuses the respective functions of oral and silent reading.

Having criticized round robin reading, the chapter concluded with descriptions of acceptable combinations of oral and silent reading. The chapter that focuses exclusively on basal reader materials, Chapter 13, also points out more alternatives to round robin reading. Chapter 13 should be especially helpful to teachers who have students take turns reading a basal selection aloud simply because they are unaware of alternatives. For teachers who rely on round robin reading to cover content in subjects like social studies, Chapter 14, "Content Subject Textbooks," also suggests other possibilities.

REVIEW

1. To assess your comprehension of parts of Chapter 2, the following terminology is used:

choral reading
diagnosis
elocutionary vs. cognitive view
    of reading
eye-voice span
fixation
method of introspection

regression
return sweep
round robin reading
saccade
subvocalization
vocalization

   a. Underline all the terms listed above that pertain directly to eye movements, then explain each one.
   b. Describe the developmental pattern for eye movements as an individual becomes more proficient in silent reading.
   c. Explain the meaning of these statements:

   During oral reading, the eye must accommodate itself to the rate at which the reader pronounces the words.

   Eye movements associated with oral reading are inefficient for silent reading.

   d. Re-examine the data in Table 2.1. How would the numbers be likely to change if subjects read the same material but read it orally rather than silently? What accounts for the changes?

2. Viewed from the perspective of the "silent followers," describe problems that may develop if round robin reading is used often over a long period of time.

3. Critique round robin reading from the viewpoint of the student doing the oral reading:
   a. when the material was read silently before the start of round robin reading.
   b. when the material was not read ahead of time by members of the group.

4. Explain the difference between an elocutionary and a cognitive concept of reading.

5. Describe times when it is appropriate—even necessary—to have oral reading.

6. Describe circumstances that clearly call for silent reading.

7. Subvocalization and eye movements are two topics about which teach-

ers should be knowledgeable. They should not be discussed with children, however. Why not?

8. Now that some of the key terms and concepts in Chapter 2 have been reviewed, what are your own thoughts about the chapter? For instance, what do you think about round robin reading? What are your reactions to other topics discussed?

REFERENCES

1. Adams, Marilyn J.; Anderson, Richard C.; and Durkin, Dolores. "Beginning Reading: Theory and Practice." *Language Arts* 55 (January, 1978), 19–25.
2. Allington, Richard. "The Reading Instruction Provided Readers of Differing Reading Abilities." *Elementary School Journal* 83 (May, 1983), 548–559.
3. Anderson, Irving H., and Dearborn, Walter F. *The Psychology of Teaching Reading.* New York: Ronald Press, 1952.
4. Artley, A. Sterl. "Good Teachers of Reading—Who Are They?" *Reading Teacher* 29 (October, 1975), 26–31.
5. Buswell, Guy T. *An Experimental Study of the Eye-Voice Span in Reading.* Supplementary Educational Monographs, No. 17. Chicago: University of Chicago Press, 1920.
6. Buswell, Guy T. *Fundamental Reading Habits: A Study of Their Development.* Supplementary Educational Monographs, No. 21. Chicago: University of Chicago Press, 1922.
7. Cullinan, Bernice E. (Ed.). *Chidren's Literature in the Reading Program.* Newark, Dela.: International Reading Association, 1987.
8. Duffy, Gerald D. "Teacher Effectiveness Research: Implications for the Reading Profession." In M. Kamil (Ed.), *Directions in Reading: Research and Instruction.* National Reading Conference, 1981.
9. Durkin, Dolores. "Is There a Match between What Elementary Teachers Do and What Basal Reader Manuals Recommend?" *Reading Teacher* 37 (April, 1984), 734–744.
10. Durkin, Dolores. "A Six-Year Study of Children Who Learned to Read in School at the Age of Four." *Reading Research Quarterly* 10 (1974–75, No. 1), 9–61.
11. Durkin, Dolores. "What Classroom Observations Reveal about Reading Comprehension Instruction." *Reading Research Quarterly* 14 (1978–79, No. 4), 481–533.
12. Durr, William K.; LePere, Jean M.; Pikulski, John J.; and Alsin, Mary Lou. Teacher's Guide for *Boats.* Boston: Houghton Mifflin Company, 1983.
13. Ellis, DiAnn W., and Preston, Fannie W. "Enhancing Beginning Reading Using Wordless Picture Books in a Cross-Age Tutoring Program." *Reading Teacher* 37 (April, 1984), 692–698.
14. Erickson, Sheryl E. *Conference on Studies in Reading.* Washington, D.C.: U.S. Department of Health, Education and Welfare, 1978.
15. Gibson, Eleanor J., and Levin, Harry. *The Psychology of Reading.* Cambridge, Mass.: MIT Press, 1975.
16. Gilbert, Luther C. "Effect on Silent Reading of Attempting to Follow Oral Reading." *Elementary School Journal* 40 (April, 1940), 614–621.

17. Golinkoff, Roberta M. "A Comparison of Reading Comprehension Processes in Good and Poor Comprehenders." *Reading Research Quarterly* 11 (1975–76, No. 4), 623–659.
18. Goodman, Kenneth S. "Behind the Eye: What Happens in Reading." In Harry Singer and Robert B. Ruddell (Eds.), *Theoretical Models and Processes of Reading*, 3rd ed. Newark, Dela.: International Reading Association, 1986.
19. Green, Frank. "Listening to Children Read: The Empathetic Process." *Reading Teacher* 39 (February, 1986), 536–543.
20. Guthrie, John T. "Effective Teaching Practices." *Reading Teacher* 35 (March, 1982), 766–768.
21. Hayes, Alfred S. *Language and Reading: A Linguist's View.* New York: Harcourt, Brace and World, Inc., 1969.
22. Holmes, Betty C. "The Effect of Four Different Modes of Reading on Comprehension." *Reading Research Quarterly* 20 (Fall, 1985), 575–585.
23. Huck, Charlotte S. *Children's Literature in the Elementary School*, 4th ed. New York: Holt, Rinehart and Winston, 1987.
24. Huey, Edmund B. *The Psychology and Pedagogy of Reading.* New York: Macmillan, 1908.
25. Johnson, Richard. "Reading Aloud—Tips for Teachers." *Reading Teacher* 36 (April, 1983), 829–831.
26. Karwoski, Arleeta O. "Practicing Oral Reading Skills." *Reading Teacher* 36 (March, 1983), 690.
27. Kimmel, Margaret Mary, and Segal, Elizabeth. *For Reading Out Loud: A Guide to Sharing Books with Children.* New York: Delacorte Press, 1983.
28. Lewis, William D., and Rowland, Albert L. *The Silent Readers.* The John C. Winston Company, 1920.
29. McConkie, George W. "Studying the Reader's Perceptual Processes by Computer." Reading Education Report No. 34. Urbana: University of Illinois, Center for the Study of Reading, May 1982.
30. McConkie, George W.; Hogaboam, Thomas W.; Lucas, Peter A.; Wolverton, Gary S.; and Zola, David. "Toward the Use of Eye Movements in the Study of Language Processing." *Discourse Processes* 2 (July–September, 1979), 157–177.
31. Manna, Anthony L. "Making Language Come Alive through Reading Plays." *Reading Teacher* 37 (April, 1984), 712–717.
32. Mendak, Peggy Ann. "The Use of Silent Reading in the Primary Grades." *Reading Teacher* 39 (March, 1986), 636–639.
33. Neilsen, A. R.; Rennie, B.; and Connell, B. J. "Allocation of Instructional Time to Reading Comprehension and Study Skills in Intermediate Grade Social Studies Classrooms." In J. A. Niles and L. A. Harris (Eds.), *New Inquiries in Reading Research and Instruction.* Thirty-First Yearbook of the National Reading Association. Rochester, N.Y.: National Reading Conference, 1982.
34. Rayner, Karl. "Do Faulty Eye Movements Cause Dyslexia?" *Developmental Neuropsychology* 1 (Fall, 1985), 3–15.
35. Shavelson, Richard J., and Borko, Hilda. "Research on Teachers' Decisions in Planning Instruction." *Educational Horizons* 57 (Summer, 1979), 183–189.
36. Smith, Frank. *Understanding Reading.* New York: Holt, Rinehart and Winston, 1971.
37. Stanovich, Keith E. "Matthew Effects in Reading: Some Consequences of Individual Differences in the Acquisition of Literacy." *Reading Research Quarterly* 21 (Fall, 1986), 360–407.

38. Strange, Michael C. "Considerations for Evaluating Reading Instruction." *Educational Leadership* 36 (December, 1978), 178–181.

39. Sutherland, Zena, and Arbuthnot, May Hill. *Children and Books*, 7th ed. Glenview, Ill.: Scott, Foresman and Company, 1986.

40. Trelease, Jim. *The Read Aloud Handbook.* New York: Viking Penguin, Inc., 1982.

41. Underwood, N. Roderick, and Zola, David. "The Span of Letter Recognition of Good and Poor Readers." *Reading Research Quarterly* 21 (Winter, 1986), 6–19.

42. Weiger, Myra. "Puppetry." *Elementary English* 51 (January, 1974), 55–64.

43. Wixson, Karen K.; Bosky, Anita B.; Yochum, M. Nina; and Alvermann, Donna E. "An Interview for Assessing Students' Perceptions of Classroom Reading Tasks." *Reading Teacher* 37 (January, 1984), 346–352.

Chapter 3

Reading Instruction

PREVIEW

As surprising as it may seem, not until the 1970s did a sizable number of reading educators and educational psychologists begin to scrutinize both the nature of instruction and the essential differences between instruction, practice, and assessment. Interest in such an endeavor was spawned by a number of factors, one of which was research. Of particular influence were findings about the tendency of teachers, teachers of teachers, and authors of instructor's manuals to equate practice and assessment with instruction (15, 16, 18).

Even though it can hardly be said that agreement about the nature of instruction was eventually achieved (16, 29), it is clear from the literature that whenever researchers went into classrooms to learn exactly what is done during the time scheduled for reading, findings were similar. Classroom observation studies repeatedly showed that large amounts of time are consumed by round robin reading, by many assessment questions asked in ways not likely to make them instructive, and by large numbers of written assignments originating in workbooks and ditto masters supplied by both basal and nonbasal reader publishers.

A more general conclusion to which the classroom studies pointed is that, in many instances, the major thrust behind classroom procedures is not to teach students but to cover commercially prepared material (11, 14, 18, 33). Or, to state this conclusion differently, the observation data suggest that the planning many teachers do focuses not on what they will help students learn but on what they will have students do.

Because of findings like those just referred to, Chapter 3 singles out reading instruction for special attention even though the whole of the book is concerned with the same topic. Like the material covered in the two previous chapters, the content of Chapter 3 provides background information for all subsequent chapters.

Before starting Chapter 3, you might want to read the Summary at the end in order to get an overview of its content.

Teachers are human; thus, the best of them make mistakes. However, more often and consistently than others in their profession, superior teachers catch and correct their mistakes.

Underlying this partial portrayal of the best of teachers is the fact that they are knowledgeable about subject matter and how to teach it and, further, are introspective about their decisions and efforts. Superior teachers, therefore, are capable of trial-and-error learning. This is the case because such learning is possible only when the person making the error has knowledge that is sufficient enough to allow for analyzing what went wrong and for coming up with possible remedies. This means that limitations in a teacher's knowledge both of the content of a reading curriculum and of the necessary components of effective pedagogy place corresponding limits on potential for growth.

Almost all the chapters in this book deal with content for instruction. Even though they also include descriptions of ways to teach it, instruction is the primary focus now. As is true of most topics, reading instruction can be divided in various ways for purposes of discussion. Three divisions are chosen for this chapter:

1. *Unplanned, unintentional instruction:* Something occurs by chance that is instructive for students.
2. *Unplanned, intentional instruction:* Something occurs by chance that has the potential to be instructive. The teacher consciously attempts to realize the potential.
3. *Planned, intentional instruction:* A teacher offers instruction designed to achieve a preestablished objective.

As mentioned in the Introduction to *Teaching Them to Read*, having an overview of what is to be read before the reading itself begins promotes better comprehension and retention. It is advisable, therefore, to go over the content of Figure 3.1 before proceeding.

UNPLANNED, UNINTENTIONAL
INSTRUCTION

For good or bad, unplanned, unintentional instruction is probably more effective *and* more common than anybody realizes. As emphasized in Chapter 2 when round robin reading was discussed, teachers who routinely praise correct word naming even when the student doing the naming understands little or nothing in the text, may, in an unplanned and certainly unintentional way, succeed in teaching a misconception about the nature of reading.

On the positive side, the most important thing a student might learn when his teacher takes time to find a book about castles is that reading ability is a highly useful possession. This may be the case even though the teacher's only conscious intention was to satisfy a student's curiosity about castles.

1. *Unplanned, Unintentional Instruction*
   During postreading discussions, a teacher habitually asks so many comprehension assessment questions that some inevitably deal with insignificant details.

   Outcome: Students reach an incorrect conclusion about the nature of proficient reading, namely, that it requires paying attention to, and re-membering, every single thing that a piece of text communicates.

2. *Unplanned, Intentional Instruction*
   A "teachable moment" occurs when a student refers to whales as "fish." The teacher responds by explaining why whales are mam-mals, not fish.

   Outcome: Students learn why a whale is not a fish.

3. *Planned, Intentional Instruction*
   To provide further corrective instruction, the teacher just referred to reads a colorfully illustrated expository book on the following day that tells about whales and dolphins. The book also explains why whales and dolphins are mammals, not fish.

   Outcome: Students have a more detailed understanding of the differences between fish and mammals.

4. *Planned, Intentional Instruction*
   Several derived words whose roots are known (e.g., *unhurt, playful,* and *careless*) are in the basal reader selection that will be assigned next to a reading group. Prior to making the assignment, a teacher explains the nature of derived words with the help of those examples. She tells the group that the words are in the story they will soon read.

   Outcome: Members of the instructional group learn that some words are "roots" and that certain letters can be added to them, both at the beginning and the end, to form different but related words.

5. *Planned, Intentional Instruction*
   The basal reader manual used with one reading group describes procedures for teaching the contrasting meanings of *or* and *and.* Because the description suggests suitable illustrations, includes clear explanations, and refers to sentences in the next basal selection that include *or* and *and,* the teacher follows the manual's recommendations.

   Outcome: Members of the instructional group understand the meanings of *or* and *and* and demonstrate their understanding by correctly explaining the meaning of such contrasting sentences as: *We'll have a sandwich or soup* and *We'll have a sandwich and soup.* In the postreading discussion, they are also able to explain the meaning of *and* and *or* in sentences in the basal selection.

Figure 3.1   Examples of Instruction

In any discussion of unplanned, unintentional instruction, parents can hardly be omitted. It is not accidental, for instance, that when children who acquire initial reading ability at home are studied (13, 20), a typical finding is that one or both parents are avid readers. This is not surprising, given the fact that just hearing people chuckle as they read adds a positive note to that ability. Nor is it surprising that parents who spend their free time watching television often turn out to have children who are fans of television, not of books.

The effectiveness of what is being categorized as "unplanned, unintentional instruction" accounts for such maxims as:

"Attitudes are as much caught as they are taught."

"I can't hear what you're saying for the noise of what you're doing."

"Don't do what I do. Do as I say."

UNPLANNED, INTENTIONAL INSTRUCTION

Unplanned, intentional instruction often occurs (a) as a response to one or more students' misunderstandings, overgeneralizations, insufficient information, and errors; or (b) as a way of taking advantage of unexpected opportunities, sometimes referred to as "teachable moments." Because unplanned but intentional instruction often has many of the components of instruction that is both intentional *and* planned, the discussion of instruction itself is saved for the next major section of this chapter. Here, the two sets of circumstances that often prompt unplanned but intentional instruction are considered.

Response to Errors

Students' incorrect responses take many forms; however, because teachers spend large amounts of time asking questions (11, 18, 29), errors often are incorrect answers to questions.

Because question-asking *is* so common in classrooms, it has been the subject of study for a long time (21). Recent research (9, 18, 29) has especially called attention to, and criticized, the question-answer pattern described below:

1. Teacher poses question about a piece of text students have read and calls on one student to answer.
2. If answer is correct, teacher asks another question.
3. If answer is incorrect, additional students are called on (or volunteer) until one offers desired response.
4. Another question is asked.

Even though much time is spent on the question-answer sequence just enumerated, research has demonstrated the value of other kinds of responses to students' erroneous answers (4, 9, 23, 25, 31). Minimally, for example, students should receive feedback that allows them to understand *why* a response is unacceptable. Should a series of incorrect responses be given, one teacher might decide to stop responding to each incorrect answer and, instead, switch to an attempt to walk the students through the text so she can model the act of answering the questions she poses. More specifically, if the student who responded to the first question said "A hundred gold coins" when the correct answer is "A hundred silver coins," the teacher who is about to offer unplanned but intentional instruction might begin as follows (25, p. 23):

> Let's go back through the story to answer the question again. The question is, "What was Anna to bring to court?" Read the first paragraph. . . . Does any sentence in that paragraph tell what Anna was to bring to court? . . . Jack, read the sentence that says what Anna is supposed to bring. . . .

In the face of the same series of wrong answers, another teacher may also decide that corrective instruction is needed; however, her decision is to take the time to think through a lesson before offering it the following day. In this case, the next day's lesson is what is being called "planned, intentional instruction."

But, now, let us continue the discussion of *un*planned, intentional instruction in the framework of teachable moments.

Response to Teachable Moments

One conclusion repeatedly verified during many years of observing in classrooms is that effective teachers plan carefully and are well organized. Complementing those characteristics is the ability to take advantage of unexpected opportunities to teach something that is both educationally significant and needed. Although I am not sure whether it is flexible structure or structured flexibility that characterizes the instructional programs of such teachers, I can state with certainty that these teachers take advantage of teachable moments whenever possible. The following account by a teacher illustrates her use of one such event:

> I teach third grade. This year my class is made up primarily of children whose achievement in reading is seriously hampered by a limited knowledge of word meanings. That is why I'm always looking for opportunities to give attention to vocabulary. Thanks to a boy who arrived Monday wearing an unusually colorful shirt, I'm giving time this week to the concept "pattern" and to words that go with it. Since the boy's shirt attracted much attention but little in the way of specific descriptions, I decided to work on patterns with the entire class.
>
> Today (Tuesday) after lunch, the children were surprised to find a large male paper doll on one of the bulletin boards. This Mr. Fashion was wearing a polka dot hat, a striped shirt, and checkered pants.

Once the children were seated on the floor in front of the bulletin board and had quieted down, we discussed ways of describing his clothing. Eventually, the descriptions "polka dot," "checkered," and "striped" were printed on the chalkboard next to the bulletin board. I explained that all of these words referred to patterns, after which I also printed *pattern*. (With the help of my questions, "pattern" came to be defined as "something that is repeated.") After the group reread the words on the board, I displayed three cards, each displaying a word for one of the patterns. As each word was reread, I attached the card to the bulletin board next to the appropriate piece of clothing that Mr. Fashion was wearing. We then talked about other places where the same three patterns are found. (References were made to such things as tablecloths, food packaging, and games.) Finally, I suggested to the students that it might be fun to draw their own Mr. Fashion using the same patterns but not in the same way. I suggested, for example, that someone's Mr. Fashion might be wearing polka dot trousers instead of a polka dot hat. I also reminded the children that they could use the patterns for additional clothing—shoes and ties, for instance. Finally, I mentioned that some might want to write something about their Mr. Fashion, once they finished the picture.

Originally, I thought I would follow the same procedures tomorrow afternoon, this time using a Ms. Fashion paper doll. (We had talked earlier in the year about *Ms.* when we were discussing abbreviations.) However, since almost nobody wanted to do any writing, I changed my plans. (Ms. Fashion will wear a hat made of a print fabric, a solid colored blouse, and a plaid skirt.) Everything will be done the same way except for the drawing and writing. Tomorrow, I'll show the children some of the store catalogues and sports magazines that will be left on one of the larger tables. I'll show them five large envelopes, each displaying a word for one of the patterns. Now the suggestion will be to look through the catalogues and magazines whenever free time is available in order to cut out examples of the patterns. If, for instance, a baseball player is pictured in a striped uniform, his picture will be cut out and placed in the envelope labeled *striped*. I will remind everyone that if any of the pattern words cannot be recalled, the cards placed next to Mr. and Ms. Fashion on the bulletin board will help. I also plan to say that on Friday afternoon we'll take a look at each envelope to see what has been found and, in particular, to learn if the patterns were identified correctly. Only time will tell how the plan works.

Whether it works well or not, I expect to use these vocabulary items whenever it seems appropriate. Like all the other classes I've taught, this one picks up on the words I use. In fact, when I listen to some of them, it's almost as if I were listening to myself. That's when I know the potential is there, but it was never given enough opportunities to bear fruit.

To provide a contrast, let me describe what was seen in another third grade. At the start of this observation, the teacher had just begun to work with five boys who were much more interested in a pencil than in the basal reader they were being told to open. The pencil's attraction was both the die attached to one end and the advertisement for a new furniture store printed on its side. The latter said, "Don't gamble on quality. See us first." At the time the pencil was taken from its owner, he and the other boys were doing their best to read the two sentences. Since they did anything but try hard to read the basal story—they kept insisting they had read it in second grade—a question had to be raised about why the basal reader was not temporarily laid aside in order to allow for attention to the slogan on the pencil because it had so much potential for reading comprehension. Specifically, the meaning of "Don't gamble on quality" could have been contrasted with the meaning of something like "Don't gamble on a horse," immediately establishing the opportunity to talk about literal and figurative language. Or, the words *die* and *dice* could have been written and discussed in the context of unusual ways to form plural nouns. Words like *quantity* and *quality* might also have been considered along with such questions as, When is quality more important than quantity? Is quantity ever more important than quality? Instead of doing anything like this, however, the teacher spent the time on some very poor oral reading, while the boys insisted they had read the story when they were in second grade.

Even though the reference to this classroom incident is *not* intended to convey the notion that instructional programs should proceed according to students' whims, it *is* meant to emphasize, first, that teachable moments do occur and, second, that they sometimes have greater potential than planned, intentional instruction.

PLANNED, INTENTIONAL INSTRUCTION: AN INTRODUCTION

Although it may seem like a truism to say that a classroom is a place where instruction is provided, data from classroom-observation research has painted a different picture (6, 9, 18, 33). Whereas instruction in the observed classrooms was hard to find, assignments and assessment received generous amounts of attention. Because the little instruction that *was* seen was often brief and shallow, some of it came to be called "mentioning," defined as "saying just enough about a topic to allow for an assignment related to it" (18, p. 505).

Data from research have also highlighted the similarity between the way time is used in classrooms and the recommendations in basal reader manuals (11, 14, 33). Because of the similarity, classroom activities carried out during the period of time allocated to reading were soon being portrayed not as instructing but as "moving students through materials" (11).

The essence of the conclusions from the combination of classroom studies and analyses of materials can be summed up with a reference to

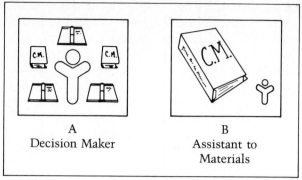

Figure 3.2 Contrasting Teachers

what is called "Teacher A" and "Teacher B," both depicted in Figure 3.2. The classroom studies describe Teacher B as being more concerned about covering commercially prepared materials than about teaching particular children. Because Teacher B abides by the recommendations in these materials, she is characterized in Figure 3.2 as "an assistant" to them. Among the by-products of such a role is little incentive to become more knowledgeable about reading and reading instruction. For Teacher B herself, the most undesirable consequence may be the omission of reflection about the meaning and significance of her work as a teacher.

Whereas Teacher B is subordinate to materials in the sense that she allows them to dictate what will be taught, and how, and even when, Teacher A makes the key decisions herself. Once decisions *are* made about necessary instructional objectives, Teacher A uses whatever materials are likely to forward her efforts to attain them. Although not directed by materials, Teacher A is knowledgeable about what is available—probably more knowledgeable than Teacher B.

When discussing what is commonly referred to as direct, explicit instruction, James Baumann (3) portrays Teacher A this way:

> In direct instruction, the teacher, in a face-to-face, reasonably formal manner, tells, shows, models, demonstrates, teaches the skill to be learned. The key word here is teacher, for it is the teacher who is in command of the learning situation and leads the lesson, as opposed to having instruction "directed" by a worksheet, kit, learning center, or workbook. (p. 287)

PLANNED, INTENTIONAL INSTRUCTION: ITS COMPONENTS

For maximum effectiveness, reading specialists now believe that teachers should consider the following whenever their intention is to provide instruction (4, 5, 7, 9, 26):

Components of a Lesson

1. Specific, preestablished objective
2. Explanations to students:
    a. what the objective is
    b. how its achievement contributes to becoming a better reader
3. Explicit instruction
4. Guided practice
5. Independent practice
6. Application in whatever students are reading

Because each component is discussed in the sections that follow, you might want to take another look at the overall picture just portrayed before continuing.

Specific Objective

It should go without saying that attempts to teach should be guided by clearly defined objectives, which, when the desired behavior is specified, are sometimes called behavioral objectives. For instance:

> Students will know what the referent of a pronoun is when the referent and pronoun are in the same sentence and the referent appears prior to the pronoun.

> Students will be able to explain the meaning of an unknown word when an appositive in the same sentence reveals its meaning.

> Students will be able to identify the root in derivatives in which the spelling of the root is altered.

Even though we should be able to take it for granted that the selection of objectives reflects students' needs, the commercialization of instruction referred to earlier can result in a curriculum that is a poor match for the individuals it is supposed to serve. This fact is portrayed in Figure 3.3, which depicts a practice that starts as early as kindergarten: Each grade has a given curriculum, often defined by commercial materials (14, 17). What is in a fourth-grade basal reader and manual, for instance, constitutes the fourth-grade reading curriculum. Even though students at each grade level are dif-

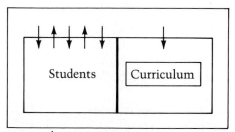

Figure 3.3   Different Students, Same Curriculum

ferent from year to year, the curriculum for each grade remains unchanged. As portrayed in Figure 3.3, it is as if an opaque wall kept curriculum directors, administrators, and teachers from seeing students in relation to what they, as particular individuals, need and are ready to learn.

An instructional program that contrasts with a curriculum defined by textbooks and grade levels is characterized by *individualized instruction:*

Individualized Instruction

1. Deals with what contributes to reading ability.
2. Concentrates on what has not yet been learned by the individual or group being instructed.
3. Has an objective that the student(s) is capable of achieving.
4. Proceeds at a suitable pace.

Conceivably, individualized instruction is possible with a group as large as one hundred—or one thousand, for that matter. For instance, showing a film whose content clearly explains an unfamiliar concept currently being studied in science provides individualized instruction for the entire audience regardless of its size.

Naturally, too, individualized instruction can be offered to a single student. In this case, the description *individualized* is merited not because someone is being taught individually but because the skill or ability receiving attention is something the student needs and is ready to learn.*

Obviously, providing large amounts of individualized instruction in the setting of a classroom is a tall order. Individualized instruction, nonetheless, is central to the concerns and decisions of effective, introspective teachers.

Such individuals, it should be noted, are not only consciously aware of what they are trying to achieve but also take the time to explain the objectives of their lessons to students. How the attainment of the selected objectives figures in becoming a better reader is explained, too. (Developing the habit of explaining the value for reading of what is to be taught is one way for Teacher B's to develop into Teacher A's. This is the case because some recommendations in teaching manuals have little or even nothing to do with reading ability.)

How one teacher explained to a group of students the value for reading of what she was about to teach follows:

> We've been working on figuring out what new words say when they have only one vowel that's not at the end. Yesterday, you'll remember, we figured out new words like these. (Teacher writes *cob, bud, pal,* and *rim* and has the students read them.) Today I want to

---

* In the late 1950s, an antibasal reader movement supported what was then called "individualized reading programs" (24, 35). At the core of such programs was support for the use of literature rather than textbooks to teach reading and also for opportunities for students to select the books from which they would learn to read. This brief background information is offered now to discourage confusion between that antibasal reader movement and the topic being discussed: individualized instruction.

show you how to figure out by yourselves new words that have *two* vowels. In the words we'll be talking about, the second of the two vowels is *e*, and it's at the end of the word—for example, a word like this. (Teacher writes *pale* on the board.) Knowing how to pronounce these kinds of words will be helpful when you come across a word you don't know that has two vowels like this word on the board, one of which is a final *e*.

To sum up, then, planned, intentional instruction originates in an objective chosen because (a) its realization advances proficiency in reading and (b) it pertains to a skill, an ability, or an understanding that the students do not have but are ready to acquire. To make the lesson maximally meaningful, the teacher states explicitly what she is about to teach and also explains its usefulness for readers.

Instructional Procedures

Teachers caught in the act of teaching are likely to be engaged in a variety of behaviors—imparting information, explaining, using examples and non-examples, modeling, posing questions, and so on. The procedure referred to as *modeling* has received the greatest amount of attention in recent years. Modeling is an attempt to demonstrate, or act out, a particular behavior or thought process (19, 28, 29). A teacher working on the use of structure to recognize derived words, for instance, verbalizes the thoughts she herself might have if faced with the job of working out the pronunciation of the unknown word *dislocation*. Because examples of such modeling appear in Chapter 10, "Structural Analysis," none are provided now.

The illustrations in Chapter 10 help explain why Scott Paris characterizes modeling as "making thinking public" (27). Whatever the definition, the emphasis on "show them" reflects the belief that the likelihood of an objective's being realized is directly related to the extent to which the instruction is explicit.

Let's continue now with what else is listed under "Components of a Lesson."

Guided and Independent Practice

Reflecting the importance of monitoring student progress, the next recommended step for a lesson is guided practice. Such practice may be written or oral. Guided practice gives students a chance to do or use under the supervision of a teacher what they presumably learned. With an instructor available and watching (or listening), prompt feedback is possible. When all goes well, it will usually be praise. Should problems develop, feedback can range all the way from a few explanatory comments to reteaching the lesson.

Once students seem to have attained the objective of a lesson, the next step is to get them involved with further practice, this time done independently. Following that comes application, one of the most important components of a lesson.

Application

Teachers who are in the habit of asking, *"Why* am I doing what I'm doing?"* are not likely to omit giving students an opportunity to use what they are learning in the context of "real" reading. With such teachers, students who have been taught how to figure out the pronunciation of words with a given spelling pattern get a chance to read a selection that includes unfamiliar words composed of that pattern. Or, to cite another illustration, students who have been taught that clauses sometimes add information about the subject of a sentence get assigned reading that includes sentences with clauses serving that function. All this is to say that if students do not have the chance to experience the practical value of what they are being taught, lessons soon become little more than something one learns to endure in the course of being a student.

Because of all the widespread, highly publicized criticism that has been directed at basal reader materials in recent years, some of the updated versions do show attempts to coordinate at least some manual recommendations with selections in the basal readers. Nonetheless, the absence of such coordination is still easy to find (12). Using a randomly selected lesson in a second-grade manual, let me list just some of the times when no connection exists between the manual's recommendations and the basal story children will soon read:

> A recommendation for teaching the prefixes *un-* and *re-* is offered even though not a single derivative in the basal story starts with either prefix.
>
> Another recommendation is to have the children read ten known words, each with *ar* in one of its syllables. The stated purpose is to review one of the blends that *ar* records. Although two words in the basal selection are *start* and *cart,* neither is referred to in the manual. It is unclear, therefore, why *ar* is singled out for attention, especially when an examination of the basal selection uncovered ten words containing *er.*
>
> A workbook assignment is recommended that is said "to provide practice with character." Practicing character turns out to be answering three multiple-choice questions about a brief paragraph whose content bears no relationship to the basal story.

What these few illustrations help emphasize is that even though basal reader series show some improvements, the need for a Teacher A continues.

A Summary

In an article about comprehension, Mary Shoop (34) makes the following analogy, which is useful for summarizing what has been said about the components of instruction no matter what the objective is:

Teachers must train students to comprehend just as pilots are taught to fly. While students are learning the basics of comprehension, teachers act as flight trainers, modeling comprehension processes and providing opportunities for practice. After sufficient ground school instruction and demonstration runs, students must be allowed to become the pilots. Teachers must then serve only as navigators, implementing strategies which allow students to take responsibility for comprehension and being available for direction as needed. The teacher's goal in guiding comprehension is moving the student to the point of flying solo, comprehending print independently. (p. 671)

PLANNED, INTENTIONAL INSTRUCTION: SOME PRECAUTIONS

In theory, it is difficult to dispute the efficacy of offering instruction made up of the components just discussed. Each part has a contribution to make to successful, efficient learning. Nevertheless, putting into practice what seems theoretically desirable *may* have undesirable consequences. Objectives that do not reflect the requirements of reading or of students' needs, practice and application that never get beyond workbook exercises to real reading—these are some of the problems that are possible but not inevitable. Therefore, as a way of bringing the discussion of planned, intentional instruction to a close, we offer some guidelines that can prevent explicit instruction from turning into a monotonous, unexamined routine.

Some Guidelines for Teaching

Objectives
- Whether instruction is planned or spontaneous, a definite objective ought to guide its development. (It goes without saying that the objective should be one that, if realized, advances students' reading ability.)
- Keeping the objective in mind ("*Why* am I doing what I'm doing?") minimizes the likelihood of wandering away from what is necessary for realizing the objective. It also discourages the tendency to turn means into ends in themselves.
- Whenever instruction is offered at the time students demonstrate they do not understand something, no need exists to explain the significance of the instruction. In such instances, the value for solving a real problem is apparent.

The Instruction Itself
- Teaching reading is not delivering one lecture after another. To view it that way runs the risk of replacing reading with lessons about reading.
- Instruction should not be allowed to become an end in itself. Keeping it in close and obvious contact with students' current reading (assigned or voluntary) helps avoid that pitfall.
- Just as variety is the spice of life so, too, does variety characterize in-

struction that keeps students attentive. Replacing tedious explanations with modeling and, for instance, involving students by posing problems and questions allow for variety as well as for the likelihood that students will listen and watch and think.

■ Whatever form instruction takes, it should be no longer or more detailed than achievement of the objective requires. Teachers, like preachers and authors, need to work at knowing when to quit.

■ The nature of instruction should be matched to the abilities of students. Whereas some children require detailed, slow-paced explanations, others profit most from instruction that moves along at a fairly fast pace.

Practice and Application
■ With practice, "rules were made to be broken." For example, even though it was recommended that instruction should be followed by supervised and independent practice, there are times when instruction is so obviously successful (or students are so obviously bright) that instruction can be immediately followed by application.

■ Viewing practice only in the context of workbook exercises is highly restrictive. In fact, as often as possible, practice should be connected with, not detached from, meaningful reading. Supervised practice, for instance, might be a teacher-guided reading of certain parts of a selection. Whenever practice is carried on in the context of purposeful reading, it closely resembles application.

■ One of the best ways to provide both practice and application is to allow students time for self-selected, uninterrupted reading.

What has now been said can be summed up by stating that superior teachers do not rely on recipes—not even on good recipes. Rather, they have cookbooks in their heads from which they make different selections at different times, always based on what needs to be taught to whom.

SUMMARY

It is natural to find in a book entitled *Teaching Them to Read* fairly continuous attention to instruction. To provide background for subsequent descriptions of instruction dealing with specific topics, Chapter 3 discussed reading instruction more globally. To start the discussion, instruction was divided into three kinds differentiated by the descriptions (a) unplanned, unintentional; (b) unplanned, intentional; and (c) planned, intentional.

The first combination of descriptions, unplanned and unintentional, acknowledged that students learn many things from what a teacher says, asks, or does even though what was said or done was spontaneous and never thought, or intended, to be instructive. The maxim "We teach what we are" reflects both the existence *and* effectiveness of unplanned, unintentional instruction.

The next type of instruction discussed, unplanned but intentional, is especially characteristic of highly effective teachers. Two facts account for this. First, they have the ability to make the most of unexpected opportunities to teach something and, second, they are able to respond with on-the-spot help when evidence of a deficiency becomes apparent. As Chapter 3 explained, on-the-spot instruction stands a good chance of being successful because students readily identify it as an attempt to solve a problem. Such instruction thus comes across as being less contrived than does some of the intentional, planned instruction that has been seen in classrooms and that is promoted in basal reader manuals.

Intentional, planned instruction received generous coverage in Chapter 3 not only because it is essential but also because it can turn a reading program into an unending series of lectures if it is overused or if certain precautions listed in Chapter 3 are not taken into account.

A chapter on instruction could hardly omit instructors; consequently, Chapter 3 discussed teachers in the context of Teacher A, the decision-maker, and Teacher B, the assistant to commercial materials. Such a context made it natural to point out how the commercialization of instruction commonly results in inappropriate curricula. To counteract that problem, individualized instruction was described and endorsed. It can be said, in fact, that the overriding goal of *Teaching Them to Read* is to increase both the number of Teacher A's and the amount of individualized instruction that is available in classrooms everywhere.

REVIEW

1. Chapter 3 categorizes instruction as (1) unplanned and unintentional, (2) unplanned and intentional, (3) planned and intentional.
   a. Explain each category.
   b. To supplement the content of Figure 3.1, describe one example of each of the three types of instruction. (Examples need not be confined to reading instruction, especially if your present knowledge about teaching reading is meager.)

2. Chapter 3 lists and then discusses the components of planned, intentional instruction. What are the components? Why is each component considered to be necessary?

3. How does the concept "individualized instruction" fit into the picture of planned, intentional instruction portrayed in Chapter 3?

4. Many people believe that instruction will be effective to the degree that it includes explicit explanations. That is why modeling is promoted as one effective way to instruct.
   a. Explain the meaning of *modeling.*
   b. Explain how modeling can enter into two lessons. The first is concerned with helping students understand that authors infer infor-

mation as well as state it directly; the second, with helping students understand the significance of commas for comprehending text.

5. First, what is *feedback* and, second, how does it help promote both successful and efficient learning?

6. Keeping in mind the characteristics of Teacher A and Teacher B, explain the following observation: Some teachers mature with experience whereas others merely age.

REFERENCES

1. Anderson, Linda M.; Evertson, Carolyn M.; and Brophy, Jere. "An Experimental Study of Effective Teaching in First Grade Reading Groups." *Elementary School Journal* 79 (March, 1979), 193–223.

2. Baumann, James F. "The Effectiveness of a Direct Instruction Paradigm for Teaching Main Idea Comprehension." *Reading Research Quarterly* 20 (Fall, 1984), 93–115.

3. Baumann, James F. "A Generic Comprehension Instructional Strategy." *Reading World* 22 (May, 1983), 284–294.

4. Baumann, James F. "Implications for Reading Instruction from the Research on Teacher and School Effectiveness." *Journal of Reading* 28 (November, 1984), 109–115.

5. Baumann, James F. "The What, Why, How, and When of Comprehension Instruction." *Reading Teacher* 39 (March, 1986), 640–646.

6. Berliner, David C. "Academic Learning Time and Reading Achievement." In John T. Guthrie (Ed.), *Comprehension and Teaching: Research Reviews.* Newark, Del.: International Reading Association, 1981.

7. Commission on Reading. *Becoming a Nation of Readers.* Washington, D.C.: National Institute of Education, U.S. Department of Education, 1984.

8. Duffy, Gerald G. "Fighting Off the Alligators: What Research in Real Classrooms Has to Say about Reading Instruction." *Journal of Reading Behavior* 14 (1982, No. 4), 357–373.

9. Duffy, Gerald G. "From Turn-Taking to Sense-Making: Toward a Broader Definition of Reading Teacher Effectiveness." *Journal of Educational Research* 76 (January–February, 1983), 134–139.

10. Duffy, Gerald G.; Roehler, Laura R.; and Rackliffe, Gary. "How Teachers' Instructional Talk Influences Students' Understanding of Lesson Content." *Elementary School Journal* 87 (September, 1986), 3–16.

11. Duffy, Gerald G.; Roehler, Laura R.; and Putname, Joyce. "Putting the Teacher in Control: Basal Reading Textbooks and Instructional Decision Making." *Elementary School Journal* 87 (January, 1987), 355–366.

12. Durkin, Dolores. "An Attempt to Make Sense Out of a Senseless Basal Reader Lesson." *Illinois Reading Council Journal* 14 (Spring, 1986), 23–31.

13. Durkin, Dolores. *Children Who Read Early.* New York: Teachers College Press, Columbia University, 1966.

14. Durkin, Dolores. "A Classroom-Observation Study of Reading Instruction in Kindergarten." *Early Childhood Research Quarterly* 2 (September, 1987), 275–300.

15. Durkin, Dolores. "Reading Comprehension Instruction in Five Basal Reader Series." *Reading Research Quarterly* 16 (1981, No. 4), 515–544.

16. Durkin, Dolores. "Reading Methodology Textbooks: Are They Helping Teachers Teach Comprehension?" *Reading Teacher* 39 (January, 1986), 410–417.

17. Durkin, Dolores. "Testing in the Kindergarten." *Reading Teacher* 40 (April, 1987), 766–770.
   Durkin, Dolores. "What Classroom Observations Reveal about Comprehension Instruction." *Reading Research Quarterly* 14 (1978–79, No. 4), 481–533.
   Gagne, Robert M. *The Conditions of Learning and Theory of Instruction.* New York: Holt, Rinehart and Winston, 1985.

20. Greaney, Vincent. "Parental Influences on Reading." *Reading Teacher* 39 (April, 1986), 813–818.

21. Guszak, Frank. "Teacher Questioning and Reading." *Reading Teacher* 21 (December, 1967), 227–234.

22. Guthrie, John T. "Effective Teaching Practices." *Reading Teacher* 35 (March, 1982), 766–768.

23. Hoffman, J. V.; O'Neal, S. F.; Kastler, L. A.; Clements, R. O.; Segel, K. W.; and Nash, M. F. "Guided Oral Reading and Miscue Focused Verbal Feedback in Second-Grade Classrooms." *Reading Research Quarterly* 19 (Spring, 1984), 367–384.

24. Jacobs, Leland B.; Vite, Irene; Sperber, Robert; Veatch, Jeannette; McCune, Mary A.; and Noel, Ann Ragland. *Individualizing Reading Practices.* New York: Bureau of Publications, Teachers College, Columbia University, 1958.

25. Meyer, Linda A. *Strategies for Correcting Students' Wrong Responses* (Technical Report No. 354). Urbana: University of Illinois, Center for the Study of Reading, December 1985.

26. Office of Educational Research. *What Works.* Washington, D.C.: U.S. Department of Education, 1986.

27. Paris, Scott G. "Using Classroom Dialogues and Guided Practice to Teach Comprehension Strategies." In Theodore L. Harris and Eric J. Cooper (Eds.), *Reading, Thinking, and Concept Development.* New York: College Entrance Board, 1985, 133–144.

28. Paris, S. G.; Newman, R. S.; and McVey, K. A. "Learning the Functional Significance of Mnemonic Actions: A Microgenetic Study of Strategy Recognition." *Journal of Experimental Child Psychology* 34 (December, 1982), 490–509.

29. Pearson, P. David, and Dole, Janice A. "Explicit Comprehension Instruction: A Review of Research and a New Conceptualization of Instruction." *Elementary School Journal* 88 (November, 1987), 151–165.

30. Rosenshine, Barak. "Synthesis of Research on Explicit Teaching." *Educational Leadership* 43 (April, 1986), 60–69.

31. Rosenshine, Barak. "Teaching Functions in Instructional Programs." *Elementary School Journal* 83 (March, 1983), 335–351.

32. Rouk, Ullik. "Separate Studies Show Similar Results of Teacher Effectiveness," *Educational R & D Report* 2 (Spring, 1979), 6–10.

33. Shannon, Patrick. "Commercial Reading Materials, a Technological Ideology, and the Deskilling of Teachers." *Elementary School Journal* 87 (January, 1987), 307–329.

34. Shoop, Mary. "InQuest: A Listening and Reading Comprehension Strategy." *Reading Teacher* 39 (March, 1986), 670–674.

35. Veatch, Jeannette. *Individualizing Your Reading Program.* New York: G. P. Putnam's Sons, 1959.

Part II

Reading
at the Beginning

For a long time, the term readiness has been associated with beginning reading instruction. In fact, "When are children ready to learn to read?" is a question many people have asked for many years.

Regardless of that association, readiness is as important for successful learning by adults as it is for children who are becoming readers. Evidence for this is widespread, but let's take as an example something as far removed from reading as chemical engineering. Even though professors who plan a college curriculum in chemical engineering are not likely to use the term readiness, prerequisites—which are at the core of readiness—are taken into account. Specifically, undergraduates majoring in chemical engineering will never be advised to enroll in a course such as Mass Transfer if they have not already had Physical Chemistry, the prerequisites for which include Analytical Geometry and Calculus.

In spite of the encompassing significance of readiness, the first chapter in Part Two, Chapter 4, covers readiness for the most part from the perspective of prerequisites for success with beginning reading. It is only natural, therefore, that Chapter 5 is about "Reading in the Kindergarten." This is a logical sequence because it is now taken for granted that reading instruction will be offered in some form to kindergartners. Because reading instruction is also found in a number of nursery schools, Chapter 5 should be pertinent for instructors at that level, too. And, it should be added, parents who wonder about their responsibilities insofar as reading and preschool children are concerned will also have some of their questions answered in both Chapter 5 and Chapter 4.

As you read Part Two, view Chapter 4 as providing something like a theory of readiness for beginning reading and Chapter 5 as one that illustrates how the theory is put into practice.

Chapter 4

Readiness for Reading

PREVIEW

As the Introduction to Part II indicated, Chapter 4 deals for the most part with the question, When are children ready to learn to read? To understand both the answer given and the reasons for it, some knowledge of the original conception of readiness for beginning reading is necessary. Chapter 4 refers to this earlier view as the "traditional" conception not only because it was the original one but also because its influence on the timing of beginning instruction was unusually persistent. Currently, knowing about the traditional conception of readiness is important for a reason explained in Chapter 5: The traditional conception has been resurrected and is enjoying a second round of influence over many early childhood educators. To witness the new influence is to be reminded of Santayana's well-known observation, "Those who cannot remember the past are condemned to repeat it."

Another reason for including historical material in Chapter 4 is that it shows how the timing of an idea is often more influential for its acceptance or rejection than is its quality or validity. The failure to keep this in mind accounts at least in part for some of the bandwagons that show up in the reading field with some regularity.

Following the historical sections, the focus of Chapter 4 shifts to a discussion of what "being ready" really means and of how readiness for reading can be assessed. Chapter 4 also discusses a conception of early reading and writing ability referred to as "emergent literacy."

The fact that successful learning at any level depends on the learner's readiness explains why the concluding section in Chapter 4 deals with instruction that goes beyond beginning reading. To emphasize the significance of readiness at all levels, this last section includes descriptions of more advanced reading instruction that give explicit attention to the prerequisites required if the objectives of the instruction are to be realized.

To establish purposes that can guide your reading of Chapter 4, examining the questions in the Review section now is recommended.

A detailed history of the readiness concept applied to beginning reading can be found elsewhere (20, 21). Only that part of the past that seems necessary for understanding the conception of readiness that *Teaching Them to Read* supports is covered here.

HISTORICAL PERSPECTIVE

As soon as the teaching of reading moved out of the kitchen into one-room schoolhouses and from there to buildings organized by grade levels, a close association developed between first grade and beginning reading. That union was eventually ruptured by a development that became apparent in the 1920s: interest in objective measurement viewed as a way to make psychology "scientific" (52). One consequence of the interest was national surveys of children's achievement in school. Others were the disclosures in the surveys that retentions in first grade were more common than had been thought and that inadequate achievement in reading was the common cause (15, 34, 42).

Logically, a study of unsatisfactory achievement would take into account such multiple and commonsense causes as poor instruction, inappropriate instructional materials, large classes, and low IQs among the children. In the 1920s and 1930s, however, the factor singled out as the culprit is identified in a pronouncement often found in the professional literature of that period: First graders are having problems learning to read because they were not ready when instruction began (15, 34). Why deficiencies in reading were attributed exclusively to a lack of readiness and, second, why delaying the timing of instruction was proposed as the way to resolve the problem can be explained with a brief review of the school of psychology most influential at the time. This requires a reference to psychologist G. Stanley Hall.

Early Psychological Beliefs

Hall, you may recall from psychology courses, had a striking influence on interpretations of human behavior at the start of this century. Prominent in Hall's writings was his belief in the unique importance of heredity. Equally apparent was his acceptance of the theory of recapitulation, which Hall himself explains as follows:

> The most general formulation of all the facts of development that we yet possess is contained in the law of recapitulation. This law declares that the individual, in his development, passes through stages similar to those through which the race has passed, and in the same order. (31, p. 8)

Hall's emphasis on heredity and recapitulation theory promoted a view of human development that stressed *a predetermined nature that unfolds in stages.* This interpretation of growth had a pronounced effect on Hall's students, who included Arnold Gesell. Because the concept of readiness is central to Gesell's work and also because his research and publications were uniquely influential during the 1920s and 1930s, he plays a leading role in this attempt to explain why (a) lack of readiness and (b) postponed instruction were thought to be the cause and the solution for beginning reading problems.

Arnold Gesell was a physician; thus his interest in the maturation process is not surprising—nor is his description of maturation as something that occurs in distinct stages (28, 29). Such a description clearly shows the influence of G. Stanley Hall. Hall's influence is also apparent in Gesell's proposed explanation of how children advance from one stage to the next. Bypassing such possible causes as learning and practice, Gesell singled out what was called at various times "intrinsic growth," "neural ripening," and "automatic and unfolding behavior."

Early Interpretation of Beginning Reading Problems

How Gesell's views of child development account for how first-grade reading problems were explained, starting in the late 1920s and continuing for decades thereafter, is summarized below. The summary clarifies why postponed instruction was offered as the solution for problems.

Traditional View of Readiness

1. A child's development takes place in stages that follow one another in an inevitable order.
2. Advancement from one stage to the next is the result of maturation (internal neural ripening) that occurs automatically with the passing of time.
3. The ability required to learn to read comes into existence at one of these stages.
4. Reading problems disclosed by the surveys suggest that most beginning first graders have not reached that particular stage of development and thus are not ready to learn to read.
5. The solution is to postpone reading instruction so that with the passing of time, the children will become ready.

Mental-Age Concept of Readiness

Given the circumstances of the 1920s, contentment with a concept of readiness that equated it with some vague stage in a child's development was not likely to persist. After all, that hardly reflected the interest in exact measurement that characterized the times. Not unexpected, therefore, were the subsequent efforts to define with more precision the stage of development thought to ensure success with reading.

New group intelligence tests affected the form these efforts took, because their availability fostered studies of the relationship between intelligence and reading achievement. As early as 1920, for example, one researcher claimed that first graders who had problems learning to read had mental ages of less than six years (16). Other researchers soon made proposals to establish a certain mental-age level as a requirement for starting instruction (2, 34, 56).

The type of thinking reflected in these reports was crystallized in a 1931 article that became widely known and uncommonly influential for a long time (39). Written by Mabel Morphett and Carleton Washburne, the report described the reading achievement of first-grade children when one particular method was used in one school system (Winnetka, Illinois). Based on the children's achievement as it related to mental age, the authors concluded:

> It seems safe to state that, by postponing the teaching of reading until children reach a mental age level of six and a half years, teachers can greatly decrease the chances of failure and discouragement and can correspondingly increase their efficiency. (39, p. 503)

How seriously Washburne took his own proposal is demonstrated in an article he wrote in 1936 entitled (in keeping with the prevailing psychological views) "Ripeness." Washburne observed:

> Nowadays each first grade teacher in Winnetka has a chart showing when each of her children will be mentally six-and-a-half, and is careful to avoid any effort to get a child to read before he has reached this stage of mental growth. (54, p. 127)

Evidence of how seriously other educators took the Morphett-Washburne proposal is in reading methodology textbooks that appeared not long after their report and also in some published as many as ten and twenty years later. In fact, textbooks published in the 1960s still took this proposal seriously.

Reasons for Acceptance of Mental-Age Concept

Now that you know how influential the Morphett-Washburne proposal was, you may wonder why findings from a study of one teaching method in one school system were accepted as being applicable to all children. You might also wonder why the acceptance persisted. A subsequent section answers the latter question; here, the one that asks why the Morphett-Washburne proposal was accepted so quickly is considered.

To begin, the proposal matched perfectly the temper of the times in which it was offered. It supported the "doctrine of postponement," since most children entering first grade do not have a mental age of 6.5 years. It also reflected the notion that development proceeds in stages—in this case, defined by mental age—and it honored the measurement and testing movement by being precise and "objective."

Early Objections to Mental-Age Concept

Even though the mental-age concept of readiness was quickly and widely accepted for reasons just cited, objections were still raised. The most important came from Arthur Gates, a well-known specialist in educational psychology. Conclusions reached in a number of his studies merit attention not only because they raised serious questions about the mental-age concept but also because they were conducted soon after the Morphett-Washburne article. Here, only two studies are discussed.

In 1936, in an article entitled "Reading Readiness: A Study of Factors Determining Success and Failure in Beginning Reading," Gates and Guy Bond described reading achievement in four first-grade classes (26). Of relevance to the present discussion is that in March, the ten lowest achievers were identified and assigned tutors. By June, all ten were enjoying success. Referring to that success, Gates and Bond wrote:

> The study emphasizes the importance of recognizing and adjusting to individual limitations and needs . . . rather than merely changing the time of beginning. It appears that readiness for reading is something to develop rather than merely to wait for. (26, p. 684)

Another study reported by Gates in 1937 reinforced the same conclusion (25). In this case, different methods of teaching reading and the achievement that resulted were examined. Commenting on the findings, Gates observed:

> Reading is begun by very different materials, methods, and general procedures, some of which a pupil can master at the mental age of five with reasonable ease, others of which would give him difficulty at the mental age of seven. (25, p. 508)

As the two reports indicate, a concept of reading readiness emerged from Gates's research that was at odds with the Morphett-Washburne description. Within the Gates frame of reference, considerable importance was assigned to the type and quality of instruction offered. In addition, questions were raised about the wisdom of postponement and of equating readiness with a particular mental age.

Essentially, Gates's message was simple: Improve your instruction and watch the children read! Apparently, the Morphett-Washburne proposal was more appealing because just as the publications of the 1930s and subsequent decades provide ample evidence of the prolonged acceptance of the mental-age concept of readiness, so too do they reveal how little attention went to

Gates's findings. His simply did not move with the stream of popular thought. What did, though, were further descriptions of the child thought to be ready for reading. To illustrate, in the Thirty-Eighth Yearbook of the National Society for the Study of Education, published in 1939, the following are cited as being "requisites of readiness for reading" (30, p. 195):

Keen interest in reading
Reasonably wide experiences
Facility in the use of ideas
Ability to solve simple problems
Ability to do abstract thinking of a very elementary type
Ability to remember ideas, word forms, and the sounds of words
A reasonable range of vocabulary
Command of simple English sentences
Good health, vision, and hearing
Ability to see likenesses and differences in word forms and to
discriminate sounds of words
Normal speech organs
Emotional stability
Some degree of social adjustment

With such a list—as well as with other checklists still in use—it is easy to forget that the concern is beginning reading, since the requirements appear to be for something much more difficult.

Reading Readiness Tests

Other efforts to describe the child who is ready to read account for readiness tests, which are referred to in the literature as early as the 1920s (6, 47). The initial versions of these tests were usually composed of subtests that dealt with vocabulary and visual and auditory discrimination. Each type of subtest is described next.

When a subtest focused on vocabulary, children were usually asked to circle or underline a picture that went with a word named by the person administering the test, generally a teacher. Or the administrator might be directed by the test manual to read aloud a particular sentence; again, children were told to select from a row of pictures the one that pertained to its content.

Subtests for visual discrimination also relied on pictures. In this case, the *unverified* assumption was that the ability to see similarities and differences in pictures is directly related to the ability to distinguish among similar and dissimilar letters and words. That the same unverified assumption held for geometrical figures also seems to have been accepted, as many of the early visual subtests focused on shapes. Now a child was asked to look at the first figure in a row and to underline all the others that were the same (or different).

Evidently the people who constructed readiness tests assumed that sooner or later phonics would be taught. This is suggested by the frequent inclusion of auditory discrimination subtests, typically involving rhyme. Now the administrator named each picture in a given row and had the children underline or circle all the pictures whose names rhymed with the name of the first one. Sometimes, but less often, an auditory subtest dealt with initial sounds in words. In this case, the person administering the test might say: "Put your finger under the picture of the boat. I'll name the other pictures in this row. Listen, because you are to draw a line around the one whose name begins with the sound you hear at the beginning of 'boat'."

In addition to explaining how the tests were to be administered, readiness test manuals usually suggested that results be used diagnostically. That is, subtest scores were to be studied in order to identify each child's particular strengths and weaknesses. What happened in practice, however, was quite different, as is explained next.

Reading Readiness Programs

When it was generally agreed in the 1930s that most beginning first graders are not ready to read, a decision had to be made about what to do while they were "growing into readiness." The description for the product of that decision is *reading readiness program.*

Content of Readiness Programs. Although called by the same name, the content of readiness programs varied from school to school. Some of the variation, no doubt, reflected differences among teachers, but some reflected conflicting viewpoints about the nature of readiness. More specifically, educators who believed that the passing of time automatically results in readiness also concluded that the content of a readiness program need not be directly related to the reading process. On the other hand, educators who believed that what occurred as time passed had some effect on readiness were more likely to focus on objectives similar to those assessed in readiness tests.

What also promoted attention to the tests—and this turned out to be uniquely influential over several decades—was the appearance of reading readiness workbooks, many of which came from companies that published the readiness tests. Whether or not this was so, the content of the tests and the content of the workbooks were very similar. In time, the content of the workbooks and the content of the readiness programs were also similar— which is to say that the *commercialization of instruction* is hardly a new phenomenon.

Duration of Readiness Programs. In theory, a readiness program was for "unready" children and would last until they became "ready." In practice, the typical procedure was to administer a readiness test close to the start of first grade. Evidently the purpose was not to learn whether some children might be ready for reading but, rather, to see how much time all children were to spend in a readiness program. The assumption seemed to be that it was good for everybody—ready or not.

If a school had decided that the shortest amount of time for participation in a readiness program was, let's say, two months, then the first graders with the highest readiness test scores were in a readiness program for two months. The remaining children participated for longer amounts of time, often determined somewhat arbitrarily and without consideration of individuals.

Reasons for Questionable Practices.   One reason for the questionable practices just described was the large number of children typically found in first grade. Ideally, readiness programs should have been highly individualized and should have included only children who seemed unready. Being responsible for large numbers of children—sometimes as many as forty—teachers were hardly able to achieve the ideal.

Further, the idea of readiness and of readiness programs was new. In addition, the programs were viewed not humbly but as a means for solving all the reading problems. No wonder they were greeted with what now seems like naïve enthusiasm, which, among other things, may have fostered the notion that readiness programs are good for everybody, ready or not.

Why the content of the programs was often sterile and routine also has a very human explanation. When first-grade teachers were suddenly called on to do something other than teach reading at the start of the year, many, if not most, must have felt insecure, to say the least. After all, a good program—whether for readiness or something else—is not created overnight. It is no wonder, then, that readiness workbooks seemed highly attractive when plans were made for a readiness program.

Reasons for Maintenance of Questionable Practices.   Even though it is easy to see how questionable practices developed when readiness programs were a novelty, it is difficult to understand why they persisted from the 1930s into the 1960s and, in some instances, even longer. Among the collection of reasons is the tendency of schools to be conservative (55). They often want to keep what they are doing and sometimes actively resist change.

With readiness programs, unchanging and sometimes questionable routines were also linked to instructional materials, specifically to readiness workbooks. As mentioned, not long after the programs came into existence, the workbooks appeared. And they came, sometimes two and three to a set, as part of basal reader programs. Because the vast majority of elementary teachers rely on basal materials, readiness workbooks were used, too, and not always because their content allowed for individualized instruction. As one first-grade teacher explained not too many years ago, "Our principal buys readiness workbooks, so we use them."

One more reason other questionable practices continued for so long relates to the tendency of educators to place too much faith in test scores. This was the case with readiness scores even though researchers examining their predictive value raised questions almost from the time the tests first appeared (22, 27). The critics did have some effect on the content of revised editions, but they had little effect on their use. Even now, readiness tests are published because they are purchased.

Another factor needs to be mentioned in this attempt to explain the persistence of certain practices connected with readiness assessment and readiness programs. It is that psychological conceptions of human growth and development changed very little from the early 1920s until the late 1950s, due mostly to the influence of Gesell, his students, and his disciples (43).

Willard Olson, another psychologist, has to be mentioned because he was especially popular among educators of young children. His ideas about child development, expressed in terms of "organismic age," were not contrary to Gesell's (40), nor was the notion of "developmental tasks," a term Robert Havighurst used (32). And so, having little reason to do otherwise, schools continued with the routine practice of administering readiness tests in first grade and of having every child—ready or not—participate in a readiness program. But then came Sputnik and, with it, a revolution in education.

A NEW ERA

Major educational changes hardly occur on one specific day; nonetheless, it is customary to designate the start of midcentury changes by citing the date when the Soviet Union launched Sputnik I: October 4, 1957. Expectedly, the launching of a satellite by a foreign power produced a variety of repercussions in the United States. Too loud to be ignored were the criticisms of public school education, which increased the already existing debate about the quality of instruction in American schools (7). Now the debate stressed the inferiority of our educational endeavors compared to those of the Soviet Union (5, 14).

One result of the new criticism was an atmosphere characterized by the plea, "Let's teach more in our schools, and let's teach it earlier!" Such an atmosphere, as time has demonstrated, fostered rapt attention to new proposals from psychologists. Relevant to this chapter's consideration of readiness are proposals that highlighted both the learning potential of young children and the unique importance of the early years for intellectual development.

Different Emphases in Psychology

One of the first books to receive the blessing of the post-Sputnik era was *The Process of Education* (9) by Jerome Bruner. This book is a psychologist's account of a ten-day meeting convened "to discuss how education in science might be improved in our primary and secondary schools" (9, p. vii). Of relevance to the present discussion is the chapter entitled "Readiness for Learning," introduced with the statement, "We begin with the hypothesis that any subject can be taught effectively in some intellectually honest form to any child at any stage of development" (9, p. 33). People who read all of Bruner's book will find little that is startling in the statement. It simply urged in a somewhat different way that the schools take another look at how they organized and presented instruction in such fields as science and mathematics. However, when the statement was quoted out of context— and it often was—it fostered what could only be called wishful thinking about the learning potential of young children.

That was the beginning. Later, in 1961, a book by another psychologist became unusually popular. *Intelligence and Experience* (35), by J. McV. Hunt, was a review and reinterpretation of earlier research that had examined the effects of training and practice on certain aspects of development. According to the original interpretation, readiness to learn—whether a motor skill or an intellectual skill—was the product of maturation, not of such environmental factors as training or practice. In the interpretation Hunt proposed, a great variety of practice and experiences was said to affect the emergence of an ability. Especially highlighted in Hunt's hypothetical explanation was the critical importance of *early* experiences.

Because of books like the two just cited, it was natural that the young child's environment emerged as a popular topic for discussion. Predictably, it was the theme of another book from which it became fashionable to quote. *Stability and Change in Human Characteristics* by Benjamin Bloom (8) appeared in 1964. Like Hunt's work, Bloom's was a detailed reexamination of earlier research—in this instance, of long-term studies concerned with the development of certain measurable characteristics. Concluding that the most rapid period for the development of many characteristics— including intelligence—is in the first five years of life, Bloom again stressed the crucial importance of the child's early environment.

New Social Concerns

At the start of the 1960s, in the midst of the excitement about early environmental factors, another development occurred. In this case, it was a new interest in an old problem: Children from the lowest socioeconomic levels start school with disadvantages that preclude adequate achievement. Why such a concern was unusually vocal and widespread at this particular time is found in political, social, and economic factors (45). Why the concern led to plans for prekindergarten schooling for "culturally disadvantaged" children—plans later formalized in Head Start programs—was clearly related to the psychological climate of the times.

Persistence of Traditional Views

What cannot be overlooked is that well-known leaders in early childhood education still clung to the traditional interpretation of readiness. In 1960, for example, Helen Heffernan wrote:

The restlessness and anxiety of our times have been expressed in trying to force down in the curriculum learnings for which the child is neither physiologically or psychologically ready and for which he sees no need. We have a mountain of evidence to prove that a perfectly "normal" child—I.Q. 100—cannot learn to read until he is about six years six months old. Any attempt to drive him may result in some evidence of reading but at an excessive cost in physiological and psychological damage and at great risk of impairment of his interest in reading. When the time comes he can master it readily. (33, p. 316)

The same message, embellished with slightly different details, also came from the pens of Frances Ilg and Louise Ames, both closely associated with the Gesell Institute of Child Development. In their book, *School Readiness,* published in 1964, the two complained about the new developments with an argument that existing studies contradicted:

Much, in fact rather too much, has been written about the formal teaching of reading in the preschool years. . . . Research has shown that most efforts . . . do not succeed in teaching the child to read. Even if they do, such a child's advancement over his contemporaries is usually not maintained. (36, p. 324)

In Conclusion

At opposite ends of a continuum ("Everybody is ready at four!" versus "Nobody is ready at six!"), the two positions described here are nonetheless alike in that research data support neither. Meriting attention, too, is that the conception of readiness that emerged from the earlier studies by Gates and his associates still attracted little attention. But that is not surprising, given the fact that changing the timing of instruction is a much easier solution than is changing the nature of an instructional program.

The position taken in this book is like the one of Gates. Consequently, the next section deals with that concept of readiness with the help of an article written in 1959 (3) by another well-known educational psychologist, David Ausubel.

PROPOSED DEFINITION OF READINESS

Readiness, Ausubel proposed, "is the adequacy of existing capacity in relation to the demands of a given learning task" (3, p. 246). Each part of his definition is now examined in order to point out what the whole of it implies, first, about the nature of readiness for beginning reading and, second, about ways to assess it.

Existing Capacity

Nothing that is known indicates that heredity alone determines a person's capacity to learn, nor does anyone insist that only environmental factors count. At various times, it is true, both nature and nurture have each been assigned exaggerated importance; nonetheless, it is generally agreed that an individual's capabilities at any given time are the result of an interplay among genetic endowment, maturation, experiences, and practice.

Demands of the Learning Task

According to Ausubel's definition, what it takes to be successful with beginning reading depends, first, *on the method used* to teach it *and*, second, *on how the method is executed.* A methodology that has children learn to identify whole words, for instance, has requirements that are not identical to what is necessary when beginning instruction focuses on letter-sound correspondences. When one reason to provide children with opportunities to write is to allow reading ability to emerge, different requirements exist. But even with the same methodology, demands may differ because of the variation in what teachers do with a method. Not to be overlooked, either, is that the pacing of instruction makes a difference.

Adequacy of Capacity in Relation to Demands

The most important feature of Ausubel's definition is the explicit attention it gives to the relational aspect of readiness. This feature points up that readiness for reading has a *two*fold focus: (a) children's abilities *in relation to* (b) the nature of the instructional program.

A Summary

How Ausubel's conception of readiness has been interpreted to apply to reading is summarized in Figure 4.1. Please examine that diagram now along with the commentary about Figure 4.1.

IMPLICATIONS OF THE DEFINITION

One implication of Ausubel's conception of readiness pertains to how questions ought to be posed. To ask, "Is the child ready to begin to read?" is, according to Ausubel's definition, incorrect. This is the case because in failing to account for the kind and quality of instruction that is available, the question overlooks the relational aspect of readiness. A more correct question, therefore, asks, "Is the child ready to be successful with this particular kind and quality of instruction?" Even this concern is less than perfect, however, because it assumes that the instructional program is "a given." The ideal question, then, is: Considering the child's particular abilities and interests, what type of instruction can make the greatest use of what he or she is able to do and learn?

Admittedly, some of you may conclude that such a question is too idealistic and thus is not helpful. If this conclusion does resemble your thoughts, at least allow the correct question to help you understand that some children are unsuccessful with beginning reading because the pre-established instructional program, which often comes directly from commercial materials, does not use what they know and can and like to do. Or, to make this very important point differently, an all too common practice is to expect children to adapt to a program rather than to offer instruction that has been adapted to their particular abilities and interests (18).

Another implication of Ausubel's conception of readiness has to do with assessment. If, as Ausubel states, *readiness is the adequacy of existing capacity in relation to the demands of the learning task*, it follows that the only meaningful way to test for adequacy is to give children opportunities to learn to read in order to see what their capacity actually is. The definition further suggests that the opportunities should vary in the methodology they represent, because it is possible that a child can be successful with one method but not with another. By observing what a child does or does not learn from each method, much can be gleaned about that child's readiness and also about the kind of instruction that makes the best use of his or her abilities and interests.

To make all of this more specific, illustrations of assessment featuring typical kindergarten activities are offered next.

VARIED LEARNING OPPORTUNITIES

Time in every kindergarten is spent taking attendance, which allows teachers to look for behavioral signs of readiness for reading. Specifically, at the beginning of the year, a teacher can take attendance by showing first names on cards. Later, the children indicate their presence by selecting their name card and putting it on an attendance board. This simple routine can teach a child to read his name and others' names as well. In addition, it helps a teacher learn which children remember (read) names easily, which have more difficulty, and which remember few if any names.

Art activities provide other opportunities to assess readiness. This is the case because finished products in art provide a reason for kindergartners to learn to print their names and, later, to write captions and to read those composed by others. Pertinent to this discussion is that the same activities give an observant teacher the chance to identify children for whom writing might be an easy way into reading, to identify those who remember whole words with a minimum of exposure to them, and to become aware of still others for whom the motor skill of writing is a formidable task or for whom it is difficult to compose even the briefest caption.

Reading to children is another activity found in kindergartens. Even though this should always be for enjoyment, a story can be used occasionally to learn even more about the children's readiness for reading. Let's as-

Figure 4.1 Readiness for Success with Beginning Reading Instruction

Commonly, people interested in children's readiness for reading focus on the
children, specifically, on what they can and cannot do. In contrast, the content
of Figure 4.1 recognizes the equal significance of the available instruction for a
child's success (or failure) with beginning reading.

   Because children of the same age differ in abilities and interests due to
both hereditary and environmental factors, it can be inferred from Figure 4.1
that an instructional program should be composed of different methodologies.
More specifically, programs should include opportunities (a) to learn to read
whole words, (b) to learn the sounds that letters record, and (c) to learn to print
letters and write simple text.

   The content of Figure 4.1 can be summed up by saying that changing the
timing of beginning instruction without ensuring the delivery of instruction that
is eclectic in nature is not the way to promote maximum success for a maximum
number of children.

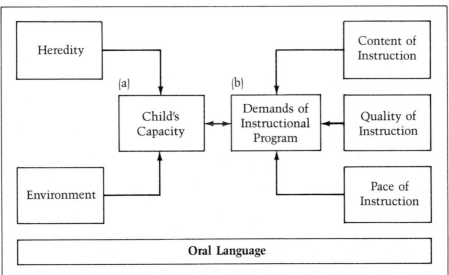

Heredity		Content of Instruction
(a)	(b)	
	Child's Capacity ⟷ Demands of Instructional Program	Quality of Instruction
Environment		Pace of Instruction

Oral Language

Summary: Whether children are ready to acquire beginning reading ability depends on the match that exists between (a) what they know, understand, and are able to do, and (b) what the instructional program requires for success. What *is* required is determined by the *content* of the instruction offered, the *quality* with which the instruction is delivered, and the *pace* at which the instruction progresses. Underlying all this is the dependence of success in reading—no matter what the instructional program might be—on oral language.

sume, for example, that two recent stories were about Ping, a duck. Let's also say that two children in the class are Paul and Penny. The kindergarten teacher decides, therefore, to print *Ping* on the chalkboard, allowing for the question, "Does anybody [pointing to the *P*] have a name that starts the way *Ping* starts? If you do, I'll write your name with Ping's." Soon the board shows:

Ping
Penny
Paul

Other questions (their number and kind should be determined by the children's abilities and interest) follow: "Does anybody know the name of the letter [pointing to *P*] at the beginning of these three names? ... Have you ever seen any other word that begins with this letter *P*? If you have, what is it? ... Now there are five words on the board that begin with *P*. I'll read them all. As I do, listen to see if you can hear how they all start with the same sound. ... Can someone make the sound that these names start with? ... I'll say the words again. Watch how I put my lips together when I start to say each one. Listen to the way each word starts. ... Can someone think of other words that start the way *Ping, Paul, Penny, Punch,* and *Pat* begin? If you can, I'll write them, too."

On another day, another word and letter might receive attention; or the teacher might decide to repeat the attention given *P* using different words to illustrate the sound it records. Whatever the decision, the opportunity exists for children to respond and—and this is the point being stressed—for a teacher to identify who among them has skill in auditory discrimination. At the same time, the teacher may become aware of other kindergartners who appear to have no understanding of what is meant by "begin with the same sound."

Perhaps these few illustrations are enough to give specific meaning to the proposal made earlier for assessing readiness: Give children varied opportunities to begin to read and write and note what they are able to learn. Implied even in the few illustrations are other important ideas.

ASSESSMENT, READINESS INSTRUCTION, AND READING INSTRUCTION

One way to deal with the additional ideas is through descriptions of two children in the kindergarten class just referred to.

Paul. *Paul shows signs of being mentally slow. Even his physical movements are sluggish and awkward. When the teacher wrote* Ping *on the board and asked whether anyone had a name that began with the same letter, he remained silent. A concentrated look* *from the teacher plus a nudge from the child next to him (Mary Anne) eventually led to Paul's volunteering his name. It is doubtful that he would have mentioned it had these hints from others been missing. Once his name appeared on the board, Paul seemed interested in the discussion, although he remained silent during all of it.*

The question of relevance here is, What did both Paul and his teacher learn from the discussion and questions? For his teacher, the situation provided further evidence of Paul's slowness. Even though the letter being highlighted was in his name and he had seen it written many times before, Paul did not seem to be aware that his name and Ping's begin the same way. It is also unlikely that Paul understands the concept "sound alike" applied to parts of words.

For Paul himself the situation was special because everybody was talking about his name. He did not remember anyone telling him before—they had, actually—that the first letter in his name is *P.* Nor did he seem to know until the day of the *Ping* lesson that other words start with *P.*

But what about Mary Anne? What did the same discussion and questioning mean for her?

Mary Anne. *Mary Anne is an alert child who doesn't believe in hiding her candle under a bushel basket. In the discussion of words beginning with P, she was quick to say she knew its name because it was in her big sister's name (Pat). She said she could write her sister's name and her mother's and daddy's names, too. As the discussion proceeded, she enjoyed making the sound that p represents—this seemed new for her—and quickly recalled words beginning with it.* Punch, princess, *and* Pat *were her contributions when the teacher inquired, "Can anyone think of some words that begin the way* Ping *begins?" (Mary Anne was eager to explain that* Punch *was the name of the detergent her family used to wash clothes.)*

Obviously, results of the discussion and questions for Mary Anne were totally different from what they were for Paul. With both children, however, the teacher had an opportunity to look for behavioral signs of readiness. In the case of Mary Anne, much was learned—including the fact that she had already begun to read. She knew the name of *p,* enjoyed making the sound it represents in *Ping,* and was able to name words beginning with *p.* That she did some writing at home and was attentive to words in her environment also became clear.

While the teacher was seeking out behavioral signs of readiness, what was Mary Anne learning? For the most part, the discussion and questions helped her recall and use what she already knew. Two new learnings were the understanding that words have a beginning sound and that the sound that *p* represents is /p/.* The teacher's assessment efforts, therefore, provided an opportunity for Mary Anne to have reading instruction, specifically, instruction in phonics.

What the discussion and questioning turned out to be for both Mary Anne and Paul is summarized below:

	Assessment	Readiness Instruction	Reading Instruction
Paul	X	X	
Mary Anne	X		X

STILL MORE ABOUT THE NATURE OF READINESS

Another important point about readiness can be made by describing one more child in the same kindergarten.

Joey. *Joey is an enthusiastic participant in all activities. At first, he generally went to the blocks at free-choice time; however, quiet table games and puzzles soon became attractive. He also is an inevitable joiner whenever the teacher provides other choices: "Today I'm going to be reading a story over in that part of the room" or "Today I'm going to be playing a game" (such as bingo played with numerals, letters, or words). When words enter into a game, Joey is both involved and successful because of his wonderful ability to remember words with minimal help. He learned to read all the days of the week as a result of quick, early morning discussions related to "What day is today?" The attention given to September and October in connection with a calendar put those words into his reading vocabulary, too.*

Word games have allowed Joey's observant teacher to hear him make informative comments. When Sunday was used he observed, "Sandy's name looks like a short Sunday." On another day when the teacher wrote silk on the board in connection with a discussion of fabrics and textures, Joey quickly observed, "That almost looks like salt." Asked, "Where did you see salt?" he explained, "It's on our salt shaker at home."

Interestingly, Joey's excellent visual memory is not matched by excellence in auditory discrimination. In fact, he rarely responds when the teacher makes requests like: "I'm going to say two words. Tell me whether they start with the same sound or a different sound: tree, fence."

---

* A detailed discussion of phonics, including the isolation of sounds, appears in Chapters 8 and 9.

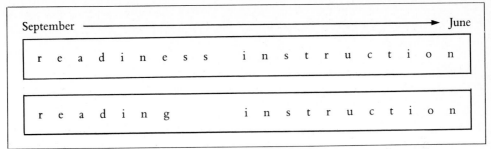

Figure 4.2 Curriculum Reflecting Realistic Understanding of Readiness

What all the observations about Joey correctly indicate is that in some ways he is more than ready for reading—he has already begun. In other ways, however, he is still learning to be ready. Here, the important implication is that efforts to assess readiness should not have an either-or focus. That is, a teacher's thoughts ought *not* to be, "Is he or is he not ready?" but, rather, "In what ways is he ready and in what ways is he not?" This more correct concern means that readiness instruction and reading instruction go on simultaneously. With Joey, for instance, reading ability is developing as a result of help with whole word identification. *At the same time,* the attention going to sounds is readiness instruction for him. Graphically, this point is made in Figure 4.2.

Notice the essential difference between the conception portrayed in Figure 4.2 and the traditional practice of separating readiness programs from reading programs, which is portrayed in Figure 4.3. Among the results of the unrealistic separation displayed in Figure 4.3 is the notion of "prereading skills." The distinction made between prereading and reading skills has, unfortunately, fostered attention to abilities that are not even related, let alone necessary to reading. The irrelevance is generously illustrated in Figures 4.4 to 4.8, which show pages from reading readiness workbooks that provide "prereading" exercises. Please examine the workbook pages and the commentary about each one before proceeding.

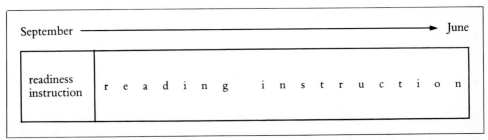

Figure 4.3 Curriculum Reflecting Either/Or Concept of Readiness

(text continues on p. 100)

Figure 4.4 Questionable Activity for Visual Discrimination Practice

The ability to see that some pictures are the same and some are different reveals ▶
nothing about an individual's ability to discriminate among letters or words;
nonetheless, pictures as well as geometric shapes continue to be used in reading
readiness workbooks. The page shown in Figure 4.4 illustrates another
characteristic of the workbooks: very few items per page. (This helps to account
for the sizable amount of time spent on coloring pictures in workbooks and ditto
sheet exercises.)

The point to remember is that work with visual discrimination should
concentrate on single letters at first, beginning with comparisons of no more
than about three or four arranged in columns, not rows. (Making visual
comparisons is easier when the objects being compared are placed under each
other.) Teachers also need to keep in mind that children who can name letters
have no need for this work. After all, how can they remember the names of
letters if they are unable to make distinctions among their shapes? Because
readiness materials have many pages of visual discrimination exercises, finding
out whether children can name letters is an early obligation for kindergarten
teachers.

This point leads to a third reminder: Children who are unable to name
letters may have adequate visual discrimination ability but may not have had the
opportunity to learn the names. Consequently, some instruction in letter naming
should be provided before conclusions are reached about a child's visual
discrimination ability.

Source: Virginia Polish, *Starting Off with Phonics* (Cleveland, Oh.: Modern Curriculum Press, 1986), p. 29. Reprinted with permission of Modern Curriculum Press, Inc.

Figure 4.5   Another Questionable Exercise for Preparing Children to Read

The workbook page in Figure 4.5 shows a visual discrimination exercise—three ▶
items in all—that focuses on patterns. Children are to draw lines connecting
identical patterns. (It needs to be kept in mind that children who are able to
name letters and even words may have problems with a page like this one even
though it is offered as help for preparing children for reading. Such a possibility
suggests another point for teachers to remember: What is said to get children
ready for reading should not be more difficult than learning to read.)

Typically, work with patterns is grouped under "Visual-Motor Skills."
When it is, the usual task is to make a simple pattern look exactly like a more
complex one. Authors of such exercises claim that the ability to make one
pattern look like another tells something about maturation, which, in turn,
reveals information about a child's readiness for reading. Such claims continue
to be made even though research data have consistently contradicted them (1,
10, 41, 46).

Not surprisingly, visual-motor tasks were popular when Arnold Gesell was
a leading figure in the field of child development. As the next chapter shows,
Gesell-like thinking is again influencing early childhood education in the form of
support for tests referred to as "developmental" (18). These tests assess such
motor skills as hopping and walking a balance beam and such visual-motor
abilities as copying patterns. The return of support for a Gesell-like view of what
constitutes readiness helps account for the large number of visual-motor
exercises in current readiness workbooks.

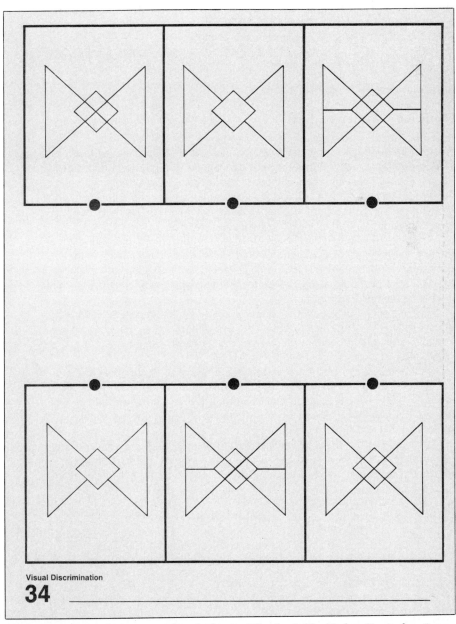

Visual Discrimination
34

Source: Virginia Polish, *Starting Off with Phonics* (Cleveland, Oh.: Modern Curriculum Press, 1986), p. 34. Reprinted with permission of Modern Curriculum Press, Inc.

Figure 4.6 Misnamed Task

Presumably, auditory discrimination exercises are included in reading readiness
workbooks to prepare children for phonics. Phonics instruction, in turn, attends
to connections between letters and speech sounds as a way of helping children
figure out unfamiliar words. All this makes it necessary to raise a question about
the workbook page in Figure 4.6, because the required task has nothing to do
with discriminating among speech sounds.

Clearly, the exercise has much to do with world knowledge. Although, as
the first chapter in this book demonstrated, world knowledge makes major
contributions to comprehension, the page should hardly be labeled ''Auditory
Readiness.'' Nor should teachers who assign the page shown in Figure 4.6 think
it will prepare children for phonics.

Figure 4.6 raises yet another question, namely, Will children remember the
directions after they are read to them? (It goes without saying that children who
are able to read the directions themselves should hardly be using the
workbook.)

On the positive side, teachers can use this page to discuss the content of
the pictures, to name what the children are unable to name, and, eventually, to
decide whether what is pictured makes a noise. If the children are still
interested, they can be asked to circle in each row the picture that shows
something that makes a very loud noise.

The message in these final suggestions is that teachers often have to use
workbook pages—if they feel they must be used—in ways and for purposes
different from the recommended use. If such adjustments are not made, much
time will be wasted.

Section Two
(Loud & Soft Sounds)

In each row there are three pictures. In one picture a loud sound is being made. In another picture a softer sound is being made. In the third picture no sound is being made. Circle the picture in which a loud sound is being made.

—7—

Source: William Wittenberg, *A Word Recognition Program: Auditory Readiness* (Baldwin, N.Y.: Barnell Loft, Ltd., 1981), p. 7. Copyright 1981 Barnell Loft, Ltd. *Word Recognition Program.*

Figure 4.7 Problems with Rhyme

Figure 4.7 shows another three-item page that has children draw lines to
connect pictures whose names rhyme. A more common format for rhyming
exercises is several rows of pictures. In this case, the children circle or underline
all the pictures in a row whose names rhyme with the name of the first picture.
Regardless of the format, questions have to be raised both about spending time
on rhyme and about the way "rhyming words" is commonly defined.

Spending time on rhyme as part of a phonics program is questioned, first,
because a reader hears nothing when an unknown word is encountered. The
ability to hear that certain words rhyme is therefore of no relevance.

The second question pertains to the fact that rhyming words are often
described in manuals and by teachers—and even by researchers (48)—as "words
that end with the same sound." In one kindergarten, a teacher used just such a
definition with the following results. After giving two examples of words that
rhyme, she asked the children for others. Immediately, one boy suggested
"kitten" and "spoon," indicating he had paid very close attention to the
teacher's definition. It quickly became clear, however, that the teacher did not
find the response acceptable, as she went on to praise a second child who
suggested "kitten" and "mitten."

In addition to offering accurate definitions, teachers must be certain that
whenever pictures are used for work with auditory discrimination, each is
assigned the same name by all children. A picture of an addressed envelope, for
instance, might put "envelope" into the head of one child but "mail" and
"letter" into the heads of two others. The problem here is that by the time all
the pictures on a page are named, some children will have finished the page,
especially if similar pages were done earlier.

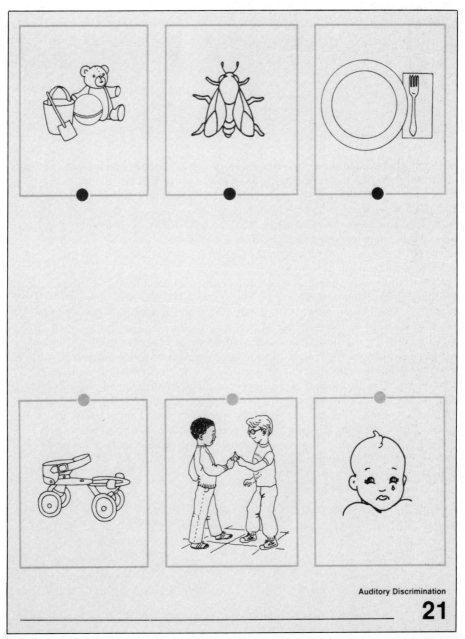

Auditory Discrimination

21

Source: Virginia Polish, *Starting Off with Phonics* (Cleveland, Oh.: Modern Curriculum Press, 1986), p. 21. Reprinted with permission of Modern Curriculum Press, Inc.

Figure 4.8 Busy Work

Even though this page shows that reading readiness workbooks eventually do
attend to letters, the page nonetheless illustrates busy work. It also illustrates the
large amount of mislabeling that occurs; what is required for the page shown in
Figure 4.8 has nothing to do with letter recognition.

The same page also raises a question about the ability of children to
understand, much less remember, the directions, which, presumably, a teacher
reads aloud. But the most fundamental question is whether something like this
exercise is necessary or even helpful.

Such questions prompt some educators to recommend that the concept
"readiness" be abandoned, for it is no longer useful (49). However, because
readiness viewed as a prerequisite is a most important concept for anyone
teaching at any level, the recommendation seems to be a case of throwing out
the baby with the bathwater. Or to put it differently, just because reading
readiness workbooks continue to provide large numbers of highly questionable
exercises does not make the concept "readiness" any less useful or important.

A definition that should help teachers of young children spend time on
relevant activities is one that suggests: *Readiness instruction is reading instruction
in its earliest stages.* Teachers who keep this equation in mind are not likely to
conclude that marching children through readiness workbooks is the best way to
prepare them for reading. The equation should also put doubt in the mind of
anyone who is considering buying workbooks. Not to be forgotten is that what
does not sell soon goes out of print.

Section Four
(Letter Recognition)

Draw lines to connect the boxes that have the same letters. Use a different colored crayon for each line, and do not draw your lines across a box.

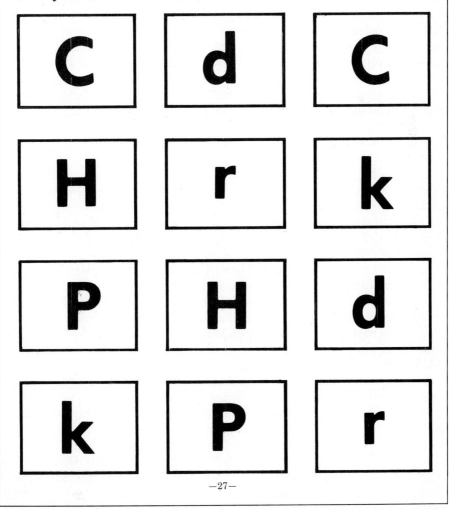

—27—

Source: William Wittenberg, *A Word Recognition Program: Motor-Visual Readiness* (Baldwin, N.Y.: Barnell Loft, Ltd., 1981), p. 27. Copyright 1981 Barnell Loft, Ltd. *Word Recognition Program.*

EMERGENT LITERACY

Anyone who keeps up with the literature on early reading is bound to come across the term *emergent literacy*. Some background information about this concept follows.

Emergent literacy refers to a view of reading ability that conceives of it as something that begins very early in a child's life—long before entrance into school (49). For people who accept the rather loose definition of reading ability that underlies the notion of emergent literacy, a child's pointing to a picture in a book or, perhaps, turning the pages in a magazine is evidence of the start of reading ability. Such ability is then thought to progress very slowly and gradually during the preschool years, hence the description "emergent." "Literacy" rather than "reading" is used because educators' interest in the roots of reading ability fostered other interest in what is known about preschoolers' ability to write. The latter is commonly discussed now in the context of *invented spelling*, a topic dealt with in the next chapter.

The facts that some preschoolers acquire reading ability and, further, that certain ones seem more interested in writing than in reading were uncovered in longitudinal studies done in the United States in the early 1960s (17) and somewhat later in a study done in England (12). It wasn't until the late 1970s and early 1980s, however, that widespread interest in emergent literacy became apparent in the literature (13).

As with any highly enthusiastic interest that occurs in reading from time to time, the one in emergent literacy may have negative as well as positive consequences. On the positive side, the attention to emergent literacy should move educators away from the belief that readiness occurs at some given point in a child's life, whereupon reading instruction can commence. Put differently, the concept should prompt acceptance of the point of view communicated earlier in Figure 4.2. With such acceptance, rejection of the prereading exercises shown in Figures 4.4 through 4.8 is inevitable.

On the negative side, the possibility exists of generalizing about young children's abilities without sufficient evidence. Overgeneralizing is possible because the more recent reports of early readers and writers are of very small numbers of children whose accomplishments are told in anecdotal reports (23, 38, 44). Even though the accounts are interesting and often informative, they are far removed from the type of research required for reliable generalizations about young children's abilities and interests.

Another possible problem is related to the fact that the children described in the reports usually come from highly literate, professional families (49); yet those who describe their achievements often minimize the significance of such backgrounds for the development of early literacy. It is almost as if what is acquired is learned "naturally," interpreted to mean without the help of adults or, for example, of older siblings (49, 51, 53). Insufficient attention to the influence of the environment could encourage teachers of young children to have unrealistically high expectations. Given the fact that children of poverty will make up larger and larger proportions of our schools' populations in the near future, such expectations could be problematic.

Finally, the widespread interest in young children's early efforts to write has already moved some educators to propose that writing should be taught before reading instruction is offered (11). Here one must ask, "Is it any more defensible to claim that all children should be taught to write first than it is to insist that the only way to start teaching reading is by attending to the sounds that letters record?"

The point of all this is as follows: The most defensible posture for teachers to take as they put together a beginning literacy program is one that recognizes (a) that children entering school are very different in what they know and have experienced, and (b) that the best way to accommodate the largest number is to provide a program marked by eclectic methodology executed in ways of interest to young children. An example of such a program is described in the next chapter. Before this chapter concludes, readiness beyond beginning reading is discussed.

READINESS AT LATER LEVELS

Even though readiness is most often referred to when the timing of beginning reading is discussed, its significance for success at subsequent levels should not be forgotten by teachers of older students. After all, every step of the way to becoming a proficient reader has certain requirements, which is what the readiness concept is all about.

Whether viewed in the context of the Ausubel definition or in the category of requirements or prerequisites, readiness beyond the beginning may be one thing or a combination of things that could include—depending on what is to be taught—an attitude, an experience, a skill, or an understanding. Let me illustrate prerequisites with some examples.

If students find it difficult to follow a sequence in written discourse, their teacher might decide to help by instructing about words that signal sequence (for example, *first, later, next*). Before that can be done, she needs to make sure the students are ready. In this case, being ready means (a) having an understanding of what is meant by sequence, (b) being able to identify the selected signal words, and (c) knowing what they mean. Any prerequisite that is missing needs to be taught first.

To cite another example, if a story takes place in years gone by, preparing students to read it might include more than teaching new vocabulary. Specifically, if a central character runs from house to house to warn neighbors of an approaching fire, students need to know that at the time the story took place, telephones were nonexistent. Otherwise, it will be hard to understand why such an inefficient and possibly dangerous means was chosen for dealing with the emergency. Providing the necessary background information, therefore, constitutes another example of readiness instruction.

In another instance, a teacher may find several similes in a selection that a certain group of students will be reading. She decides, therefore, to teach them about similes signaled by *as . . . as,* since that is the construction the author of the selection uses. In this case, readiness for learning about similes includes understanding "comparison." If *as dark as a big bottle of black ink* is one simile in the selection, another requirement might be information about bottles of ink, since students brought up on ball-point pens may not know about ink in bottles.

The need for teachers of older students to take readiness into account almost invariably shows up when something like a chapter in a social studies textbook is about to be read. Now, readying students may require attention to how the author organized the chapter, what the author does to explain technical terms, how the end-of-the-chapter questions can be used to guide the reading, and how certain graphic aids (such as maps and graphs) are to be interpreted.

Teachers who want to learn whether students can distinguish among five short vowel sounds must also consider readiness requirements, one of which is an understanding of "short vowel sounds." A second-grade teacher who overlooked prerequisites was observed working with seven children who had been given a list of short, one-syllable words they could read. The teacher began by asking, "What's the first word in the list that has a short vowel sound?" Silence resulted. The teacher continued, "The first word says 'slow.' Do you hear any short vowel sound in 'slow'?" Now some said "yes" while others were saying "no." Clearly there was confusion, in this case originating in the children's failure to remember the meaning of "short vowel sounds." Eventually, the teacher did what should have been done in the first place: review the meaning as well as the individual sounds.

It is possible that teachers sometimes bypass attention to prerequisites in order to save time. Yet what the second-grade teacher just referred to demonstrated is that attending to review is a way to save, not waste, time. It is also a way to maximize success for students.

SUMMARY

The nature of readiness for starting to read is the central theme of Chapter 4. It merits detailed attention because success at the start is crucial for building self-confidence.

In considering the best time to start teaching reading, educators and psychologists who dominated the scene from the 1920s to the 1950s correctly gave attention to readiness when they asked, "When are children ready to be successful with reading?" Many answered, "When they have a mental age of about 6.5 years." Others turned to special testing as a way to find an answer; thus was born the reading readiness test. Routinely, the concern of people administering these tests was not for the possibility that some beginning first graders might be ready for reading but, rather, for how long a readiness program ought to last.

The chapter identified flaws in the early interpretations and use of the readiness concept. One was an exaggerated appreciation of the contributions that heredity and maturation make to readiness. In contrast, the position taken in Chapter 4 is that what constitutes a given child's abilities is affected not only by genetic endowment and maturation but also by prior experiences and learnings.

The point especially emphasized in the chapter is the need to look at instruction as well as at students' abilities when readiness is considered. With the twofold focus, the question earlier psychologists and educators asked—Is the child ready?—is incomplete, and thus incorrect. It assumed that success with different kinds of reading instruction requires the same abilities and that readiness, therefore, has a single meaning that can be assessed in a test. Or maybe the assumption was that there is only one way to teach reading, and so the question to ask is, "When are children ready to be successful with it?"

Whatever the explanation, Chapter 4 tried to show that the correct and complete question is more specific, for it asks, "Is the child ready to succeed with this particular kind and quality of instruction?" Such a question recognizes the *equal* significance of the child's abilities and the instruction. Stated differently, it reflects the relational aspect of readiness, which is underscored in Ausubel's conception of readiness as being "the adequacy of existing capacity in relation to the demands of a given learning task" (3, p. 246). This concept has implications for how readiness can be assessed: Give children varied opportunities to learn to read. What they do or do not learn tells something not only about their readiness but also about the way of teaching reading that takes advantage of their abilities and interests.

Using such assessment procedures, teachers commonly learn that most children are neither totally ready nor totally unready. Such awareness ought to encourage schools to give up the idea that "getting ready to read" and "beginning to read" occur at separate points on some time line, as well as the related practice of having a readiness program followed by a reading program. Instead, *readiness instruction* will be viewed as *reading instruction in its earliest stages.* Such an equation is supported by another concept discussed in Chapter 4—emergent literacy.

The chapter ended by stressing that the readiness concept has as much significance for middle- and upper-grade teachers as for those at the kindergarten and first-grade levels. With examples, Chapter 4 underscored the need for all teachers to think through prerequisites whenever they make plans to attain a particular objective. The same examples also served to show that progress in learning to read is a matter of moving from what is known to what is new but related.

REVIEW

1. Explain how G. Stanley Hall's conception of human development fostered the original ("traditional") view of readiness for beginning reading instruction.

2. Describe how Arnold Gesell's ideas about (a) development and (b) what promotes development also contributed to the initial conception of readiness for reading.

3. What *is* the traditional interpretation of readiness?

4. Now that you have described the traditional interpretation, tell why a mental-age stipulation was added to the traditional description.

5. Describe the studies done by Arthur Gates, which are referred to in this chapter. Next, explain how his findings contradict the traditional interpretation of readiness.

6. How are Arthur Gates's and David Ausubel's conceptions of readiness similar?

7. In what sense did the post-Sputnik years communicate hypotheses that are directly opposite to the hypotheses that supported the traditional interpretation of readiness?

8. Let's assume you accept Ausubel's definition of readiness. How would you respond to a teacher who made the following request in October: "I teach first grade and am required to use the _____ basal reader series.* All the children are doing just fine with the exception of two boys. Apparently they are not yet ready to read. What readiness materials would you recommend for them?"

9. Explain what is meant by "the commercialization of instruction." What are some possible negative consequences of the commercialization for kindergarten?

10. Teachers at all grade levels need to consider whether students are ready to learn what has been planned for them to learn. State one instructional objective related to reading and then specify what students need to know or to be able to do to make the objective attainable.

REFERENCES

1. Arter, Judith A., and Jenkins, Joseph R. "Differential Diagnosis—Prescriptive Teaching: A Critical Appraisal." *Review of Educational Research* 49 (Fall, 1979), 517–555.
2. Arthur, Grace. "A Quantitative Study of the Results of Grouping First Grade Children According to Mental Age." *Journal of Educational Research* 12 (October, 1925), 173–185.
3. Ausubel, David P. "Viewpoints from Related Disciplines: Human Growth and Development." *Teachers College Record* 60 (February, 1959), 245–254.
4. Backman, Joan. "The Role of Psycholinguistic Skills in Reading Acquisition." *Reading Research Quarterly* 18 (Summer, 1983), 466–479.

* The required series starts with phonics and moves at a fairly brisk pace.

5. Benton, William. *This Is the Challenge.* New York: Associated College Presses, 1958.
6. Berry, Frances M. "The Baltimore Reading Readiness Test." *Childhood Education* 3 (January, 1927), 222–223.
7. Bestor, Arthur E. *Educational Wastelands: The Retreat from Learning in Our Public Schools.* Urbana: University of Illinois Press, 1953.
8. Bloom, Benjamin S. *Stability and Change in Human Characteristics.* New York: Wiley, 1964.
9. Bruner, Jerome. *The Process of Education.* Cambridge: Harvard University Press, 1960.
10. Chall, Jeanne S. "A Decade of Research on Reading and Learning Disabilities." In S. Jay Samuels (Ed.), *What Research Has to Say about Reading Instruction.* Newark, Del.: International Reading Association, 1978.
11. Chomsky, Carol. "Write First, Read Later." *Childhood Education* 47 (March, 1971), 296–299.
12. Clarke, Margaret M. *Young Fluent Readers.* London: Heinemann Educational Books, 1976.
13. Clay, Marie M. *Reading: The Patterning of Complex Behavior.* Exeter, N.H.: Heinemann Educational Books, 1972.
14. "Crisis in Education." *Life* 49 (March 24, 1958), 26–35.
15. Dickson, Virgil E. *Mental Tests and the Classroom Teacher.* New York: World Book Co., 1923.
16. Dickson, Virgil E. "What First Grade Children Can Do in School As Related to What Is Shown by Mental Tests." *Journal of Educational Research* 2 (June, 1920), 475–480.
17. Durkin, Dolores. *Children Who Read Early.* New York: Teachers College Press, Columbia University, 1966.
18. Durkin, Dolores. "A Classroom-Observation Study of Reading Instruction in Kindergarten." *Early Childhood Research Quarterly* 2 (September, 1987), 275–300.
19. Durkin, Dolores. "A Language Arts Program for Pre-First Grade Children: Two-Year Achievement Report." *Reading Research Quarterly* 5 (Summer, 1970), 534–565.
20. Durkin, Dolores. *Teaching Young Children to Read,* 4th ed. Boston: Allyn and Bacon, 1987.
21. Durkin, Dolores. "When Should Children Begin to Read?" In Helen M. Robinson (Ed.), *Innovation and Change in Reading Instruction,* Sixty-Seventh Yearbook of the National Society for the Study of Education, Part II. Chicago: University of Chicago Press, 1968.
22. Dykstra, Robert. "The Use of Reading Readiness Tests for Prediction and Diagnosis: A Critique." In Thomas B. Barrett (Ed.), *The Evaluation of Children's Reading Achievement.* Newark, Del.: International Reading Association, 1967.
23. Dyson, Anne Haas. "Oral Language: The Rooting System for Learning to Write." *Language Arts* 58 (October, 1981), 776–784.
24. Educational Policies Commission. *Universal Opportunity for Early Childhood Education.* Washington, D.C.: National Education Association, 1966.
25. Gates, Arthur I. "The Necessary Mental Age for Beginning Reading." *Elementary School Journal* 37 (March, 1937), 497–508.
26. Gates, Arthur I., and Bond, Guy L. "Reading Readiness: A Study of Factors

Determining Success and Failure in Beginning Reading." *Teachers College Record* 37 (May, 1936), 679–685.

27. Gates, A. I., Bond, G. L.; and Russell, D. H. *Methods of Determining Reading Readiness.* New York: Bureau of Publications, Teachers College, Columbia University, 1939.

28. Gesell, Arnold L. *Infancy and Human Growth.* New York: Macmillan, 1925.

29. Gesell, Arnold L. *The Mental Growth of the Preschool Child.* New York: Macmillan, 1925.

30. Gray, William S. "Reading." *Child Development and the Curriculum,* Thirty-Eighth Yearbook of the National Society for the Study of Education, Part I. Bloomington, Ill.: Public School Publishing Co., 1939.

31. Hall, G. Stanley. *The Psychology of Adolescence.* New York: D. Appleton, 1904.

32. Havighurst, Robert. *Human Development and Education.* New York: Longmans, Green, 1953.

33. Heffernan, Helen. "Significance of Kindergarten Education." *Childhood Education* 36 (March, 1960), 313–319.

34. Holmes, Margaret C. "Investigation of Reading Readiness of First Grade Entrants." *Childhood Education* 3 (January, 1927), 215–221.

35. Hunt, J. McVicker. *Intelligence and Experience.* New York: Ronald Press, 1961.

36. Ilg, Frances, and Ames, Louise B. *School Readiness.* New York: Harper and Row, 1964.

37. Jenkins, Frances. "Editorial." *Childhood Education* 3 (January, 1927), 209.

38. Martinez, Miriam, and Teale, William H. "The Ins and Outs of a Kindergarten Writing Program." *Reading Teacher* 40 (January, 1987), 444–451.

39. Morphett, M. V., and Washburne, C. "When Should Children Begin to Read?" *Elementary School Journal* 31 (March, 1931), 496–503.

40. Olson, Willard. *Child Development.* Boston: D. C. Heath, 1949.

41. Paradis, Edward, and Peterson, Joseph. "Readiness Training Implications from Research." *Reading Teacher* 28 (February, 1975), 445–448.

42. Reed, Mary M. *An Investigation of Practices in First Grade Admission and Promotion.* New York: Bureau of Publications, Teachers College, Columbia University, 1927.

43. Resnick, Lauren B. "Social Assumptions As a Context for Science: Some Reflections on Psychology and Education." *Educational Psychologist* 16 (Spring, 1981), 1–10.

44. Schickedanz, Judith A., and Sullivan, Maureen. "Mom, What Does U–F–F Spell?" *Language Arts* 61 (January, 1984), 7–17.

45. Shaw, Frederick. "The Changing Curriculum." *Review of Educational Research* 36 (June, 1966), 343–352.

46. Sippola, Arne E. "What to Teach for Reading Readiness—A Research Review and Materials Inventory." *Reading Teacher* 39 (November, 1985), 162–167.

47. Smith, Nila B. "Matching Ability As a Factor in First Grade Reading." *Journal of Educational Psychology* 19 (November, 1928), 560–571.

48. Stanovich, Keith; Nathan, Ruth G.; and Vala-Rossi, Marilyn. "Developmental Changes in the Cognitive Correlates of Reading Ability and the Developmental Lag Hypothesis." *Reading Research Quarterly* 21 (Summer, 1986), 267–283.

49. Teale, Wiliam H., and Sulzby, Elizabeth. "Emergent Literacy As a Perspective

for Examining How Young Children Become Writers and Readers." In W. H. Teale and E. Sulzby (Eds.), *Emergent Literacy.* Norwood, N.J.: Ablex Publishing, 1986.

50. Templeton, Shane. "Literacy, Readiness, and Basals." *Reading Teacher* 39 (January, 1986), 403–409.
51. Thomas, Karen F. "Early Reading As a Social Interaction Process." *Language Arts* 62 (September, 1985), 469–475.
52. Thorndike, Robert L., and Hagen, Elizabeth. *Measurement and Evaluation in Psychology and Education.* New York: Wiley, 1969.
53. Torrey, J. W. "Reading That Comes Naturally: The Early Reader." In T. G. Waller and C. E. MacKinnon (Eds.), *Reading Research: Advances in Theory and Practice,* vol. I. New York: Academic Press, 1979.
54. Washburne, Carleton. "Ripeness." *Progressive Education* 13 (February, 1936), 125–130.
55. Wayson, W. W. "A New Kind of Principal." *National Elementary Principal* 50 (February, 1971), 8–19.
56. Zornow, T. A., and Pachstein, L. A. "An Experiment in the Classification of First-Grade Children through Use of Mental Tests." *Elementary School Journal* 23 (October, 1922), 136–146.

Chapter 5

Reading in the Kindergarten

PREVIEW

Anyone who keeps up with the professional literature on reading cannot help but conclude that "young children and reading" is a popular topic. At the same time, they cannot help but acknowledge that consensus hardly characterizes recommendations for beginning reading instruction. Some persons, for example, recommend teaching nothing but phonics; others come close to saying that writing should be taught first. Whether public school classes should be available to four-year-olds and whether kindergarten ought to be a full- or half-day program are other questions to which individuals and groups respond with anything but accord.

A major problem facing authors who write chapters with titles like "Reading in the Kindergarten" is that the kind of research required for taking a verifiable position on all these issues has not been done. Although anecdotal accounts of children and classrooms are available along with short-term studies, long-term research that permits scrutiny of both the future outcomes as well as the present effects of various kinds of interventions comes close to being nonexistent. Given this situation, Chapter 5 proceeds as follows. It starts with what are thought to be defensible guidelines for developing programs designed to bring beginning reading ability into existence. Because omitting a description of current kindergartens is equivalent to keeping reality out of the picture, a summary of findings from a classroom-observation study of kindergarten classes is also included. Subsequently, suggestions are made to teachers that consider current practices and also provide alternate ways for helping young children acquire both reading and writing ability.

A discussion of six guidelines for people responsible for kindergarten programs starts the chapter. The six were chosen because of their special relevance for beginning reading instruction. They were also selected because the description of current kindergarten programs later in the chapter shows that one or more of the guidelines are often disregarded.

GUIDELINE ONE: PROVIDE ECLECTIC METHODOLOGY

Based on the assumption that entering kindergartners are ready to learn to read in different ways (2, 8, 9), the first guideline has to do with the need for eclectic methodology—that is, for an instructional program that offers kindergartners opportunities not only to read but also to write and to learn letter-sound correspondences.

Recommending three different means for bringing reading vocabularies into existence is not meant to foster the conclusion that the three are to be kept apart as teaching and learning progress. Even though each methodology may be scheduled at different times in order to ensure that each is offered, keeping the three kinds of instruction separate "no matter what" represents a failure to appreciate how they often mesh when teachers and schedules allow them to do so. For example, anyone who has taught is aware that sooner or later children learning to read words will often—not inevitably—want to write as well as to read the words. Whenever this occurs, reading and writing new words should be a joint activity no matter what a schedule suggests.

Thinking of the three methodologies as being distinct and separate also overlooks the possibility that children learning to read words that start with the same letter and sound may, at some point, comment about the twofold similarity. Such an observation makes it an ideal occasion for giving explicit attention to a given letter-sound correspondence even though it may have been scheduled for a later date.

To cite one final illustration, keeping the three methodologies apart hardly acknowledges that children who inquire about the spelling of a word have the chance when an answer is given not only to learn to spell and write it but also to learn to read the word.

One way to summarize all this is to say—as did Chapter 3—that schedules should be marked by flexible structure. They should never be so compartmentalized as to keep apart related learnings and activities. Another way to summarize the discussion is to say—as did Chapter 3—that some of the most effective classroom instruction is intentional but unplanned.

GUIDELINE TWO: CONSIDER PRINT AWARENESS AS A PREREQUISITE FOR CHILDREN'S SUCCESS WITH BEGINNING READING

Success at the start is of unique importance for any kind of learning. This means that teachers of young children need to be cognizant of those under-standings basic for success with beginning reading. What *is* basic is often described with the term *print awareness.* Print awareness refers to under-standings about written language that are acquired slowly, steadily, and often early among children brought up in highly literate environments. Such children commonly arrive in kindergarten—or even nursery school—knowing a great deal about written language. Others, in contrast, have little knowledge of the conventions of print and thus have to start at the begin-ning. The need for teachers to attend to the beginnings of print awareness with *some* children is the reason for listing its basic elements in Figure 5.1.

Whether preschoolers or kindergartners, whether at home or in school, children acquire print awareness gradually with the help of many interac-tions with text. Such contacts may be in the mode of reading or writing, hence the term *emergent literacy* to describe the slow but steady progres-sion of children's ability to read and write (6, 15, 16, 23).

In classrooms, helping children acquire print awareness is accom-plished not with one-day lessons but with many meaningful experiences that involve written language. Because the experience of being read to has great potential for developing both print awareness and an understanding of *metalinguistic terms*—the topic discussed next—how children ought to be read to is dealt with later in some detail.

Child:

1. Knows that words exist in a written as well as a spoken form.
2. Knows the difference between a graphic display that is a word and one that is not.
3. Knows the difference between a letter and a word.
4. Understands that empty space marks the end of one word and the beginning of the next.
5. Understands that words (in English) are read in a left-to-right direction.
6. Understands that lines of text are read from top to bottom.
7. Understands that, like spoken language, written words make sense.

Figure 5.1 Basic Elements of Print Awareness

GUIDELINE THREE:
BE SURE CHILDREN UNDERSTAND
THE LANGUAGE OF INSTRUCTION

Even very young children repeatedly demonstrate an understanding of language, initially as listeners. However, understanding language and understanding the language used to talk about it are different. The latter, which is necessary when language becomes an object of study, is commonly referred to as *metalanguage* (language about language). Metalanguage includes such terminology as *word, letter, sentence, beginning of a word*, and *beginning sound in a word*. As is true of print awareness, metalinguistic terminology is taught most effectively not with definitions or a single lesson but by providing children with a number of experiences in which the terms are used and illustrated.

The fact that teachers cannot take it for granted that students understand metalanguage has been verified many times during classroom observations. In one kindergarten, for example, the teacher wrote *you* and *me* on the board, then asked, "How many words did I just write?" With much enthusiasm a group of children responded, "Five!" (I was impressed with both the quick counting and the confusion about the meaning of *word* and *letter.*)

At another time, I had been invited to observe in a classroom occupied by four- and five-year-olds. It was early in the school year, and the teacher was working on visual discrimination. She had placed word cards in the slots of a chart and was asking individuals in a small group to find any two words that were the same. (Earlier work had concentrated on smaller combinations of letters, beginning with comparisons of just two.) All went well until the teacher pointed to a card displaying *Monday* and asked if anyone could find the same word on the chalkboard. (At the start of the morning, *Monday* and *October* had been written and discussed.) Now, in contrast with the earlier work, nobody could. Upon reflection, the children's failure to respond was no longer unexpected, although at the time it was because of the earlier success. *Monday* had been printed on the board in large, white letters, whereas much smaller letters in black appeared on the card. Clearly, what these children needed to learn was the meaning of *same* and *different* applied to words. Eventually, they needed to learn that to all of the following, the same response must be given: Monday, MON-DAY, *Monday*, and Monday .

GUIDELINE FOUR: ALLOW TIME
FOR READING TO CHILDREN

Anybody who has read Chapter 2 in this book is not likely to be surprised to learn that some of the most memorable and positive recollections people have of elementary school are the occasions when teachers read to them.

The common occurrence of such recollections suggests the first two points that need to be made about reading to children, namely, it should be frequent and enjoyable. When reading *is* a consistently enjoyable experience, it also is a means for developing positive attitudes toward books and reading and for fostering children's interest in acquiring reading ability themselves.

Even though enjoyment is the key concern, additional consequences of significant value should not be overlooked. Sometimes, as an incident in a kindergarten demonstrated, nothing special is required to achieve the "extras" except to read the book. In this case, the kindergarten teacher read a story about a dog that was listened to with rapt attention. When the story ended, several children commented simultaneously and could not be understood; consequently, the teacher reminded everyone of the need to take turns. Eventually, many took a turn. One child said the animal in the story was like her grandmother's dog. Another said that was impossible because the dog in the story wasn't real. And another referred to the discrepancy between how the story ended and how he thought things would turn out. All in all, it was an excellent discussion that revealed excellent comprehension. That made the teacher's next procedure both unexpected and unnecessary. Perhaps mimicking the practices of basal manuals, the teacher posed a series of questions (How many . . . ? What color was . . . ? Where did . . . ? When did . . . ?). By the time the questions were answered, a group of squirming five-year-olds had replaced the group of engrossed discussants. Afterward, the teacher explained the questions with a reference to "helping children with comprehension." Because helping children comprehend what is read to them is important, examples of *desirable* help follow.

Help with Comprehending: Prereading

One of the most interesting illustrations of an appreciation for the need to prepare children for a story refers not to a teacher but to a girl in third grade who was about to read her revised version of *The Three Pigs* to some kindergartners. (The children's teacher had read the original the day before.) The third grader began by saying that she had revised the story of *The Three Pigs*, after which she explained the meaning of "revise." She next told her audience a little about Austria, the setting for her revision. Finally, she explained the meaning of "asthma," an affliction from which the wolf in her version suffered. She then read her illustrated tale to a most attentive group.

In another room, a teacher prepared for an expository selection, *Look at Your Eyes*, by printing and reading *pupil*. The children provided the more familiar meaning whereas the teacher explained in simple terms the meaning relevant for the book she was about to read. To help the children understand other information in the book, she showed them how smiling changes the appearance of one's eyes by covering the lower part of her face with paper and asking the children whether they could tell when she was smiling by looking at her eyes. The teacher next used several volunteers to show the class, one small group at a time, how the pupil of the eye gets smaller when light—in this case, a flashlight—is directed toward it. Somewhat excited, the children nevertheless settled down when the teacher proceeded to read about their eyes.

Also recognizing the value of prior, relevant knowledge for comprehending, a teacher in another kindergarten reviewed the three fruit juices that had been discussed thus far (orange, apple, grapefruit) and their origins. She then mentioned that she had found a beautifully illustrated book about another fruit juice (pineapple), after which she brought out a pineapple. Once that was discussed and felt, the teacher read the book that told about pineapple trees and where they grow.

Because graphs for other topics had been made earlier, one postreading activity was the preparation of a graph entitled "Our Favorite Juices." Listed at the left-hand side in large letters were *apple, grapefruit, orange,* and *pineapple.* (Responses showed that orange juice was the overwhelming favorite.) An art project concluded the work, for which the children drew pictures of the sources of the four juices and labeled each with a word selected from the graph.

Help with Comprehending: Postreading

What the teacher just referred to did with a book about pineapples demonstrates that plans to help children comprehend should not concentrate on prereading possibilities *or* postreading activities. This is not an either-or consideration. Nonetheless, the present section is confined to postreading possibilities.

The first example is described by the kindergarten teacher who planned and carried out the activities:

> Today I read *One Kitten for Kim.* Briefly, the story is about a child whose cat had eight kittens. His parents said he could keep only one and must find homes for the remaining seven. He succeeds in finding one for each, but ends up with seven other pets because he traded the kittens to get the homes.
>
> After the story was read, I encouraged the children to tell what they thought Kim's parents would say about the new pets. I was hoping the children would conclude that Kim's parents would not want seven new pets anymore than they wanted seven kittens. I was pleased that several of the children did understand this, even though others did not until we discussed it.
>
> To help the children follow the sequence of events, I had them draw pictures of Kim's trip around the neighborhood and the trades he made. Later, we pasted the pictures on a long, narrow sheet of paper and rolled them through our television (a shoebox with an opening). As the pictures appeared, the children retold the story. I

took the tale one step further by having the children consider what Kim's parents would do with all the new pets.

I was pleased with the results. The children seemed to understand the subtle humor of the story and enjoyed making the pictures and retelling the story. I felt that it was an effective activity for listening comprehension.

This account is useful in making the point that what ought to be done either before or after something is read depends not only on the children but also on the nature of the material. Whereas *One Kitten for Kim* provided an appropriate occasion for giving explicit attention to sequence, *Herbie the Hippo*, read to other kindergartners, allowed for attention to the fact that stories that are different on the surface may have the same underlying theme.

Herbie the Hippo is about a baby hippopotamus who wants to be a bird but, with the help of a variety of experiences, learns it is better to be "his own self." Once an open-ended discussion of the story was concluded, the teacher in question inquired of the children, "Have you ever wanted something, didn't get it, and later were glad you didn't get it?" After the children responded to the personal question, the teacher asked, "Can you remember other stories I've read that told about somebody, sometimes a person and sometimes an animal, who was like Herbie in that they, too, wanted to be somebody else, but then decided it was better to be who they were?" Once the three related stories were recalled and reviewed, the teacher asked, "Can you think of one title that would be a good one for all four stories?" (Titles had been discussed earlier.) After a number of suggestions were made, it was decided that "Be Glad You're You" was the best title offered. A consideration of why it was the best ended the postreading discussion.

As anyone who has read to young children knows, they sometimes want to have certain stories read more than once. Whenever that happens, postreading discussions for each repeated reading can bring out different features of the story—for instance, a particular character and her or his behavior, an especially humorous or suspenseful episode, how one event could not have happened had another not occurred earlier, how the story might have ended differently, and interesting sounding words.

Not to be overlooked are postreading discussions that serve the purpose not only of helping children recall what was read but also of finding out why a book was *not* enjoyed. Having observed a lack of interest on the part of her students, one recently observed second-grade teacher had the courage to use a postreading discussion for the second purpose after she finished reading *Freckle Juice*. The children's complaints included, "It was too long and draggy," "It wasn't very exciting," and "No kid could be that dumb."

The moral of this frank discussion is that teachers need to choose stories with care. They should keep in mind that children have little patience with excessive detail and slowly moving plots. Like us all, they enjoy suspense—but not too much—and happy endings. Stories of children and animals are usually attractive, as is a book whose theme or content relates to their own experiences.

Charlotte Huck offers additional advice:

> *Anyone reading a story . . . should have read it in preparation for sharing it orally. In this way the reader can emphasize particularly well-written passages, read dialogue as conversation, anticipate the timing of amusing remarks, and be able to look up from the book . . . to see children's reactions. (18, p. 716)*

Help with Print Awareness and Metalanguage

How reading to children can be used to help develop print awareness and, in addition, to review or teach metalinguistic terms are the last of its contributions to be discussed. This is an appropriate time, therefore, to review the elements of print awareness listed in Figure 5.1 as well as the definition of *metalanguage.*

Children who arrive in kindergarten already reading typically divide among those whose ability is limited to identifying a certain number of words, those who can read easy books, and those who can manage surprisingly difficult text. Not to be forgotten are those who can do some writing. But not to be overlooked, either, are children who arrive at school having had few meaningful contacts with print.

The great variety found in most classes supports the position that at the beginning of the year, kindergarten teachers should assume that many students will benefit from explicit attention both to the conventions of print and to metalinguistic terms. In this case, working with an entire class has the advantage of allowing the most advanced children to ask questions that may be instructive for others. How reading to children can sometimes be used to promote print awareness and teach metalinguistic terms is the concern now.

When reading does serve these purposes, books with few words on a page, preferably printed in large type, should be sought. Alphabet books, for instance, can help give meaning to the terms *letter, word,* and *beginning of a word.* Depending on the children—and on the alphabet book—they might function successfully in assigning meaning to *beginning sound in a word.*

Reading (and showing) stories told with one or two sentences per page provides additional opportunities not only to clarify the meaning of *word* but also to demonstrate how empty space defines word boundaries—that is, indicates where one word ends and the next begins. On other occasions, reading pictureless text is useful in helping children understand that reading is not a matter of holding a book, looking at pictures, and saying whatever comes to mind, but, instead, is directly controlled by the words on a page.

Whenever it seems appropriate to do so, the short verses customarily read aloud to young children can be printed (and enlarged) on chart paper to teach even more about reading. Even though some verses will have been memorized, teachers who use a pointer as the children "read" a verse in unison can show overtly the one-to-one relationship between spoken and written words as well as the left-to-right, top-to-bottom direction of print.

Enlarged copies of brief stories make available what are commonly called "shared book experiences." Using these "big books," teachers have the opportunity not only to bring children into contact with written words in meaningful contexts but also to illustrate facts like the end of a line does not always mean the end of a thought. In turn, this brings into existence an opportunity to deal with punctuation—again in a meaningful setting. Don Holdaway (17, 22), one of the early advocates of shared literary experiences with big books, reminds teachers that access to an overhead projector means that the pages of a book can be put on transparencies to obtain the enlarged print.

Still other material suitable for shared reading experiences is *predictable books*. Lynn Rhodes defines a predictable book as one having text that, at times, is either sufficiently repetitive or predictable that children "can chant the text right along with the teacher" after it has been read once or twice (24, pp. 511–512). Well-known examples of predictable, patterned verses and stories include *Oh, A'Hunting We Will Go*; *Brown Bear, Brown Bear*; *The Three Billy Goats Gruff*; *The Gingerbread Man*; *The Three Bears*; and *The House That Jack Built*. (As Figure 2.3 showed, material suitable for choral reading often includes predictable text.)

Cases in which phrases or sentences are repeated intermittently make it natural to print them on the board. If certain words are repeated regularly in a predictable order, it might be a time to display them, too. Either way, attention can eventually go to selected words—enough for some children to learn them well enough to be able to identify them apart from the context in which the words were originally embedded.

Three entries in the References at the end of this chapter (3, 24, 32) are especially helpful in the lists of predictable books they include and in the specific suggestions made for using predictable books to promote print awareness, to teach metalinguistic terms, and to get reading vocabularies started.

GUIDELINE FIVE: MAKE GENEROUS USE OF LANGUAGE EXPERIENCE MATERIAL

In this book, "language experience material" encompasses any noncommercial text that deals with the interests and experiences of an individual or a particular group. Whether the words are identical or only similar to what one or more children said is thought to be less critical than that the content be current and relevant. Within such a framework, text like that in Figure

5.2 is "language experience," and so too are the following child-generated or teacher-child generated items:

> Invitations, thank-you notes, messages for greeting cards, letters to parents, and questions to pose to visitors.
> Reactions to pictures, books, or a movie.
> Directions for making something, getting somewhere, or conducting an experiment.

Two questions teachers often ask about language experience material are stated and answered below:

1. *Should language experience material be used with an entire class?* The most ideal use involves one child, which means that classrooms in which teacher aides are present should offer numerous opportunities for highly personal uses of language experience material. Reality being what it is, unassisted teachers usually work with small groups because the whole class should be involved only when an experience is of compelling interest to everyone. In the case of the text shown in Figure 5.2, for example, the class composed it with the help of the teacher's questions about what had been done and seen. The more detailed attention that went to the text later involved only seven of the most advanced children.

2. *How does a teacher decide when to use the children's words, when to modify them, and when to do most of the composing herself?* This question calls for another reference to the dependent relationship between objectives and teaching procedures, because some reasons to use language experience material (e.g., to show the connection between oral and written language) make it essential to write exactly what children say, whereas others point in different directions. If what children say, for instance, is not spoken in sentences and if one preestablished objective for the material is to teach that a period signals the end of a

---

Yesterday was Tuesday. We went for a walk to Hessel Park. We saw squirrels eating acorns that had fallen to the ground. They held them in their hands like people. The leaves are turning colors. We played in the park and got hot. Mrs. Urbank got red in the face from running.

Figure 5.2 Children's Recollections of a Walk to a Park

sentence, a teacher will need to compose sentences based on the fragments.

To explain more specifically the effect of objectives on the development and use of experience-based text, two examples are offered. The first describes how a kindergarten teacher worked at achieving the following objectives:

Objectives: To teach what is meant by *word.*

To teach the function of empty space in establishing word boundaries.

After lunch, a magician from the community put on a show for kindergarten and first-grade children. Subsequently, one kindergarten teacher wisely took advantage of the special event to work on the two objectives just named. Following is the conversation that took place after the children had made spontaneous comments about the show. (In this case, the interest of all children in the topic allowed for whole-class work.)

Teacher: To make sure you don't forget some of the things we saw the magician do, I want to write them for you here [pointing to the chalkboard]. Who wants to tell us one thing the magician did?

Kevin: He pulled a rabbit out of a hat!

Teacher: He sure did. Let me write what you said, Kevin. Say it one more time.

Kevin: He pulled a rabbit out of a hat.

Teacher: Who remembers something else that the magician did? Margie, what did you see him do?

Margie: Pick a black ace out of a deck of cards.

Teacher: Yes, he did that, too. Let's see now. Kevin said, "He pulled a rabbit out of a hat." What do you want to say?

Soon the chalkboard displayed the account shown in Figure 5.3.

To realize the two preestablished objectives, procedures similar to the following should be used. They are listed now to reinforce a guideline re-

He pulled a rabbit out of a hat.

He pulled an ace out of a deck of cards.

He threw up lots of balls and always caught them.

Figure 5.3 An Account of an Experience

ferred to before: *How* anything ought to be done depends on *why* it is being done.

> *To teach the meaning of* word *and the use of empty space to show word boundaries, a teacher should:*
>
> **1.** Say aloud each word as it is written. This permits children to watch talk become print.
> **2.** Read the entire account *in a natural speaking fashion,* pointing to each word as it is identified.
> **3.** Suggest to the children that they might like to read it. (As the children "read," the teacher reads along with them, all the while moving her hand or pointer across each line of text from left to right.)
> **4.** Point to and read words that appear more than once. If the children are interested, let them "read" these words again.
> **5.** Make a comment like, "There are so many words up here!" Then count them, pointing to each one. Show how a space separates one word from another. Next, have the children count the words. Point to each as it is counted.
> **6.** Reread the entire account. Encourage the children to read along.

In addition to specifying what a word is and indicating the function of space to show word boundaries, the procedures just described (a) demonstrated how words are read from left to right; (b) showed that identical words have the same spelling; (c) gave the children a chance to pretend they can read; and (d) gave them the opportunity to learn some words. If the group had been fairly small or if the help of an aide was available, the teacher might have asked each child for her or his favorite word. Named words could have been quickly printed on small cards to be taken home to be read to parents and anyone else willing to listen. The cards could also be used to initiate individual and personal collections of word cards.

The objectives of the second example of a kindergarten teacher's use of experience-based text are listed below.

Objectives: To demonstrate the value of print for preserving information.

To reinforce the usefulness of reading ability.

As in so many kindergartens, the schedule in this one begins with attention to the day's weather, a topic of interest to young children because it affects their play life. On one Monday morning the teacher commented,

"This certainly is a beautiful morning, isn't it? Was last Monday as nice as it is today? Can someone tell us what it was like last Monday?" Responses begin with guessing and end with the conclusion that nobody remembers. Thus it is time for the teacher to propose, "If I write words that tell us about today, then next Monday we can look at what I write, and the words will tell us. We won't have to work so hard trying to remember." A discussion of current weather then begins and leads to the printing of *sunny* and *clear* at the left side of a wide sheet of paper. By the end of the week, the sheet shows:

Monday	Tuesday	Wednesday	Thursday	Friday
sunny	cloudy	cold	rainy	sunny
clear	warm	dark	windy	clear
		windy		

A couple of weeks later, this teacher makes another proposal: "We seem to use the same words over and over, don't we? [Points to and reads *sunny, clear*, and *windy*.]. If I put these words on cards, then instead of writing them every day I can just pick out the right cards." Soon, a weather chart with slots for cards is attached to a bulletin board. Meanwhile, all the children work hard at remembering what each word on a card is so that they will be able to select appropriate descriptions. And so, reading vocabularies expand still more.

GUIDELINE SIX: INFORM PARENTS ABOUT THE KINDERGARTEN PROGRAM

Increasingly, the contributions of parents (and grandparents) to the development of literacy in preschoolers is being recognized (8, 10, 25, 31). What should be recognized more often than is the case is the need for educators to provide opportunities for parents to learn about the goals of a kindergarten program and the means chosen to promote literacy. The latter topic is especially important because parents do not always understand how something like language experience materials or "big books" can be more effective—and interesting—for fostering literacy than is a workbook.

Because some kindergartners ask for help with printing at home, parents should also be informed about the type of printing the school teaches. Given the fact that most adults know how to print only capital letters, a copy of the printing system used should be made available. (See Figure 5.4 for an example of one model.) To be emphasized with parents is that the model is intended not to foster unrealistic standards for kindergartners but, rather, to help them learn to print. Such an ability makes parents ready to provide help, should it be requested by their children.

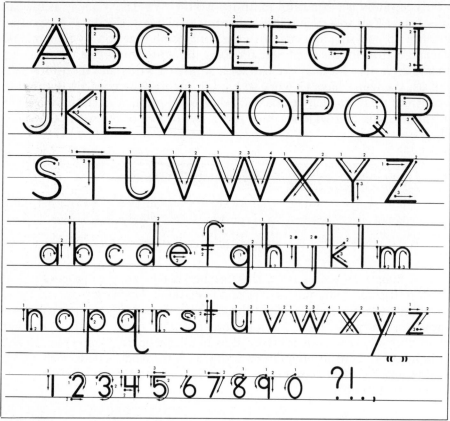

Figure 5.4 A Model for Printing

Source: Used with permission from Zaner-Bloser *Handwriting: Basic Skills and Application,* © 1984 Zaner-Bloser, Inc.

Simple discussions of print awareness and of the importance of meta-linguistic terms are appropriate for parent meetings, too, since adults who are far removed in time from their own experiences with beginning reading and writing will not know about the foundations for literacy. Something like the checklist shown in Figure 5.5 can be used in specifying what is important (and why) before, during, and after a child's participation in a kindergarten program.

EXISTING KINDERGARTEN PROGRAMS

As mentioned at the start of this chapter, the six guidelines discussed were selected for attention, first, because all are important and, second, because of findings in a study of kindergartens (12). Only the findings that relate to

Parent Self-Help Checklist

	Yes	No
1. I read aloud to my child every day.	____	____
2. If my child asks for it, I'll read the same book aloud repeatedly.	____	____
3. When I read aloud, my child sits on my lap or very close beside me and is in a position to follow along in the book.	____	____
4. My child has seen me read frequently.	____	____
5. My child has seen a man and a woman reading.	____	____
6. There are books, magazines, and newspapers in our home.	____	____
7. My child has books of his/her own and a place to keep them.	____	____
8. Books and magazines are an important part of my gift-giving for each child.	____	____
9. Our conversations go beyond daily functions like eating, dressing, bathing. For example, we talk about what happens in our family and neighborhood, and why things are done the way they are.	____	____
10. I give my child opportunities to express himself/herself through art, play, and talking.	____	____
11. I am a concerned and interested listener, showing my child that his/her feelings and interests are important to me.	____	____
12. My child knows I value reading as much as I do watching television.	____	____
13. I control the amount of time my child spends watching TV, and the types of programs.	____	____
14. I provide many interesting and varied experiences for my child, such as visits to parades and fairs, restaurants, cities, and towns of different sizes, concerts, church, beach, mountains, lakes, rivers, nature walks.	____	____
15. I provide plenty of paper, pencils, and crayons or a chalkboard for play activities.	____	____
16. We play games that help my child see differences and likenesses in objects in our home.	____	____
17. My child has a library card and has a chance to use it regularly.	____	____
18. I transmit a positive attitude towards schools and teachers.	____	____
19. My child's hearing and vision are checked regularly.	____	____
20. I am sure my child receives a balanced diet.	____	____

Figure 5.5   A Checklist for Parents

Source: Nancy J. Smith, The Parent Self-Help Checklist from "A Self-Help Checklist for Parents on Their Role in Reading Readiness," *The Reading Teacher*, March 1984, p. 670. Reprinted with permission of the International Reading Association.

topics already discussed either in the present chapter or in Chapter 4 are referred to in the following sections.

Use of Developmental Tests

One finding should bring to mind the previous chapter, since it has to do with the frequent use of Gesell-like developmental tests. In fact, one of the most popular tests was the Gesell *School Readiness Test* (14), which, like the other tests administered, is heavily weighted with motor tasks (e.g., skipping) and visual-motor tasks (e.g., tracing lines and copying patterns). How seriously results of the tests were taken by administrators and teachers alike is surprising when it is kept in mind that researchers have always questioned the value of such tests for describing a child's readiness for something like learning to read (1, 4, 21). Reasons cited for giving a developmental test, either during the spring prior to the start of kindergarten or at the beginning of the kindergarten year itself, sounded as if it were the 1920s or 1930s. For example:

"To see who is developmentally ready"
"To identify those who should stay home for a year"
"To decide who will go to our prekindergarten motor class"
"To spot maturity levels and determine readiness for reading"

The frequency of explanations like these is the reason the Preview for the previous chapter stated that "Currently, knowing about the traditional conception of readiness is important for a reason that will be explained later in Chapter 5: The traditional conception has been resurrected and is enjoying a second round of influence over many early childhood educators."

Preestablished Programs Determined by Commercial Materials

Even though fifteen school systems were in the study, the kindergarten programs themselves were strikingly similar (12). The uniformity hardly matched the contention that the developmental tests just referred to were used to identify differences in entering kindergartners. Without question, the combination of (a) readiness workbooks published by basal reader companies, and (b) traditional subject matter for kindergarten (e.g., colors and shapes) accounted for the similarity.

Although the children were tested periodically on what was being taught, results were used not to allow for individualized instruction but to prepare for parent conferences or marking report cards. Typically, a close correspondence existed between "academic" items on report cards and the content of workbooks.

What was seen throughout the year of observing could not help but bring to mind Figure 3.3, which is reproduced here as Figure 5.6.

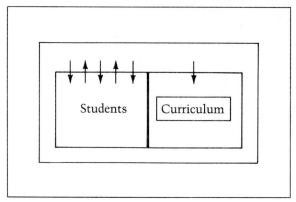

Figure 5.6 Different Students, Same Curriculum

When the observed teachers were asked whether they thought reading ought to be taught in kindergarten, answers for the most part were negative. This was unexpected since phonics was never missing from any schedule. The most developmentally oriented teachers explained their opposition to teaching reading with responses that were again reminiscent of the 1920s and 1930s:

> "Reading is a skill that can be taught, but when the child is ready it takes two weeks. At age five, you spend eight months. At age seven, it takes two weeks."

> "Five and a half-year-olds have the ability to move from left to right but not to return. They are visually not ready. If they are not forced, it will happen naturally and more easily."

> "I believe that if they're ready, they'll read in spite of me."

Why teachers accepted phonics instruction but rejected teaching reading was unclear until one teacher said:

> "Phonics is not reading instruction because we only teach letters and sounds, not words."

The implied distinction between teaching phonics and teaching reading might account for the pattern identified when phonics was taught: Sounds were related to pictures and letters, not to written words. Often seen, then, is what is called *decontextualized* instruction. This refers to instruction offered in a way that does not relate what is being taught to how to read. It thus turns reading instruction into an end in itself.

Although phonics instruction comprised most of what was done with reading in the observed kindergartens, some attention did go to identifying words. For the most part, the words that received attention were those introduced in the readiness workbooks. (The selected words were said by the publishers to be necessary for their first-grade materials.) It should be noted, too, that at no time—even in the case of the classroom observations that occurred early in the school year—was anything done to promote print awareness or to clarify metalinguistic terms. Nor for the whole of the year was much use made of language experience material.

Whenever teachers gave special attention to one child or a group, the help was designed to reteach what had been taught earlier to the whole class. It was as if the goal was to bring everyone up to a certain standard of achievement defined by commercial materials. That such a possibility was in fact the case was verified in the response of at least one teacher. Asked what she thought was especially difficult about teaching kindergarten, she replied, "There is great variation in what comes to you." She then added, "But by the end of the year, they're more leveled out."

Even though none of the teachers interviewed openly complained about the expectation to use workbooks and to teach certain sounds and certain words to every child, it seems realistic to conclude that they and the very large number of teachers who were not observed hardly want to be subservient to commercial materials. The following sections, therefore, are meant to help teachers who are expected to spend time on certain sounds and words but who are still unwilling to let commercial materials define not only what they will teach but also how they will go about teaching it.

PLANNING A KINDERGARTEN READING PROGRAM

Underlying the forthcoming recommendations is a point of view developed in the previous chapter and portrayed in Figure 4.1. It would be helpful, therefore, to review Figure 4.1 and the commentary about it.

Diagnostic Orientation

Even though plans for a kindergarten program often—and should—change as more information is obtained about the children the program is intended to serve, the six guidelines listed earlier in this chapter imply types of planning that are both possible and desirable right at the start. Because so much time is now spent at the beginning of the kindergarten year on whole-class instruction in color, shape, number, and letter identification, early plans should include individual diagnosis for those topics to ensure that necessary instruction is provided and unnecessary instruction avoided.

Why similar individual testing for print awareness and metalinguistic terms is not considered to be mandatory can be explained in two ways. First, there is not enough time at the start to test everything that is important. Second, as illustrated earlier, attention can go to print awareness and metalanguage in ways that will not be boring for the most advanced children.

Time constraints is also a reason early attempts to uncover existing reading and writing ability are not considered essential. The other reason is that the schedule described in the next section allows teachers to learn close to the beginning of the year which children are already doing some reading and writing. The same schedule also allows for different levels of instruction for different children.

A Possible Schedule

Even though every kindergarten teacher needs a schedule, not every teacher needs to follow the same one. The schedule to be described, therefore, is just a sample. Although the sample schedule is for a half-day program, it indirectly suggests how the additional time provided by full-day programs can be used to advantage.

Sample Schedule

8:30– 8:45	Attendance taking; attention to date, weather, and current interests
8:45– 9:10	"Academic" period for one group; assignments and/ or free-choice activities for remaining children
9:10– 9:35	Groups reversed for "academic" period
9:35– 9:55	Music
9:55–10:30	Bathroom, recess, snack
10:30–11:00	Art
11:00–11:25	Storytime
11:25	Preparation for home

With all the attention that has gone to the need for flexible scheduling, it is taken for granted that divisions of time in any schedule change whenever the need exists either for more or for less time for something. Unexpected interest on the part of the children or, for example, an instructional objective that turns out to be too easy or too difficult are some of the many reasons for teachers to be flexible.

Possible Content and Materials

On the assumption that the need for flexibility has been emphasized sufficiently, some of the blocks of time shown in the sample schedule are now discussed.

8:30–8:45	Attendance taking; attention to date, weather, and current interests

Children's names, combined with calendars and the weather, provide continuous opportunities not only for children to talk about what interests them but also for teachers to initiate literacy. Because children's interest in their own names never seems to wane, it can be used to work on instructional objectives related to:

names of letters
capitalization
spacing between words
printing
alphabetical order
letter-sound correspondences

Using name cards (approximately 5 by 12 inches), children can learn early to take attendance by placing their card in a chart with pockets provided for that purpose. One positive by-product of children's involvement with attendance taking—in addition to saving a teacher's time—is a heightened awareness of who is absent. As a result, an absentee's return to school will be greeted with unusual enthusiasm, something likely to contribute to that child's positive feelings about school (9).

Discussions of calendars, which should be large enough that numbers and words are easily seen, inevitably include birthdays. In time, a visual display such as the one in Figure 5.7 might be placed on a bulletin board. As Figure 5.7 shows, names of the children are written in large print on whichever train car displays the month in which their birthday occurs. (Notice that the engine is at the left, thus encouraging a left-to-right scanning.) By the time the train is taken down—nothing should be displayed so long that it becomes neither eye- nor mind-catching—some children will be able to read all the words shown; others will know considerably fewer. The more important point is that all have had the opportunity to learn words in a meaningful context that is of personal interest.

Weather is another topic rich in opportunities for expanding literacy. What one teacher did with weather-related words was described in an earlier section of this chapter. A bulletin-board display entitled "April Showers" was used by another teacher. In this case, blue construction paper covered the board to which were attached clouds (gray) and raindrops (white).

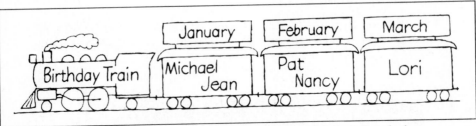

Figure 5.7 Personalizing the Acquisition of a Reading Vocabulary

Objectives	*Procedures*
To teach the meaning of "fall" and "autumn." To introduce sequence of seasons.*	1. Used first day of autumn to introduce fall. Printed it on board and pronounced it. Named other seasons too. Also talked about different meanings of fall with help of sentences like, "Don't fall off your chair" and "Try not to fall when you play." 2. On the following day, introduced autumn as a word that can be used in place of fall. Read a story about the fall as a time of changing colors in leaves. 3. The next day took children to the park to collect leaves. Upon return to school, used them to remention fall and autumn and to provide practice in counting and naming colors. 4. A week later, read story about squirrels gathering nuts to prepare for winter. (Also showed children some nuts.) Used story to review fall and autumn and to introduce the fall season as one that is followed by winter and preceded by summer. Showed sequence of four seasons with time line.

*The teacher chose the second objective because of an answer from one of her more sophisticated kindergartners. Asked, "When does spring come?" the child responded, "In the fall."

Figure 5.8   Preplanned Instruction

Printed on the raindrops were words suggested by the children when they discussed activities suitable for rainy days (e.g., *read, write, draw, color, play a game*). Some children expressed interest in illustrating a particular activity, after which they copied the appropriate word from the board to serve as a description.

How another teacher used the four seasons of the year to realize two purposes is described in Figure 5.8. In addition to illustrating carefully made plans guided by preestablished objectives, the content of Figure 5.8 makes the point that work with topics such as weather or seasons is not necessarily confined to a given period or to one type of activity. More specifically, attention to seasons may originate in work with a calendar but may also expand to include a walk in the neighborhood, attention to colors and counting, and even the use of a simple time line.

9:35–9:55	Music

Even though the fun and freedom of music should never be stifled with nagging efforts to include reading and writing in a kindergarten program, occasions do arise when attention to written language can add to the music as well as to children's literacy. A much enlarged copy of a page from a song book, displayed for all the children to see, will show how notes tell singers when to go up and down with their voice and also how the written words tell them what to say as they sing.

If attention is going to musical instruments, perhaps with the help of recordings, a bulletin-board display of labeled pictures showing something like horns, violins, and drums can add specificity to the instruction. If the instruments are those of the kindergarten rhythm band, pictures with iden-tifying labels will still be of interest—perhaps of even greater interest. Ap-propriate to refer to here is an article by Frances Smardo (26) that tells of a field trip taken by children to hear a symphony orchestra. "Back at school, their teacher read them *The Philharmonic Gets Dressed* by Karla Kuskin, which humorously explains how the 105 men and women in the orchestra get ready for a concert and travel into town with their bulky instruments" (p. 700).

As young children learn songs, additional ways to feature written lan-guage are possible. In a song about four farm animals, with a verse for each animal, a picture of the appropriate animal can be shown each time a new verse is begun. Later, when the song is repeated, the teacher can show the same pictures, this time with identifying labels. After the procedure has been used on a number of occasions, the teacher might next hold up cards on which only an animal's name is written, asking, "Who can tell me what this animal is?" And then, "Let's sing that verse."

With other songs, only one word might be highlighted. A song about children's games, for instance, provides an opportunity to call attention to *games*. (It might also be a time to compare *games* and *game* on the chalk-board.) A song called "Getting to Know You" can naturally lead to attention to *you*.

On days when children are unusually restless, music functions well in providing for movement as well as for attention to certain words. Such days might be the time to have children (accompanied by suitable music) *tiptoe*, walk *slowly* and then *quickly, clap loudly* and then *softly*. It might also be an opportunity—depending on the children—for looking at, and talking about, words composed of two words (*tiptoe, raindrop, chalkboard*). Or it might be an appropriate occasion to discuss the meaning of *opposite* applied to words like *slowly* and *quickly*, and *loudly* and *softly*. Were this done, reading *Push, Pull, Empty, Full* by Tana Hoban would be an excellent com-plementary activity. Using large photographs of objects, animals, and people (e.g., gumball machine, turtle, and human hands and feet), the author of this book helps pinpoint the meaning of such descriptions as *many* and *few*, *together* and *apart*, and *heavy* and *light*. Reading such a book leads naturally to drawings made by the children for which they can print antonyms to serve as captions.

10:30–11:00	Art

Signing names to artwork, writing simple captions about a picture, labeling objects in a display of clay figures—all of these are highly appropriate activities for helping children become both artist and author. But other opportunities occur, too. Once children are familiar with the concept *circle*, magazine pictures showing circular objects can be collected, labeled, and made into a book. Hooked to a string or wire, strung low enough for the children to reach, shape books may eventually look something like the ones in Figure 5.9.

Although elaborate covers are unnecessary, any booklike collection of pictures (including homemade picture dictionaries) creates the need not only to illustrate a cover but also to spell and write words for titles. At another time, bookmarks can be made and decorated with designs or words.

A bulletin-board display of artwork provides even more contacts with print. After children draw self-portraits, their pictures can be displayed under the title, "Who Are You?" Later, when the same children draw pictures of their homes, "Where Do You Live?" is the title for the bulletin board. The positive feature of such titles is that they can be used to talk about question marks, to discuss the use of capital letters, and to provide practice in reading hard-to-remember but important words like *what, who, where,* and *why* in meaningful contexts.

Even though there is no intention here to portray art as being nothing more than a means for dealing with written text, one further example of an art activity seen in a kindergarten is described, because it is useful in emphasizing that what is done with any activity depends on children's abilities and interest.

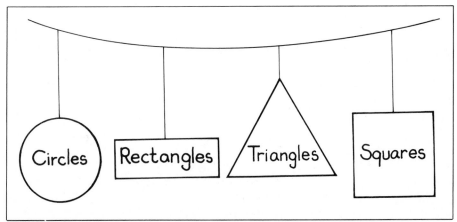

Figure 5.9   Products of Work with Geometrical Shapes

After discussions about safety (coupled with a walk to examine traffic lights), the children made their own lights using construction paper:

In the case of the observed kindergarten, attention only went to identifying the colors of the lights and to the meaning of *top, middle,* and *bottom* when it came time to paste the three circles. With more advanced children, other possibilities exist:

1. Call attention to *red, yellow,* and *green,* now printed on cards of the same size.
2. Have children match word cards:

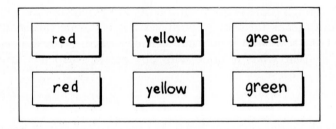

3. Name and talk about red, yellow, and green objects.
4. Provide practice in identifying *red, yellow,* and *green* in preparation for attaching small word cards to the traffic lights:

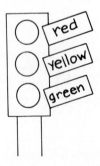

Now that a number of illustrations have shown how meaningful contacts with print can be provided in periods set aside for other subjects, the discussion shifts to what was referred to in the sample schedule shown earlier as the "academic" periods.

TEACHING THE ACADEMICS

You probably noticed in the schedule that two twenty-five minute periods were assigned for "academics." For each period, only part of a class will be working with the teacher to allow for suitable instruction. Assumptions that support the need for different instruction for different children are made explicit below:

1. Just about every child in a kindergarten is ready to acquire literacy to some degree.
2. Because children entering kindergarten vary considerably in what they know, understand, and can do, instruction ought to be offered to subgroups of children organized on the basis of needs. Because of time restrictions, subgroups may have to be limited to two. Membership in each group will vary from day to day depending on what is being taught.
3. Whenever possible, teachers should also work with individuals or very small groups to provide extra help or extra challenge. When an aide is available, such extras ought to be the rule, not the exception.

One further reminder also merits explicit attention: Subject matter should be taught in ways that link it with children's everyday experiences. Instruction with numbers, for instance, should make generous use of such materials as clocks, calendars, license plates, birthday cards, rulers, store catalogs, and toy telephones. To do otherwise, one author warns, is to make "reading and writing in the kitchen with a parent" so at odds with "school reading and writing" that the child will conclude that the two are essentially different (27).

Possible Subject Matter

Keeping reality in mind—specifically, a school district's expectations for kindergarten—it is possible that topics eventually covered in academic periods might have to include (a) shape, color, number, and letter identification; (b) word identification; (c) auditory discrimination of speech sounds; (d) letter-sound correspondences; and (e) printing. Whether mandated or not, it is assumed that all teachers will do whatever is possible throughout the whole of a kindergarten program to extend and deepen children's oral vocabularies.

One possible way—there is no one "right" way—to sort out topics for

①	Shape identification Color identification Number identification Math*
②	Word identification
③	Letter identification Printing Auditory discrimination Letter-sound correspondence Composing
④	Oral language

⑤	"Open time" to allow for:
	    extra help
	    extra challenge
	    special whole class projects

*In the attempt to be realistic, math is included because a sizable number of kindergarten teachers are expected to use a mathematics workbook.

Figure 5.10 One Possible Division of Subject Matter

five academic periods per week is shown in Figure 5.10. On which day of the week any given topic is covered will vary not only across different kindergartens but also within a single kindergarten. Which topic in a group of topics is covered will also vary. With the first group shown in Figure 5.10, for example, a teacher might attend on one day to nothing but colors. The next week, however, a planned activity may deal with counting and naming different geometrical shapes shown in a variety of colors. Meanwhile, time allotted to art, music, and storytime may include attention to one or more of the same topics.

Each cluster of topics shown in Figure 5.10 is now discussed, starting with the one below. Shape identification is used here to illustrate two approaches to teaching, both of which serve well in realizing instructional objectives.

> Shape Identification
> Color Identification
> Number Identification
> Math

One, which we can call an "informal" approach, has been illustrated many times in the chapter. Use of this approach to teach shapes, for instance, was described in the earlier section on "Art." A second approach, which is a more carefully planned and sequenced type of teaching, is illustrated below in "Plans for Instruction." The illustration serves not only as a contrast for what was described in the section "Art" but also as an example of how attention to "circle" does not eliminate attention to other topics.

Plans for Instruction

Objectives	Procedures
1. To introduce the concept "circle."	1. Begin a discussion with the question, "Does anybody know what a circle is?" (Print circle on chalkboard.)
	2. Show and discuss circular objects. (Later, display them on a table with the sign circles.)
	3. Show and discuss pictures of circular objects. (Save for bulletin board.)
	4. Assemble and discuss bulletin board entitled "Circles," showing pictures of circular objects each labeled circle.
2. To reinforce children's understanding of circle.	1. Show red cutout circles of identical size. Discuss the similarity in color and size. Then show other circles that vary in both size and color. With questions, help children conclude that the concept "circle" encompasses variation in size and color but not shape.
	2. Let children paste cutout circles of different sizes and colors on paper, making a design if they wish. While the pasting is being done, write Circles on each paper. Display papers in the classroom.
3. To introduce s to denote plural.	1. Prepare a bulletin-board display entitled "Circles" showing cutout circles of various sizes and colors. Below each one write Circle.
	2. Discuss the display with the children. Have them read all the labels. Ask whether the labels and the title are

Objectives	Procedures
	exactly the same. To emphasize the difference, write on a chalkboard:

Circle

Circles

Read the two words. Discuss the one difference. Explain that s at the end of a word sometimes shows it means more than one. Write, read, and discuss other pairs of words:

girl	boy	color	day
girls	boys	colors	days

Objectives	Procedures
4. To summarize attention to circles.	1. Prepare a circle-shaped scrapbook for pictures of circular objects. Write Circles on the cover, and label each picture Circle. Show and discuss the scrapbook. Put it with other books that can be used at free-choice time.
5. To help children begin to print letters composed of circles.	1. Have children make circles in the air.
	2. Have children trace circles drawn on dittoed sheets.
	3. Have them make their own circles on paper.
6. To practice printing o.	1. Using the chalkboard, print known words that include o. Name and discuss the words and call attention to the o's.
	2. Show children a sample of paper with o's printed on it. (Lined paper, which makes more demands of children, can be used later.) Distribute paper and have them try to print o's. Remind them that the ability to make o will help them write words that have an o in them.
7. To practice printing c.	1. Follow the same procedures, emphasizing that c is an unfinished circle.

While reading the teaching plans for circles, which would require different amounts of time with different groups, you probably noticed that they incorporated ideas emphasized earlier. More specifically, the plans show how instruction can bring together such related learnings as vocabulary knowledge, the identification of written words, and the beginning of skill in printing. The same plans exemplify how practice in word identification can be provided by such sources as bulletin-board displays and scrapbook collections of labeled pictures. The plans should also have made the point that productive teaching does not just happen but is, instead, the fruit of thoughtful, knowledgeable decisions based, first, on the needs of children and, second, on the kinds of materials, procedures, and assignments that allow for the achievement of what they need to learn.

Let's move on to the next topic listed in Figure 5.10.

Word Identification

Generally—and again, there is no one, inevitably "right" way to introduce reading—young children who are just starting to be readers profit at first from being exposed to connected text—a sentence, for instance, as opposed to an isolated word. This is the case because, as listeners and speakers, they are accustomed to utterances that exceed one word. Contacts with connected text also permit the development of print awareness and an understanding of metalinguistic terms. For these reasons, it is advisable to work for a while with the whole class, using a combination of language experience material, big books, predictable books, and whatever else is useful in calling attention to relevant text. Not to be overlooked is that in the course of the children's various contacts with print, teachers have many opportunities to collect information about who knows what.

Meanwhile, individual words can be taught—that is, displayed, named, discussed, renamed—when the children are learning about circles (as was illustrated) or, perhaps, about colors. More specifically, when a color is identified and discussed, a teacher might choose to write its name on a chalkboard or large sheet of paper so the children can see what it looks like. Eventually, several color words might be summarized on a chart showing differently colored pieces of paper with labels identifying each one. By this time, all the colors will be familiar, and some children will be able to read the names as well.

Later, perhaps in connection with painting, mixing colors to make another one might be demonstrated. A meaningful summary for such an experience—and more reading practice as well—can be one or more bulletin-board displays. For example:

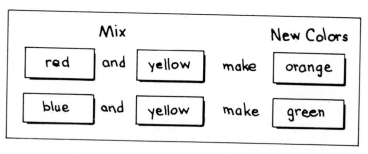

Snack time also allows for meaningful attention to individual words, at first to the children's names. In the beginning, place cards can both display names and simplify who sits where. Later, menu cards can be left at each child's place until the majority of children are able to read most of the few words that cover menu possibilities.

At another time, repeated attention to high-frequency words (for example, *is* and *a*) can be achieved with sentences that are completed with pictures:

It is a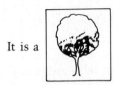

In sentences like the one above, small picture cards replace unknown words. If the words are printed on the backs of the picture cards, they can be used to show the unknown words. (At times, children can complete sentences with their own pictures.)

Other types of sentences allow for attention to a way to form plurals. For instance:

I like a

I like

Again, words are printed on the backs of the cards; they should also be printed on a chalkboard in a way that makes apparent how they are the same and how they are different:

flower

flowers

Pictures standing for words is known as *rebus* reading. Although it should not be used too often or for too long, rebus reading can be helpful at the beginning when reading vocabularies are limited.

Exactly how to initiate and expand reading vocabularies is the subject of the next chapter, "Whole Word Methodology." For that reason, the discussion now shifts to consider the next cluster of topics shown earlier in Figure 5.10:

> Letter Identification
> Printing
> Auditory Discrimination
> Letter-Sound Correspondences
> Composing

Although listed separately from "word identification," these topics are related. For instance, one way to call attention to the details of a word being taught is to have children name its letters. Writing the word serves the same function. In addition, it is known words that ought to be used when the concern is developing ability in auditory discrimination or teaching the sound a particular letter records. Known words such as *September, Saturday*, and *sunny*, for instance, can help in teaching about the sound that *s* represents.

Probably the next statement that needs to be made about the cluster of topics shown above is that the order in which they are listed does not indicate a necessary sequence for teaching them. This means that when children are learning the names of letters—and there is no one "right" sequence for teaching them—they may also be learning to print the letters. On the other hand, progress in learning letter names should not be impeded by motor skills that, as yet, only allow for scribbling. (See Figure 5.11 for samples of variation in kindergartners' ability to form letters.) Worthy of explicit attention, too, is that perfectly formed letters is not the goal of printing instruction, just as perfectly spelled words at the beginning is not a requirement for composing.

The fact that the message is more important at the beginning than correct spelling has received a large amount of attention under the heading *invented spelling*. Because of the widespread interest and some misunderstandings, invented spelling is discussed in the commentary about Figures 5.12 through 5.16. Please examine and read those pages now.

Oral Language

The dependence of literacy on oral language is so pervasive that spending sizable amounts of time adding to children's world knowledge, concept development, and oral vocabularies should be a taken-for-granted responsibility in all classrooms. The importance of concepts and vocabulary ex-

Tom	Rita	karen	Bob
Lori Jo	Amy	Scott	David

Figure 5.11 Printing at Midyear in Kindergarten

plains why one kindergarten teacher conducted a number of experiments with water; then, following each one, she wrote about it with the children's assistance. (Some of the text is in Figure 5.17.) Results of the experiments included an understanding of new concepts and vocabulary (e.g., *liquid, freeze, solid, steam, boil,* and *evaporate*). Other results included additions to the children's reading vocabularies, as well as some understanding of sequence and how a reader might follow one.

Much more is discussed about developing oral vocabularies in Chapter 11.

Independent Activities

As the sample schedule for a kindergarten pointed out earlier in this chapter, an "academic period" has some children working with the teacher while others spend time on free-choice activities and assignments. To have independent work proceed smoothly, thus freeing a teacher to give uninterrupted attention to instruction, it may be necessary at the beginning to allot time for letting children become accustomed to working on their own. When that is the purpose, both assignments and free-choice activities are supervised so that expectations can be explained and reinforced. If a teacher aide is available, the need to have children practice working on their own is eliminated, as she or he can supervise while the teacher instructs.

It should be emphasized that a well-prepared aide can do much more than just supervise. In one kindergarten, for example, the aide's initial responsibility is to supervise activities selected by the children from among prescribed possibilities that include, at the beginning of the year, blocks, trucks, dolls, dishes, and telephones. Possibilities are gradually altered to

(text continues p. 147)

Figure 5.12 Composing: Early Efforts

All the examples of children's writing shown in Figures 5.12 through 5.16 were found in kindergartens (Figures 5.12, 5.13, 5.14), first grades (Figure 5.15), and second grades (Figure 5.16) long before "invented spelling" became a much discussed topic.

The writing shown in Figure 5.12 was done by a kindergartner soon after her teacher had read the class a story about sea serpents. The fact that this child wrote a caption for her picture and added her name is not unexpected, since from the beginning of the kindergarten year either the teacher or a volunteer parent was available to write whatever children requested.

In the study of kindergarten classes referred to earlier in the chapter (12), one teacher encouraged children to say something about their pictures, which she wrote in a notebook. When she was interviewed later, the teacher said she printed what the children had said on their artwork "after school." Considering the value of letting children see their words being turned into print, the timing of this teacher's printing has to be questioned. *"Why am I doing what I'm doing?"* does not appear to have been considered.

Figure 5.13 Useful Writing

The kindergartner's writing shown in Figure 5.13 was part of a response to a suggestion made by her teacher near the end of the year. The class had been talking about summer as a time to vacation, after which the teacher suggested that the children might like to draw a picture of where they would want to go on a vacation if they had a choice. The list shown in Figure 5.13 was on the back of one child's picture.

Again, the fact that this child listed what she would bring on a vacation is not surprising, because the teacher had frequently made lists on the board to serve as reminders for a variety of purposes. (Stressing the usefulness of reading and writing ability is something that is not done with sufficient frequency even though it is the usefulness of literacy that prompts some children to try to read and write before they ever get to school.)

The samples of kindergartners' writing shown in Figure 5.13, and earlier in Figure 5.12, reflect the eclectic methodology available in their classrooms. At times, words were taught, which is reflected in *see, books, paper,* and *dolls.* It is also clear that phonics was taught in a way that made apparent its usefulness for writing as well as for reading. That attention also went to printing instruction is evident, as is the fact that communication is what is valued, not perfectly formed letters.

All of these comments are made to reinforce the fact that early literacy does not develop in a vacuum but, rather, is fostered by numerous and meaningful opportunities to acquire the various components of literacy. This needs to be kept in mind because of the tendency of some researchers to act and write as if teaching has not taken place when children read and compose early (29).

Reacting to this tendency, Karen Thomas writes the following in a report of her study of early readers: "It is both an oversimplification and an injustice to the parents in this study to suggest that reading was the sole and natural act of the child" (31, p. 473). Later in the report, after describing how parents had fostered the early abilities of their children, this researcher makes other comments worth repeating. Reacting to descriptions like "natural readers" and "natural literacy," Thomas notes: "Use of these terms raises interesting questions. Do all those children who do not learn to read 'naturally' become unnatural learners of reading? If learning to read is 'natural,' are teachers less culpable if children fail to read? . . . The term 'natural' takes the teaching onus off responsible adults and, as a term, can be misleading in that reading is not an innate and involuntary response" (p. 474).

Gams
Crds
cririg Books
Books
paper
crans
Pers
Traks
Dolls
Paper Dolls

Figure 5.14 More Kindergarten Writing

Like the previous samples, the composing shown in Figure 5.14, which was done toward the end of kindergarten, reflects a wonderful understanding of the nature of alphabetic writing. The fact that young children—in some instances, preschoolers—are able to achieve such understanding is the source of the excitement about invented spelling. (In some ways, "invented" is not the best description, since the spelling referred to is remarkable not because it is "made up" but because it reflects, and is constrained by, the nature of alphabetic writing.)

One fourth-grade teacher's question ("Are invented spellings okay at my level?") suggests the need to add to this commentary the reminder that the goal of schooling is still standard spelling. The same question also calls for attention to the fact that one of the many kinds of research still to be done is studies of the *later* effects of invented spellings. Or, as Margo Wood states in a very informative article (34), "Longitudinal studies of children who engage in invented spelling as preschoolers are needed to determine the effect, if any, of these early activities on the development of proficiency in standard spelling" (p. 715). Wood goes on to say that "Some maintain that early inventive spellers will learn to read and spell more easily than children who have not attempted to write before learning to read. . . . This is theoretical supposition, however, in an essentially unexplored area" (p. 715).

How writing ability progresses is illustrated in Figure 5.15 (first graders) and in Figure 5.16 (second graders).

it was a antalope it lived in a field it had a baby. The End

Amy AD A Dragon
A Dragon is big. big.
My Dragon is Sik.
My Dragon is very very, tall?

Figure 5.15 First-Grade Writing

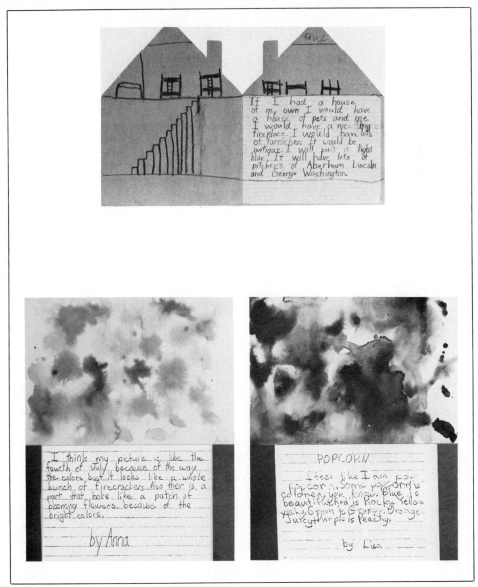

Figure 5.16 Second-Grade Writing

include such activities as writing on small chalkboards or slates, working puzzles, and playing with sequence cards, concept cards, or bingo cards that, at different times, display colors, numbers, letters, and words. Eventually, three learning centers are established (Listening, Reading, Writing), and the aide divides her time among them. Now, children can be found involved

```
                    Ice

1.    We put water into the freezer.

2.    The water is a liquid.

3.    The water is freezing.

4.    The water is a solid.

5.    The water is ice.
```

```
              Float and Sink

Some things float.

Some things sink.

Things heavier than water sink.

Things lighter than water float.
```

Figure 5.17   Summaries of Water Experiments

with activities such as listening to stories on earphones, making signs for block constructions, dictating descriptions of pictures to the aide, and playing with a variety of number and word games as well as with an old typewriter.

As you read through this chapter, you may have noticed other possibilities for assignments. Some are repeated below. As they are described for the second time, you will see that many have children drawing. This is often necessary at the start when literacy skills are limited. Eventually, possibilities for both assignments and free-choice activities increase considerably.*

---

* Keeping children profitably occupied is always a concern of teachers whose goal is to provide individualized instruction. You might find it helpful, therefore, to record in a notebook the many suggestions for independent assignments that appear in subsequent chapters.

Listed in the order in which they are referred to in the chapter, the following are suggestions for independent activities:

Children draw pictures of the sources of four fruits (apple, grapefruit, orange, and pineapple) and label each with a word selected from a large graph.

Children draw pictures depicting opposites (*laugh, cry; up, down; cold, hot*) and print or copy appropriate antonyms to serve as captions.

Children draw pictures to portray a storybook character's trip around the neighborhood and the trades he made.

Children make homemade dictionaries, composed of pictures cut from magazines and store catalogs. Each picture is labeled, and a cover is appropriately decorated.

Children draw self-portraits (labeled) for a bulletin-board display. Each picture shows a child's name.

Children draw their home for a bulletin-board display entitled "Where Do You Live?"

Children cut out circles of different sizes and colors, then paste them on a sheet of construction paper to make a design. Each sheet is labeled *Circles.*

Children engage in rebus reading by drawing pictures to complete simple sentences.

When kindergarten teachers are expected to use one or more workbooks, they can also be used for independent work. Presumably, pages will be selected on the basis of their intrinsic worth and on the kinds of practice children need. Whenever such pages provide something of value that *is* needed, teachers should not hesitate to supplement a page with additional items of their own, because—as illustrated in the previous chapter—most workbook pages are extremely limited in content even when a page has children do something useful.

SUMMARY

The purpose of Chapter 5 is to show with many examples how kindergartners who vary in experiences and ability can be accommodated with suitable help in all the language arts. The chapter began by presenting guidelines to those people responsible for planning or executing a kindergarten program that offers opportunities to learn to read and write. Anyone familiar with the previous chapter should not have been surprised to see that the first guideline underscored the need for eclectic methodology if the greatest number of five-year-olds are to succeed in acquiring the beginnings of literacy. Because literacy *is* the concern, importance was assigned to (a) helping children learn about the conventions of print, (b) making sure that children understand the language of instruction, and (c) reading to children. How big books, predictable text, and language experience material function in achieving a variety of objectives was discussed, too.

To show how and when everything can receive attention, Chapter 5 offered a sample schedule. One point made repeatedly is that no schedule should keep apart related topics or interests. Stressed again, therefore, was the need for schedules marked by a flexible structure that encourages teachers to respond to children and events rather than to the hands on a clock.

Chapter 5 can be said to have succeeded in realizing its main objective if it provides help to kindergarten teachers who are expected to teach certain subject matter with workbooks but who are convinced that it can be taught in ways that are more appropriate for, and of greater interest to, five-year-olds. The chapter can also have realized its purpose if it was able to demonstrate that using nothing but reading readiness workbooks with a whole class is not the best way to promote success in acquiring reading ability—and certainly not the best way to offer experiences that make attending kindergarten an enjoyable way to spend one's time.

REVIEW

1. Let's start the review of Chapter 5 with a request to explain each of the following terms:

   print awareness   invented spelling
   metalanguage   predictable text
   eclectic methodology   decontextualized instruction

2. Alert kindergarten teachers learn a great deal about a child's readiness for reading by observing day-by-day behavior. Even in grocery stores, behavioral signs of readiness are noticeable. Recently, I was in a store and observed a girl of about three or four who, penny in hand, walked to a gumball machine. Taped to it was a sheet of paper displaying three handprinted words: *out of order.* Upon seeing the sheet, the child turned and asked a woman who was passing by, "What does that say?" "It says 'out of order'," the woman answered. "What does that mean?" the little girl inquired. "It means the machine doesn't work. I hope you didn't put your money in." "No," responded the child and walked away. Specify the behavioral signs of readiness that became apparent during the very brief conversation just described.

3. To help specify the meaning of *word,* one kindergarten teacher uses dashes between words when she prints sentences. For instance:

   I – am – five.

For the same purpose, another teacher lists brief sentences on a ditto sheet and has the children place a small paper square under each word. Which procedure is better? Why?

4. In a book entitled *Reading Readiness*, a suggestion for developing readiness is similar to what appears below.

> Have the children close their eyes. Ask them to be as quiet as possible. Play a record of sounds (e.g., slamming door, bird noises, barking dog, drum). Have the children identify as many of the sounds as they can.

What do you think about the suggestion? If followed, will it promote readiness for reading?

5. Chapter 5 provides a brief description of what was found in a classroom-observation study of forty-two kindergarten classes. State the major problems identified during the observations and in the interviews conducted with the teachers.

6. A number of guidelines presented throughout Chapter 5 were selected for discussion *because* of what was learned in the study of kindergartens. Pinpoint the ones that seem especially important when the findings of the kindergarten research are kept in mind.

7. At one point, Chapter 5 suggests:

> Work with reading ought to begin with connected text, move from there to individual words, and from there to parts of words.

First, explain with examples what the suggestion means. Second, explain why the recommendation is made.

REFERENCES

1. Arter, Judith A., and Jenkins, Joseph R. "Differential Diagnosis—Prescriptive Teaching: A Critical Appraisal." *Review of Educational Research* 49 (Fall, 1979), 517–555.
2. Backman, Joan. "The Role of Psycholinguistic Skills in Reading Acquisition: A Look at Early Readers." *Reading Research Quarterly* 18 (Summer, 1983), 466–479.
3. Bridge, Connie A.; Winograd, Peter N.; and Haley, Darliene. "Using Predictable Materials vs. Preprimers to Teach Beginning Sight Words." *Reading Teacher* 36 (May, 1983), 884–891.
4. Chall, Jeanne S. "A Decade of Research on Reading and Learning Disabilities." In S. Jay Samuels (Ed.), *What Research Has to Say about Reading Instruction*. Newark, Del.: International Reading Association, 1978.

5. Chomsky, Carol. "Write First, Read Later." *Childhood Education* 47 (March, 1971), 296–299.

6. Clay, Marie. *What Did I Write?* London: Heinemann Educational Books, 1975.

7. Combs, Martha. "Modeling the Reading Process with Enlarged Texts." *Reading Teacher* 40 (January, 1987), 422–426.

8. Durkin, Dolores. *Children Who Read Early*. New York: Teachers College Press, Columbia University, 1966.

9. Durkin, Dolores. "A Language Arts Program for Pre-First Grade Children: Two-Year Achievement Report." *Reading Research Quarterly* 5 (Summer, 1970), 534–565.

10. Durkin, Dolores. "Poor Black Children Who Are Successful Readers: An Investigation." *Urban Education* 19 (April, 1984), 53–76.

11. Durkin, Dolores. *Teaching Young Children to Read*, 4th ed. Boston: Allyn and Bacon, 1987.

12. Durkin, Dolores. "A Classroom-Observation Study of Reading Instruction in Kindergarten." *Early Childhood Research Quarterly* 2 (September, 1987), 275–300.

13. Early Childhood and Literacy Development Committee of the International Reading Association. "Joint Statement on Literacy Development and Pre-First Grade." *Reading Teacher* 39 (April, 1986), 819–821.

14. Gesell Institute of Child Development. *School Readiness Test*. Lumberville, Penna., 1978.

15. Henderson, Edmund H. *Learning to Read and Spell: The Child's Knowledge of Words*. DeKalb: Northern Illinois University Press, 1981.

16. Hiebert, Elfrieda H. "Developmental Patterns and Interrelationships of Preschool Children's Print Awareness." *Reading Research Quarterly* 16 (1981, No. 2), 236–259.

17. Holdaway, Don. *The Foundations of Literacy*. New York: Scholastic, 1979.

18. Huck, Charlotte. *Children's Literature in the Elementary School*, 4th ed. New York: Holt, Rinehart and Winston, 1987.

19. Martinez, Miriam, and Teale, William H. "The Ins and Outs of a Kindergarten Reading Program." *Reading Teacher* 40 (January, 1987), 444–451.

20. Melvin, Mary P. "First Moments in Reading." *Reading Teacher* 39 (March, 1986), 632–634.

21. Paradis, Edward, and Peterson, Joseph. "Readiness Training Implications from Research." *Reading Teacher* 28 (February, 1975), 445–448.

22. Park, Barbara. "The Big Book Trend—A Discussion with Don Holdaway." *Language Arts* 59 (November/December, 1982), 815–821.

23. Read, Charles. *Children's Categorizations of Speech Sounds in English*. Urbana, Ill.: National Council of Teachers of English, 1975.

24. Rhodes, Lynn K. "I Can Read! Predictable Books As Resources for Reading and Writing Instruction." *Reading Teacher* 34 (February, 1981), 511–518.

25. Roser, Nancy, and Martinez, Miriam. "Roles Adults Play in Preschoolers' Response to Literature." *Language Arts* 62 (September, 1985), 485–490.

26. Smardo, Frances A. "Using Children's Literature As a Prelude or Finale to Music Experiences with Young Children." *Reading Teacher* 37 (April, 1984), 700–705.

27. Spencer, Margaret. "Emergent Literacies: A Site for Analysis." *Language Arts* 63 (September, 1986), 442–452.

28. Squire, James R. "Instructional Focus and the Teaching of Writing." *Ginn Occasional Papers, No. 1.* Lexington, Mass.: Ginn and Company, 1983.
29. Teale, William H. "Toward a Theory of How Children Learn to Read and Write Naturally." *Language Arts* 59 (September, 1982), 555–570.
30. Templeton, Shane. "Literacy, Readiness, and Basals." *Reading Teacher* 39 (January, 1986), 403–409.
31. Thomas, Karen F. "Early Reading As a Social Interaction Process." *Language Arts* 62 (September, 1985), 469–475.
32. Tompkins, Gail E., and Webeler, MaryBeth. "What Will Happen Next? Using Predictable Books with Young Children." *Reading Teacher* 36 (February, 1983), 498–502.
33. Willert, Mary K., and Kamii, Constance. "Reading in Kindergarten: Direct vs. Indirect Teaching." *Young Children* 40 (May, 1985), 3–9.
34. Wood, Margo. "Invented Spelling." *Language Arts* 59 (October, 1982), 707–717.

Part III

Instruction:
Words

As was underscored as early as Chapter 1, the underlying assumption of *Teaching Them to Read* is that "reading" and "comprehending" are synonymous. One implication of the equation is that all instances of instruction in reading should have as their ultimate goal improvement in students' ability to comprehend. Similarly, all the topics in this third section have something to do with comprehension. The relevance of the topics for comprehending can be explained with the help of the following display:

Facilitating Comprehension	→	Assigned Text
Attending to new vocabulary		
Activating or adding to world knowledge		
Establishing purpose(s) for reading		

Even though knowing all the words in a given piece of text is no guarantee it will be comprehended, knowing too few puts comprehension out of reach. That is why decisions about what to do with new words must be resolved when plans are made for preparing students for assigned reading. What to do with new vocabulary, and why, is explained in Chapters 6 through 10.

Because the meanings of words are more important than their pronunciations, Chapter 11 focuses on ways to add to the number of words that students understand. Earlier, when Chapter 10 deals with prefixes and suffixes, it explains how students can be taught to work out meanings whenever new vocabulary includes derived or inflected words.

Because knowing the meaning of individual words does not automatically add up to an understanding of connected text, the need exists for comprehension instruction. The importance of such instruction is reflected in the fact that all the chapters that make up the fourth major section of Teaching Them to Read deal with that topic.

Chapter 6

Whole Word Methodology

Preview

Introducing the topic discussed in Chapter 6 calls for repeating a recommendation made earlier when reading in the kindergarten was the
concern: Instruction ought to begin by bringing children into contact
with large pieces of meaningful text, move from there to words, and
from there to parts of words in the context of print to speech relationships. The relevant point to emphasize for Chapter 6 is the recommendation to teach some words before attention shifts back and forth
between whole words and letter-sound correspondences. This recommendation stems from the conviction that the use of known words
to teach that letters stand for speech sounds fosters an understanding
of how words are recorded. In no sense, then, does the recommendation question the contention that "a beginning reader must at some
point discover the alphabetic principle: that units of print map onto
units of sound" (17, p. 363).

The foregoing comments require emphasizing yet another
point: The content of Chapter 6 has as much relevance for middle-
and upper-grade teachers as for those working with younger children.
Admittedly, students' knowledge of letter-sound relationships and
word structure reduces progressively the number of words that need
to be taught as wholes; nonetheless, whole word methodology can
never be abandoned. Irregularly spelled words like *acre, anxious, cari-
bou,* and *coyote,* which are in an alphabetic list of words introduced
in one fourth-grade basal reader, explain the need for whole word
instruction.

One final reminder is that the suggestions in Chapter 6 for teaching words apply equally to new vocabulary for a basal reader selection and to new vocabulary taught to prepare students for a chapter
in a social studies or science textbook.

This chapter, plus Chapters 7 through 10, focus on ways for developing students' reading vocabularies. (An individual's *reading vocabulary* is all the words that she or he knows in their written form and whose meanings are understood.) Only words that are known at the level of *automaticity*—that is, can be read "without thinking"—facilitate comprehension (1, 9, 17). This is the case because the ability to name words instantaneously allows readers to fix their attention on meaning. Or, as Keith Stanovich concludes after reviewing research concerned with comprehension, "the key mechanism that allows capacity to be allocated to comprehension is the efficient identification of words" (17, p. 369). An addition to Stanovich's conclusion would go something like: The key mechanism that allows word identification to be automatic is practice. Words that can be identified automatically constitute a person's *sight vocabulary*.

To summarize:

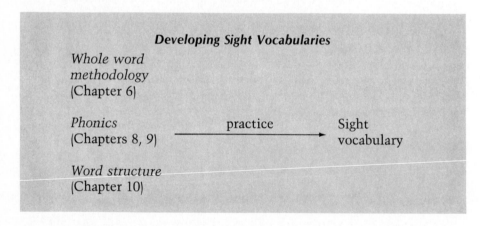

Early emphasis is placed on the importance of practice because classroom observations show that the amount provided for new or troublesome words decreases steadily as grade level increases (7, 8). This is the case whether the new vocabulary is in a basal reader or in something like a social studies textbook. For many students, one obvious consequence of too little practice is an inability to name large numbers of words. Frank Green describes the consequence more dramatically as he observes, "Reading is often a trial, with each word a problem solving crisis" (11, p. 536).

In need of early emphasis, too, is that substantial sight vocabularies are no guarantee of successful comprehension. Signs like the following remind us of that:

> No shoes.   No shirt.   No service.

Attached to the door of a restaurant, this warning is useful in demonstrating that comprehending, in this case, requires the ability not only to read the six words but also to link them into a cause-effect relationship. Nonetheless, knowing the six words *is* the foundation for concluding that in this restaurant, the effect of not wearing shoes or a shirt is not having food or drink served.

With all these reminders in the background, let's proceed to consider one way to bring reading vocabularies into existence: whole word methodology.

WHAT WHOLE WORD METHODOLOGY IS

Naming an unknown word for an individual or a group is whole word methodology. Consequently, a parent who answers, "Elm" when his or her child looks up at a street sign and asks, "What does that say?" is using whole word methodology. So, too, is the teacher who writes and reads *muscle*, *tendon*, and *sinew* after showing a film that deals with the meaning of the three words.

At one time, whole word methodology was commonly referred to as the *look-say method* to contrast it with other methods that call attention to parts of words. The fact that whole word methodology is also called the *sight method* has led some people to conclude erroneously that a "sight word" is one that was initially introduced by somebody using whole word methodology. As explained earlier in the chapter, the term *sight* pertains not to how a word was taught or learned but to the fact that it is known at the level of automaticity—that is, is known "on sight."

Regardless of the label attached to it, whole word methodology is simply a matter of naming words. Because anyone who can read is able to use the method, some explanation does seem necessary as to why an entire chapter is devoted to this topic.

One reason is that a single identification by a teacher rarely leads to permanent retention by students. Because nothing less than permanent recall can be the goal of school instruction, it is imperative that professional teachers know how to foster retention. That explains why the chapter considers such topics as *cues* and *practice*.

Because students must be able to read many more words than those they happen to inquire about, the professional teacher also needs to know which words to select for whole word methodology. When it ought to be used, therefore, is considered now.

WHEN TO USE WHOLE WORD
METHODOLOGY

At the time children are just starting to be readers, whole word methodology is used routinely. It is used even with *regularly spelled words* (e.g., *no, red, boy*) whose pronunciations are predictable on the basis of their spellings.

This is the case because beginners lack *decoding* ability. (Decoding is using the spelling and/or structure of an unfamiliar word to learn its pronunciation.)

Because independence in coping with unknown words is a most important goal for instructional programs, whole word methodology should be used less and less as students learn more and more about decoding. However, as explained in the Preview, irregularly spelled words like *colonel, quay, suite,* and *vein* make whole word methodology something that may need to be used even with better readers.

To sum up, then, when to use whole word methodology depends on (a) the nature of the unknown words, and (b) students' decoding ability. (As Chapter 7 explains, the context in which unfamiliar words are found is a third relevant variable.) Factors to consider when whole word methodology *is* used are dealt with next.

SOME GUIDELINES FOR WHOLE WORD METHODOLOGY

The core of whole word methodology is simply naming words; nevertheless, certain guidelines need to be followed. Guidelines having to do with the type of word receiving attention are considered in the sections that follow.

Function Words

Even when teachers of beginners make a conscious effort to select words for instruction that are both meaningful and of interest, it isn't long before they find it necessary to get into children's reading vocabularies words that are neither meaningful in and of themselves nor of interest. I refer to words like *the, but, of,* and *is.* Such words are called *function words* and include prepositions, conjunctions, auxiliary verbs, pronouns, articles, and the various forms of the verb *to be.* Function words require attention fairly early because they specify relationships among the components of a sentence. They thus allow for phrases, clauses, compound subjects, compound verbs, and compound sentences. For instance:

> Mike drove into snow at work.
> Mike, who drove into the snow, went home early.
> Mike and Tom drove into a pile of snow.
> Mike drove into snow and got very angry.

Because function words hold the structure of text together, they are sometimes referred to as *structure words.* Examples of the type of function (or structure) word commonly found in more advanced text are shown on the next page.

The men were afraid. <u>Nevertheless</u>, they kept walking.
The sun was too hot. <u>Therefore</u>, they went home.
You may go out. <u>However</u>, be back by nine o'clock.

As the examples point out, the more difficult function words typically connect meaning from one sentence to the next. Because this *is* the role they often play, attending to such words in the context of intersentence relationships is one piece of the very large responsibility called "teaching comprehension."

Whether simple (*or, the*) or more advanced (*meanwhile, anyway*), the nature of function words suggests the following guideline for teachers: *Whenever a function word is taught, present it in the context of other known words.* The context may be as short as *pencil or pen* or as long as the one used by a first-grade teacher when she provided instruction for *and.* This is what the teacher did.

She started by praising members of an instructional group for all the color words they had learned. While the children recalled the colors, she wrote (and read) the names of the colors in a way that allowed for extra space between each one and that stretched the words across the chalkboard—to the great delight of the onlookers. The teacher then started to reread the words, this time saying "and" between the first and second colors. Immediately she stopped to observe, "Oh, oh. I put in a word that isn't here. Did anyone hear the word I said that isn't on the board?" Immediately the children responded, "And!" The teacher continued, "If I'm going to say 'and', I had better write it. Watch me write 'and'." Each time it was written between two color words, the children named, spelled, and renamed it. Finally, the entire line of words was read with considerable enthusiasm and obvious pride.

Now it was time for additional practice that made use of cards prepared ahead of time. They displayed contexts like the following.

come and go	one and four = ____	tall and thin
Jean and Bill and Tom	girls and boys	August and September

At the end, *and* was printed alone, then read, spelled, and read again. And so a very interesting presentation of an uninteresting word came to a close.

What happens when first-grade teachers (and all others) do *not* give sufficient attention to function words is pinpointed in an account of an observation in a second grade:

When I observed this week in a second grade, I was reminded of the discussion we had in class about the critical importance of a large sight vocabulary that includes function words. Almost as soon as I entered the room, the teacher asked if I would listen to several children read in order to check their ability to identify the new words in a story they had read earlier. Without waiting for an answer, she gave me a copy of the words she wanted checked.

The first child, a boy by the name of Dwayne, brought his chair close to mine in a corner of the room and after spending a short time to get acquainted, he opened his basal to read. Since his reading group had read the story at least once before, he seemed a little bored to have to read it again, but read it he did.

What I especially noticed as Dwayne read served to reinforce the fact that a function-word vocabulary is of great importance for comprehending. Dwayne was able to read all but one of the ten new words listed, including *helicopter*; but he stumbled over, or missed, an average of 5 to 9 function words per page. Partly because he had read the story before, but mostly as a result of his inability to identify function words readily, the story must have been little more than a word-naming exercise. Dwayne became tired very soon and seemed to miss the basic point of the story as he read things like "They found the helicopter in the building" when the text stated "They found the helicopter on the building."

Later, when the children were at music, I discussed my findings with the teacher. To my great surprise, her response to my reference to problems with function words was that children "should know them when they get to second grade," and that all she had time to do is "let them practice the words in the stories they read." I felt very disappointed with her apparent lack of concern about constantly reoccurring words and came away realizing their importance more than ever before. It makes me wonder how much second- and third-grade children's comprehension deficiencies result from the problems they have with these basic words that are often critical to the meaning of all kinds of text.

Other Text-Dependent Words

Sometimes the classification *function word* is contrasted with the classification *content word*. The contrast lies in the fact that although function words derive their meaning from other words in the same context, content words are meaningful in and of themselves (nouns, verbs, adjectives, adverbs). The difference suggests that new content words do not always need to be presented in the company of other words—assuming students know their meanings when the words are spoken. More specifically, if students know and have even experienced the meaning of fog, it can be written alone when presented as a new word for reading.

On the other hand, certain types of content words require a context to the same degree that function words do. Two types of content words that are always text-dependent, homonyms and homographs, are defined below and illustrated in a variety of contexts.

Homonyms are words that are spelled the same but that have different meanings. The difference in meaning is generously illustrated below with the help of the homonym *hand*.

I've hurt my hand.

One hand is missing from the clock.

Please hand me the scissors.

She makes all that pottery by hand.

They're always ready to lend a helping hand.

You have to learn some things first hand.

He got a big hand after his talk.

They lead a hand-to-mouth existence.

He rules his family with a heavy hand.

Homographs are words that are spelled the same but that have different pronunciations and meanings. How contexts determine both pronunciation and meaning is illustrated in the sentences that follow.

They live close to us.
Please close the door.

The wind is noisy tonight.
Did you remember to wind the clock?

He had tears in his eyes as he read the lines.
The tears in their clothing suggested they had fought.

The young does ran through the forest.
Sally does that constantly.

Although homonyms and homographs always need to be placed in a context if correct conclusions about them are to be reached, another type of content word, one called *homophone*, requires a context only initially. Once students can read a homophone, its spelling is sufficient to indicate its meaning. This is illustrated next.

Homophones are words that are pronounced the same but that have different spellings and meanings. Thus:

If I could, I would go with you.
The wood is finally burning.

He can tell a great tall tale.
The dog's tail wagged and wagged.

I'll meet you tonight at eight.
This meat is too tough to chew.
They'll have to mete out the water carefully.

The suggestions for teaching content words can now be summed up as follows. Because content words have meaning in and of themselves, most do not have to be taught in the context of other words. (This assumes that the word being taught has a meaning that is known when the word is spoken.) Two types of content words, however, must always be presented in a context, since it is the context that defines, in one case, the meaning (homonyms) and, in the other case, both the pronunciation and the meaning (homographs). A third type of content word requires a context when it is taught initially; however, once students know the word, the spelling suggests its referent. Content words falling into this third category are homophones.

Contractions

One of the many puzzling features of commercially prepared materials is their use of sentences like *They do not like the game* prior to *They don't like the game.* The sequence is puzzling because children use contractions in their speech long before they say something like—if they ever *do* say it—"I do not want to go with you."

A second puzzling feature of the same materials is the type of prolonged attention that contractions receive once they finally appear. The detailed but *unnecessary* attention will probably be recalled from your own experiences with the help of both Figure 6.1 and the following description of what took place in a third grade. It would be best to examine Figure 6.1 first, because what is shown there fosters classroom practices like the one described next.

During this particular observation, the teacher was directing a lesson whose objective was the ability to identify, and know the meanings of, eight contractions listed on the board. Apparently, the words had been practiced earlier because all three boys—the poorest readers in the class—were able to read most of them unassisted. Following the identifications, sentence cards were displayed. Now the teacher's request was to read a sentence silently and then explain its meaning. For the first one (*Don't cross in the middle of the street*), one boy explained, "It means you're not supposed to cross in the middle of the street. You're supposed to go to the corner." Even though the meaning of all the other sentences was explained equally well, which was evidence of the boys' understanding of the contractions, the teacher still asked them to name the two words for which each contraction substituted and to name the letters that each apostrophe replaced. Now, fidgeting, guessing, and errors were characteristic. Clearly the lesson had become not only too demanding but—and this is the point to be underscored—it also exceeded the requirements of reading.

For teachers, this incident has a twofold message. First, keep in mind the basic requirements of reading and, second, do not go beyond them even though workbook exercises do. This guideline is especially important to follow when working with slower children who, for the sake of their self-esteem, need all the success and encouragement they can get.

The foregoing description of common practices with contractions may have prompted the question, "Is detailed attention to the unique structure of contractions ever warranted?" The answer is, "It depends." If students are curious about the appearance of a contraction the first time they see one, all that needs to be said is something like, "You'll see that mark—it's called an 'apostrophe'—in a few other words, too." Once additional contractions have been introduced with whole word methodology and it thus becomes time to teach the meaning of *contraction*, something specific needs to be said about the fact that the apostrophe serves to contract two words into one. Now it is appropriate to contrast and discuss the details of pairs like:

don't	can't	I'll	she's	they're
do not	cannot	I will	she is	they are

Once the term *contraction* is understood, no further need exists to talk about what is substituted for what. Instead, the concern is, Do students understand the meaning of contractions when they are embedded in sentences?

USING WHOLE WORD METHODOLOGY: AN ILLUSTRATION

Before whole word instruction is illustrated, let me list two reminders for its use.

Reminders for Using Whole Word Methodology

1. At first, insufficient decoding ability means that unfamiliar words have to be identified for students. Words that are of interest should be selected initially. Soon, function words along with any other words that appear in the materials children are asked to read must get attention. If children are expected to do written assignments on their own, words like *draw* and *underline* need to be taught, too.
2. As grade level increases, so too does the number of new words in both basal reader selections and chapters in content subject textbooks. The time required for dealing with new vocabulary can be reduced by allowing students to figure out on their own any words they are capable of decoding. If the remaining words are still excessive in number and time is limited, it ought to be used for the most part to attend to those words that relate to the central ideas in the text. If a new word is *fuchsia*, for instance, and it is used in the text merely to describe the color of flowers, it might be skipped entirely for two reasons: First, knowing *fuchsia* has nothing to do with the main plot in the story and, second, *fuchsia* is an uncommon word.

Figure 6.1 Needless Exercise with Contractions

All the basal reader programs have a very large number of exercises similar to the one in Figure 6.1. For example, the series from which the page shown in Figure 6.1 is found has two workbooks for each reader. Combined, the two have thirty-five pages dealing with contractions. The exercises start in first-grade materials and continue throughout grade two.

As you know from your own experiences as an elementary school student, these kinds of exercises have been offered for some time. In earlier years, workbook pages were unadorned; the more recent materials, however, are often colorfully decorated, as is the worksheet shown in Figure 6.1. The change has two consequences: The cost of the materials increases while the number of items per page decreases.

As the page in Figure 6.1 illustrates, attending to contractions in isolation obscures their meaning. Placing them in a sentence (e.g., *She's at home.*) that is contrasted with another sentence that shows the words the contraction replaces (*She is at home.*) would be more helpful.

At some time, too, certain contractions need to be contrasted with possessive nouns, as in the advertisement *It's Pop's for Pizza!*

"A BELL FOR THE CAT," 41-47

Introducing the Page: Read and discuss the meaning of the title. For the first half of the page, have pupils write the contracted forms of the words given. For the second half of the page have pupils write the two words that comprise the contraction.

Additional Activity: Have pupils create oral sentences using the contractions on this page, or written sentences if they are capable of doing this.

2 to 1 and 1 to 2

1. she is

she's

2. he is

he's

3. it is

it's

4. here is

here's

5. here's

here is

6. she's

she is

7. he's

he is

8. it's

it is

46   Decoding: contractions with is

Source: From Teacher's Edition of Studybook for *Little Dog Laughed* of the Ginn Reading Program by Theodore Clymer, et al.: © Copyright, 1987, by Silver, Burdett & Ginn Inc. Used with permission.

Because preparations for reading a basal selection are—or ought to be—a time for attending to new vocabulary, the following illustration describes a third-grade teacher working with four of the eleven words cited in a basal manual as being new in a story that nine students will soon read. (The remaining seven words are regularly spelled and have meanings likely to be familiar.) The four words are *hummingbird, honey, experiment,* and *touch.*

As you read through the lesson, notice how the attention to the four words allows for imparting background information. This suggests that even though "Attend to new vocabulary" and "Activate or add to relevant world knowledge" have been listed as separate responsibilities in preparing students for assigned reading, dealing with one often contributes to the other.

Vocabulary Instruction

Teacher: It takes a lot of letters to name the most important character in the story you'll be reading today. I'll write just three of them. [Prints *hum*.] How do you pronounce this?

Group: Hum.

Teacher: I'll add more letters. [Adds *ming*.] Now what do all these letters say?

Group: Humming.

Teacher: Right. What does "humming" mean, Billy?

Billy: Humming is like singing, but there aren't any words. You don't have to open your mouth either.

Teacher: I have to add one more part to this word so that you'll know whom you'll be reading about. [Adds *bird*.] Today the story is about what?

Group: A hummingbird.

Teacher: Right you are. I've never seen a hummingbird around here. They're tiny birds, and they make a humming noise. That's how they got their name. Let me show you some pictures of hummingbirds. The ones in your reader are very small.

The teacher proceeds to show colorful pictures, which elicit comments from some of the children. The teacher then continues:

Teacher: The story is about a hummingbird, but it's also about [teacher finishes by printing *honey* on the board]. Who knows this word? . . . Nobody? I bet you'll know it if I write something else. [Adds to board so that it shows *bee and honey*.]

Michael: I know. Honey!

Teacher: Right. I thought you'd think of honey if I wrote *bee*. [Erases *bee* and *and*.] Have any of you ever eaten honey?

Mary Ann: My mother puts it on toast, but it makes me sick.

Trish: Sometimes my mother puts it in carrots when she's cooking.

Teacher: Yes, honey is sweet, so it's good on toast and in carrots.

Mary Ann:	It's too sweet and sticky. It makes me sick.
Teacher:	Mary Ann, when you read the story you'll have to see whether the hummingbird agrees with you. When all of you read the story you'll find a fairly long word, and I'm not sure you'll know what it means so we better look at that, too. [Writes *experiment.*] What is this word?
Billy:	It says "ex" at the beginning and "ment" at the end, but I don't know the rest of it. I don't think I've ever seen that word before.
Teacher:	Maybe not. Scientists use it a lot. Does anyone know what it is? . . . No? It says "experiment." What is it?
Group:	Experiment.
Teacher:	Rob, you weren't even looking at *experiment.* You'll never remember it if you don't look at it when you read it. Let's all look at this word. What is it everyone?
Group:	Experiment.
Teacher:	What does "experiment" mean? Does anyone know what an experiment is?
Billy:	It's when you try something, and you have to be careful because it might blow up. The other night on television, two guys did an experiment and it almost killed them.
Teacher:	That was one kind of experiment, Billy. Not all experiments are dangerous. In fact, I'm carrying on an experiment right now at home. I have two plants that are the same. I'm watering one every week and the other about every ten days. I'm trying to learn which amount of water is better. It's not dangerous, but it's an experiment because I'm trying to learn something by doing different things and then looking at the results. That's what your story for today is about. Someone is trying to find out something about hummingbirds. And it has to do with honey.
Trish:	I bet I know what happens. Some bees sting the hummingbird because they both want honey.
Teacher:	I can't tell you because then there wouldn't be any mystery. Before you find out what happens, there's one more word I want you to look at because you might have trouble figuring it out. [Prints *touch.*] Can anyone read this? Jim?
Jim:	Touch? [Pronounces it to rhyme with *couch.*]
Teacher:	Jim, have you ever heard a word that sounds like "touch"? [Repeats Jim's pronunciation.]
Jim:	I don't think so. I guess I don't know what it is.
Teacher:	Let's see if you do now. [Writes *touch football.*] Jim, think about what I just wrote. What does this word [points to *touch*] say?
Jim:	Touch. Touch football.
Teacher:	Yes, in this case *touch* means a kind of football game in which

you touch rather than tackle the players. [Erases *football*.] In the story about a hummingbird, it will just mean to touch something—the way I'm touching Mary Ann's shoulder. Jim, I think I know why you first thought this word said "touch" [pronounces it to rhyme with *couch*]. With this word [writes *couch* directly under *touch*], we do say "couch." We give that /ou/ sound to the digraph *ou*. But in "touch," the vowel sound is /ŭ/. All this shows the importance of asking—what question should you always ask after you think you've figured out a new word?

Group: Does it make sense?

Teacher: Correct. The reason I wrote *touch football* is to show you how words you can read help with words you're not sure of. There are other words in the story about the hummingbird that are new, but the way they're spelled should tell you what they say. If you have problems, be sure to read all the other words in the sentence. They'll help, too. To make sure you don't have problems with the words we've been talking about now, let's read them a few more times. Be sure to look at each word when you say it.

After the story is read silently, the teacher shows the group phrase and sentence cards, each containing at least one of the seven new words that were not taught before the reading. How the children decoded them is discussed. Sentences using the words that were presented before the reading was begun are used next. By having individuals read the cards aloud, the teacher learns which, if any, of the eleven new words are causing problems and thus require further attention.

COMMENTS ABOUT THE ILLUSTRATION

The teacher just referred to did a number of things that promote word learning, two of which will be discussed: (a) used students' experiences, and (b) requested attention to the new words.

Used Students' Experiences

Throughout the instruction, the teacher related the words she was teaching to students' experiences. Stated differently, she connected the new words with something already familiar. Connecting the new with the known is desirable, because it facilitates both learning and retention.

Other kinds of connections also help when new vocabulary is the concern. These connections are based on meaning and thus are referred to with names like *conceptual groups* and *semantic categories* (18). Whatever the name, the idea is that attending to a new word, not in isolation but as a member of a group of words that have something in common, makes that word more meaningful as well as more memorable.

Usually, the new vocabulary in content subject textbooks lends itself more readily to semantic groups than does basal reader vocabulary. A social studies chapter about a given country, for instance, is likely to have new words that can be grouped under headings like *Location, Resources, Population,* and *Occupations.* There will be times, nonetheless, when at least some of the new vocabulary for a basal story can be grouped, too. In a tale about a cross-country journey taken by pioneers, for instance, the new vocabulary includes *journey, country, anxious, caravan, mountain, peak, valley, desert, steep,* and *canyon.* Because this story comes close to the end of the second of two readers said to be for third grade, a teacher may decide— regardless of the manual's suggestions—to preteach only *journey, country, anxious,* and *caravan,* the assumption being that the students can decode the other six words.

Once the story is read, the heading *Cross-Country Journey* can be written on the board, first to allow for a review of the meaning. Afterward, the six words that were not pretaught, all of which relate to the journey, can be listed under the heading in any order that allows the teacher to pose questions designed to have students trace the journey using the listed words as prompts. As a result of this procedure, the teacher will be learning whether the six words were correctly decoded and, even more important, whether the meanings are known. In the end, the teacher will have collected information about vocabulary, decoding ability, and comprehension.

For another look at grouping words to facilitate learning, please see Figure 6.2 and the commentary about it.

Let's move on to discuss a second important feature of the lesson described earlier for words like *experiment* and *honey.* The first is "used students' experiences"; the second is "requested the students' attention."

Requested Attention to New Words

In its skeleton form, whole word methodology requires that a word be written and identified. ("The word I just wrote is 'fence'.") Learning theory suggests a further requirement: Be sure students look at the word *when* it is identified. At first, a reminder to get students to look at a word when it is named—which is what the third-grade teacher did in the illustrative lesson—may seem unnecessary because it appears to be little more than common sense. Be that as it may, visits to classrooms reveal many instances in which the importance of such a directive is overlooked. Let me cite just one example.

Using round robin reading, a second-grade teacher was with a group of ten. Pertinent to the present discussion is what happened while one child was reading aloud. When he was first asked to read, he immediately had difficulty with *toward,* so he looked up to the teacher for help. She told him what it said, and he continued. A few lines later he encountered *toward*

Figure 6.2 New Vocabulary and Semantic Groups

New vocabulary for a story in a basal series that claims to teach words "in conceptually related sets" is in Figure 6.2. (The story tells about the disastrous effects when a circus arrives in a small Western town.) Teachers adhering to the manual say to students, "You'll learn some words about the West," prior to attending to vocabulary. As is shown, only four words are "about the West"; other possible ways to group words, therefore, are suggested.

Students who are knowledgeable about phonics and word structure should be able to figure out all the new words with the possible exception of *pedestal*. The root of *manageable* may present problems; however, knowing that *manage* is the root and that *un* and *able* are affixes are conclusions that well-taught students should reach. Whole word methodology, therefore, may be required only for *pedestal* and *manage*.

Because the meaning of a number of the words may not be known, one possible decision is to work with all twenty words before reading begins. All can be listed on a ditto sheet, grouped according to the categories shown in Figure 6.2. After identifying and discussing the meaning of *pedestal, manage,* and *unmanageable,* a teacher can allow time for each student to work out the pronunciation of the other words and, further, to consider why they are grouped as they are. (Meanwhile, the teacher helps other students.) Once the allotted time ends, the teacher returns to the group to check pronunciations and the students' understanding of what the words mean. Whenever possible, the discussion should link the words with the story. Students who know it is about a circus, for instance, can be asked, "Why would *sequin* be in the story?" Such questions help with new words and with developing necessary background information and interest in reading the story.

The manual's recommendations for handling new vocabulary are briefer than what has been suggested. Extra time spent on vocabulary, however, saves time by allowing for independent, successful reading. The time-consuming, page-by-page reading referred to in manuals can thus be bypassed.

New Vocabulary: Grade 4			Some Semantic Categories	
			noise	*animals*
midway**	pedestal	livestock** (W)	grumble	camel
grumble*	lash*	unmanageable**	shrill	livestock
distract*	shift*	snare*	uproar	
camel*	swarm*	saddle* (W)		*to do*
sequin*	arena*	cactus* (W)	*opposites*	*something*
shrill*	uproar*	coax*	arena	grumble
wrestle*	range* (W)		range	wrestle
				shift
				coax
* phonics				distract
** word structure				lash
(W) "words about the West"				swarm

For the story about the West, preparations can be made one day, followed by the assignment to read the story. (Presumably, preparations include establishing purposes for the reading.) On the second day, the story is discussed in relation to those purposes. Another postreading activity can focus on sentences taken from the story that include one or more new words. Attending to the sentences allows for a check on vocabulary and for whatever extra work with the words seems to be warranted. One "extra" can be two worksheets suggested in the manual. (Twelve worksheets go with this selection.) Unfortunately, the two exercises deal with word recognition, not identification. Why identification should be the concern is explained later in the chapter.

once more, again did not know it, and again looked up to the teacher. Soon it was another child's turn to read aloud; however, had the first one continued and come across *toward* once more, it is safe to predict that he still would not know it. Why not? Each time the teacher named it, he was looking at her, not at *toward*.

Because of what has been seen in many classrooms, the following guideline clearly needs to be emphasized: *Encourage students to look at a word at the time it is being identified.* Implied in this guideline are two others:

1. New words should not be presented to as many as an entire class.
2. Whole word instruction should not begin until everyone is paying attention.

PRACTICE

Even when students do attend to a new word at the time they are being told what it is, the one experience is rarely sufficient to put the word in their sight vocabulary. To achieve that end, it is generally necessary to provide students with more than a single opportunity to think (or say) "honey" as they look at *honey*.

Ideally, multiple responses, or practice, allow for noting what distinguishes a word from all other words. In turn, it is the *distinctive features* that prompt a correct response. To clarify what is meant by the distinctive features of a word, a discussion of *cues* is necessary.

Cues

Applied to word learning, a cue is what the learner uses to establish a connection between a given word (stimulus) and what it says (response). Or, to put it somewhat differently, one or more features of a written word are selected as a prompt for its identification. If what is selected fixes the correct response permanently, it is a *relevant* cue. If it offers only temporary assistance and eventually fosters confusion and erroneous responses, it is *irrelevant*. With classroom illustrations, let me cite examples of the latter. (Subsequent chapters deal with relevant cues.)

An abundant use of irrelevant cues occurred in a first-grade classroom near the beginning of the year when the teacher was reviewing color words. As she wrote each on the chalkboard, she used a different colored piece of chalk. The word *blue*, for instance, was written with blue chalk, *yellow* with yellow chalk, and so on. Predictably, when she finished writing the words, the children had no difficulty remembering them. Equally predictable is that those who did not know the words before this colorful lesson would not know them any better when they appeared later in books or written with white chalk or black ink. Why? The teacher used an irrelevant cue (color) to help establish connections between visual stimuli (words) and correct responses to them.

To help children establish connections, some teachers still outline the configuration of words. (This was once a common practice.) When introducing *funny*, to cite an illustration, they show:

The problem with explicit attention to contour is made clear below and is the reason configuration is an irrelevant cue.

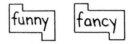

Another example of an irrelevant cue was identified in a classroom in which *look* was a new word. After writing it, the teacher commented, "This word says 'look'. It's easy to remember because it has two eyes in the middle—just what you use when you look at something." Even though this observation might help temporarily, dependence on two "eyes" in the middle for remembering *look* inevitably leads to confusion, specifically, when *book* or perhaps *foot* needs to be learned.

Elsewhere, a teacher was preparing for a story by introducing new words, one of which was *monkey*. As with the other words, the teacher wrote *monkey* on the chalkboard and identified it. She next told the students they would be reading about a monkey; she also said there was an easy way to remember the word that said "monkey." At this point she explained that, like a monkey, the word has "a tail at the end." If it happened that the only word in our language "ending with a tail" was *monkey*, the teacher's comment might help. However, other words not only end in *y* but also begin with *m* and, further, are about the same length as *monkey* (for example, *money*). The teacher's "help" thus called attention to a highly irrelevant cue.

Two further examples of irrelevant cues need to be cited because they were found in work done by two student teachers *after* they read an earlier version of this chapter. Their assignment was to describe practice to help children remember a function word. Correctly, one student chose *and*; the other, *the*. Correctly, too, each sample of practice presented the function words in contexts. Unfortunately, however, one student printed *and* in red—all the remaining words in each sentence were printed in black—and the other took the time to form *the* with yarn. In addition to using irrelevant cues, the two students demonstrated how easy it is to work hard on the wrong things. It isn't just industry, therefore, that separates superior teachers from others.

To discuss (and, hopefully, to discourage) teachers' uses of irrelevant cues is not to deny that children use what is irrelevant quite on their own. Here I cannot help but recall a child who, when shown ten word cards, quickly identified all ten words. Later, new cards were prepared for the same words, after which the child looked at *famous* as if she had never seen it before. In one sense, she had not. When the original card displaying *famous* was examined, it was found that a small piece of one corner had been torn off. Apparently, what this student had been responding to was a three-cornered card, not *famous*. What she had been relying on was an irrelevant cue that was outside the word itself.

Another irrelevant cue that students use is pictures—for instance, those in their readers. Because manuals often advise teachers to tell children to "look at the picture" when they cannot recall a word, pictures as cues for word identification requires further discussion.

The discussion begins with a reference to a classroom in which a child, who was reading aloud, was unable to recall the word *school*. His teacher suggested, "Look at the picture," which showed a building that was obviously a school. Immediately the puzzled reader said "school," not even looking at the symbol for it.* I believe it is safe to say that when he encountered *school* again, the same problem occurred.

This negative response to an unfortunately common practice is not meant to deny the significance of pictures for instruction. To the contrary, for pictures are *very* helpful at all grade levels in specifying word meanings and promoting oral discussions. Some that are in books also succeed in pricking students' curiosity to the point that they want to read the text that goes with the pictures. (In contrast, pictures that reveal the story reduce motivation.) I have also been in classrooms in which carefully selected pictures prompted students to write imaginative stories and descriptions. Nevertheless, as cues for word identification, pictures are irrelevant.

With all the attention that has now gone to irrelevant cues, you must wonder what could possibly be left that is relevant. To answer, let's first consider the meaning of relevant cue: permanent features that distinguish things. One permanent feature of a written word is the sequence of its letters. (The fact that sequence *is* a distinctive feature is made apparent in words like *tap, pat,* and *apt*.) Because of the significance of letter sequence, some teachers have children spell words when they are being taught. Name, spell, and rename are the requests these teachers make, especially when students still know very little about letter-sound correspondences. Fostering attention to sequence can also be accomplished with questions about contrasting words. For instance, if *soap* is known and a new word is *soup*, the two can be written one under the other to allow for a comparison, which helps make apparent the similarities and differences.

Besides letter sequence, other cues that are relevant for learning words

---

* The frequency of this warrants repetition of an earlier reminder: Be sure students look at a word *when* it is being named.

are letter-sound correspondences, which are sometimes referred to as *graphophonic cues.* The fact that the structure of a word is a relevant cue accounts for *structural cues.*

Now that cues applied to word learning have been discussed, it is time to turn our attention to the goal of word practice.

The Goal of Practice

As both research data and our own experiences confirm, the ability to identify most of the words that appear in a body of text is essential for comprehending it. (Knowing the words is also essential for developing self-confidence as a reader.) The same two sources tell us, too, that the faster such identifications are made, the easier it is to comprehend.

Since automatic identification *is* the goal of word practice, it is necessary for teachers to understand the difference between word *identification* and word *recognition.* Identification refers to the ability to name a stimulus (e.g., *five* or *5*) directly without any external prompt. Recognition, on the other hand, is the ability to name the stimulus with a prompt.

Actually, word recognition should be very familiar to us all because of the large number of word recognition exercises that commercial materials have always provided. You will recall, I am sure, workbook pages composed of lists of words in boxes:

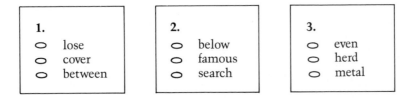

Reading from the basal manual, our teacher was apt to say something like: "Find box number one. Look at all the words in that box. Find the word *cover* and draw a line under it." To provide practice in taking tests, more recent versions of the same type of exercise are likely to be accompanied with directions that state: "Find the word *cover.* With your pencil, fill in the oval in front of the word *cover.*" Whether students are underlining or filling in ovals, the exercise just referred to deals with word recognition, because a word is named not independently but with the aid of a prompt. In this case, the prompt is offered by the teacher when she says the target word.

Teachers in the habit of asking, "*Why* am I doing what I'm doing?" may choose to use workbook pages like the one just described but are likely to change the task to word identification by having students produce, not choose, words. This can be accomplished by asking individuals to read all the words in a given box.

The same teachers will also be pleased to find some exercises in workbooks that do provide practice in identifying words. For an example, see Figure 6.3. (The page is from the teacher's edition of the workbook; thus answers are listed.)

Teachers can also prepare their own worksheets by sorting words in need of practice into groups like the following, to which written directions are added to supply even more word practice:

child

father

pony

aunt

Underline all the words
that have to do with people.

Practice like this is desirable, as it fosters attention to meaning as well as to naming.

The display in Figure 6.4 synthesizes what has now been said about word recognition, word identification, and comprehension. An important component omitted from the display is practice, which accounts for the progression that takes a person from "cannot name the word" to "identifies the word instantaneously."

Additional Comments about Practice

Comments that still need to be made about word practice have to do with the questions, "How much practice is necessary to ensure automatic identifications?" and "Should all new words receive similar amounts of practice?"

How Much Practice Is Necessary to Ensure Automatic Identifications? Even though "It depends" is not the most helpful or welcome answer, it is, nonetheless, the correct one for such reasons as the following.

To begin, whether a word is of interest makes a difference, which explains why children learn to read their own names with minimal practice. Interest is also the reason that students who have recently seen a television documentary about penguins find it easier to remember *penguin* than do peers who missed the program. It goes without saying—or should—that individuals who have no idea what a penguin is are not even ready to learn to

The Word's the Thing

If you were writing a story about the sky, you might call it **blue, gray, rainy, sunny,** or even **angry**—but you probably wouldn't call it **bossy** or **prickly.** You could say that **blue, gray, rainy, sunny,** and **angry** are **sky words,** because you can use them to describe the sky.

Find words to describe the sea, people, a city, and weather in this list and write your words in the boxes that follow. You may want to use some words more than once. You might want to add some of your own.

rainy	windy	hot
bossy	blue	snowy
noisy	kind	crowded
interesting	rough	stormy
mean	friendly	busy

Possible responses are given. Have pupils read and explain their answers.

SEA WORDS

blue	noisy
rough	
stormy	
windy	
rainy	

PEOPLE WORDS

bossy	noisy
interesting	
mean	
kind	
friendly	

CITY WORDS

noisy	hot
crowded	rainy
busy	snowy
	windy

WEATHER WORDS

rainy	rough
windy	
snowy	
hot	
stormy	

22   Language: descriptive words

Figure 6.3 Practice in Identifying Words

Source: From Teacher's Edition of Studybook for *Barefoot Island* of the Ginn Reading Program by Theodore Clymer, et al.: © Copyright, 1987, by Silver, Burdett & Ginn Inc. Used with permission.

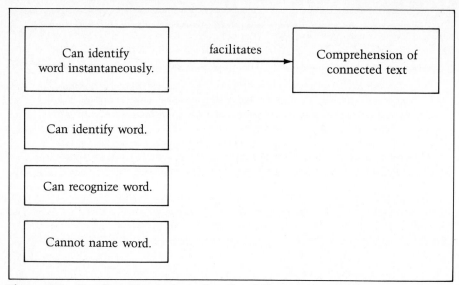

Figure 6.4   Reading Vocabulary: Levels of Knowing a Word

read *penguin* because, for them, it is nothing more than a string of seven letters.

Because the ability of a word to evoke a mental image helps make the word memorable (13), that factor needs to be considered, too. But, as you should see by now, the picture being drawn of the factors that determine what is sufficient practice shows mingled, not distinct, variables. This is the case because a word can hardly be of interest if its meaning is vague or unknown; and if the meaning is unknown, mental imagery is ruled out. Although confounded, the three variables referred to do support generalizations like: The easiest words to remember are content words whereas the most difficult ones to recall are function words.

It should be noted that once students know about letter-sound correspondences and word structure, the amount of practice required for learning words is reduced, because that knowledge allows for the use of relevant cues to recall words. Teaching phonics and structural analysis is important, therefore, not only for enabling students to cope on their own with unknown words but also for reducing the time that must be allotted to practice to put a word into an individual's sight vocabulary.

Should All New Words Receive Similar Amounts of Practice? As just suggested, more practice is necessary to learn function words than content words. The fact that function words are more difficult to remember, however, is not the only reason they merit more practice. Another is their importance. As brought out earlier in the observations made by a person visiting a second grade—and as our own experiences as readers make clear—function words such as *in* and *on* not only occur with considerable frequency but also make important differences insofar as constructing meaning is concerned.

Reading specialists are naturally interested in high-frequency words. One of the earliest efforts to identify them was made by Edward Dolch in the 1930s (6). Figure 6.5 shows his well-known list of 220 *service words,* so-called because their regular appearance in print makes knowing them highly serviceable or useful. (You will notice in Figure 6.5 that most but not all the words listed are function words.) Subsequently, other reading specialists pursued the task of identifying high-frequency words. For instance, in an article entitled "The New Instant Word List," Edward Fry (10) offers what he says are the 300 words that show up most frequently in written text. He further claims that "half of all written material in English is composed of just the first hundred Instant Words and their common variants" (p. 284). (By *variant* Fry means the inflections that are added to roots, such as *-s* and *-ing.*)

Even though factors like cultural change and the availability of computers result in high-frequency lists that vary somewhat from the collection of service words proposed by Dolch, the list he compiled is reproduced in Figure 6.5 because it is the best known and, further, is the standard against which more recently compiled lists are often compared.

With or without such lists, anyone who knows English is aware of the value of being able to identify automatically such frequently occurring words as *was, the, to,* and *it.* They are also aware that with the exception of color and number words and others such as *time, people, water, sound,* and *animal* (10), nouns appear much less frequently. Whether in anybody's list or not, teachers who expect to have students carry out written assignments independently assign importance to words like *underline, circle, draw, picture,* and *describe.*

The conclusion about practice that this discussion reaches is: The more frequently students are apt to encounter a word, the more frequently should that word be practiced.

Another point, one made earlier, needs to be repeated, as it also relates to questions about word practice. The point has to do with comprehension, specifically with the fact that when the new vocabulary in a selection that students will be asked to read is excessive and time is limited, the words that relate to the central ideas in the text should get more prereading and practice time than the other words. Such words can be selected when a teacher examines the selection she plans to assign in order to make decisions about what needs to be done to facilitate comprehension.

Anyone who takes the time to examine basal manuals quickly learns that new vocabulary and word practice receive too little attention, whether the words are important or not. By grade four, and sometimes as early as grade three, having students look up new words in a glossary is often the extent of the "help" offered. Flaws like this are the reason this chapter illus-

a	could	had	may	said	under
about	cut	has	me	saw	up
after		have	much	say	upon
again	did	he	must	see	us
all	do	help	my	seven	use
always	does	her	myself	shall	
am	done	here		she	very
an	don't	him	never	show	
and	down	his	new	sing	walk
any	draw	hold	no	sit	want
are	drink	hot	not	six	warm
around		how	now	sleep	was
as	eat	hurt		small	wash
ask	eight		of	so	we
at	every	I	off	some	well
ate		if	old	soon	went
away	fall	in	on	start	were
	far	into	once	stop	what
be	fast	is	one		when
because	find	it	only	take	where
been	first	its	open	tell	which
before	five		or	ten	white
best	fly	jump	our	thank	who
better	for	just	out	that	why
big	found		over	the	will
black	four	keep	own	their	wish
blue	from	kind		them	with
both	full	know	pick	then	work
bring	funny		play	there	would
brown		laugh	please	these	write
but	gave	let	pretty	they	
buy	get	light	pull	think	yellow
by	give	like	put	this	yes
	go	little		those	you
call	goes	live	ran	three	your
came	going	long	read	to	
can	good	look	red	today	
carry	got		ride	together	
clean	green	made	right	too	
cold	grow	make	round	try	
come		many	run	two	

Figure 6.5   The Dolch Basic Vocabulary of 220 Service Words

trates how attention to new vocabulary and practice can be worked into basal lessons.

Anyone who observes in a variety of grade levels will also learn that efforts to make word practice interesting are more obvious in primary-grade classrooms than in those beyond grade three or four. One possible reason is the questionable belief that older students are too sophisticated to enjoy the embellishments that teachers of younger children rely on to make practice appealing. (See Figure 6.6 for examples of how primary-grade teachers used bulletin-board displays for word practice.) Even though teachers are not entertainers, superior ones do try to make word practice at least somewhat interesting. Making such an effort is important because involvement and achievement go hand in hand.

Halloween
Every day starting on October 1, a paper ghost is added to a bulletin board. Appearing on each is a word selected by the children as being especially difficult. Daily, all the ghosts on the board are read until thirty-one have accumulated by the time Halloween arrives.

Autumn
Prompted by the plentiful supply of apples available, a teacher attached a large paper tree to a board. She also cut out red paper apples on which words in need of practice are printed along with other words to provide a context (e.g., *far away*). Whenever a child reads an apple correctly, the teacher attaches it to the tree. At the end, the apples are picked, allowing the group to review all the words. Using the same procedure, this teacher uses a pine tree and ornaments in December. (Other possibilities: cornucopia and fruit, net and fish, mailbox and envelopes, jar and cookies)

Questions/Answers
Phrase cards on a board allow a teacher to ask questions and children to respond by reading the cards. If the teacher asks, "When you're crossing the street, where should you *not* go?" the card displaying *between cars* provides the answer.

Jack and the Beanstalk
To highlight a much-enjoyed story, one teacher put a tall, thick stalk (green paper rolled tightly) on a board, attached to which were long leaves on which phrases had been printed. Also on the board were paper figures of both Jack and the giant. Children take turns being one or the other. With the selected figure in hand, the climb is attempted. Misread words bring the child crashing to the ground, after which another child has a chance to attempt the climb. Successful climbers get to keep a figure temporarily.

Figure 6.6   Interesting Word Practice

That some small embellishment is all it takes to make practice attractive was demonstrated when I was visiting regularly in a fourth grade in which there were two boys with major deficiencies in reading. Although the teacher's desire to help was praiseworthy, the help itself was not. Day after day, nothing but a flash-card technique (word card is held up and one or more students name the word) was used. Day after day, it elicited little enthusiasm and, seemingly, little learning. What the teacher was illustrating, in fact, is that *more* is not always a remedy—especially not more of the same.

To help, a slight alteration was suggested that created an unexpected amount of enthusiasm from the boys: List and number on the chalkboard brief phrases or sentences containing troublesome words. Have the boys take turns selecting number cards from a bag, which indicate the phrases they are to read. A correct response means the card can be kept; an incorrect one means it goes back into the bag.

Because persons still in the process of acquiring proficiency in reading need to be willing to risk making mistakes, a final point worth making is that practice ought to take place in a nonpunitive setting. That is, students should see practice as something designed to help them, not as a time for teachers to identify and criticize errors. This indicates that a teacher comment like the following should be the rule rather than the exception: "I noticed yesterday that you were mixing up some words. Let's go over them again, and then I'll ask you to do this worksheet so that we can find out if they're still causing problems."

Having reviewed some features of effective practice, let's move on to examples.

The procedures one fourth-grade teacher follows merit initial attention. Typically, she has two instructional groups—sometimes three. Either way, she prints all the new basal words on cards of different colors, one word per card. (The colors indicate grammatical functions.) As words are taught, they are removed from the alphabetized card collection so that they can be practiced intermittently. If review is conducted by the teacher, word combinations like the following might be displayed on cards. Students read the combinations and, if it seems necessary, explain the meaning:

forlorn personality	enormous appetite
sociable adults	shrill siren

At other times, words selected for practice might be arranged in some random way on an assignment sheet. Now the job for the students is to write the words in meaningful pairs. For example:

uncommonly helpless	piteously inferior
unbelievably ancient	discouragingly endangered

At another time, the task might be to organize randomly placed words into conceptual sets, each to be assigned a classification. To illustrate:

Noise

crunch	whine	rustle	shriek
bleat	chirp	slam	whimper
crackle	mutter	growl	thud

If more teachers took word practice as seriously as this one in fourth grade, it seems safe to predict that comprehension problems would be substantially reduced.

More ideas for word practice follow.

- Compose sentences based on a selection just read. Each sentence should include at least one new word. Show one sentence at a time to the members of an instructional group. (Each member has two small cards, one displaying *yes,* the other *no.*) At the snap of your fingers, the students hold up one of their cards to indicate that the content of the sentence does or does not correspond to what they just read. (Similar procedures can be used with cards showing *fact* and *opinion,* or *true, false,* and *sometimes.*)

- If appropriate pictures are available, students can match their content with descriptions composed of words still in need of practice—descriptions like *Anticipation was written on their faces* and *An evening of magnificent beauty.* For less advanced students, descriptions might be *a mountain peak* and *hoar frost* or, easier still, *a cloudy day* and *toward the house.*

- Partial sentences composed of words that students are learning can be used to write complete sentences—for instance, *The bulk of their problems, An elderly man,* or *among flowers and shrubs* and *by the side of the building.*

INDEPENDENT READING AND PRACTICE

A number of researchers claim that the most beneficial practice is reading extended pieces of text—books, magazines, newspapers, and so forth—that can be comprehended without assistance. Or, as Stanovich states, "many things that facilitate further growth in reading comprehension ability—general knowledge, vocabulary, syntactic knowledge—are developed by reading itself" (17, p. 364).

Because some teachers carry in their heads the puritanical notion that only if something is difficult can it possibly be "good," the value of reading easy material is pinpointed in the list on p. 186.

> ### Benefits of Reading Independent-Level Material
>
> 1. Allows for the consolidation and realistic use of what has been taught.
> 2. Moves attention away from individual words to the meaning of connected text.
> 3. Fosters good habits insofar as rate is concerned.
> 4. Adds to the reader's knowledge of the world.
> 5. Promotes self-confidence and, with it, a greater interest in reading.

Teachers who appreciate the potential of extended reading always make certain that they do not become so intent on teaching skills that they never develop readers. They also make certain that classroom libraries reflect students' interests. One observed teacher who kept interests in mind had a classroom collection that included series like the Nancy Drew books; cartoon, riddle, and joke books; and other books dealing with such topics as judo. Aware that some students are intimidated by length, this same teacher made sure that books with relatively few pages were available. Keeping difficulty in mind, she saw to it that free-choice materials allowed for selections that would foster confidence, not insecurity.

Realistically, it has to be acknowledged that the mere availability of suitable and interesting books is not always sufficient to get students to want to read them. This means that teachers sometimes have to take special steps to change their minds. Allowing students to make their own selections (and doing away with such obligations as book reports) is one helpful step; however, if freedom of choice is to have any meaning, what is available must be known. Therefore, each time all or part of a classroom library is changed, the new possibilities must be announced—some might even be advertised—by showing a few illustrations or by reading just enough from each to spark curiosity about the rest of the book.

Other steps that teachers have taken to motivate reading are described next.

■ Whenever students show special interest in a topic, our school librarian and I seek out books that pertain to it. Together, we usually succeed in finding material written at a level that each child can handle. Initially, I meet with the group of interested children to discuss the topic, to distribute books, and to set a date for a subsequent meeting. Often, postreading discussions are as mature as any that adults might have. One bonus feature is the opportunity that the discussions give to less able readers to make significant contributions for, very often, the content of their books is just as informative as that found in more difficult sources.

- Because my contacts with students are often impersonal, I meet as often as I can with individuals, ostensibly to discuss what they have been reading on their own. At such times, I am more eager to learn how children feel about reading than to assess abilities or deficiencies. These meetings give me a chance to recommend books or to find some that match expressed interests. I especially try to find out the questions that are important to students and then try to locate books that might offer answers.

- If children enjoyed a book, they may, if they wish, tell in writing why they enjoyed it. Recommendations are displayed on a board to assist anyone who is looking for a book. If multiple copies of a really good book are available, I feel no compunction about asking certain students to read it. We first meet as a group so that I can introduce the book and set a date for getting reactions. When we meet again, I am ready with questions, but I ask them only if something is needed to get a discussion started. If the children appear to have enjoyed a book, I am also ready to show others by the same author or similar books by different authors.

- Many of the new informational books—even those written at fairly simple levels—are more interesting than textbooks. Students like them better, too. That's why I encourage groups to do extra reading on topics that originate in social studies and science texts. With the supplementary reading, we often get contradictory information, which results in lively discussions and, very often, in further reading.

- Sometime each year I suggest the possibility of looking for interesting new words in self-selected books. To fan some interest, I couple the suggestion with a few examples I've come across in my own reading. (I always go out of my way to let students know that I am an avid reader.) At some designated date, interested students and I get together to discuss our findings.

- By the time children get to third grade, some are effective oral readers. With guidance from me or the school librarian, they select books that kindergartners and first graders will enjoy. After reading the books silently, they read them aloud to small groups of younger children.

- Whenever parents or other adults in the community have interesting hobbies, I invite them to tell my students about them. I then try to find books that relate to the hobbies. Parents who have traveled and have taken slides also speak to us. Again, I work with our librarian to find books about the places each person has been to.

- Into some of the library books in my room I tuck cards that make a request. (Students call them the "Would you" cards.) One is: "Would you pretend that you're the author of this book as you read it? When you're finished, be ready to tell which parts of the book were the hardest to write." A card in another book might ask, "Would you get a friend to read this book when you're finished? Together, the two of you can make a mobile whose parts will show drawings of characters or scenes or happenings in the book. Later, you can use the mobile to tell others about the story."

Some references at the end of the chapter offer more suggestions for promoting interest in reading books (4, 14, 16). Others tell of books that children especially enjoy (3) and name others that are easy to read (2, 5).

SUMMARY

Identifying new words as wholes was the main subject of Chapter 6. Naming whole words, usually referred to as whole word methodology, was recommended as the way to get reading vocabularies started.

When reading ability *is* just getting started, all new words have to be directly identified, since children lack the ability to decode them themselves. At that point, words that merit attention are those that (a) are of special interest, and (b) appear in whatever material the children are expected to read. Once children are able to use graphophonic and structural cues to recognize new or forgotten words, whole word methodology enters into instruction only when a word is so irregularly spelled that the most advanced decoding ability will not help in getting it figured out.

Any teacher using whole word methodology at any grade level needs to decide whether to introduce a new word alone or in the context of other known words. Helpful with such decisions is the division of words that catalogs them as content and function words. Although the former do not always require a context, the latter do because, by themselves, they are meaningless. Content words that always need a context are homonyms and homographs.

Just as the nature of new words determines whether a context is needed, so too does it affect the amount of practice required for automatic identifications. Because the most meaningful words are the easiest to remember, a safe assumption is that function words require more practice than do content words. But both kinds will require some practice, a fact not always recognized, especially in the middle and upper grades.

Essentially, practice (repeated responses to a written word) allows for attention to relevant cues—that is, to the features of a word that distinguish it from all other words. The importance of relevant cues for permanently correct identifications is the reason Chapter 6 spent considerable time illustrating cues that are relevant and, in particular, cues that are irrelevant. The importance of automatic identifications for comprehension is the reason the chapter also included a discussion of practice.

REVIEW

1. Chapter 6 recommends teaching together—whenever possible—words that are related. This recommendation suggests the following: To re-

view terms used in Chapter 6, explain each one in the two charts shown below in a way that makes implied relationships explicit.

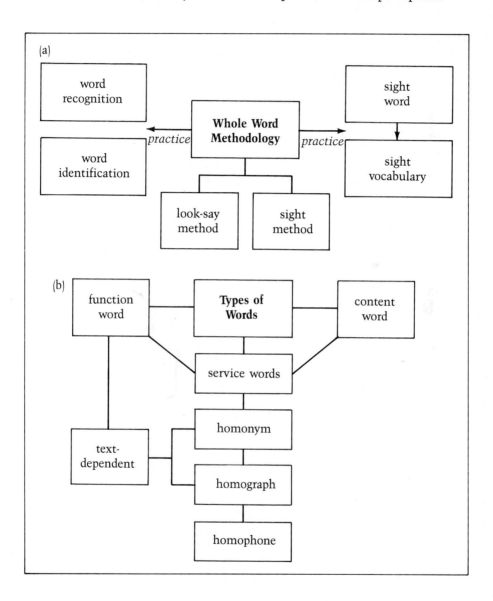

2. Since the new words that children figure out on their own with the help of graphophonic and structural cues still require practice, why shouldn't all new vocabulary be identified by a teacher?

3. Color as an irrelevant cue is discussed in Chapter 6. Is the following assignment another example of encouraging use of irrelevant cues? Explain your response.

A ditto sheet shows a list of sentences, each containing a word that names a color. Directions ask children to read each sentence and underline the color word with a crayon of the same color.

4. Using what you learned earlier in Chapter 1, cite reasons why the following statement is correct.

   Those who presuppose that students will be able to comprehend a piece of text as long as they can read all the words do not understand the comprehension process.

5. Even though Chapter 6 is primarily concerned with one way for developing reading vocabularies, a number of points are made that have significance for any instruction. What *are* some of these points?

REFERENCES

1. Adams, Marilyn J., and Huggins, A. W. F. "The Growth of Children's Sight Vocabulary: A Quick Test with Educational and Theoretical Implications." *Reading Research Quarterly* 20 (Spring, 1985), 262–281.
2. Bissett, Donald J., and Moline, Ruth E. "Books in the Classroom." *Language Arts* 53 (May, 1976), 504–509.
3. Children's Book Council and IRA. "Children's Choices for 1987." *Reading Teacher* 41 (October, 1987), 34–53.
4. Cullinan, Bernice E. (Ed.). *Children's Literature in the Reading Program.* Newark, Del.: International Reading Association, 1987.
5. Cunningham, Pat. "Books for Beginners." *Reading Teacher* 34 (May, 1981), 952–954.
6. Dolch, Edward W. *Problems in Reading.* Champaign, Ill.: Garrard Press, 1948.
7. Durkin, Dolores. "A Six Year Study of Children Who Learned to Read in School at the Age of Four." *Reading Research Quarterly* 10 (1974–1975, No. 1), 9–61.
8. Durkin, Dolores. "What Classroom Observations Reveal about Reading Comprehension Instruction." *Reading Research Quarterly* 14 (1978–1979), 481–533.
9. Fredericksen, John. "Sources of Process Interaction in Reading." In A. M. Lesgold and C. A. Perfetti (Eds.), *Interactive Processes in Reading.* Hillsdale, N.J.: Lawrence Erlbaum Associates, 1981, 361–386.
10. Fry, Edward, "The New Instant Word List." *Reading Teacher* 34 (December, 1980), 284–289.
11. Green, Frank. "Listening to Children Read: The Empathetic Process." *Reading Teacher* 39 (February, 1986), 536–543.
12. Nemko, Barbara. "Context versus Isolation: Another Look at Beginning Readers." *Reading Research Quarterly* 19 (Summer 1984), 461–467.
13. Paivio, Allan. "Mental Imagery in Associative Learning and Memory." *Psychological Review* 76 (May, 1969), 241–263.
14. Pillar, Arlene M. "Individualizing Book Reviews." *Elementary English* 52 (April, 1975), 467–469.

15. Rash, Judy; Johnson, Terry D.; and Gleadow, Norman. "Acquisition and Retention of Written Words by Kindergarten Children under Varying Learning Conditions." *Reading Research Quarterly* 19 (Summer, 1984), 452–460.
16. Ryan, Florence H. "Taking the Boredom Out of Book Reports." *Elementary English* 51 (October, 1974), 987–989.
17. Stanovich, Keith E. "Matthew Effects in Reading: Some Consequences of Individual Differences in the Acquisition of Literacy." *Reading Research Quarterly* 21 (Fall, 1986), 360–406.
18. Wixson, Karen K. "Vocabulary Instruction and Children's Comprehension of Basal Series." *Reading Research Quarterly* 21 (Summer, 1986), 317–329.

Chapter 7

Contexts

PREVIEW

Verbal contexts, the focus of this chapter, consist of known words, some of which were likely to have been learned from teachers using whole word methodology. That is why the previous chapter discussed whole word teaching. The concern of this chapter is the use of verbal contexts by readers to get help with recognizing words that are unfamiliar in their written form. A number of instances of such help were referred to earlier. You will recall, for example, the third-grade teacher who added the known word *football* after *touch* when the latter word caused problems for an instructional group.

The importance of being able to use contexts that may be as brief as two words is directly related to the importance of independence. More specifically, students who have the ability to use the known to get help with recognizing the unknown are much less dependent on outside help—on a teacher or dictionary, for example—than are other students who lack that ability.

Because contextual cues lie outside the word causing problems, they can be thought of as interword cues. In contrast, the cues or prompts that derive from the spelling of an unknown word (graphophonic cues) or from its structure (structural cues) are intraword help. Together, the three types of cues provide readers with considerable assistance—assuming they are sufficiently knowledgeable to make use of it. This explains why it can be said that the chapters covering contextual, graphophonic, and structural cues share the same underlying theme: helping students acquire independence in coping with words not yet in their reading vocabulary.

As Chapter 7 considers contextual cues, it divides them into syntactic and semantic cues. You learn as you continue through the chapter that work with syntactic and semantic cues can get started even before children are able to read. This is possible because spoken language provides listeners with contextual cues to the same degree that written material makes these cues available to readers. This means that Chapter 7 has content that is relevant for teachers who work with nonreaders as well as for teachers whose students are fairly proficient.

This chapter starts with another reference to the third-grade teacher mentioned in the Preview, because her writing *football* to help students recognize *touch* allows for comments about contextual cues that should be kept in mind throughout the chapter.

INTRODUCTORY COMMENTS

The first point to be made about the word *football* is that it provided assistance only to students who knew about the game called "touch football." How previous knowledge enters directly into the availability of contextual cues is illustrated even more clearly with the two contexts below:

The United States flag is red, ———, and blue.

The flag of Spain is red and ———.

For readers who know the colors of the two flags referred to, the contexts above are so helpful that the correct words can be "recognized" with certainty even when the symbols for them are no more than blanks.

Now let's return to *touch football* to make a second point, namely, that the reason *football* offered help with *touch* is not only because touch football had been experienced—directly by playing it or indirectly by watching it—but also because at some point the word *touch* was mentioned in connection with the game. Stated differently, *football* provided assistance because *touch* was in the third-graders' oral vocabulary and was associated with a particular way of playing football. That allowed them to think "touch" in the context that the teacher supplied. Conceivably, children can play "touch football" without ever learning its name. For them, writing *football* after *touch* makes little difference in their ability to cope with *touch*. This suggests that contextual help is not some unalterable given but, instead, has an existence that depends on readers' oral vocabularies, which, in turn, are closely tied to experiences and knowledge about the world.

The third point in need of early attention is that the use of cues, whether contextual, graphophonic, structural, or a combination of the three, results in word recognition, not word identification. The implication of this is that the third-grade students referred to earlier need to practice *touch* in order to be able to identify it—eventually "on sight." And, as mentioned, sight words comprise contexts. This fact indicates that sight vocabularies are significant not only for comprehending but also for the contextual cues they provide.*

Probably the most basic point to make about contexts is that they only exist in text in which most words are known. A sentence like the following, for example, in which three of its five words are unknown, can hardly be thought of as a context:

A _____ _____ at _____.

To make sure students have opportunities to use contexts for help with unknown written words is one reason that excessively difficult material should be bypassed.

Having considered important points about contexts, let's move on to examine two kinds of cues: syntactic and semantic. Because it is not possible to discuss two topics simultaneously, syntactic and semantic cues are dealt with separately even though proficient readers use the two kinds of cues jointly.

SYNTACTIC CUES

Syntactic derives from the word *syntax,* which has to do with the construction or word order of sentences. In any language that is *positional,* how words are ordered is very significant. This is the case because positional languages such as English rely heavily on word order to convey meaning. Because word order is so critical, rearranging words usually affects meaning or may destroy it altogether. This is illustrated in these sentences:

They painted the house yellow.	The horses play.
They painted the yellow house.	Play the horses.
Painted they yellow the house.	Horses play the.

The nature of positional languages explains why a sentence can be defined as a series of words arranged in an order that yields something meaningful. The nature of positional languages also explains why word order is patterned in certain ways that are predictable. The fact that words are sequenced only in certain ways places constraints on the kinds of words that fit at given points in sentences. It is these constraints that allow for syntactic cues. In sentences like the ones below, for example, syntactic cues

---

* This chapter is concerned with the use of contextual cues to recognize the visual form of a word whose meaning is known. Chapter 11 looks at contextual cues to see how they help readers reach a conclusion about the meaning of a word.

(prompts that derive from word order) indicate that all the blanks can be filled only with nouns:

> The _____ can sing.
> The talented _____ can sing.
> The talented and ambitious _____ can sing.

If *The* were replaced by *These* in the sentences above, the syntactic constraints would be even greater; all the missing words would have to be plural nouns.

Admittedly, knowing that an unfamiliar word is a plural noun—or a verb or an adjective or whatever—does not provide a reader with direct help in recognizing that word. Nonetheless, constraints that derive from syntactic cues serve the reader well in eliminating possibilities. When constraints that derive from syntax are combined with constraints originating in *semantic cues,* an even larger number of words can be eliminated from consideration as a reader wonders, "What *is* that word?"

SEMANTIC CUES

The fact that words in sentences are ordered only in certain ways brings syntactic cues into existence. It is the fact that language makes sense that accounts for *semantic cues.* For readers, semantic cues are sources of help for unknown words that derive from the collective meaning of the words they know. How semantic cues add to the constraints that originate in syntactic cues is illustrated in the sentence below, in which the blank represents an unknown word.

> The children are playing _____ the park.

In this instance, the position of the unknown word in the sentence points to its being a preposition; however, the collective meaning of the known words indicates that only certain prepositions are semantically acceptable. Replacing the blank with *at, in, outside,* or *beyond,* for example, makes sense whereas replacements such as *into, on,* or *between* do not. What is being illustrated, then, is that slots in sentences are constrained both syntactically and semantically.

It should be noted that semantic cues, unlike syntactic cues, are not confined to the sentence in which an unfamiliar word is embedded. This is the case because text is composed of sentences that are linked semantically. For instance:

> This room is hot. Turn on the _____.

The construction of the second sentence shown above clearly indicates that the unknown word is a noun. Semantic cues in the same sentence are less generous; a large number of nouns make sense. *Faucet, radio, television, light,* and *road* are a few that are semantically acceptable. However, when the meaning of the previous sentence is taken into account, a reader's thoughts should immediately turn to a noun like *fan.*

Why it is often wise for readers not only to keep the previous sentence(s) in mind but also to read ahead when an unknown word is encountered is demonstrated next:

> The _____ in the pot is still wet. Don't water that plant.
> When you feed the dog, be _____. He might bite.
> I don't use _____ in my tea. It makes it too sweet.

The last context is useful for reviewing the fact that contextual help is dependent on a reader's experiences and the knowledge they yield. What teachers need to keep in mind is that individual experiences make the notion "meaningful" somewhat subjective. This was brought out during a recent visit to a classroom. Reading aloud, one boy said, "The men went into the horse" in response to the sentence *The men went into the house.* Because the teacher had been stressing that reading must make sense, she naturally asked, "Kevin, does it make sense to say that men went into a horse?" "Yes," responded Kevin without hesitation. "Once on TV, I saw men marching into a wooden horse to hide there."

The moral of this story pertains not only to the significance of experiences but also to the need for readers to consider graphophonic cues as well as cues originating in a context. After all, *house* is not "horse" no matter what a child's experiences may have included. As shown in the following sections, giving attention to the combined use of contextual and graphophonic cues can get started very early.

ORAL CONTEXTS

Even though young children are not consciously aware that making sense is the essence of language, they display an intuitive knowledge of that fact every time they speak. It is that tacit knowledge that makes practice in using contextual cues possible even before children are able to do any reading.

How one kindergarten teacher who knows the value of contextual cues for readers worked with a group of eight is depicted below.

Teacher: Does anyone know what a detective is?
Vincent: I do. He catches robbers.
Maria: Sometimes he gets shot, too.
Teacher: Yes, that's true. Vincent, how is a detective able to catch a robber?
Vincent: If somebody knows him, they can tell the police.

Teacher:	But what if nobody does? Maybe he's wearing a mask, and nobody knows who he is. What then? Might he do something in the store he's robbing that will help a detective find him later?
Joan:	The other night on television a robber had wet shoes and left puddles in the store. That's how come he was caught.
Teacher:	What do we call something like puddles—or maybe fingerprints? What do you call what a detective uses to catch a thief?
Peter:	I know. They're clues. He uses clues.
Teacher:	Good for you. Has anyone else heard the word *clue* before?
Michael:	I have. I have a detective game at home.
Teacher:	Good detectives know how to use clues, don't they?
Maria:	They use them to find people who kill people, too.
Teacher:	Yes, they do. Today I want to find out if *you* would make good detectives. I'm going to give you a clue by saying something. I won't say everything, though. I'll leave out a word at the end; but if you listen, you'll be able to tell me the word I'm thinking of but don't say. Listen now. See if you can tell me the word at the end that I don't say. In our room, we have fifteen girls and only nine—who can finish it?
Group:	Boys!
Teacher:	Say, you really *are* good detectives. You certainly know how to use clues. I'll have to make it a little harder. This time if you think you know the word I don't say, raise your hand. Here goes. When we draw pictures, we use crayons or _____.

Correctly, the kindergarten teacher referred to above started with brief sentences that had familiar content. She used the word *clue* rather than *cue* because the former has meaning for children. She also provided maximum contextual help by omitting a word at the very end of her sentences. On another day, both to shift the position of the omitted word and to vary how practice is carried on, the same teacher might deal with contextual cues by commenting as follows:

> Sometimes, parents know so much about us that it seems they know what we're thinking even before we say it. They can almost read our minds, can't they? Let's see whether you can read *my* mind. I'll say something, but I'll leave out one word. I'll think of the word but won't say it. When I come to the word that I'm thinking of, I'll raise my hand. Listen. Every Monday morning at ten, Mrs. _____ comes to our room for art. What word did I leave out?

To provide even more variety, pictures are useful. Now, children select displayed pictures in order to complete sentences spoken by the teacher. For example:

> To keep us dry, we can carry an _____. (picture of an umbrella)
> My favorite pet is a _____. (pictures of a dog, a cat, and a bird)

The children in the park are _____. (picture of children on swings)

The last two sentences allow for attention to the guideline that should be used in evaluating children's responses: Any response is acceptable as long as it is syntactically and semantically consistent with the rest of the context. In the third example above, meaningful responses include "swinging," "having fun," and "playing."

Even though this section is meant to highlight early use of contextual cues by using spoken language, the fact that most kindergartners can read some words should not be overlooked. After all, even limited reading vocabularies are sufficient to make available practice in arranging words in a meaningful order. Known words can be printed on small cards, for example, so children can put them together—perhaps on the floor—in ways that convey meaning:

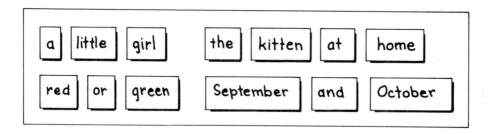

ORAL CONTEXTS AND MINIMAL GRAPHOPHONIC CUES

Teachers who remember to ask "Why am I doing what I'm doing?" combine the use of contextual cues with the use of graphophonic cues as soon as possible. With all the phonics now being taught in kindergarten, the combination of spoken contexts and graphophonic cues becomes available early.

Including graphophonic cues is desirable not only because it brings children closer to what is available when they read but also because it makes phonics instruction meaningful. As pointed out in Chapter 5, when phonics instruction comes directly from workbooks, it is often decontextualized. In contrast, when letter-sound correspondences are used in the way that will be described, the value of knowing about sounds is made apparent.

To illustrate early use of oral contexts plus minimal graphophonic cues, one teacher's procedures are described below.

Teacher: [Holds up card showing *t*.] We've just been talking about the sound that goes with this letter. Again, tell me some words that begin with that sound.

Danny: *Tell* starts with it.

Kim: So does *two* and *ten* and *tall*.

Teacher: Well, you certainly know lots of words that begin with the sound that goes with *t*. I wonder, though, if you can think of one certain word that starts with *t*. I'll think of it but won't say it. See if you can tell me what it is. Listen. Right now we have two pets in our room. One is a _____. Which of our pets am I thinking of? . . . How did you know I was thinking of the turtle? . . . Why did you know I *wasn't* thinking of the gerbil? What if we had a tiger for a pet? Might I have been thinking of that?

Letter cards similar to the one referred to in this illustration can be used with riddles: "Who can think of something that starts with this letter—think of its sound—and that we wear on our hands?" Since some children remember words with minimal amounts of practice, it is sometimes advisable to print on the board whatever words are suggested by contextual cues and an initial letter—*mittens*, for example. Many teachers have been pleasantly surprised at the number of words some children remember as a result of casual but meaningful opportunities to see what specified words look like.

INSTRUCTION: CONTEXTUAL CUES

As demonstrated in the illustrative work with kindergartners, initial attention to contextual cues does not make explicit the role they play in helping readers recognize words that are visually unfamiliar. At some point, however, students need to be helped to understand that written words they do know often help with those they don't know. More specifically, they need to learn "how to think their way through a problem situation . . . " (3, p. 417). That is, they need to become *strategic readers who have systematic plans for coping with problems* (11).

Some teachers initiate explicit attention to the use of contextual cues to solve word problems when students misread a word or simply do not know what a word is. Others start in a way that is illustrated next. The teacher is speaking to an instructional group:

As you know, when people read they sometimes come across words they don't know or have forgotten. There are a couple of ways in which readers can help themselves whenever that happens. I want to talk today about one way. It's as simple as using the words you can read to help you with the ones you can't read. To show how this works, I'm going to write a sentence on the board. I'll use words you can read. [Writes *The boy almost _____ on the bone.*] Let's pretend that a word you can't read is where this blank is. Since you know all the other words, let's read them together. Clap when you get to the blank, and then go on and read the rest of the sentence.

In this case, one student immediately volunteers, "I know what the word is. It's 'choked' because once I almost choked on some fish bones."

The teacher says in response, "That's just the word I wrote on this card. Please look at this word, everyone. What is it?"

Once *choked* is read by all, the teacher prints it in the blank and asks the group to reread the sentence. She then continues:

Karl suspected the missing word was "choked" for two reasons. To begin, the words I wrote suggested it might be "choked" because it makes sense to say that a person almost choked on a bone. For Karl, the right word came into his head quickly because he remembered the time he himself almost choked. So he did what we all should do when we come across a word we don't know: Read the words you *can* read to see whether they remind you of anything you know. Let's try more sentences. By the way, can anyone think of a word besides "choke" that also makes sense in this sentence?

When one student offers "coughed," the teacher erases *choked*, prints *coughed* in its place, and then asks the group to read the sentence once more. Now she comments:

A bone certainly might make a boy—or anyone—cough, but I think if it did, we'd say something like "The bone got stuck in the boy's mouth and made him cough." I don't think we'd say that he coughed *on* the bone. I believe "choked" is about the only word that fits where this blank is—although, come to think of it, a word like "gagged" fits, too. *I* usually say that somebody choked on a bone, but "gagged" makes sense, too.

The teacher continues with other sentences—these are printed on cards—in order to reinforce the point that deciding what word fits in a blank is helped by reading all the other words and by thinking about what they mean. The last two sentences the teacher uses are from the basal reader selection that the group is to read next. Identifying their source is something this teacher makes sure she does, because it makes apparent the usefulness for reading of what is being done. It thus promotes transfer, which is the essence of effective instruction.

Written practice following instruction can take a variety of forms, three of which are illustrated below:

I want to ＿＿＿＿＿＿ the horse.
    look   see

Did you hear the dog ＿＿＿＿＿＿?
                 bark   beg

They ＿＿＿＿＿＿ the noise.

Don't ＿＿＿＿＿＿ your hair.

I go to sleep ＿＿＿＿＿＿.

I drank all the milk. Now the glass is ＿＿＿＿＿＿.

Wash your face first. ＿＿＿＿＿＿ get dressed.

The bike has only one ＿＿＿＿＿＿. Where should I put my foot?

With written practice like that shown above, it is important for teachers to keep two points in mind. First and foremost, be sure students understand that a blank space is presumed to be a word that is unknown and, further, that the practice is to show how words that are known often help readers with others that are not. Second, allow time whenever possible for students to explain how they decided on the word to put in a blank. (For exercises like these, the emphasis is on "Does a word make sense syntactically and semantically?" not on "Is it spelled correctly?") Such discussions are helpful because they allow teachers to examine the thought processes students are using and also because the thoughts described by one student may help other students who are listening. Even thoughts that lead a student astray can be enlightening.

Because the spelling of an unknown word is always available to readers, a question might be raised about instruction and practice that eliminate the possibility of using graphophonic cues. For anybody who wonders about the advisability of restricting help to contextual cues, let me stress one point: The purpose of work like that just described is to make clear to students as often as seems necessary that the ultimate standard used to evaluate decisions about unfamiliar words is described by the question, Does it make sense? Attending only to contextual cues emphasizes "making sense" and is often required when beginning instruction overemphasizes phonics. Children, for example, who respond to a sentence like *I would have torn my dress if I didn't see the nail* with "I would have turn my dress if I didn't see the nail" may need further practice in using contextual cues. On the other hand, the child who reads *The canary flew out of the cage* as "The bird flew out of the cage" needs to be reminded that the spelling of an unknown word must be used in conjunction with the help that known words offer.

All this underscores a point made earlier: A balanced use of all available cues characterizes the behavior of able readers whenever they encounter a word that is unfamiliar visually.

INSTRUCTION: CONTEXTS
AND MINIMAL GRAPHOPHONIC CUES

When children are not yet able to use complete spellings to figure out unfamiliar words, minimal graphophonic cues, coupled with the availability of contextual cues, can be featured. Now the purpose is to show how contextual cues suggest sensible possibilities and how graphophonic cues determine which is correct. That objective underlies the work of one teacher, which is described next.

I've written a sentence on the board and, as you can see, one word is missing. [*On Saturday we're going to* _____ *our car.*] Who wants to say what the missing word might be? . . . Okay. Josh thinks it's "sell." Does anyone think it might be something else? ... There have been four more very good suggestions. "Buy," "trade," "wash," and "clean" are good because they all make sense. However, the letter with which the missing word begins is on the back of this card. What letter is this? ... Since it's *w*, what is the missing word? ... Yes, only "wash" starts with *w*. Let me show you what "wash" looks like when it's written. I'll write it in the blank in this sentence.

At another time, the same teacher may elect to give explicit attention to the value of minimal graphophonic cues (plus contexts) when she's helping children learn new words in a basal selection she is about to assign. For illustrative purposes, the ensuing modeling by a teacher covers just two words, *forest* and *roar*. (You will recall that modeling is "a talk-through procedure" in which a teacher attempts to make explicit the processes used to realize a goal [12].) Sentences taken from the basal selection are on the board. The fact that they are found in the selection is made clear.

> All the animals lived in a f_____.
> The lion said, "I will r_____ so loud all will hear me."

The teacher begins:

As I mentioned, the story you'll be reading is about animals and tells how one of them helped an elephant who had a broken leg. I think you'll be able to read all the animal names—like "lion," for instance—but you might not know some other words. Let me tell you how I'd go about figuring them out if I were reading the story and didn't know them. I'll start with this first sentence. You'll find it in the story. The word I don't know starts with *f*. This is the way I'd think. First I'd read the words I know. "All the animals lived in a." Oh, it's probably "forest." All the animals lived in a forest. That makes sense. They live in a zoo, too, but that doesn't start with *f*. Now I'll do the next sentence. It's in the story, too. "The lion said, 'I will (blank) so loud all will hear me'." It could be "yell" since that makes a lot of noise, but "yell" doesn't begin with *r*. Let's see. What do lions do that's loud and starts with *r*? Oh, sure. Roar. Lions roar. "The lion said, 'I will roar so loud all will hear me'."

INSTRUCTION: CONTEXTS
AND ADDITIONAL GRAPHOPHONIC CUES

In the same basal reader, another selection is about birds. One sentence in the text states: *Some eagles have bald heads.* Because the manual suggests that *bald* is a new word, the sentence can serve to make two points. First, students who know about bald eagles will have much less trouble deciding what *bald* says than will others who may not even be aware of what an eagle is. Even so, the latter should still know from the context that the unknown word tells something about *heads*. Keeping that in mind, along with the sound that *b* records, may lead to the conclusion that the word is *big*. Such a conclusion—which makes sense—demonstrates that instruction eventually needs to focus on the use of more than one letter (plus contextual cues). In fact, a sentence like the one about the eagle can be used for such instruction.

The need to make use of more than one letter might also be encouraged as follows. In this case, the sentence below is on the chalkboard:

The water was d_____.

The teacher starts:

We've been talking about the fact that, by using words we know plus the sound that a beginning letter stands for, we can sometimes decide what a new word is. With this sentence on the board, we're going to pretend it ends with a word we don't know. As you can see, it starts with *d*. It's a word that tells about the water. What do you suppose it is if it begins with *d*? [Given the purpose of the lesson—to demonstrate the need to rely on more than the first letter—the teacher has in mind a number of suitable words starting with *d*.] The first volunteer suggests "dirty." "Yes," responds the teacher, "we've all seen dirty water, but the word in the sentence ends with *k*." [Adds *k* at the end.] If the word starts with *d* and ends in *k*, can it be 'dirty'?" Although the children agree it cannot, none is able to think of a word that starts with *d*, ends with *k*, and makes sense. Consequently, the teacher adds a sentence to the board:

There were no lights. The water was d_____k.

Several children simultaneously call out "dark." This is followed by a discussion of the fact that help for a word can often be found in other sentences and that such help, plus some of the letters in the unknown word, will sometimes be enough to decide what the word is.

Additional sentences that can be used in ways similar to what was just illustrated are shown on the next page.

They got into the b_____ and left fast.
They got into the b_____k and left fast.
The robbers came at about six o'clock.
They got into the b_____k and left fast.

Don't t_____ the page.
Don't t_____ch the page.
Your hands are too dirty. Don't t_____ch the page.

When students are aware that words are decoded syllable by syllable and when they are proficient in blending sounds to produce syllables, instruction can focus on the use of a context, plus the initial syllable in an unfamiliar word, to get the latter figured out. Now, text like the following is appropriate either for instruction or practice:

You can use a pen or pen_____. Don't hur_____ with your work.
Turn in a good pa_____. In fact, make it ex_____ good today.

A lesson in which a teacher is focusing on the use of contexts and initial syllables might proceed as follows. In this case, the instruction starts just after the teacher has demonstrated procedures for using the spelling of *cactus* to arrive at its pronunciation.

Teacher: It took a fair amount of time to get *cactus* figured out, and that's okay if it's necessary. However, if "cactus" is in a story that takes place in a desert, you might not need to work on all of it, letter by letter and sound by sound. Let's say, for instance, that a sentence in the story is "I only saw one cactus plant." Now, knowing how the first syllable is pronounced might be enough to suggest the word is "cactus," especially since it's followed by the word "plant." After all, in a desert the most common kind of plant—if there are any at all—is a cactus. I've written some sentences on these cards. They're in the next story you'll be reading, so let's see if you can figure out some of the new words if I just write the first syllable. Again, be sure to read all the words in the sentence before you decide what the word is when I write its first syllable.

Some of the new words in a basal selection (*silver, mountain, escape, tiny*), placed in the sentences in which they occur but with only their initial syllables printed, are:

The spider spun a sil___ web.
It's on the other side of the moun___.
They tried to es___ by running.
All they needed was a ti___ bit of sun.

The teacher shows the first sentence card [*The spider spun a sil___ web.*] and says:

Teacher:	Please read this sentence to yourselves. Who can pronounce the first syllable in the word that goes here [points to *sil___*]?
Joe:	I know what the whole word is. It's "silly."
Teacher:	"Silly" does begin with *s, i, l.* Joe, how do you pronounce a syllable spelled *s, i, l?*
Joe:	"Sil."
Teacher:	That's correct. One vowel but not at the end. "Sĭl" *is* the first syllable in this word, and "silly" starts with that syllable. "The spider spun a silly web." Does everyone think "silly" is the word that tells about the web?
Mary Pat:	I'm not sure "silly" makes sense. At least I don't think webs are silly looking.
Bob:	I was thinking of "silver." I usually think of webs as being white, but silver is a better way to talk about their color.
Teacher:	Any other thoughts about this word? . . . None? I'll finish printing the word, since both "silly" and "silver" describe something and both start with the syllable "sĭl." [Adds *ver.*]
Bob:	I thought I was right.
Teacher:	Joe pronounced the first syllable correctly but, usually, spider webs are quite beautiful and perfect and not at all silly. Let's all take a look at the word. What is it?
Group:	Silver.
Teacher:	Please read the sentence, because this is one you'll see when you read the story later.
Group:	The spider spun a silver web.
Teacher:	Here's another sentence you'll find. Again, I only printed the first syllable of the new word. [Shows card that displays *It's on the other side of the moun___.*] Please read this sentence to yourselves to see what the last word might be.
Bob:	I think I know this word, too. It's "mountain."
Teacher:	Pronounce *m, o, u, n* for us, Bob.
Bob:	Moun.
Teacher:	Correct. "Mountain" begins that way, and it makes sense to say that something is on the other side of the mountain. How about another word that makes sense and starts with the syllable "moun?" Any suggestions? . . . The only other word that *I* can think of that starts this way and has more than one syllable is "mounted," as in "They mounted the horses." But that cer-

tainly doesn't make any sense here. I'll finish printing this new word. [Adds *t*, *a*, *i*, and *n*.]

Bob: I'm right again!

Teacher: Yes, you are, Bob. You've been correct twice because you thought of the pronunciation of the first syllable and then of a word that starts that way that makes good sense in the sentence. That's what everyone should do when they come across a new word. If it has more than one syllable, think about the pronunciation of the first syllable and then think of a word you know that starts that way and fits with all the other words. Let's take another look at this new word. [Points to *mountain*.] Tommy, you don't seem to be looking where I'm pointing. Everybody, what is this word?

Group: Mountain.

Teacher: Please read the sentence together.

Group: It's on the other side of the mountain.

Teacher: I guess you'll have to read the story before you find out what it is that's on the other side of the mountain.

Tom: I bet it's a wild animal or something like that.

Teacher: You'll just have to wait to find out, Tom. By the way, Tom, what is this word? [Points to *mountain*.]

Tom: Mountain.

Teacher: Good. Okay, everybody, please read this sentence again.

Group: It's on the other side of the mountain.

Using the same procedures, the teacher attends to two additional words, *escape* and *tiny*, since they also appear for the first time in helpful sentences. Together, all the work done with the four words is intended to help the students understand that:

1. The meaning of known words should be considered both first ("What word makes sense here?") and last ("Does this word make sense?).
2. The spelling of an unknown word must be considered along with the collective meaning of the known words. That is, "contextual and graphophonic information should be used in an integrated manner" (13, p. 369).
3. Sometimes, the spelling of less than the whole word—for instance, its initial syllable—suggests the word fairly quickly. The entire spelling is then useful in verifying or questioning the tentative conclusion.
4. At times, the entire spelling of a word must be considered almost immediately. This is the case when two or more words come to mind that start with the same syllable and make sense in the context. (How to use entire spellings to decode words is the focus of the next two chapters. How to use the spelling of a word to divide it into syllables is explained, too.)

All that has now been said about work with contextual cues and with a combination of contextual and graphophonic cues is summarized in Figure 7.1.

MORE EXTENSIVE CONTEXTS

Thus far, "context" has been confined to limited amounts of text—in some instances, to just a few words. This should not obscure the fact that much larger pieces of discourse are contexts and also that they offer readers help with new or forgotten words. A story, for instance, usually takes place in a certain setting and has particular kinds of characters, both of which may allow readers to anticipate certain words. By anticipating them, readers are in a better position to recognize them. Knowing this, teachers should at times raise questions before a story is read not only to cover background information but also to call attention to words that may or may not be in the students' reading vocabularies.

Let's take a story about hiking in the mountains to show how this might be done. To prepare students who live far from mountains to read it, a teacher can begin by saying: "Since the story you'll be reading next is about a boy who took a three-day hike in the mountains with his dad, I was wondering whether any of you have done that or have seen mountain hikers on TV or in a movie." This introductory comment could lead to a discussion that reveals the need to clarify the difference between a hazardous type of mountain climbing and the recreational activity of hiking in the mountains. As soon as it seems timely to do so, the discussion can be structured with

---

Spoken Context

1. Spoken sentence with omitted word at the end.
2. Spoken sentence with omitted word anyplace in the context.

Spoken Context and Minimal Graphophonic Cues

3. Spoken sentence with omitted word whose beginning letter is named or shown.

Written Context

4. Written sentence with omitted word. Children select suitable word from listed possibilities.
5. Written sentence with omitted word. Children fill in the blank with a suitable word.

Written Context and Partial Graphophonic Cues

6. Written sentence with initial letter of target word supplied.
7. Written sentence with initial and final letters of target word supplied.
8. Written sentence with first syllable of target word supplied.

Figure 7.1 Progression in Using Contextual Cues

questions designed to highlight certain words. Two possible questions and the vocabulary in the story that prompted them are listed below:

> In the city, we usually walk on sidewalks. Where do people walk when they are in the mountains or the woods? (*trail*)

> Because the two people you'll be reading about spend two nights where there are no hotels or motels, what will they have to have? (*tent, sleeping bag, flashlight, fire*)

Teachers who pose questions to call attention to certain words and who keep that purpose in mind accept reasonable answers but also make sure that preselected words are eventually mentioned even if they themselves have to name them. To illustrate, if the first question listed above brings responses like "on a dirt road" and "on a path," both are accepted. Afterward, a teacher can add, "The word the author of the story uses is 'trail' [which is written on the board]. The author talks about the boy and his dad following a trail, which, of course, is a path. What is this word on the board?"

Attending to vocabulary in the way just described is not sufficient to put words into students' sight vocabularies; however, it does allow for meaningful attention to new words and for establishing an appropriate mental set for the reading that will be done.

MISCUE ANALYSIS

The many references to contextual and graphophonic cues makes this chapter an appropriate place to refer to work initiated in the early 1960s by Kenneth Goodman (7, 8).

At the time, Goodman and his colleagues were attempting to learn about the mental processes that take place during reading by analyzing individuals' oral reading of unfamiliar text. For the analyses, each response to a word was cataloged as "expected" (says the word on the page) or "observed" (what the reader said). In turn, observed responses were referred to as *miscues*, which, when analyzed, were said by Goodman to be "windows on the reading process." (The term *error* was avoided, as that has only negative connotations. A miscue, on the other hand, may be positive, as when a reader responds to *lad* with "boy," or negative, as when a word like *tried* is read as "tired.") Emphasized in Goodman's work is that reading is not naming words but is, instead, a sense-making process achieved only when a reader uses both the words on the page and what he or she knows to construct something meaningful.

Writing in the early 1970s, Goodman (8) asserted that "reading instruction in the last four decades has been word oriented" (p. 8). He went on to say that "miscue research has led us away from a word focus to a comprehension focus" (p. 8). And, as he continues, Goodman provides a summary of points made in this chapter:

Three kinds of information are available to the reader. One kind, the graphic information, reaches the reader visually. The other two, syntactic and semantic information, are supplied by the reader as he begins to process the visual input. Since the reader's goal is meaning, he uses as much or as little of each of these kinds of information as is necessary to get to the meaning. He makes predictions of the grammatical structure, using the control over language structure he learned when he learned oral language. He supplies semantic concepts to get the meaning from the structure. In turn, his sense of syntactic structure and meaning make it possible to predict the graphic input so he is largely selective, sampling the print to confirm his prediction. (p. 9)

The question to pose now is, What is the significance for teachers of the miscue research and, in particular, of its underlying assumptions?

To begin, it holds an obvious message for any teachers who still cling to the use of round robin reading and, in the process, bestow praise not so much for signs of comprehension as for an exact rendition of the words on a page. Goodman's conception of successful reading has equally obvious implications for teachers working with nonstandard and nonnative speakers of English. He says, for example:

Rejection or correction by the teacher of any dialect-based miscue moves the reader away from using his own linguistic competence to the teacher's expected responses to the text. Word-for-word accuracy, in a narrow sense, becomes the goal rather than the meaning. . . . In encouraging divergent speakers to use their language competence . . . and accepting their dialect-based miscues, we minimize the effect of dialect differences. In rejecting them, we maximize the effect. (9, pp. 11–12)

As suggested, Goodman's philosophy emphasizes that "number of miscues" is much less significant for decisions about needed instruction than is "types of miscues." How the latter enter into instructional decisions is discussed in Chapter 16 under the heading "Monitoring Oral Reading to Establish Instructional Needs."

Now it is time to supplement suggestions already made for practice with contextual cues with a few others.

PRACTICE

Before additional ideas for practice are examined, it is advisable to review Figure 7.1 in order to see again how instruction and practice progress over time. The following samples of practice exemplify the first type of written practice listed in Figure 7.1.

Samples of Practice: At the Beginning

As suggested, early written practice can have children make selections from words they are able to read, which are then written in blanks. For such practice, choices might be systematically varied in ways illustrated on the next page.

Choices

Our _____ helps us.   grammatically
     teach   teacher   dissimilar

He _____ the wall.   graphically similar
    painted   pained

Don't run so _____.   semantically similar
    quickly   fast

Can you _____ this?   nonsense
    to   in

Practice might also take the form shown below. In this case, all the words that are syntactically and semantically acceptable are to be underlined.

> baby
> girls
> The boxes are on their way to school.
> boys
> children

> us
> up
> They are now on school.
> in
> at

Once children acquire some spelling ability, filling in blanks with words they themselves provide becomes an option. (The focus is on making sense, not on correct spellings. Children, therefore, should feel free to take the risk of misspelling a word if they think it fits a context.) Initially, single sentences can be used:

> I got _____ skates for my birthday.
> It will soon be _____ to go home.
> We were eating at the time the door _____ open.

Later, practice should allow for reinforcing the fact that help with a word may lie in a sentence different from the one in which it is embedded:

> Greg forgot to water the plants. They _____.
> I was so _____. I ate everything in sight.

Because variety *is* the spice of life, foreign words can replace blanks. In this instance, students write a suitable English word above each foreign word. One author (10) suggests the following sentences, in which Italian words provide the variety:

> The gana bit the mailman on the leg.
> They returned the books to the biblioteca.
> The man stopped his car when the luz a di traffic turned red.

Samples of Practice: Later On

Filling in blanks with words that are acceptable syntactically and semantically is something you probably experienced in taking tests. It is usually referred to as the *cloze* procedure. *Cloze* comes from the word *closure*, a term associated with Gestalt psychologists, who maintain that human behavior is motivated by the need for wholeness or completeness.

The relevant point now is that cloze procedures can be used not only to provide practice in using contextual cues but also for assessing comprehension. Specifically, if students will be reading an expository (informational) selection about how birds keep warm in the winter, they can be asked to fill in the blanks in a paragraph like the one shown below. In this case, an added bonus is practice with some of the new words used in the selection.

If you live where it's cold, you won't see many _____ in winter. Most _____ south. The ones who stay have ways to keep _____. To begin, birds can lower their body _____. This _____ the amount of heat they need to stay _____. Birds also _____ to make more heat in their bodies. To save the heat they have, they grow more _____. The ones that really keep them warm are called _____. To _____ themselves from the cold _____, they _____ on the inside branches of _____ trees. That is why you don't _____ many birds during the _____.

Once students begin to receive instruction about grammar, cloze exercises can focus on whatever part of speech is being taught. Sentences like the following, for example, highlight nouns:

The _____ in the _____ will soon arrive.
These old _____ aren't of _____ anymore.
Chuck and his _____ went _____ early.

Practice: Concluding Comments

In the course of visiting a classroom not long ago, I had the opportunity to ask three third-graders what they were doing in their workbooks. (They were filling in blanks in sentences with words that were listed at the top of the page.) None was able to offer any better explanation than "Writing words." My question, "*Why* are you writing words?" resulted in silence.

This experience suggests the need to reinforce some points made earlier in the chapter.

First, children should be helped to understand right from the beginning that blanks in sentences symbolize unknown words. Second, exactly how words they know help in coping with words they do not know should be clarified. To do this, children should have the chance to explain why they wrote (or chose) the words they did. Finally, as often as possible, attention to contextual cues should use text taken from selections that students have read or will read. That a given selection *is* the source of the text should be pointed out. This is helpful in specifying the connection between (a) what is being taught and practiced, and (b) how to be a better reader.

SUMMARY

The thesis developed in Chapter 7 is that in a piece of text, the words that readers know combine to form a context. This context permits them to make inferences about words that are unknown. In developing this overall message, the chapter made the following six more specific points:

1. Known words provide a context only when their number is considerably larger than the number of unknown words. Too many unknown words, in fact, eliminate contextual cues. One implication of this is to avoid the use of overly difficult material.
2. The context provided by known words is helpful only with words that are in the reader's oral vocabulary. Stated differently, contexts assist with words that are unfamiliar visually but that are familiar in their spoken form.
3. The help with an unknown word that derives from a context does not reveal its identity directly. Rather, it helps indirectly by placing constraints on what the unknown word can be.
4. Because language makes sense, one kind of constraint stems from the meaning of known words. Such help, therefore, is said to be semantic in nature.
5. English is a positional language; thus, words are ordered in certain patterned ways. This allows the position of an unknown word in a sentence to place additional constraints on what it can be. Because this source of help lies in the construction of a sentence, it is said to be syntactic in nature.
6. English words are recorded with letters that stand for sounds, which means that the spelling of an unknown word is another source of help for deciding what it is. When this help, which is referred to as graphophonic cues, is combined with the help that is rooted in a context, the decoding process is both simplified and speeded up. This is important, because it is only correct *and* fast decoding that facilitates the comprehension process.

In addition to making these points, Chapter 7 showed with numerous illustrations how instruction progresses from spoken to written contexts and from the use of contextual cues to the combined use of contextual and graphophonic cues. Although Chapter 7 demonstrated the value of all these cues, it also explained that using them results in recognizing words, not identifying them. Practice is still required for word identification.

REVIEW

1. Chapter 7 mentioned that the cloze procedure is useful in assessing comprehension. With that in mind, see how well you can fill in the

blanks in the text below with words that are contextually appropriate and that reflect the content in Chapter 7.

English is a (a) _____ language in which word order is critical for determining (b) _____. The arrangement of words that makes up a sentence is referred to as its (c) _____; consequently, when the position of an unknown word in a sentence helps to identify it, that help is called a (d) _____ cue. Syntactic cues offer assistance by establishing the (e) _____ (f) _____ of an unknown word. For instance, in the sentence "Many _____ were in the room," syntax signals that the omitted word is a (g) _____ (h) _____ functioning as the subject of the sentence.

Just as language as a whole makes sense, so, too, do individual phrases and sentences. The sense, or meaning, communicated by phrases and sentences offers a second type of contextual help. Because it has to do with meaning, it is called a (i) _____ cue. The sentence "Many _____ were in the room" provides minimal semantic help; one like "The swing went up and _____" provides (j) _____ semantic help.

Because the (k) _____ use of syntactic and semantic cues often provides important assistance with new or forgotten words, children should be encouraged to consider them whenever they have a problem with a word. Sometimes—as in "The swing went up and _____"—contextual cues will provide so much help that just about all words except one can be (l) _____ from consideration. Most of the time, however, contextual cues will have to be used in conjunction with the help that derives from the (m) _____ of the unknown word. That is why beginning instruction in (n) _____ goes along with early work with contexts.

2. Four points about contextual cues were made at the start of Chapter 7:
   a. The availability of contextual cues is affected by the reader's world knowledge.
   b. Contextual cues only help with words that are in the reader's oral vocabulary.
   c. The use of contextual cues allows for word recognition, not word identification.
   d. Contexts exist only when an individual can read most of the words in a selection.

   Explain the meaning of each statement. Include examples in your explanations that are different from those in Chapter 7.

3. Keeping in mind that able readers use all available cues, explain the placement on the continuum shown below of five different responses to *cloak*, which is embedded in the sentence *The woman wore a cloak*.

Best _____ Worst

cloak   coat   cape   clock   choked

4. Chapter 5 defined "decontextualized instruction" and Chapter 7 referred to it.
  a. What is decontextualized instruction?
  b. Go through Chapter 7 so that you can explain how the teachers described in the chapter avoided decontextualizing their instruction.

5. Chapter 3 defined "modeling" and Chapter 7 referred to it.
  a. What is modeling?
  b. Describe how one teacher described in Chapter 7 relied on modeling while working with contextual and minimal graphophonic cues.

REFERENCES

1. Anderson, Linda M.; Evertson, Carolyn M.; and Brophy, Jere. "An Experimental Study of Effective Teaching in First Grade Reading Groups." *Elementary School Journal* 79 (March, 1979), 193–223.
2. Dewitz, Peter; Carr, Eileen M.; and Patberg, Judythe P. "Effects of Inference Training on Comprehension and Comprehension Monitoring." *Reading Research Quarterly* 22 (Winter, 1987), 99–119.
3. Duffy, Gerald G., and Roehler, Laura R. "Teaching Reading Skills As Strategies." *Reading Teacher* 40 (January, 1987), 414–418.
4. Duffy, Gerald G.; Roehler, Laura R.; and Rackliffe, Gary. "How Teachers' Talk Influences Students' Understanding of Lesson Content." *Elementary School Journal* 87 (September, 1986), 3–16.
5. Durkin, Dolores. "Is There a Match between What Elementary Teachers Do and What Basal Reader Manuals Recommend?" *Reading Teacher* 37 (April, 1984), 734–744.
6. Durkin, Dolores. "What Classroom Observations Reveal about Reading Comprehension Instruction." *Reading Research Quarterly* 14 (1978–79, No. 4), 481–533.
7. Goodman, Kenneth S. "Analysis of Oral Reading Miscues: Applied Psycholinguistics." *Reading Research Quarterly* 5 (Fall, 1969), 9–30.
8. Goodman, Kenneth S. (Ed.). *Miscue Analysis: Applications to Reading Instruction.* Urbana, Ill.: National Council of Teachers of English, 1973.
9. Goodman, Kenneth S., and Buck, Catherine. "Dialect Barriers to Reading Comprehension Revisited." *Reading Teacher* 27 (October, 1973), 6–12.
10. Karstadt, Roberta. "Teach Context Clues with Foreign Words." *Reading Teacher* 31 (October, 1977), 72.
11. Paris, Scott; Lipson, Marge; and Wixson, Karen. "Becoming a Strategic Reader." *Contemporary Educational Psychology* 8 (July, 1983), 293–316.
12. Rinehart, Steven D.; Stahl, Steven A.; and Erickson, Lawrence G. "Some Effects of Summarization Training on Reading and Studying." *Reading Research Quarterly* 21 (Fall, 1986), 422–438.
13. Stanovich, Keith. "Matthew Effects in Reading: Some Consequences of Individual Differences in the Acquisition of Literacy." *Reading Research Quarterly* 21 (Fall, 1986), 360–406.

Chapter 8

Phonics: Content

PREVIEW

To ensure that teachers and prospective teachers who are using this textbook have enough knowledge of phonics to permit children to achieve proficiency in decoding, two chapters cover phonics. The first deals with what to teach; the second, with how to teach it.

The two-chapter treatment is not meant to imply that phonics instruction is more important than other kinds. Rather, the two-part coverage is based on the assumption that there is a body of content to learn and that knowing it well is a prerequisite—although not a guarantee—for teaching phonics effectively. It also should be kept in mind that effectiveness is determined by one criterion: the ability of children to decode unknown words correctly and rapidly (6).

To help you keep track of what you do and do not know, Chapter 8 provides intermittent self-testing. This permits you to monitor your understanding of what has been discussed. If deficiencies are apparent, do some rereading and rethinking. With effort on your part, you should come to the end of Chapter 8 knowing what needs to be taught.

It is recognized that some individuals who read Chapter 8 are very much at home with all the content discussed. For those people in this category, Chapter 8 can serve to reconfirm and refresh what you know. Serving these functions, the chapter will add to your security when you are either teaching phonics or giving children opportunities to use what has been taught.

It is also recognized that some individuals know very little about phonics when they begin Chapter 8. If you are in this group, plan to spend ample time studying Chapter 8. In particular, use the results of the tests to monitor what you are learning and, perhaps, to pinpoint the section or sections that need to be studied again.

Typically, individuals who start with little knowledge of phonics have thoughts like, "If I'm having problems remembering all this, how can children be expected to learn it?" What needs to be remembered in such cases is that children acquire decoding ability slowly and gradually over as many as three or four years. The task for children, therefore, is essentially different from what it is for anyone who starts Chapter 8 knowing very little about phonics.

English has an *alphabetic writing system*. This means that words are written with letters that represent speech sounds. The nature of our writing system explains why a substantial portion of the subject matter for phonics is about letter-sound correspondences.* Because knowledge of letter-sound relationships, such as the one that exists between *b* and /b/, is applied to syllables, additional subject matter pertains to ways for dividing unknown words into syllables.

Before the content of phonics is identified and discussed, a few introductory comments are in order.

INTRODUCTORY COMMENTS

Phonics instruction serves one purpose: to help readers figure out as quickly as possible the pronunciation of unknown words. When unknown words are in their oral vocabulary, the pronunciation allows readers to do what is essential for comprehension: access their meaning. ("Oh, sure, that's 'pendulum'. We have a big one in our grandfather clock at home.") Proficiency in decoding is useful, therefore, only when the word being figured out is familiar orally.

It should also be kept in mind that oral vocabularies allow decoders to modify approximately correct pronunciations. Take the word *lawyer* as an example. If a reader did not know *lawyer* in its written form and applied what had been taught in phonics to decode it, the pronunciation "law-yer" would result. For the reader who is familiar with *lawyer* in its spoken form, modifying the approximately correct pronunciation ("law yer") to make it the correct one ("loi yer") is easy—especially when *lawyer* is in a context, which will generally be the case.

One further point to emphasize is that the help that derives from a knowledge of letter-sound correspondences is affected by the extent to which readers can apply that knowledge with flexibility. Because of the significance of this point for teachers, let me elaborate on it with an example.

Some of the most important content taught in phonics has to do with factors that affect the sounds that certain letters record. Most often, the letters are vowels. This content is usually presented in the form of generalizations.** For example, it is generally correct to say:

> When there is one vowel in a syllable and it is not in final
> position, that vowel stands for its short sound, as in *at, clash,*
> *ten, stretch, him, glint, not, shock, up,* and *snub.*

---

* To distinguish between letters and sounds, two slash marks are used when the referent is a sound. For instance, *b* stands for /b/ in words like *big* and *cub.*

** All the generalizations discussed in this chapter and in Chapter 10 are listed together at the end of Chapter 10.

To show how flexible decoding works, let's assume a student is reading and encounters the sentence *He's putting in a post for the fence.* We'll further assume that *post* is not in this individual's reading vocabulary. The point emphasized here is that various options are available to deal with *post.* One student might use the three consonant sounds (plus the helpful context) to reach a correct and quick conclusion both about the pronunciation and about the meaning of *post.* (This is possible, it must be kept in mind, only when *post* is familiar orally.) Another student may apply the generalization stated above and arrive initially at the pronunciation "pŏst." Having been taught to ask, "Does this make sense?" the student rejects that pronunciation because it fails to suggest a familiar word. A different strategy should then be used. In this case, trying out different sounds for *o* is a good first step to take, because it is vowel letters that vary the most in the sounds they record. One immediate possibility is to replace the short sound for *o* with its long sound, which, when done, produces a recognizable word that makes sense in the given context.

The future value of achieving the correct pronunciation for *post* becomes apparent when words like *postpone, poster,* and *postage* need to be read. The value of knowing how to pronounce *post* is also apparent when the prefix *post-* is introduced with the help of derivatives like *postpaid, postwar,* and *postdate.*

These three introductory points are summarized below.

1. The pronunciation of a printed word allows a reader to access its meaning only when the word is in the reader's oral vocabulary (*pendulum*).
2. A reader's ability to shift from approximately correct pronunciations to correct pronunciations depends on that individual's familiarity with the word in its spoken form (*lawyer*).
3. Although English words are written with letters that represent speech sounds, the correspondence between letters and sounds is not so consistent that generalizations can predict sounds with absolute accuracy. Therefore, it may be necessary for decoders to try additional sounds for one or more letters when the sound predicted by a generalization does not produce a recognizable word. The spoken version of the word (plus the context) allows readers to conclude that they have arrived at a pronunciation—that is, at a word—that makes sense (*post*).

As many as twenty years ago, Roger Brown, a well-known linguist, was making the same points:

The usefulness of being able to sound a new word depends on the state of the reader's speaking vocabulary. If the word that is unfamiliar in printed form is also unfamiliar in spoken form the reader who can sound it out will not understand the word any better than the reader who cannot sound it. . . . The real advantage in being able to sound a word that is unfamiliar in print, only appears when the word is familiar in speech. The child's letter-by-letter pronunciation, put together by spelling recipe, will, with the aid of context, call to mind the spoken form. There will be a click of recognition, pronunciation will smooth out, and meaning will transfer to the printed form. (1, p. 69)

Now that the dependence of decoding ability on oral language has been demonstrated in a variety of ways, let's proceed to the subject matter for phonics instruction.

CONSONANTS

Beginning instruction in phonics focuses on the sounds that letters record. Initially, consonants usually get attention because they are more consistent than vowels in the sounds they represent. Even though some vowel sounds should be taught before all the consonants are covered, the present discussion deals with all the consonants. Afterward, vowels are considered. Because the presentation is for adults who already know something about the alphabetic system of English, it is not meant to be a model for teaching phonics to children.

The ensuing discussion of consonants divides them into single consonants, consonant clusters, and consonant digraphs.

Single Consonants

The quickest way to identify the consonants is to say they are all the letters in the alphabet except *a, e, i, o,* and *u.* Each word listed below begins with the sound commonly recorded by the initial consonant.

bell	fun	jam	lie	not	run	van	yes
dog	how	kit	me	pie	to	we	zoo

The listed words, you will notice, include *yes* and *we* in which *y* and *w* function as consonants. When *y* and *w* function as vowels is considered later. Now, the five consonants not listed (*s, c, g, q, x*) are discussed.

The sound customarily associated with *s* is the one that starts *see* and ends *bus.* Other words show it also stands for a sound associated with *z* (e.g., *was, husband, resort, exercise, busy*).* Because /s/ is more common, students should be taught to try that sound first. If /s/ does not produce a recognizable word, it can be replaced with /z/.

C and *g* also record two sounds each. They are traditionally referred to as the *hard* and *soft* sounds. The four sounds are illustrated in Table 8.1.

---

* Throughout the chapter, an advisable procedure is to read illustrative words aloud to ensure that the sound being identified is heard.

Letter	Hard Sound	Examples	Soft Sound	Examples
c	/k/	cut, sac	/s/	cent, nice
g	/g/	go, pig	/j/	gem, page

Table 8.1 Soft and Hard Sounds: C and G

The job for you now is to hear and remember the four sounds so that when a later section explains when each sound is likely to occur, a description such as "the soft sound for *c*" will immediately bring to mind a particular sound.

A consonant that need not be taught early is *x*, because it is not used frequently. This is fortunate because, as Table 8.2 demonstrates, *x* stands for a variety of sounds. The term *blend*, which is in Table 8.2, refers to two or more sounds that are synthesized or combined. Specifically, /ks/ refers to the result when /k/ and /s/ are produced in quick succession. The two different blends that *x* represents cannot be pronounced apart from words; consequently, chalkboard displays such as the following are helpful when instruction is about one or both blends:

box   exist

[boks]   [egzist]

The guideline that should be taught for *x* follows: When *x* is the initial letter in a word, it stands for /z/. Otherwise, it most often stands for the blend /ks/.

The letter *q* is another consonant requiring attention, in this case for two reasons. First, because *q* is always followed by *u*, it is *qu* that should be the focus of instruction, not just *q*. (Students ought to be taught to look at *qu* as if it were one consonant.) The second reason is that *qu* records either /kw/ or /k/. Words illustrating the two possibilities are in Table 8.3.

Children should expect /kw/ when *qu* starts a syllable, as in *quest* and *frequent*. They should also be taught to expect /k/ when *qu* represents the

Single Sound		Examples	Blend of Sounds		Examples
1.	/z/	xylophone anxiety	2.	/ks/	ox, next, explain
			3.	/gz/	exalt, exert

Table 8.2 Possible Sounds for X

Blend of Sounds	Examples	Single Sound	Examples
/kw/	queen, acquire	/k/	plaque, unique

Table 8.3   Possible Sounds for <u>QU</u>

final sound in a word, as in *plaque* and *clique*. *Qu* rarely appears in anything but initial or final positions, but when it does not, it stands for /kw/, as in *square*.

The most important points to remember, then, are that *qu* commonly stands for /kw/ in initial position and for /k/ in final position. Overall, /kw/ occurs with much greater frequency.

Testing

Before taking the first minitest, you might want to restudy the section "Consonants."

The first test is in Figure 8.1. As with all the tests, *cover the material under the horizontal lines; answers are provided there.* You are advised to write answers and then check them with those at the bottom of Figure 8.1.

Consonant Clusters

It has been emphasized that decoding must be both correct and quick if it is to contribute to the comprehension process (6). The importance of cor-

---

I. Write "hard" or "soft" to describe the sound for each of the six underlined letters:

a<u>g</u>ain _____   <u>c</u>ite _____   su<u>gg</u>est _____ _____   a<u>cc</u>ent _____ _____

II. Using slash marks and letters, indicate the sound(s) recorded by each underlined letter or letters:

e<u>x</u>act   _____   <u>s</u>ea<u>s</u>on _____ _____   <u>qu</u>ell   _____

baro<u>qu</u>e _____   <u>X</u>ero<u>x</u> _____ _____   he<u>x</u>agon _____

I. hard
   soft
   hard, soft
   hard, soft

II. /gz/
   /s/, /z/
   /kw/
   /k/
   /z/, /ks/
   /ks/

Figure 8.1   Consonant Sounds: Self-Testing

rectness is obvious. The importance assigned to speed is rooted in the fact that is is difficult for readers to hang on to the meaning of as little as a sentence if they have to invest considerable effort in deciding what a certain word in that sentence is. The significance of efficiency explains why it makes sense to attend to consonant clusters.

A *consonant cluster* is two—rarely three—consonants that often appear as successive letters in a syllable. The clusters that usually receive attention follow.

Consonant Clusters

bl	cr	fr	pl	sk	sn	sw	scr
br	dr	gl	pr	sl	sp	tr	str
cl	fl	gr	sc	sm	st	tw	spr

Two points need to be made about clusters. The first is that each letter comprising a cluster stands for one sound. The cluster *st,* for instance, stands for a blend of /s/ and /t/. The cluster *scr* represents a blend of three sounds: /s/ + /k/ + /r/.

The second point for teachers to keep in mind is the need to pronounce correctly the blends that clusters represent. Assigning ''ker'' to *cr,* for example, or to suggest incorrectly that *bl* stands for ''bul'' will not be helpful when students have to decode words like *crawl* and *blaze.*

Consonant Digraphs

As just explained, each letter comprising a consonant cluster stands for a sound. A word such as *glen,* therefore, has four letters and four sounds. *Consonant digraphs* are essentially different. A digraph, which is always two letters, stands for one sound that is unlike the sound associated with either of the two letters that make up the digraph. The letters *sh,* for instance, are a digraph and do not record the sound associated with *s* (*six*) or with *h* (*hen*). This is illustrated in *she.*

To review what has been said about consonant digraphs and consonant clusters, consider the following examples:

sky (three sounds)	twin (four sounds)	disc (four sounds)
thy (two sounds)	thin (three sounds)	dish (three sounds)

The consonant digraphs taught in phonics are listed below. Words in parentheses illustrate their sounds.

Consonant Digraphs

th (the, thin)	sh (shut)
ph (phone)	ch (champ)
gh (tough)	ng (ring)

Comments about consonant digraphs follow.

The digraph *th* records two different sounds, as *them* and *thin* demonstrate. One, called the *voiced* sound, is heard in *them, the, there,* and *feather.* The other, the *voiceless* sound, occurs in *thin, thorn, thirst,* and *both.*

If you have difficulty hearing the difference between the two sounds, the following contrasts will help if each contrasting pair of words is read aloud:

Words with Voiced Sound	*Words with Voiceless Sound*
thy	thigh
bathe	bath
either	ether
breathe	breath
clothe	cloth
teethe	teeth

The sound that merits initial attention is the voiced sound for *th*, because that is in such high-frequency words as *the, there, them,* and *these.*

The digraphs *ph* and *gh* are considered together because they stand for the same sound, one customarily associated with *f* (*phase, rough*). *Ph* occurs much more frequently, which is good because *gh* is less predictable in what it records. Variations include:

When *g* is followed by *h* in initial position (*ghost, ghetto*), it does not function as a digraph. Instead, it stands for the hard sound of *g*.

Sometimes, *gh* records no sound or, as is sometimes said, it is "silent" (*high, caught*).

What makes all of this less complex than it may appear is that *gh* does not show up in words with any frequency.

The common sound for *ch* is the initial sound in *chop* and *chimp* and the final sound in *such* and *branch*. Comments about two additional sounds follow.

In words of French origin, *ch* stands for the sound associated with the digraph *sh*, as is illustrated in *chef, chamois,* and *chauffeur*.

In words of Greek origin, *ch* stands for the sound associated with *k*, as is illustrated in *chord, character,* and *chasm*.

ng

The digraph *ng* stands for a sound that cannot be produced alone. The sound, therefore, is identified indirectly for students by pronouncing "ang," "eng," "ing," "ong," and "ung." This is a digraph that never occurs in initial position. Instead, *ng* follows vowels (e.g., *sing, length*).

Testing

The second minitest is in Figure 8.2. (Don't forget to cover the bottom half of the page.) Before taking the test, it would be helpful to restudy the sections "Consonant Clusters" and "Consonant Digraphs."

I. Following each word, write the number of sounds of which it is composed.

A. clam _____   C. quench _____   E. anthrax _____   G. shrill _____
B. champ _____   D. sting _____   F. sprint _____   H. brush _____

II. Explain why each statement below is *incorrect*.

A. "Draw a line under all the blends in these words."

B. "Can you hear that digraph at the beginning and at the end of 'church'?"

C. "A consonant cluster is a blend."

I. A. 4   C. 5*   E. 7**   G. 4
B. 4   D. 4   F. 6   H. 4

---

*k-w-e-n-ch

**a-n-th-r-a-k-s

II. The three statements confuse terms that refer to letters and terms that refer to sounds:

A. It is impossible to underline sounds.

B. Letters (digraph) cannot be heard.

C. A cluster *stands for* a blend of sounds.

Figure 8.2 Consonant Clusters and Digraphs: Self-Testing

VOWELS

Like the discussion of consonants, the treatment of vowels divides them into single letters and pairs.

Single Vowels

The letters associated with vowel sounds are *a, e, i, o,* and *u.* (As will be illustrated, *y* and *w* function as vowels, too.) Each of the five letters stands for what has traditionally been called a *short* sound and a *long* sound. The ten sounds are in the following words in which they are in initial position.

Words Illustrating Short Vowel Sounds	*Words Illustrating Long Vowel Sounds*
at	age
end	eat
if	ice
odd	old
up	use

It is advisable to read the ten words aloud until you are able to pronounce five short vowel sounds and five long vowel sounds.

On the assumption that the description "short *u* sound" now evokes a particular sound—one that starts words like *us, under, ugly* and *umpire*—the *schwa* sound can be discussed. Its symbol is /ə/. The need for children to know about /ə/, which is a deemphasized short *u* sound, is bound up with the fact that vowel sounds in unstressed syllables are commonly (not inevitably) reduced to /ə/. This is illustrated in the words below, in which each underlined letter represents /ə/.

sóda   alóne   promóte   sýmbol   áccident

Before proceeding, be sure you know what the schwa sound is and that you do hear it in all the unstressed syllables in the five illustrative words.

When the final syllable in words is spelled with a consonant followed by *le* (e.g., *able, candle, gargle,* and *rifle*), the schwa sound is in these syllables, too.* This is demonstrated below:

a bəl   can dəl   gar gəl   ri fəl

If you are sure of what is meant by "long and short vowel sounds"— for instance, if you are able to pronounce the ten sounds and, in addition,

---

* When children are learning a word like *purple,* it is taught as a whole word. Later, in order to help students cope on their own with words like *idle, possible, example,* and *staple,* explicit information about these final syllables is necessary.

you know about the schwa sound and understand when it occurs—then you are ready to consider the next topic: pairs of vowel letters and the sounds they represent.

Vowel Digraphs

Like consonants, certain pairs of vowels stand for one sound that is different from the sound associated with either of the two vowels. Like consonant digraphs, therefore, vowel digraphs must be viewed by decoders as a unit. (As the list below shows, *w* and *y* figure in three vowel digraphs.) The eight digraphs that require attention, along with words that illustrate the sounds they represent, follow:

Vowel Digraphs

oo (cool, cook)   oi, oy (oil, oyster)
ew (grew)   ou, ow (out, owl)
au, aw (auto, awl)

Comments about the eight vowel digraphs follow.

oo

When double-*o* occurs in the same syllable, the two letters commonly represent what is called the long sound for *oo*. This sound is in *cool* and in *loose, food, ooze, stoop, cocoon,* and *aloof.* The less common sound, referred to as the short sound for *oo*, can be heard in *cook, stood,* and *wool.*

Students who expect vowel letters to vary in the sounds they represent try the long sound for *oo* first whenever double-*o* is in a syllable of a word that needs to be decoded. If that sound does not produce a recognizable word that fits a given context, the next step is to try the short sound.

ew

A common sound for the digraph *ew* is the same as the long sound for *oo.* This is illustrated in words like *stew, dew,* and *shrewd.*

au	aw

The sound that both *au* and *aw* represent is in words like *author, pauper, awkward,* and *straw.*

The digraph *aw* is useful in illustrating a point made earlier: decoding focuses on syllables, not words. Implied in the commentary about the sound that *aw* records, therefore, is that *a* and *w* are in the same syllable. Consequently, what has been said about the sound that *aw* represents applies to words like *awe* and *awning* but not to others such as *away* and *aware* (*a way, a ware*).

The sound that both *oi* and *oy* stand for starts words like *oil* and *oyster* and is also a part of such words as *hoist, avoid, soy,* and *decoy.* As the digraph *oy* demonstrates, *y*, like *w*, may function as a vowel.

The sound that *ou* and *ow* both represent is in *south, mountain, coward,* and *allow.*

Ow requires additional attention because, although it does function as a digraph in *coward* and *allow,* in other instances it does not. The "other instances" are discussed later but are referred to in passing in case any of you thought of words like *low* and *show* when *ow* was identified as a vowel digraph.

Vowel Sounds: Summary

Even though a technical analysis of English words reveals more than fifteen vowel sounds, the fifteen discussed figure in phonics instruction. To review the fifteen, and to prepare you for the next minitest, the following list should be helpful. (Because the schwa sound is being equated with an unstressed short *u* sound, it is not listed separately.)

Words Illustrating Vowel Sounds

1. at	6. aim	11. cool (stew)
2. end	7. eat	12. cook
3. if	8. ice	13. auto (law)
4. odd	9. old	14. oil (boy)
5. up	10. use	15. out (owl)

Testing

The next minitest is in Figure 8.3. The requests in Figure 8.3 are meant to help you know whether you remember what has been said about short and long vowel sounds, vowel digraphs, and the schwa sound. Again, cover the lower part of Figure 8.3; the answers appear there. Use the results to decide if a need exists to restudy vowel sounds. Subsequent sections assume you know what has been said about them thus far.

I. In the words below, underline every letter that records /ə/.

| idol | cement | maintain | alone | Honda |
| stampede | canyon | even | human | identity |

II. In the words below, underline all the letters that stand for *long vowel sounds*.

| coax | stood | gable | ambulance | quail | reptile |
| pass | tepee | mundane | chintz | stray | too |

III. In the words below, underline all the letters that represent *short vowel sounds*.

| bronco | fantastic | cube | digraph | litmus | hobo |
| wool | exact | ethnic | booth | medley | result |

IV. In the words below, underline all the letters that function as *vowel digraphs*.

| autumn | seem | vowel | roost | know | dawn |
| royal | lounge | monsoon | quite | broil | tea |

I. idol cement alone Honda canyon even human identity

II. coax gable ambulance quail reptile tepee mundane stray too

III. bronco fantastic digraph litmus wool exact ethnic medley result

IV. autumn vowel roost dawn royal lounge monsoon broil

Figure 8.3 Vowels: Self-Testing

SYLLABLES

Syllables are basic to decoding, since they are the unit on which decoders should focus. Decisions about syllabic divisions in unknown words, therefore, are important.

As the previous chapter showed, once an unknown word *is* segmented into syllables, the first syllable, plus contextual help, is sometimes enough to allow a reader to recognize the whole of it. This is illustrated in a sentence like *They are studying rep___, starting with snakes.* (This context was chosen to remind you once again of the dependence of decoding ability on world knowledge and oral vocabularies.)

Because of the basic importance of syllables for decoding, let's start with a definition: A *syllable* is a vowel sound to which one or more consonant sounds are commonly added. Stated differently, a vowel sound is the nucleus of a syllable, which means there are as many syllables in a word as there are vowel sounds. Single-syllable words like the following highlight the fact that the number of syllables in a word equals the number of vowel sounds, *not* the number of vowel letters:

squeeze   voice   lounge   guide

Because a vowel sound *is* the nucleus of a syllable, it is possible for a syllable to be composed of only one letter—always a vowel. For instance:

e voke   o zone   a ble   i tem

SYLLABLE GENERALIZATIONS

When a word is unknown in its written form, readers can use the sequence of its letters to arrive at a conclusion about syllables so that the decoding process can proceed. Generalizations for syllabication, therefore, are concerned with visual features of words. Before the generalizations are listed and discussed, a generalization already referred to needs to be reconsidered to see how it, too, helps with syllable segmentation.

I refer to this generalization: *Every syllable must have a vowel sound.* Even though this statement is about sounds, not about sequences of letters, it is still relevant for dividing unknown words into syllables. Specifically, it allows readers to know with a quick visual inspection that a word like *strength* can be no more than one syllable even though it is spelled with as many as eight letters. When decoders know about vowel digraphs, the same generalization prompts an identical conclusion about a word like *awl*.

Knowing that every syllable must have a vowel sound also helps with multisyllabic words by letting decoders know when it is time to quit insofar as segmenting a word is concerned. Take *bauble* as an example. Once it is divided between *u* and the second *b* (*bau ble*), decoders can correctly conclude that additional syllables are impossible. They thus know it is time to decide how the two syllables are pronounced.

The other four generalizations for syllabication are in Figure 8.4. The commentary on the page facing Figure 8.4 can help you understand the generalizations.

Once you think you do understand the generalizations about segmenting words, and, in addition, have committed them to memory, you are ready to take the next minitest, which constitutes Figure 8.5.

FACTORS AFFECTING SOUNDS

It has been emphasized that initial instruction in phonics deals with consonants because they are more consistent than vowels in the sounds they represent. The difference becomes very apparent as the following sections pinpoint certain predictable variations, which are described in generalizations.

The generalizations are taught to provide students with a strategy for coping with variation. Or, as Richard Venezky has observed, "They must learn, first, that many spellings have alternate pronunciations and, second, that certain clues exist for determining which pronunciation to use in a given word" (9, p. 2).

Consonant Generalizations

Two generalizations for consonants describe when c and g are likely to record their hard and soft sounds. (Be sure you have the four sounds clearly in mind.) The third generalization focuses on g only. The first two generalizations are in Figure 8.6.

Recalling the generalizations for c and g stated in Figure 8.6 allows you to see that c and g represent predictable sounds in all the words below.

accent	receive	suggest	gene
inspect	section	gumbo	gargle
price	article	gypsum	figure
circus	consonant	ego	page
disc	clasp	ginger	growl

Although use of the generalizations about c and g usually results in correct conclusions about the sounds they represent, dealing with g in particular may require trying "the other sound." The three words below illustrate the need for versatility:

get   give   girl

The three words were selected to make another point, namely, that some words that include c and g are taught before children know anything about hard and soft sounds. In the case of the three words just listed, each is likely to be taught as a whole word with no explicit attention to the sounds that individual letters record.

One more generalization is stated before the next minitest. It deals with g when it is followed by u. The generalization is in Figure 8.7.

Keeping in mind the generalization stated in Figure 8.7, you can understand why in all the words listed below, g stands for a predictable sound.

gum	guild	vogue
gull	guitar	rogue

Testing

Sounds for c and g predicted by the generalizations that have been discussed are the focus for the next minitest. Because the test has to do with so-called regularly and irregularly spelled words (insofar as c and g are concerned), be

Figure 8.4   Syllable Generalizations

First, read all four generalizations to get a general picture of their content. As you do this, notice how each generalization focuses on visual cues, that is, on letters and their sequence.

Next, study the first generalization, making sure you see how each illustrative word does in fact illustrate the content. Using the generalization, divide each example into syllables using slash marks to note syllable boundaries. Doing this, you should notice (a) that in *kindergarten* and *fantastic,* the generalization is used three and two times, respectively; and (b) that in *panther* and *dolphin,* the digraphs *th* and *ph* function as single consonants.

Now move to the second generalization. This describes the VCV (vowel-consonant-vowel) pattern, whereas the first generalization dealt with the VCCV pattern. As you consider the second generalization, be sure you see how the illustrative words exemplify the pattern. Also, make certain you can divide the words into syllables. As you do this, you should notice that (a) the digraph *au* functions as a single vowel in *author* and *authentic;* and (b) that dividing *authentic* into three syllables makes use of two generalizations, both of which should now be familiar.

Then examine the third generalization in order to compare it with the second one. The comparison should point up that both focus on the VCV pattern. The third generalization makes the point, however, that when the consonant is *x,* a different syllabic division is called for. That is, *x* is in the same syllable as the vowel that precedes it. The difference can be summarized as follows:

$$VCV \qquad V \times V$$
$$V\,CV \qquad V \times\ V$$

Again, be sure you see how each illustrative word exemplifies the content of the third generalization.

Finally, read the fourth generalization, the content of which should be familiar.

When you feel you understand, and have committed to memory, the four generalizations for dividing unknown words into syllables, you are ready to take the next minitest, which is Figure 8.5. Again, cover the bottom part of the page until you are ready to check your answers.

1. When two consonants are between two vowels (*window*) a syllable division usually occurs between the consonants (*win dow*). For example:

textile	bamboo
panther	dolphin
canteen	kindergarten
fantastic	accent

2. When one consonant is between two vowels (*pilot*), a syllable division usually occurs between the first vowel and the consonant (*pi lot*). For example:

motel	below	oval	away
flavor	solo	author	authentic
erode	idol		

3. When *x* is the consonant that is between two vowels (*exit*), *x* and the preceding vowel are in the same syllable (*ex it*). For example:

oxen	taxi	Texas	exile
buxom	example	maximum	axiom
axle	exact	lexicon	

4. When a word ends in a consonant followed by *le* (*idle*), the consonant plus *le* are the final syllable (*i dle*). For example:

candle	dimple	bugle	ruffle
scramble	title	article	garble
temple	possible		

Divide the following pseudowords into syllables using slash marks to show where one syllable ends and the next begins.

1. ximdle	6. arfeple	11. jownar
2. dowx	7. voog	12. gebthor
3. shigur	8. dilque	13. ciftaung
4. cuxot	9. quawz	14. thoipder
5. gik	10. vipho	

1. xim dle (4)	8. dilque (5)*
2. dowx (5)	9. quawz (5)
3. shi gur (2)	10. vi pho (2)
4. cux ot (3)	11. jow nar (2)**
5. gik (5)	12. geb thor (1)
6. ar fe ple (1) (4)	13. cif taung (1)
7. voog (5)	14. thoip der (1)

The numbers in parentheses following the pseudowords refer to the numbers in the list of generalizations in Figure 8.4. (For all the words, knowing when to stop dividing derives from this generalization: Every syllable must have a vowel sound. When that is the only generalization used, it is indicated with 5.)

It is suggested that you do not proceed with the chapter until you are sure you know the generalizations for dividing unknown words into syllables.

*As discussed earlier, English words do not end in *u*. Consequently, when *qu* stands for the final sound in a word, the word ends with *que*, as in *clique* and *baroque*.

**In this case, *ow* is functioning as a vowel, thus the pattern is VCV.

Figure 8.5 Dividing Words into Syllables: Self-Testing

When *c* and *g* are followed by *e, i,* or *y* (*cent, cite, cyst; gem, gin, gym*), they usually record their soft sounds. For example:

*ce*dar	*ci*ty	*cy*nic
*ge*ntle	*gi*raffe	*gy*psy

Otherwise, *c* and *g* generally stand for their hard sounds.* For example:

*ca*ge	*co*at	*cu*t	sa*c*	fa*c*t
*ga*me	*go*t	*gu*m	wa*g*	*g*row

*This generalization can also be stated as: When *c* and *g* are not followed in a syllable by *e, i,* or *y,* or are the final letters in a syllable, they generally stand for their hard sounds.

Figure 8.6 Generalizations: C and G

When *gu* is in a syllable that includes a vowel other than the *u* (*guess*), *gu* functions as a single consonant and records the hard sound for *g*. For example:

guest   guard   guilt   guide   vague*   brogue*

*English words do not end in *u*; therefore, when *gu* stands for the final sound in a word, the word ends with -*gue*. This parallels what was said earlier about *qu* when it stands for a final sound, as it does in *antique* and *clique*.

Figure 8.7   Generalization: <u>GU</u>

sure you understand the explanation of "regularly spelled" and "irregularly spelled" that follows.

If *c* or *g* occurs in a word and stands for the sound that a generalization predicts, the word is considered regularly spelled (e.g., *accident, gypsy*). On the other hand, if *c* or *g* is in a word and stands for a sound other than the one that a generalization suggests, the word is considered to be irregularly spelled (e.g., *cello, gill*). Once you have firmly fixed in your mind the meanings of "regularly spelled" and "irregularly spelled"—and understand and have committed to memory the generalizations about *c* and *g*—you are ready to take the next minitest. It is Figure 8.8. As you take the test, remember that generalizations are concerned with syllables, not words. Again, cover the bottom of Figure 8.8 to derive maximum benefit from the test.

Vowel Generalizations

Before discussing visual features of syllables that suggest likely sounds for vowel letters, it might be helpful to review long and short vowel sounds, since they are referred to in the generalizations that will be covered. Some of the generalizations also refer to "silent" letters—that is, to letters that do not add a sound to a syllable. Displaying the diacritical marks that are often helpful to children at the beginning, the following words are offered as a review of ten vowel sounds and as an illustration of "silent" letters.

ăt   měn   hǐm   ŏdd   ŭs
āte̸   mēa̸n   hī   ōde̸   ūse̸

As you can see when the generalizations are discussed, each word above is regularly spelled. Now, "regularly spelled" describes a word in which each letter in each syllable—or pairs of letters if a digraph—stands for the sound predicted by a generalization. In such words, silent letters are also predictable, based on a generalization.

The five generalizations for vowel letters are in Figure 8.9. Comments about the generalizations face Figure 8.9.

If you have given ample time to the five generalizations about vowel sounds, you should be able to see why it is said that there are five types of syllables in English words. The five are described in Figure 8.10.

For now, a "regularly spelled word" is one in which *c* and *g* represent the sounds predicted by the generalizations that have been discussed. Divide the words below into syllables (using generalizations stated earlier); then put a check after any word that is *not* regularly spelled.

1. lilac __	9. grade __	17. igloo __
2. giggle __	10. fugue __	18. toxic __
3. impinge __	11. giddy __	19. cancel __
4. social __	12. cymbal __	20. girth __
5. chance __	13. target __	21. cascade __
6. curve __	14. infect __	22. concern __
7. gimmick __	15. rascal __	23. engine __
8. icicle __	16. gear __	24. gigantic __

The following words should *not* be checked:

lilac	curve	fugue	rascal	cancel	engine
impinge	icicle	cymbal	igloo	cascade	gigantic
chance	grade	infect	toxic	concern	

Searching through a dictionary for words for this minitest reinforced the reliability of the generalizations about *c* and *g*. Irregularly spelled words, as defined above, were difficult to find. Finding words in which *c* did not stand for predicted sounds was practically impossible. (Did you recall that in *chance*, *ch* is a digraph?)

The irregularly spelled words that should have been checked divide into syllables as follows:

gig/gle	gim/mick	tar/get	girth
so/cial	gid/dy	gear	

Figure 8.8   Sounds for C and G: Self-Testing

You can notice in the third column in Figure 8.10 that symbols for "consonant" (C) are sometimes enclosed in parentheses. This means the consonant is not an essential part of the pattern described. For instance, in the case of the first pattern listed, the single vowel in final position is all that is essential. This is illustrated in the words below.

amen (a men)   ibis (i bis)   open (o pen)

In the second type of syllable listed in Figure 8.10, the nonessential presence of the initial consonant and the essential presence of one or more final consonants is illustrated in other words:

web   inch   ant

As you study Figure 8.10, see if you can add to the illustrative words for the three remaining types of syllables.

Testing

If you think you are knowledgeable about the visual features of syllables that suggest the sounds to assign to vowel letters, you are ready for the next minitest. Because it asks for distinctions between regularly and irregularly spelled words, definitions follow:

> **Regularly Spelled Word**
> The sounds that single letters and digraphs represent, and the letters that are silent, are predicted by one or more generalizations. For example:
>
> flax   bamboo   since   vague
>
> **Irregularly Spelled Word**
> One or more single letters or digraphs in a syllable do not stand for predicted sounds. For example:
>
> host   once   two   scene

If you now understand the meaning assigned to "regularly spelled" and "irregularly spelled," it is time to take the next minitest, which is Figure 8.11. Because generalizations pertain to syllables, the words need to be segmented before decisions are made about their spellings in relation to their pronunciations. Keep in mind that a schwa sound in an unstressed syllable does not make a word irregularly spelled.

For this minitest, answers are provided at the bottom of Figure 8.11. Comments about certain words are on the page facing the test. Therefore, (a) complete the test first; (b) check your answers with those at the bottom of Figure 8.11; and (c) read the comments. Use the results of the test to decide whether you are ready to proceed with the chapter or, on the other hand, whether additional study is required.

R-CONTROLLED VOWEL SOUNDS

Previous sections described features of syllables that help decoders assign sounds to *c, g,* and *gu,* and to *a, e, i, o,* and *u.* This section extends the discussion of variation in vowel sounds. Now the focus is confined to syllables in which a vowel is followed by *r,* as is the case in *hurt* and *acorn.* With such syllables, decoders must view the vowel and the *r* following it as a unit. This accounts for the description *r-controlled vowel sounds.* R-controlled vowel sounds are three different blends that can be identified with the help of three words:

her   far   or

Figure 8.9 Vowel Generalizations

At the start read all the generalizations. With each, make certain you see how ▶
the two words in the parentheses exemplify the spelling patterns described. As
you study the generalizations, keep in mind that all the spelling-sound patterns
pertain to syllables, not to words.

Now return to the first generalization to read it carefully. Notice that all
the syllables in *ethnic* and *cactus* exemplify the generalization. In *textile*
(tex tile), only the first syllable illustrates its content.

Then go on to the second generalization, which also deals with syllables
that have one vowel letter. By contrasting the first two generalizations, you will
see the significance of the position of a vowel for the sound it is likely to record.
Just counting vowels, then, is insufficient.

Next read the third generalization. You should now understand why it
does not describe words like *oil* and *monsoon*. Notice that *ow* in *snow* stands
for the long *o* sound, not for the sound heard in *cow* and *allow*. The variation is
the reason children need to be ready to try both sounds whenever *ow* occurs in
an unknown word.

At this point you should be ready to consider together the fourth and fifth
generalizations. The two deal with contrasting patterns:

VCe   VCCe

These two generalizations describe the significance for pronunciations of the
number of consonants that separate a vowel from final e. (Be sure you
understand why *rogue* illustrates the content of the fourth generalization: *gu*
functions as a consonant when it is in a syllable that has more vowels than just
the *u*.)

Finally, look at all the illustrative words in Figure 8.9 to see how often final
e's are silent. Notice, too, that final e's frequently signal information about
sounds for other letters occurring in the same syllable. In a word like *pace,* for
instance, the final e signals that a is likely to stand for its long sound and that c
is likely to stand for its soft sound.

Before leaving Figure 8.9, be sure you understand, and have committed to
memory, the five generalizations.

1. When one vowel is in a syllable and is not the final letter (*ramp, cactus*), that vowel generally stands for its short sound.
   For example:

act	snub	ethnic	campus
bunch	dim	shock	textile

2. When one vowel is in a syllable and is the final letter (*so, veto*), that vowel generally stands for its long sound.
   For example:

she	halo	music	limbo
hi	focus	siphon	ether

3. When two successive vowels, which are not digraphs, are in a syllable (*meat, oats*), the first vowel generally stands for its long sound and the second is silent.
   For example:

aid	waif	coax	either
eel	eagle	snow	stream

4. When two vowels are in a syllable, one of which is final *e*, and the two are separated by one consonant (*ade, stroke*), the first vowel generally stands for its long sound and the final *e* is silent.
   For example:

ode	cite	cascade	abuse
safe	mete	code	rogue

5. When two vowels are in a syllable, one of which is final *e*, and the two are separated by two consonants (*else, solve*), the first vowel generally stands for its short sound and the final *e* is silent.
   For example:

since	hinge	delve	elapse
dunce	fudge	impulse	revolve

Description	Examples	Spelling Pattern
1. One vowel, at the end	me, go, she, I	(C)V
2. One vowel, not at the end	met, an, chip	(C)VC
3. Two successive vowels	meet, sea, ail	(C)VV(C)
4. Two vowels, one a final *e*	mete, cube, ace	(C)VCe
5. Two vowels, one a final *e* with the two separated by two consonants	mince, bulge, else	(C)VCCe

Figure 8.10   Types of Syllables

The three blends that are heard in *her, far,* and *or,* and the pairs of letters that represent them, are shown in Table 8.4.

Students who are aware of the need to try alternative sounds when the first one fails to produce a sensible word rely on the following three guidelines to deal with syllables in which a vowel is followed by *r*:

1. If the pair is *er, ir,* or *ur,* the blend will be the one heard initially in *urn.*
2. If the pair is *ar,* the most likely sounds are the blend heard initially in *arm.* If that blend is not productive, the one in final position in *war* should be tried. In final position, *ar* may also stand for the blend that ends *dollar.*
3. If the pair is *or,* the blend to try first is the one that comprises the word *or.* If that does not work, the next blend to try is the one heard at the end of *motor.*

These guidelines can be summarized as follows:

R-Controlled Vowel Sounds							
one blend			*three blends*		*two blends*		
er	her			far		*or*	for
ir	dirt	*ar*	cedar			world
ur	curb		wart			

Keeping the above possibilities in mind, you will know why all the following words are regularly spelled:

arbor	cinder	effort	first	burst	blizzard	hurl
motor	quart	dwarf	carve	altar	border	custard

Blends	Letters
/er/	a̲r (collar), e̲r (her), i̲r (sir), o̲r (word), u̲r (fur)
/ar/	a̲r (are)
/or/	o̲r (nor), a̲r (war)

Table 8.4 *R*-Controlled Vowel Sounds

Decoders also need to be on the lookout for syllables in which a vowel is followed by *re*. The blends that a vowel plus *re* stand for can be identified in the words listed below. These words are contrasted with five others to help you distinguish between blends recorded by a vowel plus *r* and other blends that are represented by a vowel plus *re*.

car	her	fir	for	curr
care	here	fire	fore	cure

Contrasts like those above also help children make the necessary distinctions.

Even more words in which a vowel is followed by *re* are shown below. Again, all are regularly spelled.

mare	sincere	dire	snore	pure
square	ampere	umpire	pinafore	obscure

What must not be forgotten in this discussion of *r*-controlled vowel sounds is the assumption that the vowel and the *r* occur in the same syllable. The discussion, therefore, does not apply to words like *erode* (e rode), *arise* (a rise), or *irate* (i rate).

Testing

Having considered the effect of *r* and *re* on a preceding vowel, it is time for another minitest. Once more, the task is to decide whether words are regularly or irregularly spelled. Once you have reread the section on *r*-controlled vowel sounds, try the minitest in Figure 8.12. All the words listed are in a basal reader said to be for the second half of third grade. (Be sure to cover the bottom part of Figure 8.12.)

Y FUNCTIONING AS A VOWEL

The earlier discussion of vowel digraphs showed *y* functioning as a vowel in words like *toy, employ,* and *oyster.* Alone, *y* also serves as a vowel. Before

Figure 8.11   Regularly Spelled Words: Self-Testing

To start, regular spellings for the irregularly spelled words are provided under-neath each word.

some	answer	blood	scene	aisle
(sum)	(anser)	(blud)	(sene)	(ile)
			(cene)	

swan	haste	roll	earn	busy
(swon)	(haist)	(role)	(ern)	(bizzy)

The words *some* and *sum,* and *roll* and *role,* indicate that certain irregularly spelled words are homophones. (*Earn* and *urn,* and *scene* and *seen,* are homophones, too; but in providing regular spellings, minimal changes were made to pinpoint what makes a word irregularly spelled.)

Regularly spelled words like the two below show that a schwa sound in an unstressed syllable is a pattern, not an exception:

stánza   *condénse*

The spelling of *bisque* exemplifies another pattern: VCCe, because *qu* functions as a consonant. Because *i* in *bisque* stands for its short sound, *bisque* is regularly spelled but *haste* is not.

The regularly spelled word *shallow* is a reminder that *ow* does not always function as a digraph. The second syllable in *shallow* follows the pattern of two successive vowels representing the long sound of the first one. It is thus similar to words like *stow* and *furrow.*

Finally, the word *eccentric* demonstrates the value of knowing about consonant clusters. Specifically, knowing that *t* and *r* often are successive letters in a syllable allows for segmenting *eccentric* as follows:

ec cen tric

You may have noticed as you took this test that in every word, *c* and *g* represented the sounds that generalizations predict.

Divide each word into syllable(s).
Then check the appropriate column.

	Syllable(s)	Regularly Spelled?	
		yes	no
1. gable	_____	____	____
2. reason	_____	____	____
3. some	_____	____	____
4. answer	_____	____	____
5. quail	_____	____	____
6. blood	_____	____	____
7. scene	_____	____	____
8. noodle	_____	____	____
9. stanza	_____	____	____
10. bisque	_____	____	____
11. aisle	_____	____	____
12. condense	_____	____	____
13. swan	_____	____	____
14. haste	_____	____	____
15. roll	_____	____	____
16. earn	_____	____	____
17. busy	_____	____	____
18. gender	_____	____	____
19. foible	_____	____	____
20. calculus	_____	____	____
21. shallow	_____	____	____
22. eccentric	_____	____	____

Irregularly spelled words:

some	blood	aisle	haste	earn
answer	scene	swan	roll	busy

243

Using visual cues, divide each word into syllables. If all the syllables are pronounced in ways suggested by generalizations, check that word as being regularly spelled.

	Syllable(s)	Regularly Spelled
1. entertain	_____	_____
2. perform	_____	_____
3. prove	_____	_____
4. snorkel	_____	_____
5. pour	_____	_____
6. sprawl	_____	_____
7. break	_____	_____
8. pearl	_____	_____
9. murmur	_____	_____
10. effort	_____	_____
11. eager	_____	_____
12. scarce	_____	_____
13. signature	_____	_____
14. alarm	_____	_____
15. force	_____	_____
16. rein	_____	_____

Regularly spelled words are: *entertain, perform, snorkel, sprawl, murmur, effort, signature, alarm, force.* (Presumably you kept in mind that schwa sounds in unstressed syllables do not by themselves make a word irregularly spelled.)

Are you able to provide regular spellings for the seven words that are irregularly spelled?

Figure 8.12   Regularly Spelled Words: Self-Testing

generalizations about *y* functioning as a vowel are discussed, when *y* serves as a consonant is explained.

Y functions as a consonant only when it occurs in the initial position in a syllable. Obviously, it serves that function in *yes* and *year*. It assumes the same role in *canyon* (can yon), *lawyer* (law yer), and *beyond* (be yond), because in all three words *y* starts a syllable.

The three vowel sounds that *y* represents when it is not in initial position are /ĭ/, /ē/, and /ī/. When *y* stands for each of the three sounds is considered now with the help of generalizations. The first is stated below:

> When *y* is in medial position in a syllable that has no vowel letter (*gym, cyst, system, cymbal*), it stands for the short sound of *i*. For example:

> | | | | |
> |---|---|---|---|
> | myth | crystal | syllable | pyx |
> | pygmy | mystic | syndrome | olympic |

A quick visual scanning of words like *gym, cyst, myth, crypt,* and *pyx*—should these words be unknown—is enough for a decoder to conclude that all are one-syllable words with *y* serving as the vowel that every syllable must have. Using the generalization just stated, a decoder can conclude that in each of the five words, *y* stands for /ĭ/.

Even though it is visually clear that a word like *cyst* can have only one syllable, a conclusion about the number of syllables in *crystal* is not equally apparent. It is possible it has two, if *y* is functioning as a vowel. But is it? If *y* functions as a consonant, it must start a syllable:

> cr ystal

Because *cr* cannot be a syllable, the only possible conclusion—even for the individual who has never seen *crystal* before—is that *y* is functioning as a vowel. Since that is the case, the VCCV pattern suggests that *crystal* has two syllables:

> [VC CV]
> crys tal

Now let's move to the second generalization about *y:*

> When *y* is the last letter in a multisyllabic word and it is preceded by a consonant (*fancy, pony, city, penny*), it usually records the long sound of *e*. For example:

> | | | | |
> |---|---|---|---|
> | funny | hurry | artery | autopsy |
> | candy | duty | dignity | emergency |

Because the third generalization deals indirectly with *y*, it needs to be stated in the context of the other two:

Generalizations for Y

1. When *y* is in medial position in a syllable that has no vowel letter, it stands for the short sound of *i*, as in *hymn*.
2. When *y* is the final letter in a multisyllabic word and is preceded by a consonant, it usually stands for the long sound of *e*, as in *easy*.
3. Otherwise, *y* stands for the long sound of *i*. For example:

dye	cry	nylon	dynamo	cycle
type	shy	gyrate	thyroid	python

By now you should understand why a visual inspection of all the words used to illustrate the third generalization is enough to conclude that, in every instance, *y* can function only as a vowel. This reinforces the basic importance of a generalization cited earlier: Every syllable must have a vowel sound.

A generalization stated earlier takes *y* into account in words like *day* and *pulley:* When there are two successive vowels in a syllable that are not digraphs, the first usually stands for its long sound and the second is silent. How *y* figures in this generalization is illustrated below:

day	pulley	spray	galley
[d ā y̸]	[pul l ē y̸]	[s p r ā y̸]	[gal l ē y̸]

Testing

Once you have reread the section on *y* functioning as a vowel—keeping in mind that *y* also serves as a consonant—you should be ready for the next minitest, which is in Figure 8.13. Again, it asks about regular spellings. To gain maximum benefit from the test, look at the answers only when you are ready to check your responses.

STRESSED SYLLABLES

Because English words derive from a variety of other languages, teaching generalizations about stress is not very useful. In their place, flexibility can be taught. Let me describe what this means using the word *afford* as an example. Assume it is unknown visually and is embedded in the following context:

That dress costs too much. I can't afford it.

In the second column, show the syllabication for each word in the first column. Then mark the stressed syllables. If a word is irregularly spelled, write a regular spelling in the third column.

	Syllabication and Stressed Syllable	Regular Spelling
calypso	_____	_____
abbey	_____	_____
sphere	_____	_____
blue	_____	_____
rayon	_____	_____
plenty	_____	_____
young	_____	_____
journey	_____	_____
persuade	_____	_____
phylum	_____	_____
coy	_____	_____
deny	_____	_____

Syllabication and stress: ca lýp so; ab bey; sphere; blue; rá yon; pleń ty; young; jouŕ ney; per suade; phý lum; coy; de ný.

Regular spellings: bloo, yung, jurney, perswade, denye.

Figure 8.13 Regularly Spelled Words: Self-Testing

Even though the context, plus a quick look at the spelling, is enough for some students to reach a correct conclusion about *afford*, we'll assume that is not the case. Instead, using visual cues, the decoder divides *afford* as follows:

af ford

She or he assigns the short sound to *a* and assumes for the time being that *or* stands for the blend that comprises the word *or*. After blending the sounds for each syllable, the "trying out" process and adjustments might proceed in the following way:

(1) áf fórd   (2) áf ford   (3) ăf fórd   (4) ə fórd

If the unknown word is *athlete*, the decoder's job is considerably easier even if it is in a context offering minimal help. In this case, trial-and-error efforts have little error in them:

(1) ăth lētĕ   (2) ăth lētĕ

More is said about stressed syllables in subsequent chapters. For now, this brief discussion should reinforce the important contributions that oral vocabularies make to reading.

IN CONCLUSION

The best way to conclude a chapter like the present one is to provide an opportunity for you to see what you have learned and, perhaps, what still needs to be studied. The final minitest is in Figure 8.14. In order to end the chapter on a positive note, why not go through the chapter first for a quick review, because review is the purpose of the last test. The page that faces Figure 8.14 provides answers.

SUMMARY

English words are recorded with letters that stand for speech sounds. The correspondence between letters and sounds makes it possible for readers to use the spelling of an unfamiliar word to reach a conclusion about its pronunciation. In turn, a pronunciation triggers meaning *if* the word is in the reader's oral vocabulary. This explains why the dependence of decoding ability on oral language was highlighted both at the outset and at the end of the chapter.

Even though it is unusual for a reader to have to decode isolated words, Chapter 8 laid aside consideration of contextual help in order to concentrate on subject matter for phonics. In no way, however, does the selected focus minimize the help that comes from syntactic and semantic cues. As Chapter 7 pointed out, some contexts are so rich with help that the spelling of a word needs to be used only to check on the correctness of the "answer" that contextual cues suggest. At other times, only the initial syllable in an unfamiliar word will need to be systematically decoded.

Although beginners in reading are not ready to learn about syllables, Chapter 8 emphasized at the beginning the significance of syllabication for decoding. That is why generalizations about syllabication were stated, discussed, and applied. Each generalization pointed out how visual cues (letters *and* their sequence) function in segmenting an unknown word or, as the case may be, in deciding that it has only one syllable. Visual cues were highlighted, because that is all that is available when a word is not in an individual's reading vocabulary.

A substantial portion of Chapter 8 deals with letter-sound correspondences. Like instruction in phonics, the chapter started with speech sounds that consonants record. The discussion divided into a treatment of single consonants, consonant clusters, and consonant digraphs.

Dealing with vowel sounds took up considerably more space because of the variation in the sounds that vowel letters represent. This discussion started by identifying fifteen vowel sounds. To identify them, single vowels and vowel digraphs were considered. The significance of the schwa sound for dealing with unknown multisyllabic words was explained, too. The importance of this sound is generously illustrated in dictionaries.

Chapter 8 concentrated next on the visual features of syllables that suggest the sounds to assign to *c* and *g*, and to *a, e, i, o,* and *u.* These features were the focus of generalizations. Because of the frequency with which *y* functions as a vowel and, in particular, because it represents three different vowel sounds, *y* received attention in other generalizations.

Because of the nature of English spellings, Chapter 8 offered intermittent reminders of the importance of emphasizing with students the possible need to try other sounds whenever the use of a generalization fails to produce a recognizable, sensible word. Because what is sensible depends not only on spellings but also on contexts, the need to check an "answer" with a context was not overlooked.

All this can be summarized by saying that the four tasks of the advanced decoder are to (a) make decisions about syllabic divisions and letter-sound correspondences; (b) blend the sounds in each syllable; (c) compare the pronunciation that results with words that are stored in auditory memory; and (d) decide if it is a recognizable word that is appropriate for the given context. When all this is done quickly, the comprehension process is not obstructed.

REVIEW

1. The discussion of subject matter for phonics instruction included some terms that ought to be familiar to teachers and prospective teachers. Therefore, define each of the following terms with the help of examples.

alphabetic writing system	blend
decoding	consonant cluster
letter-sound correspondence	schwa sound
syllable	regularly spelled word
digraph	

Figure 8.14 Final Test

ANSWERS:
Irregularly spelled words, followed by regular spellings, are:

one (wun)	*floor* (flore)	*pursuit* (pursoot)	*soul* (sole)
bolt (boalt)	*police* (polece)	*chamber* (chaimber)	*two* (too).
courtesy (curtesy)	*canoe* (canoo)	*squad* (squod)	

COMMENTS:
Presumably you divided the words into syllables before considering whether they are regularly or irregularly spelled. Presumably, too, you were not surprised to find /ə/ in a number of unstressed syllables, specifically, in aréna, coúrtesy, políce, quóta, canóe, fléxible, cadét, and avénge.

Hopefully, too, you remembered that *s* can stand for /s/ or /z/, as words like *courtesy* and *music* illustrate.

　　Finally, did you notice that:

■ *y* in *courtesy, guy,* and *gypsy* records predictable sounds?
■ *gu* functions as a single consonant when there is another vowel in the same syllable, which makes *guy* comparable to a word like *by*?
■ some of the words have *r*-controlled vowel sounds; specifically, *courtesy, floor, pursuit, chamber,* and *porcupine*?

　　If you had trouble with this final test, it is recommended that you give more time to reading any section that still requires studied attention.

Decide whether the words below are regularly or irregularly spelled. Then check the appropriate column. Supply regular spellings in the last column for all of the irregularly spelled words. (Change only letters that need to be changed.)

	Regularly Spelled?		Regular Spelling
	yes	no	
1. arena	____	____	_____
2. one	____	____	_____
3. bolt	____	____	_____
4. courtesy	____	____	_____
5. floor	____	____	_____
6. police	____	____	_____
7. quota	____	____	_____
8. canoe	____	____	_____
9. pursuit	____	____	_____
10. chamber	____	____	_____
11. porcupine	____	____	_____
12. flexible	____	____	_____
13. guy	____	____	_____
14. length	____	____	_____
15. squad	____	____	_____
16. phlox	____	____	_____
17. cadet	____	____	_____
18. gypsy	____	____	_____
19. soul	____	____	_____
20. avenge	____	____	_____
21. two	____	____	_____
22. twist	____	____	_____
23. bronze	____	____	_____
24. minnow	____	____	_____
25. music	____	____	_____

2. Proficient decoders work both successfully and quickly. Why is speed important?

3. What are the fifteen vowel sounds that phonics instruction covers?

4. Explain why this statement is correct:

   In *ten, line, maintain,* and *mercantile,* /n/ is in final position.

5. Why is the following generalization, taken from a basal program, useless for decoders?

   If a word has a vowel that is followed by a consonant and another vowel, divide the word after the first vowel if it stands for its long sound, as in *over* and *music.*

6. Critique another generalization found in another basal series:

   If a word has two consonants together that are not digraphs, divide the word between the consonants.

7. Cite every generalization that is pertinent for decoding the word *act.* Start with syllabication, then move to other generalizations that help with each of the three letters that compose *act.*

REFERENCES

1. Brown, Roger. *Words and Things.* New York: Free Press, 1958.
2. Calfee, Robert C., and Piontkowski, Dorothy C. "The Reading Diary: Acquisition of Decoding." *Reading Research Quarterly* 16 (1981, No. 3), 346–373.
3. Commission on Reading. *Becoming a Nation of Readers: The Report of the Commission on Reading.* Washington, D.C.: The National Institute of Education, 1984.
4. Durkin, Dolores. *Strategies for Identifying Words.* 2nd ed. Boston: Allyn and Bacon, Inc., 1981.
5. Juel, Connie. "The Development and Use of Mediated Word Identification." *Reading Research Quarterly* 18 (Spring, 1983), 306–327.
6. Perfetti, Charles A. "Language Comprehension and Fast Decoding: Some Psycholinguistic Prerequisites for Skilled Reading Comprehension." In John T. Guthrie (Ed.), *Cognition, Curriculum, and Comprehension.* Newark, Del.: International Reading Association, 1977, 20–41.
7. Stanovich, Keith E. "Matthew Effects in Reading: Some Consequences of Individual Differences in the Acquisition of Literacy." *Reading Research Quarterly* 21 (Fall, 1986), 360–406.
8. Venezky, Richard L. "English Orthography: Its Graphical Structure and Its Relation to Sound." *Reading Research Quarterly* 2 (Spring, 1967), 75–105.

9. Venezky, Richard L. "Reading: Grapheme-Phoneme Relationship." *Education* 87 (May, 1967), 1–6.

10. Zinna, Danielle R.; Liberman, Isabelle Y.; and Shankweiler, Donald. "Children's Sensitivity to Factors Influencing Vowel Reading." *Reading Research Quarterly* 21 (Fall, 1986), 465–480.

Chapter 9

Phonics: Instruction

PREVIEW

The previous chapter concentrated on subject matter for phonics instruction; this chapter deals with the instruction itself. Factors underlying recommendations for instruction include the nature of written English, research findings, my own teaching experience, and numerous visits to the classrooms of other teachers.

Because of the indisputable influence of basal reader series on classroom instruction, the opening section in Chapter 9 identifies shortcomings in some of their recommendations for teaching phonics. Such a beginning suggests that a highly desirable way to prepare for the chapter is to examine some basal manuals and workbooks.

Even though the widespread influence of basal materials is recognized, the presence of individuals who are striving to be a Teacher A is not overlooked. That is why another section in Chapter 9 responds to two questions of importance to these individuals:

1. *When* should each piece of a phonics curriculum be taught?
2. *How* should phonics be taught?

Because instruction is the main concern of the chapter, recommendations for teaching are numerous and are communicated in a variety of formats. To make the recommendations highly specific and easy to visualize, the first few lessons are described with teacher-student dialogues. The next group of lessons is communicated in a way that highlights prerequisites. This format is used to reinforce the fact that objectives of lessons cannot be realized unless students are ready to achieve them. The final series of lessons highlights modeling, because this way of teaching is especially effective when the goal of instruction is to enable students to do something—for instance, to blend sounds in order to produce syllables. Recognizing the necessity of practice for correct and quick decoding, the closing sections of Chapter 9 provide a number of ideas for practice that cover a variety of topics.

Two further points need to be made. The first is the assumption that readers of Chapter 9 are knowledgeable about the content of the previous chapter. The second point is that Chapter 9 is as relevant for middle- and upper-grade teachers as it is for those working at the primary level. In fact, Chapter 9 might be even more helpful for teachers of older students. This is possible because even though basal programs allot much space and many words to phonics in their primary-grade materials, the common recommendation for dealing with new vocabulary starting at about grade four is to send students to glossaries and dictionaries. Admittedly, phonics ought to be taught as quickly as students are able to learn it. Equally correct, however, is the contention that students should be encouraged to use what they know throughout *all* the grades. For that reason, Chapter 9 is as concerned with the use of phonics as it is with instruction for phonics.

The fact that phonics is as old as reading instruction itself means that many phonics studies have been done. However, because the quantity of the research exceeds its quality, some important questions do not have uncontestable answers (4). That is why the review of studies in the well-known book *Becoming a Nation of Readers* (2) resulted in a report of trends in existing data, not of well-documented conclusions.

Based on the available data, a pervasive theme in *Becoming a Nation of Readers* is that the phonics part of basal reader programs "falls considerably short of the ideal" (p. 43). An even more prominent theme is that the same programs "strongly influence how reading is taught in American schools"* (p. 35).

Recognizing the influence of basal reader materials as well as their flaws, this chapter starts with an overview of some of the differences in recommendations in basal programs and in the present chapter. Even though the overview takes the form of a critique, its purpose is to allow for a comparison of contrasting points of view so that choices can be made about what to teach and how to go about teaching it. The overview might also help textbook selection committees when they evaluate basal reader programs.

* The influence of these materials suggests the need to reproduce samples of manual suggestions and workbook pages in this chapter. Unfortunately, it has become almost impossible to obtain a publisher's permission to use reproductions unless the comments to be made about them are positive. This condition explains their absence in the present chapter. The omission and the reason for it point up the importance of your examining commercial materials—including phonics workbooks published by nonbasal reader companies—before, during, or after reading the chapter.

BASAL READER PRACTICES: A CRITIQUE

The discussion of differences between recommendations made here and in basal programs starts with topics relevant for pre-first-grade teachers. It then continues with a look at differences that pertain to later instruction.

At the Beginning

The existence of the previous chapter, plus the present one, is evidence of agreement with the contention that a child who is just starting to read "must at some point discover the alphabetic principle: that units of print map onto units of sound" (12, p. 363). Even so, the position taken here is that students' initial contacts with print should involve sizable pieces of text for the purpose of demonstrating the communicative aspect of print. Whenever the fact that print conveys meaning is being highlighted and a word appears more than once in the text, that word can be singled out for attention in order to make the point: same symbol, same word.

The next recommended step is instruction with meaningful words that has the development of sight vocabularies as its goal. Once words that start with the same letter and sound are known, attention can go to the fact that spellings and pronunciations are connected. How one kindergarten teacher called attention to the link between *p* and /p/ is illustrated in Chapter 4. It would be helpful for you to review that instruction now.

All these recommendations can be summarized by saying that attention to written words should focus at first on connected text, progress downward to particular words, and from there to letters viewed as parts of words. It seems logical to think that this progression makes letter-sound relationships more meaningful than does instruction that focuses immediately on sounds and then on the letters that record them (6). The latter sequence is used in the beginning workbooks of basal reader programs (3).

Preparation for Phonics

The preparation for phonics that some commercial materials recommend is illustrated in Chapter 4. This is an appropriate time, therefore, for you to re-examine Figures 4.4–4.8 and the commentary about them.

As a group, readiness workbooks give considerable attention at the beginning to auditory discrimination viewed as preparation for phonics. A typical page shows rows of pictures; a typical task for the child is to respond to a request like: "The first picture is a fan. Draw a circle around all the pictures in the row whose names start the way 'fan' starts." Even though work with auditory discrimination should help children hear that *see, sun, Saturday,* and *Sunday* start with the same sound, thus preparing them to learn the correspondence between *s* and /s/, the fact that basal workbooks attend to auditory discrimination for as long as three and sometimes even four and five years is indefensible.

Criticism of the prolonged attention stems from the fact that when a word is unfamiliar, readers hear nothing. All that is available to help is its spelling, plus the context. A second reason for questioning the amount of attention that auditory discrimination receives in commercial materials is that once children learn some letter-sound correspondences and achieve an understanding of the alphabetic nature of written words, the correspondences can be taught directly ("One sound that *a* stands for is /ă/."). Now the job for students is to remember the correspondences so that they can function in figuring out unfamiliar words.

It is likely that some basal series give what seems like unending attention to auditory discrimination because they go out of their way to avoid an explicit identification of sounds when letter-sound correspondences are taught. The avoidance is illustrated below in an abbreviated basal lesson in which the wording is changed but not the process by which this series—and others—teaches letter-sound correspondences. Because avoiding the direct identification of a sound is usually explained with a reference to the distortion of consonant sounds when they are produced apart from words, the lesson deals with *oo*. The lesson was chosen to show that indirect and obscure methods are used even with vowel sounds.

The teacher is told to put the familiar word *school* on the board, to have children read it, and to underline *oo*. The children are then asked to listen for the sound that *oo* stands for in *school*. This is followed by instructions to the teacher to use the same procedures with *book*, also familiar. At the end, the children are asked whether the sound for *oo* in *look* is the sound that *oo* stands for in *school*. (Basal manuals assume that children's responses are always correct.)

The lesson ends with a summary that goes something like: When two *o*'s are together, they stand for the sound you hear in *school* or for the sound in *book*. Listen to those words again: *school, book*. When you come to a word that has *oo* in it, you can tell what *oo* stands for by using the sounds of the other letters in the word. (Sounds for the "other letters" are taught in the same indirect way, which is why this type of instruction is referred to as implicit, as opposed to explicit, instruction.)

Unfortunately, basal series that do identify sounds directly often fail to distinguish between sounds that can be produced without major distortions and others that are impossible to produce. In the latter category are such blends as /ks/ and such single sounds as /ng/.

To sum up, then, the position here is that beginning work with phonics *should* allow time for attention to auditory discrimination. Once children have learned some letter-sound correspondences in the way illustrated in Chapter 4 and have achieved an understanding of the alphabetic nature of written words, attention to auditory discrimination can end. Additional time is thus available for the explicit identification of speech sounds and the letters that commonly record them.

Use of Rhyme

Leafing through the beginning workbooks in any basal series (and in non-basal workbooks) is enough to make clear that rhyming words are used to deal with the concept "same last sound." This has the unfortunate consequence of encouraging children to equate "words that end with the same sound" and "words that rhyme." The erroneous equation can be illustrated as follows.

If a teacher asks, "Do 'bat' and 'sat' end with the same sound?" children respond, "Yes." But if the question is, "Do 'bat' and 'get' end with the same sound?" the answer is likely to be, "No." Some teachers even report that once explicit attention goes to rhyme, it functions as a block to dealing with other sound tasks. That is, no matter what question teachers ask about words and sounds, children choose words that rhyme if they are named as possible answers.

Keeping all this in mind, the recommendation is to let children enjoy rhyme as they listen to, and sometimes memorize, pieces of text that dwell on rhyming words. Later, when the goal is to help students learn how to add and substitute sounds, words that rhyme can be used but not explicitly featured as rhyming words. Instead, the focus is on the initial part of the words. For instance:

Known words: an, say

Adding initial letter and sound to known word to decode such unknown words as:		Substituting initial letter and sound in known word to decode such unknown words as:	
can	fan	day	may
ran	tan	way	ray
man	ban	pay	bay

Why basal materials allot so much time to rhyme may have something to do with practices related to introducing vocabulary. How rhyming words are used in this context is illustrated in the recommendations that one manual makes for teaching *go*. The recommendation is approximated below.

The teacher is directed to write *gate* and *go* directly under each other and to have the children read *gate*. Subsequent questions and comments follow:

With what letter do these words begin?
Do you think both words begin with the same sound?
This new word begins like *gate* and rhymes with *no*.

It means the opposite of *stop.*
What is the new word?

Why a procedure like the one above—and it is not atypical—hardly promotes the kind of decoding ability that serves students well when they encounter unfamiliar words is too obvious to explain.

Content of Phonics Instruction

Subject matter considered to be necessary for decoders was identified in the previous chapter. Certain basal programs, however, offer much more. In one series, for example, children are eventually taught that *ou* stands for five different sounds, as is illustrated in *house, group, touch, dough,* and *bought.*

The position here is that the content covered in Chapter 8 is sufficient when ample time is spent on helping children learn how to replace a predicted sound with other sounds until they arrive at a recognizable word that fits a context. How to help students do that is described later in this chapter.

Blending Sounds

The ability to add one sound to others in order to generate a correct pronunciation (*an→ban*) is closely tied to the ability to synthesize or blend sounds. Blending is also useful in ways that are demonstrated below.

ēch	arm	ōts
ē	ar	ō
ēch	arm	ōt
		ōts

In spite of the importance of blending (1, 2, 7, 11, 17), even the basal series that recommend a direct, explicit identification of sounds and that teach much more content than Chapter 8 covers do not always include procedures for teaching blending. It seems to be taken for granted that children *can* blend—which is not correct (2). To illustrate, in one basal series, teachers are told to have the children notice the two vowel letters in the new word *like.* Even though blending has not received attention, the next recommendation is: Have the pupils pronounce *like.*

The fact that blending is omitted in those basal series that avoid the direct identification of sounds is not unexpected, because it is impossible to blend what has never been explicitly identified. Nonetheless, it is still common to find in these series such recommendations as encouraging students to try using just the consonants in a word in order to decode it. Although the use of consonant sounds is sufficient on some occasions, such use still requires the ability to blend—unless the context is so generous with help that the consonants are used only to validate a conclusion reached by using contextual cues. How to help students with blending is illustrated later in the chapter on the assumption that blending ability is the product of instruction and practice.

QUESTIONS ABOUT AN INSTRUCTIONAL PROGRAM

The previous chapter dealt with the question, What needs to be taught to promote proficient decoding? The present chapter addresses two other questions:

1. When should each component in a phonics program be taught?
2. How should the teaching proceed?

Phonics Content: When to Teach It

The need for students to see the value for reading of what they are learning and doing has been underscored in earlier chapters. Chapter 3, for instance, portrayed intentional, planned instruction as follows:

Components of a Lesson

1. Clarification of the objective and of how achieving it contributes to reading ability
2. Explicit instruction
3. Practice: supervised and independent
4. Application of what has been taught in whatever students are reading

Taken seriously, the importance of students' experiencing the value of instruction and practice means that *usefulness* is one of the most important criteria to consider when a sequence for phonics is planned. Admittedly, opportunities for children to use what is taught at the very beginning are considerably less than they are when more content has been covered. Even at the beginning, however, the promise of future opportunities merits explicit attention. Knowing the correspondence between *p* and /p/, for instance, children should be helped to see that such knowledge will eventually assist them in reading (and writing) words like *puppy, prince, play,* and *paper,* all of which can be displayed on a chalkboard and read by a teacher.

As stated in the previous chapter, consonant letters and the sounds they represent typically constitute subject matter for beginning instruction.* Exactly when each consonant ought to be taught should be affected

---

* To avoid the need for children to work at remembering the name of a letter at the time its sound is taught, the name should be known at the level of automaticity. In this way, total attention can go to what is new, namely, to the sound that the letter represents. Letter-naming ability also facilitates teacher-child communication when a teacher makes such observations as, "These two words are the same except that one ends with *d* and the other with *t*"(15).

by the words children are learning with whole word methodology and, in addition, by the frequency of their appearance in words. The latter criterion explains why *t*, *n*, and *s* merit early attention and why letters like *z*, *q(u)*, *x*, and *j* do not.

Similarity of sounds is another factor that must be taken into account if confusion about sounds is to be minimized. This criterion suggests that if the correspondence between *t* and /t/ is taught, subsequent instruction should *not* focus on the sound that *d* represents, because /d/ and /t/ are similar. Or, to cite another illustration, if children are learning that *p* stands for /p/, the correspondence between *b* and /b/ should not be taught next. To do that invites confusion.

At some point, the long and short vowel sounds require attention. Although the long sounds for *a, e, i, o,* and *u* are easier to learn, they are less useful to know. The second characteristic is the reason most commercially prepared materials deal with the short sounds first.

Once children know some vowel sounds, they are ready to understand and then apply generalizations that describe when the various sounds are likely to occur. At this point, single-syllable words should be used both to illustrate the content of the generalizations and for practice in applying the content. Now, application requires other work with blending sounds to produce syllables.

Eventually, students have to be able to cope on their own with multisyllabic words. They thus need to learn generalizations that help in getting unfamiliar words divided into syllables. This is the time, too, for offering help in putting syllables together in order to end up with a word.

Meanwhile, instruction with letter-sound correspondences continues. Now the concern is consonant and vowel digraphs and single consonants that occur infrequently in words. All the while, instructional time continues to go to blending sounds, eventually reaching the point when flexible application of what has been taught is a key concern.

The critical importance of flexibility suggests adding the reminder that concern for phonics instruction should not be so great as to obscure the fact that decoding unknown words is for the purpose of making sense out of connected text. Viewed from that perspective, the need for readers to use all available cues comes to the forefront. So, too, does the requirement of providing contexts when students are learning to use what phonics instruction has covered.

All this makes it an appropriate time for you to review Figure 7.1, which summarizes a sequence for dealing with both contextual and graphophonic cues.

Phonics Content: How to Teach It

Whenever phonics instruction is considered, a distinction must be made between (a) what successful decoders *know*, and (b) what successful decoders *do*. The distinction is necessary because it allows for decisions about the kind of instruction likely to be effective. Specifically, if a certain letter-sound correspondence is to be taught, productive instruction is likely to be composed of some combination of explanations, descriptions, and examples. On the other hand, if blending sounds to produce a syllable is the goal, then the instruction that has the best chance of succeeding is modeling—that is, verbalizing and acting out a particular strategy, in this case for blending.

Because of the importance of the distinctions just made, the sample lessons that follow are concerned with helping students *know* something. Subsequent sections provide sample lessons for helping students *do* something.

SAMPLE LESSONS: WHAT DECODERS NEED TO KNOW

One thing decoders must know are letter-sound correspondences; consequently, they are included in the initial samples of instruction. Because the first sample deals with a consonant sound, a problem related to consonant sounds is addressed first.

Teaching Consonant Sounds

The problem is the fact that consonant sounds—in particular, what phoneticians refer to as "stop sounds"—are noticeably distorted when produced apart from words. Try, if you will, saying the following sounds aloud. As you do, you will find yourself adding to each something that approximates a short *u* sound:

Stop Sounds

/b/	/p/
/d/	/t/
/g/	/k/

Why speech sounds, including vowel sounds, are altered when produced alone is explained well by Stott (13):

It is part of the very essence of language that sounds are uttered in very rapid sequences which become words. Each sound has such a fleeting existence that it is not truly reproducible outside the context of a word. Wresting it out of its natural place makes it something different, altering its length and the amount of breath put into it, and sometimes making it into a syllable by the addition of another sound. (p. 11)

It is not necessary to be a phonetician to understand, and agree with, Stott's observations. However, all one has to do is try to teach a sound to realize that some children *require* explicit identifications. That is, they require statements like: "All these words begin with *f*, so they all begin with the same sound—with the sound that *f* stands for. The sound for *f* is /f/. You'll hear /f/ at the beginning of each of these words when I read them again. Listen: *first, fall, fun, fence. . . .*"

The distortion of consonant sounds is one reason some instructors support *implicit* instruction when sounds are taught. This type of teaching requires children to extract a given sound from a spoken word, or, more commonly, from several spoken words that include the sound. In the case of the example just referred to, the underlying assumption of implicit instruction is that children *can* hear /f/ when they listen to *first, fall, fun,* and *fence.* This is the case even though the little research that has been done on this topic supports a point made above: Children are not always able to extract the separate sounds that compose words (2).

A second reason commonly offered in support of implicit instruction is that it fosters independent learning. That is, as children have experiences listening for a certain sound and associating it with a given letter, they are engaging in an activity that encourages them to make additional letter-sound associations on their own. Although this is highly desirable, nothing exists in the research literature that provides evidence for such a consequence.

Having said all this, the question to pose now is, How *should* letter-sound correspondences be taught?

When it is kept in mind that phonics is a means to an end, the guideline to follow is as simple as this: Use whatever works. When the importance of making initial instruction meaningful is also kept in mind, another guideline surfaces, namely, use words children can read so that the part of the words being singled out will be better understood, as will the nature of alphabetic writing. All this can be summarized as follows:

> At the very beginning, use known words (e.g., *to, take, turn, toy*) to call attention to the connection between a given letter (*t*) and a given sound (/t/). If children are able to extract that sound from the words, fine. If not, identify the sound for them. Once children seem to understand how spellings and pronunciations are linked, it is time for *explicit* instruction in which sounds are directly identified. This will be easier for many students; it also allows for covering content faster.

To clarify the summary statement, a sample lesson follows, which deals with a consonant sound. The second lesson described focuses on the sound that a consonant digraph represents.

Sample Lessons: Consonant Sounds

Before the first lesson is described, some preliminary comments are made in order to make the description more meaningful.

To begin, the teacher's goals are twofold: (a) to help a group of children begin to understand the nature of alphabetic writing and (b) to teach that *s* stands for /s/. Words beginning with *s* that the children learned from the teacher's use of whole word methodology illustrate the sound. (Words starting with *s* are selected because in short words, the easiest sound to perceive as a distinct sound is the one in the initial position. In contrast, the most difficult sound to hear is one in the medial position.)

In the lesson to be described, the children demonstrate their ability to extract /s/ from the illustrative words by naming other words that begin with /s/. For that reason, the teacher does not identify /s/ directly. The lesson, therefore, exemplifies *implicit* instruction. If, to the contrary, the children showed no evidence of having heard /s/ in the illustrative words, the teacher would have said something like: "The sound that *s* stands for in all these words is /s/. What sound does *s* stand for? . . . Listen for that sound at the beginning of all these words. . . . " In this case, the instruction is *explicit*.

One further point needs to be made. Because the children are just beginning to learn that letters stand for sounds, the value for reading of knowing that *s* records /s/ is not referred to until the end of the lesson.

The lesson itself follows:

Teacher: Some words you know are on the board. (The words *saw, six,* and *some* are printed in a column to make apparent that all start with *s*.) What's the same about all these words? . . . Kathryn?

Kathryn: They all have *s* at the first.

Teacher: Yes, the first letter in each is *s*. Please read these words, everybody.

Group: *Saw, six, some.*

Teacher: Did anyone *hear* something that's the same about all these words when you said them? . . . No? . . . Let's read them again. See if you hear the same sound at the beginning of all these words. Please read them and listen for the sound that all of them start with.

Group: *Saw, six, some.*

Teacher: All the words you just read start with the same sound because they all start with the letter *s*. Listen for the sound that *s* makes in all these words. Please read them again to listen for the sound for *s*.

Group: *Saw, six, some.*

Teacher: Can anyone think of another word that starts with the sound you hear at the beginning of *saw, six,* and *some?*

David: *Say* starts that way.

Teacher: Yes, David, it does. *Saw, say.* I'll write *say* under *some.* (Prints *say* under *some.*) Now there are four words that start with the same letter and the same sound. Please read them.

Group: *Saw, six, some, say.*

Teacher: How about one more word that starts with the sound you hear at the beginning of *saw* and *six*.

Amy: *Cynthia* starts that way.

Teacher: Yes, it does. *Saw, Cynthia.* But, Amy, there's something different about *Cynthia.* You'll see the difference when I write it. (Prints *Cynthia* apart from the other words.) *Cynthia* begins with the sound we're talking about, but it doesn't start with *s.* With what letter *does* it begin?

Group: C.

Teacher: Yes, *Cynthia* is a girl's name that starts with *c.* Later, we'll talk about other words like *Cynthia.* For now, let's stay with words that start with *s* and that begin with the sound you hear at the beginning of *saw.* Can anyone think of another word that starts the way *saw* begins? (Teacher erases *Cynthia.*)

Fran: *Sucker* is another word, and so is *soup.*

Teacher: Fran, you certainly know lots of words that start with the sound that's at the beginning of *saw.*

Bonnie: I know one, too. *Soap.*

Teacher: Wait a minute now until I get all these words on the board. (Adds *sucker, soup,* and *soap* to the column.) Wow! We have seven words that start with the sound of *s.* Listen. I'll read them all so that you can hear that sound. If you want, read the words with me. Let's go. *Saw, six, some, say, sucker, soup, soap.* Try to remember the sound that *s* makes. That way, when you see a word you don't know and it starts with *s,* at least you'll know the first sound. I'm going to write some words I don't think you know. Then I'll read them. When I do, you'll hear that they all begin with the same sound—with the sound that goes with the letter *s.* (Prints *sox, sun,* and *silly.*) With what letter do all these words start?

Group: S.

Teacher: Because they begin with *s,* each one starts with the sound that goes with *s.* You'll hear that sound at the beginning when I tell you what these words are. Listen. *Sox, sun, silly.*

And so the implicit instruction ends. Let's move on to another lesson whose objective is to teach the sound that *sh* represents. The students receiving the instruction know a sizable number of letter-sound correspondences and have experienced the value of that knowledge in figuring out new words. Because the teacher directly identifies the sound that *sh* records, the lesson illustrates *explicit* instruction.

Teacher: You know a lot about the sounds that letters stand for, and you've learned that knowing about sounds helps with words you can't at first read. Knowing about sounds also helps you remember new words so that you'll know them the next time you see them. In the story you'll be reading today, some of the words start with *sh*. (Prints *sh* on the board.) One of these words is a new one. The others are words you should know. In any case, I want to say something special about *sh*. You know the sound that *s* stands for. You hear it at the beginning of words like these. (Prints *sun* and *seven*.) Please read these two words.

Group: *Sun, seven.*

Teacher: You also know the sound for *h*. I'll write some words that start with *h*. (Prints *here* and *how*.) What are these words?

Group: *Here, how.*

Teacher: The point I want to make is that when *s* and *h* are together as they are in words like *shut* and *show* (prints the known words *shut* and *show*), the two letters have a special sound that isn't like the sound for *s* or like the sound for *h*. The sound that *sh* makes in words is the one we sometimes use when we want somebody to be quiet. The sound that *sh* makes is /sh/. What's the sound for *sh?*

Group: /sh/.

Teacher: Correct. Please read these two words now (points to *shut* and *show*) and listen for the beginning sound in each.

Group: *Shut, show.*

Teacher: You know other words that *end* with /sh/. I'll write some. Don't say anything, please, until I finish writing. (Prints *wish, push,* and *dash*.) Please wait until I call on you. (Points to *wish*.) What's this word, Carol?

Carol: *Wish.*

Teacher: Read this word for us, Tom. (Points to *push*.)

Tom: It says *push*.

Teacher: How about this word? (Points to *dash*.) Who can tell us what it says? Jerry.

Jerry: *Dash.*

Teacher: The story you'll be reading later is about a little girl who is very sick. A new word tells what she has. This is the word. (Prints *rash*.) What word that we just read is very much like this new one? Look at the three words that end with *sh* that we just read. Which one is like the new word?

Margie: *Dash*. The new word is *rash*, like what I had when I had the measles.

Teacher: You're right, Margie. This word is *rash*. Everyone, what is it?

Group: *Rash.*

Sue: I don't think the girl in the story has measles because when I had measles, I didn't get very sick.

Margie: When *I* had measles, I had a very bad case and was *really* sick.

Teacher: You'll just have to wait to find out what the sick girl in the story has. Right now, I want you to look at another new word. This one starts with *sh*, so you should know its beginning sound.

	(Prints *shock*.) Can someone read this word? ... It starts with /sh/ and ends with /k/. Can anyone read it now?
Gary:	*Shucks!*
Teacher:	Not quite, Gary, but you're close. I'll write *shucks* under the new word. (Prints *shucks* under *shock*.)
Margie:	I know it. It says "shock."
Teacher:	Correct. What is this word, everyone?
Group:	*Shock.*
Teacher:	What does "shock" mean? Gary?
Gary:	It means what you get from electricity.
Teacher:	That *is* one meaning. *Shock* has another meaning in the story. This is the sentence in which you'll first see *shock*. It should help with the meaning. When I write the sentence, you'll see that the new word has *ed* at the end. (Prints *Her mother was shocked when she got the news about Nancy.*) First of all, let's have Sue read the sentence.
Sue:	"Her mother was shocked when she got the news about Nancy."
Teacher:	Nancy is the name of the girl in the story who's sick. With the help of this sentence, can someone explain what *shocked* means?
Tom:	It means the mother is crying and stuff like that because she thinks her daughter is dying.
Teacher:	Well, we don't know for sure, Tom, if Nancy is dying, but what you said about "shocked" is correct. The mother is surprised at something she hears about Nancy and maybe she does cry. Mostly, "shocked" means "surprised," because something happens when you don't expect it to happen or you're surprised because somebody says something that you just didn't expect to hear. Since the word in the story is *shocked*, let me write that. (Erases *shucks* and prints *shocked* directly under *shock*. Points to *shock*.) Please look at this word, everyone. What is it?
Group:	*Shock.*
Teacher:	When *ed* is added to *shock*, what does it say?
Group:	*Shocked.*
Teacher:	Yes, *shocked*. It begins with the letters *sh* and with the sound— what sound do *shock* and *shocked* begin with, everybody?
Group:	/sh/.
Teacher:	Yes. Remember that when *s* is followed by *h*, the two letters together stand for one sound. *S* and *h* stand for /sh/. Listen for that sound as you read all the words on the board.

Teaching Generalizations

To help students understand one way to divide unknown words into syllables is the reason for the next lesson. To achieve that objective, a generalization is taught: When a word has one consonant and there is a vowel before and after it, the first vowel is in one syllable and the consonant and the vowel that follows it are in another syllable. (Words in which *x* is the consonant will be considered in another lesson.) Some comments that apply to any lesson dealing with a generalization follow.

To begin, even though every generalization can be stated in a variety of ways, critical details must be included. With the generalization just cited, necessary details are the VCV pattern and the syllabic division indicated by V CV. Further, because the generalization is applied to unknown words, it must describe visual cues.

The third point is that even though teachers *must* be able to verbalize a generalization so that they can state, explain, and discuss it, the same ability is desirable but not essential for students. What *is* necessary is that they understand the generalization and can apply it. Ronald Wardhaugh has written effectively about this:

> He [the child] may not be able to verbalize the rule any more than he could tell you how he ties his shoelaces; but just as he can demonstrate that he knows the rules for tying shoelaces by tying shoelaces, so he can demonstrate his knowledge of the rules for pronouncing c *by reading* city *and* cat *correctly. His knowledge of the rules is demonstrated by his performance and it is unnecessary for him to learn to verbalize a statement about what he has learned, that is, about what he knows. (16, p. 136)*

The lesson about the VCV pattern, as well as the lesson that is described afterward, are presented in a format designed to highlight the importance of teachers' making sure that students are ready to achieve a selected objective. Prerequisites, therefore, are identified.

Sample Lesson: Generalization for Syllabication

Prerequisites: Students (a) know what is meant by "consonant," "vowel," and "syllable," and (b) understand the significance of syllables for decoding.

Teaching the Lesson: The teacher starts by commenting, "Three of the new words in what you'll be reading today about pollution are the same in the sense that all have a vowel followed by a consonant followed by a vowel. To help you remember that, I'll use some shorthand. I'll write three letters for vowel, consonant, and vowel."

VCV

"I'll come back to these letters later because you can use them to get the three new words divided into syllables so that you can figure out what they say. Right now, I'm going to show you words you know that also have a vowel followed by a consonant followed by a vowel. They're on this chart. Please don't read them aloud yet."

music
open
paper
final

"Okay. You've had a chance to look at these words. Please read them together. . . . I'm going to ask how many syllables are in each word, so, keeping that question in mind, please read the words again. . . . How many syllables does each of these words have? . . . Correct. Two. The first word is "music." Who can spell the first syllable? Raise your hands, please. Emily. . . . Right. The letters m and u make up the first syllable. That means s, i, c is the second syllable. I'm going to use a slash mark to show where the first syllable ends and the second begins."

Eventually the chart shows:

mu / sic
o / pen
pa / per
fi / nal

"Please look carefully at these words. Like other words, they have consonants and vowels. Look at the first syllable in these four words. What kind of a letter is at the end? . . . Fine. The first syllable ends with a vowel. Okay, I have another question. Look at the words again. What kind of a letter starts the second syllable in all of them? . . . Right again. The second syllable starts with a consonant. Now my question is, 'What kind of a letter comes after the consonant?' . . . That's right. In every case, a vowel comes after the consonant. Let me draw a line under all these letters."

mu / sic
o / pen
pa / per
fi / nal

"In each word, I underlined a vowel followed by a consonant followed by a vowel. That's why I wrote VCV on the board earlier. When a word has this series of letters, the first syllable ends with the first vowel. See? This is exactly what happens in *music, open, paper,* and *final.* In *music,* the vowel letter *u* ends the first syllable and *s* and *i* are in the second syllable."

After giving similar attention to the three remaining words, the teacher says, "Let me put all this together. As I do, I'll point to certain parts of each of the four words. Please look at them so that you'll see where I'm pointing. This is what you need to remember. When a word has a vowel followed by a consonant followed by a vowel, the first syllable ends after the first vowel. Let me go back to my shorthand over here. I'll show where that syllable break comes."

VCV
V CV

"Please use these letters to answer my next questions. They're about three *new* words. Even if you can't read them, you should know where they divide into syllables. I've written the new words on this paper. Look here, please."

emit
nation
ozone

"The first word is spelled *e, m, i, t.* Do you see anything about these letters that's the same as the letters in words like *music* and *open?* . . . That's absolutely right. This new word has a vowel, *e,* followed by a consonant, *m,* followed by a vowel, *i.* What did we say about words like this? . . . Yes, the first syllable ends with the first vowel, in this case with *e.* . . . "

Similar procedures are used with *nation* and *ozone.* The instruction part of the lesson thus ends with a list that shows:

e / mit
na / tion
o / zone

After the words are divided into syllables and the generalization for syllabication is restated, attention shifts to how the words are pronounced and to what they mean. How they might be related to pollution is considered next.

Sample Lesson: Generalization for Vowel Sounds

Why the students just referred to know the sound to assign to the vowel in the initial syllables of *emit, nation,* and *ozone* can be accounted for by the fact that, earlier, they received instruction like that described next. In this instance, the objective is to teach the generalization: A single vowel in final position usually stands for its long sound.

Prerequisites: Students (a) know the long and short vowel sounds, (b) know what a syllable is, (c) understand the meaning of "final position," and (d) understand that "final position" refers to the placement of a letter in a syllable.[*]

Teaching the Lesson: After reviewing the long and short vowel sounds, the teacher prints five familiar words on the board and asks the group to read them.*

me

no

she

go

hi

Once the words are read, the teacher probes: "How many vowels are in *me?* . . . Which of its sounds does *e* stand for in *me*, the long or the short?" After asking similar questions about the remaining words, the teacher calls the students' attention to the placement of the single vowel by asking, "Where is the one vowel in all these words?"

To synthesize the relevant details, the teacher continues, "You've told me three things that are the same about all these words. You said they have one vowel, the vowel is at the end, and it stands for its long sound. Noticing all those things about words you don't know will help you figure out what they say. Now, whenever you see a word that you can't read and it has one vowel letter that's at the end, you'll know that it will have its long sound— or at least most of the time the vowel will stand for its long sound. I'm going to write all those things on the board to help you remember them." As the teacher writes, she reads:

1. one vowel letter
2. at the end
3. long sound

To show how this pertains to words in the selection that the children just read, the teacher goes through it with them. As they do this, words that entered into the lesson are found (*she* and *me*) as well as two others that did not (*he*, *so*). The teacher also discusses a word in the selection in which a single, final vowel does not have the long sound (*to*). This is done to emphasize that words must make sense—that calling *to* "toe" does not make any sense in *They ran to the house.*

The generalization taught in this lesson will be reviewed the next day when *silo, acorn, stable,* and *pony* are among the new words introduced in preparation for reading a story that takes place on a farm.

---

* Words that have all five vowel letters are preferable; however, suitable one-syllable words ending with *a* and *u* are nonexistent. One-syllable words are useful for simplifying the instruction.

SAMPLE LESSONS: WHAT DECODERS
NEED TO DO

The lessons described thus far deal with what decoders need to know. The same lessons also imply the need for students to be able to *do* something with what they know. For instance, in order to recognize the new word *shout* as quickly as possible, students have to be able to blend /sh/ and the known word *out*. Or, to cite other illustrations, they have to be able to blend /s/ and /ī/ and, on another occasion, /s/ and /ā/ in order to achieve, in these cases, pronunciations for the initial syllables in new words like *silent* and *saber*.

At its simplest level, blending is adding a sound to the initial or final parts of known words:

out*	eat	in	ape
shout	seat	chin	shape
ten	see	car	ran
tent	seen	card	ranch

Later, initial and final additions work together, as illustrated below.

can	or	in	car	ran	an
scan	for	pin	scar	ranch	and
scant	fort	pinch	scarf	branch	stand

The lesson described next is about blending sounds. Because blending is *doing* something, the instruction consists of modeling.

Sample Lesson: Adding Final Sounds to Known Words

In the lesson that follows, the teacher starts by reviewing the sound that *t* records and having the children read known words that are on the board written in a row rather than a column: *ten, for, an, car*. The teacher then proceeds by modeling blending with the expectation that the demonstration will begin to clarify the nature of blending sufficiently well that the children will eventually be able to do it themselves.

---

* Some commercial materials provide practice in adding initial sounds by using graphemic (grǎ phē′ mǐc) bases. A *graphemic base*, sometimes referred to as a *phonogram*, is composed of a vowel and one or more consonants. Examples are *-ake*, *-ine*, and *-ight*. Use of *-ight*, for example, allows for adding consonant sounds to produce words like *night*, *right*, and *bright*.

Teacher:	Please read this first word again.
Group:	*Ten.*
Teacher:	This morning I'm going to show you how you can use the word *ten*, plus the sound for *t*, to learn a new word. The new word I'm thinking of is spelled *t, e, n*—just like the word *ten*—but this word has *t* at the end. It looks like this. (Prints *tent* directly under *ten*.) This is what I do to learn what this second word is. (Points to *tent*.) I say "ten" and then add /t/. Listen as I do that. *Ten, tent.* Did you hear me add /t/ to the end of *ten*?
Group:	Yes.
Steve:	I know what a tent is. You use a tent at night when you camp outside.
Teacher:	Yes, a tent is like a home away from home. Now, Steve, you not only know what a tent is but you also know what the word that says "tent" looks like. Okay, everybody. Look up here, please. Read these two words again.
Group:	*Ten, tent.*
Teacher:	Let's read them one more time to make sure you hear yourself adding /t/ to the word *ten*.
Group:	*Ten, tent.*

The lesson deals in a similar way with *for* and *fort, an* and *ant,* and *car* and *cart.* How adding sounds to known words helps with unknown words is emphasized intermittently to make apparent the usefulness of what is being done.

Depending on how the first lesson goes, a subsequent one might attend to pairs of known and unknown words in ways that focus on adding a variety of final letters and sounds. For example:

see	her	far	four	too	pin
seed	herd	farm	fourth	tooth	pinch

Lessons that deal with adding sounds to the *initial* part of known words proceed in a similar fashion. The kinds of words that might figure in such lessons are illustrated below:

at	end	cat	it	car	air
fat	bend	scat	fit	scar	hair

low	cab	tack	lump	rug	our
blow	scab	stack	slump	shrug	scour

Blending Sounds to Produce Syllables

Once students have been helped to add sounds both to the beginning and to the end of known words, they are ready to learn how to blend sounds in unknown words to produce syllables. The syllables are then combined into a word. At first, however, blending is confined to one-syllable words.

So that you will understand what students need to do in order to decode a one-syllable word like *such* when a word like *much* is not in their reading vocabulary and the context in which *such* occurs is not very helpful (*Such a day!*), the following guidelines should be studied.

Blending Sounds to Produce Syllables

1. The first job with an unfamiliar word is to consider its syllables, because the syllable is the unit of analysis for applying generalizations. In the case of *such*, the presence of one vowel indicates one syllable.
2. Thoughts now turn to the likely sounds for *s*, *u*, and *ch*.
3. Once decisions are made about the sounds, it is time to blend them into a syllable, in this case into a word. Because consonant sounds are distorted when produced apart from words, the recommended sequence for blending begins with the first vowel in the syllable, progresses by adding preceding consonant sounds, and concludes by following the sequence of the remaining letters. All this is demonstrated below:

$$\boxed{\text{sŭch}}$$

ŭ
sŭ
sŭch

4. Returning to the context, the decoder decides whether the word generated is correct, that is, is a recognizable word that makes sense in the context *Such a day!*

One postscript to the above is this: Had the unknown word been *each*, the same steps would be taken to decode it. However, because *each* starts with a vowel, the blending procedure directly reflects the sequence of the letters:

$$\boxed{\text{ēach}}$$

ēa
ēach

To clarify still further the recommended sequence for blending sounds, more examples are shown on the next page.

lăp	ăct	sōap	mēte	voice	shawl
ă	ă	ōa	ē	oi	aw
lă	ăc	sōa	mē	voi	shaw
lăp	ăct	sōap	mēte	voice	shawl

brŭsh	rōōm	turn	ouch	hŭnt	āce
ŭ	ōō	ur	ou	ŭ	ā
brŭ	rōō	tur	ouch	hŭ	āce
brŭsh	rōōm	turn		hŭn	
				hŭnt	

The examples of blending procedures listed above should make apparent the relationship between blending and earlier lessons both for adding final sounds to known words (*ten → tent*) and for adding initial sounds to known words (*at → fat*).

Sample Lessons: Blending

To show how blending sounds to generate syllables can be taught, only the modeling part of lessons is described below.

The first lesson is offered to students who can add sounds to known words and who are now ready to use that ability to blend sounds to decode unknown words. For the example of modeling that follows, the unknown word is *owl* embedded in the context *You can hear an owl, but you can't see one in the dark.*

> This is the name of something that makes noise. The *o* and *w* act like one vowel, so there's only one syllable. Let's see. I'll try the sound for *ow* that's like the sound for *ou*. Then I'll add the sound that *l* stands for. That would be *ow → owl.* Oh sure. It's "owl." I always thought you could see an owl's eyes in the dark. Maybe not.

As part of a lesson with another group, a teacher models how to decode *ramp*, found in the sentence *In place of stairs, a ramp was used to get into the new house.*

> There's only one vowel, so this word is one syllable. One vowel not at the end probably means a short sound. That would be *ă → ră → răm → rămp. Ramp.* Probably it's a board. I've seen that with new houses. In place of stairs, a ramp was used to get into the new house.

The modeling done for *ramp* is recommended when words such as *damp* and *stamp* are not known or are not recalled when *ramp* needs to be figured out. This point is made because using initial consonant substitutions (damp → ramp, or stamp → damp) is more efficient than the procedure modeled. Nonetheless, what was modeled is something students need to know how to do when helpful words are either unknown or, as often happens, are not recalled when they would be useful.

The next example of modeling focuses on a multisyllabic word, specifically on *umpire* found in *An umpire is not always liked.* As was true of the previous illustrations of modeling, this example is offered to students as a complement to what is written on the board. By the time the modeling is done by the teacher, the chalkboard displays the following:

An <u>umpire</u> is not always liked.

| umpire | ŭm | fire | úm píre |
| um/pire | ŭ → ŭm | pire | úm pire |

The modeling itself is portrayed below.

This word is the name of something that isn't liked all the time. That doesn't help very much. There's *m* and *p* with vowels before and after. I'll divide it between them. One vowel not at the end. I'll try the short sound for *u*. I know the sound for *m*, so that's ŭ → ŭm. I can't think of any word that starts with "ŭm." I had better look at the second syllable. Oh, that looks like *fire*. Maybe it says "pire." Úmpíre. Oh, úmpire. An umpire is not always liked. Boy, that's for sure.

The modeling just portrayed allows for making two points about decoding words composed of more than one syllable:

1. After a word is divided into syllables with the help of visual cues, the pronunciation of one or more of them may result from a simple substitution—for instance, *fire* → *pire*. (Some decoders might have used another substitution for the first syllable in *umpire: am* → *um*.)
2. The pronunciation of each syllable, plus contextual cues, may be enough to bring to mind a word that is known in its spoken form. That is helpful, because the decoding process tends to make each syllable sound like a separate word (*úm píre*).

The next example of modeling allows for a demonstration of shortcuts for decoding, which are important to avoid interrupting the comprehension process. In this case, the unknown word is *bacon*. The sentence in which it occurs is *They had bacon and eggs.*

This must be something to eat. It's not *bread* because that ends with *d*. Let's see. The *c* has vowels before and after it, so I'll divide it between *a* and *c*. One vowel at the end might mean the long sound. That would be *ā* → *bā*. Oh, *bácon!* Bacon and eggs. They had bacon and eggs.

These brief thoughts allow for three further observations about decoding:

1. When contextual cues are generous, highly restrictive constraints are placed on the word being decoded. Sometimes they are so restrictive that only one word is possible. At other times, as was true of *bacon*, constraints are enough to make partial decoding productive.
2. Life's experiences and the knowledge they bring affect decoding. This means that students who have had a meal of bacon and eggs find it easier to decode *bacon* in the context cited than do others who have not.
3. Decoding one word helps with others. Having figured out *bacon*, a decoder might find it fairly easy later to figure out *beacon*. And the decoder who successfully coped with *umpire* should encounter no major problems if *empire* or *vampire* needs to be read later.

To allow for attention to other reminders, further work with a multisyllabic word is covered with a detailed explanation rather than with modeling. This time the unknown word is *infect,* and it is the only unfamiliar word in the sentence, *I don't want to infect you with my cold.*

As always, the decoder's first consideration is the context. This one indicates the troublesome word is a verb and is related to having a cold. It's something that the person with the cold doesn't want to do to somebody else.

The next focus is the word's spelling, in particular, what the spelling suggests for syllabication. Consideration of all the letters and their sequence suggests a syllabic division between *n* and *f* (*in fect*). The two vowels indicate that two syllables are the maximum number.

Having considered the syllables, the decoder's next job is to deal with the pronunciation of each one. With *infect,* knowing the word *in* provides the pronunciation of the first syllable directly. The presence of one vowel in the second syllable, which is not in final position, suggests trying a short sound for *e*. The *c* probably stands for its hard sound because it is followed by a consonant. With all this in mind, the decoder proceeds to blend sounds to learn the pronunciation of the second syllable: *ĕ* → *fĕ* → *fĕc* → *fĕct*.

Having arrived at possible pronunciations for the two syllables, the decoder is ready to consider which syllable is stressed. If *infect* is familiar orally, the sounds derived from the analysis (ĭn fĕćt) suggest both the pronunciation (infĕćt) and meaning. The achieved pronunciation is also a word that makes sense in the context.

What has now been described in some detail is summarized in Figure

Focus for the Decoder	Concern of the Decoder
Context	1. What makes sense?
Word	2. Syllabication
Each syllable	3. Letter-sound correspondence 4. Blending
Word	5. Stressed syllable?
Context	6. Does this word fit the context?

Figure 9.1   A Strategy for Decoding

9.1. Portrayed there is an outline of a strategy for decoding—that is, a systematic plan for using what is known (5). Initially, the strategy should be modeled by a teacher. To help students use it, the steps listed in Figure 9.1 can be printed on a large chart. Eventually, as students acquire greater ability in decoding, the steps will be taken practically simultaneously. Some might even be skipped. All this is to say that the discrete steps that characterize the acquisition of a new ability (strategic decoding) do not always characterize the exercise of that ability once it has been acquired.

Flexible Decoding

Assuming the word causing problems for a reader is regularly spelled and is familiar orally, the strategy depicted in Figure 9.1 is highly successful in achieving correct pronunciations. Irregularly spelled words, on the other hand, require a fix-up strategy. That is, decoders must have a plan for using alternative sounds when predicted sounds result either in an unsuitable word or in a nonword. That is why proficient decoding can be characterized as problem solving that proceeds with a systematic plan to achieve a solution that may be realized directly and quickly, or only after trial-and-error efforts.

To illustrate both direct success and trial-and-error efforts, let's say that the first time students see *flood* in print, it is in a very helpful context: *The rain keeps coming. It will flood all the basements.* In this case, the sounds that *f, l,* and *d* record, plus the students' ability to blend, plus their knowledge of basements and the fact that some get flooded when heavy rain persists, are likely to be sufficient to allow for a correct conclusion about the pronunciation of *flood* even though the double-*o* represents neither the long sound (cōōl) nor the short sound (cŏŏk).

Let's consider a different situation in which *flood* appears in a less revealing context: *Nobody wants to think about a flood.* In this instance, a reader should conclude from the context that the unknown word is the name of something. However, since many nouns make sense, the spelling of *flood* assumes importance. Noting *oo*, the reader should first try "flo͞od," then "flo͝od." Both should also be abandoned because neither produces a real word. What to do?

With one reader, trying the incorrect sounds for *oo* may be enough to suggest the correct one. With another, a trial-and-error process may be required in which other vowel sounds are used until something clicks—that is, until a recognizable, sensible word results. More specifically, the second reader tries "flŏd," "flăd," "flĕd" (a real word but not one that fits the context), "flĭd," and finally "flŭd." (Trying short vowel sounds first makes sense because of the absence of a final *e*.)

The message inherent in these illustrations is that successful decoders work differently but always with flexibility. The message for teachers is that flexible procedures do not just happen; they require instruction, modeling, and practice.

Substituting Sounds

As pointed out earlier, the ability to blend sounds to reveal the pronunciation of an unknown word (*ā → ācé*) has its roots in the ability to add sounds to known words (*it → kit; hum → hump*). On the other hand, the ability to try alternative sounds when the predicted one is nonproductive (*flăd, flĕd, flĭd, flŏd, flŭd*) is an extension of the ability to substitute sounds in known words. Types of possible substitutions are specified in Figure 9.2.

As is true of adding sounds, the only way to teach students how to substitute sounds is by demonstrating the process. Done often enough, demonstrations are usually effective.

Sample Lessons: Flexible Use of Sounds

Except for single-syllable, regularly spelled words (e.g., *nap, cool, dire, lymph*), the result of decoding is best described as an estimate of a word's pronunciation. When the word is multisyllabic and regularly spelled, the estimate is close enough to the correct pronunciation that all that may be required is an adjustment in stress (e.g., *tóx íc → tóx ic; món sóon → mon soón; í cón → í con*). At times, an adjustment will also include use of the schwa sound (e.g., *cár pét → cár pət; á wáy→ ə wáy; aṁ bú lánce → ăṁ bu lənce*). These adjustments are easy to make when the words are in the reader's oral vocabulary; they are even easier when contextual cues are available.

Oral vocabularies and contexts also help with irregularly spelled words, as demonstrated earlier with *flood*. That example of decoding also brought to the forefront the importance of a reader's ability to replace predicted sounds with others. Because such replacements involve doing something, students' ability to make them is achieved most readily when teachers model replacements. How teachers can do that is illustrated next. In

Known Word	Unknown Word	Substitution
make	cake	initial consonant
ice	ace	initial vowel
arm	art	final consonant
he	hi	final vowel
act	ant	medial consonant
bench	bunch	medial vowel

Figure 9.2 Substituting Sounds

this lesson, the unknown irregularly spelled word is *prove,* which is in the sentence *That doesn't prove a thing.*

> The sentence tells me the word I can't read is a verb, but that's about it. I had better take a look at the spelling. I can't think of any word that makes sense that starts with *pr.* Let's see. This word ends with *ve.* That means that /v/ is the last sound, that the *e* is silent, and that the word has only one syllable. I'm glad of that. Now for the *o.* *O* probably stands for its long sound because of the final *e.* I'll try blending all this, starting with *o:* ō → prō → prōvé. *Prōvé!* I've never even heard of a word like that. I'll try the short *o* sound: prŏvé. That's no better. I guess I had better keep trying other sounds for *o.* With that final *e,* I'll start with the long sounds: prāvé, prēvé, prīvé, . . . gosh, I can't even pronounce it with a long *u* sound. I'll try the long sound for *oo;* pro͞ové. Oh, sure, It's *prove.* Why didn't I think of that earlier? That doesn't prove a thing.

Subsequent to modeling like that illustrated above, the teacher might want to remind students that vowel sounds are often problems, which is why she concentrated on *o.* She might also review that /v/ in final position is recorded with *ve.* At this point, familiar words like *cave* and *dive* should be written. Finally, the teacher might want to remind the students that trying out different sounds for *o* is similar to what they did earlier when they made substitutions like:

sit	shall	must	dime	like	luck
sat	shell	mast	dome	lake	lock
set		mist			

To emphasize that vowel sounds are not always the source of problems, the same teacher might work next on *giddy* embedded in the sentence *The children were too giddy to hear what the man said.* For *giddy,* the modeling is illustrated on the next page.

The children were too something to hear what the man said. *Noisy* makes sense, but that starts with *n*. I better check the spelling. A *y* at the end is a vowel, so that's two consonants with a vowel before and after. It probably has two syllables. I'll divide between the *d*'s. The first syllable is like *kid*, so that's *jĭd*. The *y* stands for a long *e* sound. That means the second syllable is *dē. jĭddy. jĭddy?* That's a funny word. Maybe it isn't even a word. What's the problem now? Maybe *g* stands for its hard sound. That makes the first syllable say "gĭd." *Gĭddý*. Oh, *giddy*. The children were too giddy to hear what the man said. They were probably bouncing around so much they couldn't hear anything.

In this instance, the teacher might choose to show the connection between what she did with *j* and what the students did earlier when they substituted consonant sounds:

ride	back	seat	number	simple
hide	pack	heat	lumber	dimple
side	sack	meat		pimple
wide	lack	beat		
tide		bleat		

Making explicit the connection between what students know and what appears to be new is helpful not only in simplifying and clarifying what is new but also in adding to students' confidence in being successful with a new task.

PRACTICE

Until now, the focus has been on instruction provided with explanations, information, examples, and modeling. Not to be forgotten is the importance of, and need for, practice, both supervised and independent. To show the connection between lessons and practice, the purpose of a lesson is stated first in the samples of practice that follow.

Samples of Practice

Purpose: To teach the correspondence between *s* and /s/ to beginners.

Supervised practice: After writing *s* on the board and reviewing its sound, the teacher distributes two small cards to each member of the instructional group. One card displays *s;* the other is blank. The directions are to listen to the word spoken by the teacher and to hold up the card with *s* if the word starts with the sound that *s* represents. (If only a card with *s* were used, children would hold up that card whenever they saw others hold up a card whether or not they heard /s/ at the beginning of the named word. With the two cards, a choice has to be made, which allows a teacher to learn who knows what.)

Independent practice: Have children cut out pictures of objects whose names start with /s/. Each picture will be pasted on paper on which *S* and *s* are printed at the top. Later, the pictures can be labeled. (Sources for pictures are store catalogs and old newspapers, magazines, and greeting cards.)

Purpose: To teach the significance of the pattern VCV for dividing unknown words into syllables.

Supervised practice: The teacher lists and numbers words she believes are unknown. (Unknown words must be used; otherwise, students reach conclusions about syllables based on what they hear rather than on visual cues.) Individuals name the number preceding a word that they believe fits the pattern discussed. These words are printed in a second column so that they can be checked against the VCV pattern. Any word that does fit is divided into syllables and read by the teacher.

Independent practice: The task is the same. Some of the new words in the next three basal selections are printed on a ditto sheet. (Words that include *x* are omitted.) On their own, children make a second list composed of any word that fits the VCV pattern. They next use slash marks to show syllabic divisions. When the sheet is checked, the teacher reads all the words with the appropriate pattern. She reminds students that they will soon see these words in assigned reading.

Purpose: To teach how to add sounds to the beginning of known words to produce new words.

Supervised practice: The teacher lists known words on the board and has the instructional group read them. As she adds one or more letters to the beginning of a word, an individual tells her what the word is now. Someone then offers a sentence that includes the word. The same procedure is followed with the remaining words.

Independent practice: A suitable written assignment is shown in Figure 9.3.

If the focus of instruction is substituting sounds, a written assignment in which students have to change a senseless word to a meaningful one can be given. Suitable sentences are listed below.

> You'll have to six in the back seat.
> The sight from the sun helped.
> His skim is very cold.
> Please close the floor.

Add a letter to make a word. Write a sentence for each word.

Letter	Word	Sentence
1. p	_____in	1.
2. m	_____ask	2.
3. d	_____ate	3.
4. s	_____eat	4.
5. s	_____car	5.
6. b	_____last	6.
7. sc	_____rub	7.
8. sc	_____out	8.

Figure 9.3 Written Practice for Adding Sounds to Known Words

Practice in Basal Series

As the samples of practice offered thus far illustrate, meaningful practice is an extension of instruction. At times, practice also serves a maintenance function. That is, even though phonics instruction has not been offered on a particular day, one or more written assignments might be given to promote continued use of something taught earlier.

Samples of maintenance practice are offered next. First, though, the phonics practice in a randomly selected basal manual is described in order to show why teachers must be prepared to supplement, replace, or alter the practice supplied by publishers of basal series.

The teacher's manual being considered is for a reader said to be appropriate for the second semester of third grade. The reader has eighteen selections; worksheets for phonics are recommended for four of them. Some details about these worksheets are in Figure 9.4; more follow.

As Figure 9.4 shows, fifty-eight worksheets are provided for four selections, twelve of which pertain to phonics. Ten of the twelve phonics worksheets are described as practice in using consonant letters, plus contexts, to decide what a word is even though each word was taught earlier. The initial item in the first worksheet is approximated below.

Many people thought that sp_____t_ brought their food.
sports   spirits   friends

Directions for this initial worksheet are puzzling: Students are to use the consonants and the sentence to decide what the missing word is, after which they are to underline the correct meaning. For nine more worksheets,

Selection	No. of Pages in Selection	No. of Worksheets for Selection	No. of Worksheets for Phonics	Phonics Topic
1	11	12	4	Context and Consonants
2	10	12	2	Context and Consonants
3	11	18	4	Context and Consonants
9	14	16	2	Syllables

Figure 9.4   Provisions for Phonics Practice in a Basal Reader Manual

the directions are the same except the task is to underline the correct answer. Again, an illustrative item follows.

> Old airplanes were not like j__t planes.
> just   fast   jet

The two worksheets for syllables have items similar to the one below.

> The doctor put the dog on the table.
> tabl e   ta ble   tab le

Here, students are to circle the correct syllabication for the underlined word, which was taught earlier.

Clearly, this manual helps explain why *Becoming a Nation of Readers* (2) asserts that the treatment of phonics in basal programs "falls considerably short of the ideal" (p. 43).

Additional Examples of Practice

Even when students are helped to see the value of phonics instruction, it is not likely to be voted "what we like best in school." That is why efforts should be made to provide phonics practice that is interesting at least some of the time. The samples of practice that conclude the chapter are offered to help teachers who realize that attractive practice is more productive than routine exercises.

Letter-Sound Relationships. It should now be clear why the sounds that letters represent need to be known at the level of automaticity. The following suggestions for practice are meant to help achieve automaticity as well as add to children's interest in learning about letter-sound correspondences. All the examples can be adapted to different abilities and needs.

- Display cards on which a letter or digraph is printed. Distribute unlabeled pictures next. Let children take turns naming a picture and the letter with which it begins (or ends).
- With children sitting at a table, have each child select about five small letter cards. Call out words selected from a pile of word cards, but do not show them to the participants. As each word is named, the child holding the letter that records its initial sound lays that card down. The first child out of cards is the winner. To encourage careful listening, an incorrect response results in the child's getting an additional card.
- Using small boxes labeled with a letter or digraph plus a collection of small objects and trinkets, let children take turns naming a trinket and the letter with which its name begins. As this is done, the trinket is placed in the appropriate box.
- Bingo-like cards can be prepared with letters printed in the squares. As the teacher (or an able student) names a word, children cover its beginning (or final) letter if that letter appears on their cards.
- To provide for periodic summaries, scrapbooks or sound books can be assembled by having children clip pictures of items whose names begin with a selected letter and sound. If collections become large, individual books can be compiled with titles like "Vowels," "Consonants," and "Digraphs."
- Summaries can also be achieved with the help of large sheets of paper folded in accordion fashion. (Somewhere, the selected letter should be displayed. Without it, children may only think about sounds.) Pictures whose names start with the selected letter and sound are pasted in the folds. To review a letter-sound association, a child pulls out each sheet and names the pictures.
- Have each member of a group attach a paper seal (with the child's name on it) to a bulletin board. In a box, place colored paper circles (balls) on which a letter or digraph appears. The children take turns selecting a ball. If a child can name a word that begins with the sound that the selected letter records, he places that ball on top of his seal's nose. At the end, the child with the most balls being balanced is the winner.
- Table and floor games are useful for practice designed to solidify letter-sound relationships. One simple board is shown on the next page.

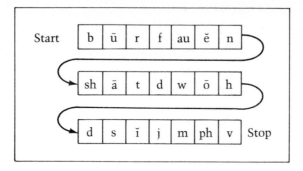

In this game, participants have to return to the starting point whenever they are unable to name a word that starts with the letter or digraph printed in a square.

Blending and Substituting Sounds. Why students need to be able both to blend sounds and to replace one sound with another should now be clear. Ideas for practice designed to help with these requirements follow.

■ Make a fishing pond by painting the inside of a box blue. For a pole, attach a piece of string to a long, thin stick. To the end of the string attach a magnet. On small, fish-shaped cards print familiar words that allow for substitutions and additions. To each card attach a paper clip. Finally, throw the fish into the pond. As children take turns catching a fish and naming the word printed on it (e.g., *rock*), pose a question like, "What would the word be if it began with *s* instead of *r?*" (The word *sock* is printed so the children can see it.) If *ran* is caught, the question might be, "What would it say if you added the letters *ch* to the end?" Correct responses allow children to keep their fish, temporarily.

Because the ability to recall relevant learnings is of critical importance for decoding, practice like the following should be helpful.

■ On small cards, write unfamiliar words that can be figured out with the help of known words plus substitutions or additions. Place the cards in a box (Surprise Box) or bag (Grab Bag). Let students select them and try to decode the words. Each successful child will be asked to tell the word that helped with the new one. Both are written on a chalkboard to display the relationship.

Because students enjoy working with bulletin-board displays, two boards that allow for practice in adding and substituting sounds are described next.

- To the bottom of a board entitled "Iceberg Hop," attach white construction paper cut to look like icebergs. On the peaks print graphemic bases (e.g., -ick, -ale, -ipe) that have been studied. Make a set of letter cards and a small paper penguin. Children choose a letter and, holding the penguin, become one by hopping from iceberg to iceberg naming words formed by combining the selected letter with the graphemic base.
- A bulletin board in the spring might feature large daisies with petals that can be rotated. Single consonants and digraphs are printed on the petals; a graphemic base is printed on the center of each flower. By moving the petals, children can make and identify words formed by the rotating letters plus the graphemic base.

More ideas for practice in blending sounds are described below.

- Each participant receives a card showing six graphemic bases. For instance:

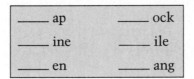

Students taken turns selecting letter cards from a deck. If a chosen letter forms a word with one of the graphemic bases and the child can read the word, he puts that letter in front of the base. Otherwise, the card is returned to the bottom of the deck. The first child to make six words is the winner.

- Cut out a small opening in the side of a shoebox. Immediately to the right print a graphemic base. On a narrow card that is longer than the box, print consonants and consonant digraphs. By slowly pulling the cardboard strip through holes in the ends of the box, children can practice adding sounds to make words.

- A written exercise allows for more practice with blending. Now, columns of words like those shown below are used:

rake	oil	each
ark	ill	ink
rain	ripe	oats
pine	and	hare

By adding a certain consonant, cluster, or consonant digraph to a row of three words (e.g., *rake, oil, each*), new words can be formed (e.g., *brake, boil, beach*).

Decoding Words in Contexts. If a balanced use of all sources of help is to characterize students' attempts to deal with unknown words, some phonics practice must focus on unknown words in contexts. You can recall from Chapter 7 a progression for combining graphophonic and contextual cues:

Supplied	*Example*
Initial letter	I can open the s___ with this key.
Initial/final letters	The cars are going too f__t.
Initial syllable	Eating ap_____ is good for your teeth.
Total spelling	They are too <u>even</u> to know who will win.

Practice that makes use of contexts and partial spellings is illustrated below.

1. Don't j__mp in the house.
2. Can you c__tch this ball?
3. I can swim in the L_k_.

> The morning was so c_ld that the children r_n to school. Wh_n they g_t there, it was too early to g_ inside. They played g_mes to k__p warm. At n_ne o'clock, the sch__l bell r_ng. They were gl_d to g_t inside the building.

An essential point to make about exercises like the two just presented is the need for students to see the connection between the exercises and what they should do and use when they come across an unfamiliar word while reading.

To show the usefulness of contexts (plus phonics) for reducing confusion with similar-looking words (e.g., *show, shove; silver, sliver; where, there; tried, tired, lighting, lightning*), other written exercises are appropriate. As the following illustrations demonstrate, they can be adapted for widely different levels of ability.

It _____ too big.
    saw   was

I want to _____ the picture.
        keep   peek

The _____ should slow down.
    terrific   traffic

Can you _____ this word?
        identity   identify

The _____ between the two boys was very long.
    conservation   conversation

With sentences like those above, the first job is to write the sensible word in the blank. The second is to use the word not selected in a written sentence. Together, the two tasks allow a teacher to learn whether all the words were correctly recognized.

SUMMARY

Underlying the content of Chapter 9 is the assumption that students can learn how to estimate the pronunciation of a word from its spelling. When the word is familiar orally, moving from an approximately correct pronunciation to the correct one is relatively easy, especially for readers who use spellings in conjunction with contextual cues. Therefore, how to use the two sources of help jointly is outlined and illustrated in Chapter 9.

A second assumption is that the materials that exert the greatest influence on classroom practices, namely, basal reader series, are flawed in a number of ways. Five shortcomings identified in Chapter 9 include (a) excessive attention to auditory discrimination, (b) rhyming words used in ways that foster confusion about the meaning of "same last sound," (c) methods for teaching letter-sound correspondences that are so obscure as to make the instruction minimally helpful, (d) omission of instruction for blending sounds and for replacing one sound with another, and (e) use of words that students are already able to read in practice exercises. The failure to provide sufficient opportunities for students to apply what they are learning about decoding when they read basal selections is another deficiency.

Having identified flaws in basal programs, Chapter 9 responds to two questions in order to help teachers who want to use basal materials with discretion: (a) What is the best sequence for teaching the components of a phonics curriculum? (b) How should the instruction proceed? The discussion of a defensible sequence called attention to usefulness and similarity of sounds as two factors that ought to affect sequence. Another factor is the difficulty of content.

The discussion of how to teach phonics made distinctions between implicit and explicit instruction. It characterized the latter as being more effective and efficient, once children understand the nature of alphabetic writing. Chapter 9 also distinguished between instruction designed to impart information and instruction whose objective is to enable students to do something. The distinction was made in order to emphasize that differences in objectives call for differences in instruction. Especially highlighted with a number of examples was modeling, portrayed as an effective way for teaching students how to do something—for instance, how to blend sounds. Blending sounds and replacing one sound with another both receive generous attention in Chapter 9 because the two topics are almost never covered in commercially prepared materials even though they are essential for proficient decoding.

Chapter 9 concludes with a sizable number of sample lessons, after which samples of practice are described.

REVIEW

1. Explain the statements that follow; then respond to the questions posed.
   a. The use of phonics allows only for word recognition. Practice is required to achieve the ability to identify the decoded word.
   b. Because decoded words need to be practiced, why bother teaching phonics? Why not reserve instructional time for whole word methodology and practice?

2. Chapter 9 recommends that known words should be used in phonics instruction, but that unknown words should be featured when the objective is to provide students with opportunities to apply what they are learning. What are the reasons for the recommendations?

3. Let's say you are teaching the correspondence between *k* and /k/. After printing and reading words that begin with this letter and sound, you ask for additional examples. One student suggests *king,* after which another immediately offers *queen.* How would you respond to the child who suggests *queen?*

4. Whenever students have to stop reading to decode a word that seems important, they should reread the sentence in which the word is embedded once the decoding is done. Why is the rereading important?

5. Using examples, explain each of the two following statements:
   a. Adding sounds to the beginning and end of words is preparation for blending sounds to produce syllables (or words).
   b. Substituting sounds in words is preparation for using with flexibility what has been taught about letter-sound correspondences.

6. Chapter 9 recommends modeling when the objective of a lesson is to teach students how to do something. With that in mind, let's assume that *group* is unknown and appears in the sentence *Schools group stu-*

dents by their ages. Demonstrate how you would model a procedure for decoding *group.*

7. Having studied Chapter 9, you should be ready to critique the two basal reader lessons described in the chapter. The first dealt with the digraph *oo;* the objective of the second lesson was to teach the new word *go.* Your critique should pinpoint flaws and make recommendations for improving each lesson.

8. At the start of Chapter 9, you were urged to examine basal reader manuals and workbooks to see what is done with phonics. Bring to class (a) an example of good instruction and/or practice, and (b) an example of instruction and/or practice that is of questionable value. Be prepared to explain your judgments.

REFERENCES

1. Chall, Jeanne. *Learning to Read: The Great Debate.* New York: McGraw-Hill Book Company, 1967.
2. Commission on Reading. *Becoming a Nation of Readers.* Washington, D.C.: National Institute of Education, 1985.
3. Durkin, Dolores. "A Classroom-Observation Study of Reading Instruction in Kindergarten." *Early Childhood Research Quarterly* 2 (September, 1987), 275–300.
4. Durkin, Dolores. *The Decoding Ability of Elementary School Students.* Reading Education Report No. 49. Urbana: University of Illinois, Center for the Study of Reading, May 1984.
5. Durkin, Dolores. *Strategies for Identifying Words,* 2nd ed. Boston: Allyn and Bacon, Inc., 1981.
6. Dyson, Anne H. "Reading, Writing, and Language: Young Children Solving the Written Language Puzzle." *Language Arts* 59 (November/December, 1982), 829–839.
7. Eeds-Kniep, Maryann. "The Frenetic Fanatic Phonic Backlash." *Language Arts* 56 (November/December, 1979), 909–917.
8. Fox, Barbara, and Routh, Donald. "Phonetic Analysis and Synthesis As Word Attack Skills: Revisited." *Journal of Educational Psychology* 76 (December, 1984), 1059–1064.
9. Juel, Connie, and Roper-Schneider, Diane. "The Influence of Basal Readers on First Grade Reading." *Reading Research Quarterly* 20 (Winter, 1985), 134–152.
10. Perfetti, Charles A. "Reading Acquisition and Beyond: Decoding Includes Cognition." *American Journal of Education* 93 (November, 1984), 40–60.
11. Richardson, E.; Dibenedetto, B.; and Bradley, C. M. "The Relationship of Sound Blending to Reading Achievement." *Review of Educational Research* 47 (Spring, 1977), 319–334.
12. Stanovich, Keith E. "Matthew Effects in Reading: Some Consequences of Individual Differences in the Acquisition of Literacy." *Reading Research Quarterly* 21 (Fall, 1986), 360–407.
13. Stott, D. H. Manual for "Programmed Reading Kits 1 and 2." Toronto: Gage Educational Publishing Limited, 1970.

14. Venezky, Richard L. "Issues in the Design of Phonics Instruction." *Ginn Occasional Papers,* Number 14. Lexington, Ma.: Ginn and Company, 1983.
15. Walsh, Daniel J.; Price, Gary G.; and Gillingham, Mark G. "The Critical but Transitory Importance of Letter Naming." *Reading Research Quarterly* 23 (Winter, 1988), 89–107.
16. Wardhaugh, Ronald. *Reading: A Linguistic Perspective.* New York: Harcourt, Brace and World, 1969.
17. Williams, Joanna P. "Teaching Decoding with an Emphasis on Analysis and Phoneme Blending." *Journal of Educational Psychology* 72 (February, 1980), 1–15.

Chapter 10

Structural Analysis

PREVIEW

This chapter continues the discussion of decoding: using spellings to achieve pronunciations. However, Chapter 10 enlarges the focus by dealing with letters that also provide cues for meaning. The chapter thus recognizes that letters like *mis-* and *re-* can help not only with the pronunciation of words such as *misteach* and *reteach* but also with their meanings. So, too, does the chapter acknowledge that letters like *-er* and *-s* offer cues for both the pronunciation and meaning of *teacher* and *teachers*.

Words such as *teach, misteach, reteach, teacher,* and *teachers* are useful in defining word structure, the concern of Chapter 10. They help, first, by illustrating that English words divide into families, members of which have the same origin. (In the case of the family just referred to, the origin, namely, *teach,* is a self-sustaining word. In the family composed of members like *inspect, spectator,* and *spectacles,* the origin is not an English word.) The existence of families accounts for the fact that words have a structure. In some instances, the structure is simple. That is, the word is a root (*teach*). In other instances, the structure is more complex and is composed of a root plus one or more affixes (*reteach, unteachable, reteaching, teacher, teachers, teaches*).

All this suggests that the previous chapter was concerned with self-sustaining roots, whereas the present one deals with self-sustaining roots to which one or more affixes (prefixes and suffixes) are added. The objective of this chapter, therefore, is to show how students can be taught a strategy for dealing with words like *burned, wishes, helpful, playfully, retie, unconquerable,* and *mismanagement.*

To prepare for Chapter 10, look over the terms below and commit to memory the meaning of any that are unfamiliar.

Word Family: Words having the same origin.*

Root: The origin of a word family. If a root is an English

---

* Commonly, basal materials erroneously assign the description "family" to words that share a graphemic base—for instance , to *tell, bell, sell, fell,* and so on.

word, it cannot be reduced (e.g., *teach* to *each*) and still remain a member of the family. Commercial materials sometimes use *stem* or *base* instead of *root*.

Prefix: A unit of one or more letters placed before a root that alters its meaning (e.g., *re*tie, *fore*tell, and *a*moral).

Suffix: A unit of one or more letters placed at the end of a root.

Derivational Suffix: A unit of one or more letters placed at the end of a root that alters its meaning (e.g., care*ful* and care*less*).

Derived Word: Composed of a root and a prefix (*re*act); a root and a derivational suffix (act*or*); or a root, a prefix, and a derivational suffix (*re*act*or*).

Inflectional Suffix: A unit of one or more letters placed at the end of a root for grammatical purposes. (Examples of inflectional suffixes, sometimes called *inflections*, affixed to roots are want*s*, box*es*, tall*er*, and slow*ly*.)

Inflected Word: Composed of a root to which an inflectional suffix is added (e.g., *doing*, *girls*, and *riches*).

Affix: Refers to a prefix, a derivational suffix, or an inflectional suffix.

Following are further examples of some of the terms defined.

Root (Base) (Stem)	Derived Word	Inflected Word
name	nameless	named
hair	hairy	hairs
draw	redraw	drawing
button	unbutton	buttons

Chapter 10 starts with background information that provides a framework for the more detailed content covered later. The framework is assembled in three ways. Initially, a description of a decoder's efforts to deal with *flawlessly* is offered. Starting the chapter this way is for the purpose of showing how contextual, structural, and graphophonic cues function jointly. The second type of background information is a description of the necessary outcomes of lessons with affixes. Here, the intent is to outline the kind of instruction that gives students a strategy for dealing on their own with both the pronunciation and the meaning of words like *flawlessly*. After that, the focus shifts to the question, When do I do all this teaching?

COMBINED USE OF ALL CUES

For purposes of discussion, let's assume it is possible not only to read a person's mind but also to describe thoughts that occur virtually simultaneously. In the portrayal of thoughts that follow, the intention is to model how contextual, structural, and graphophonic cues work together to help decoders with unfamiliar words. In this case, the word is *flawlessly*, found in the sentence *All the children danced flawlessly.*

> Let's see now. It tells how the kids danced, so this word is an adverb (contextual cue). The *l* and *y*, then, is an inflection (structural cue). It's pronounced "lē." Maybe *l, e, s, s* is another suffix, like in *careless* (structural cue). I remember when we learned that. It's pronounced with the schwa sound. That leaves *f, l, a,* and *w*. That must be the root. The *a* and *w* act like one vowel, so that means one syllable (graphophonic cue). *F* and *l* are a cluster and I know the blend they stand for (graphophonic cue). I better put all these sounds together to see what the root is: aw → flaw. Flaw. That's something that's wrong with something (oral vocabulary). With *-less* added to it, though, it means without flaws (structural cue). Oh, I see. There was nothing wrong with the kids' dancing (contextual cue). It must have been pretty good. All the children danced flawlessly.

As mentioned, the description above is a contrived portrayal of mental activities that is designed to make explicit how three types of cues function together. In reality, proficient decoders are not as concerned about a pronunciation as is the decoder depicted above. This is the case because meaning is what counts and because comprehension requires readers "to keep moving." It is likely, too, that when *flaw* is sorted out as the root, blending the three sounds of which it is composed proceeds more quickly than the contrived description suggests. It is even possible that *flaw* will be recognized once it is mentally separated from the two suffixes.

What is not contrived is the dependence of decoding on oral vocabularies. Worthy of explicit attention is that knowing the meaning of *flaw* contributed to the decoder's success in two ways. It helped with the root itself, and it also allowed for use of the decoder's knowledge of the suffix *-less*. Stated differently, it is of little value to know that the suffix *-less* means "without" unless it is affixed to a root whose meaning is known.

In addition to showing the fundamental importance of oral vocabularies as well as the combined use of contextual, structural, and graphophonic cues, the portrayal of a reader's efforts with *flawlessly* suggests the need for a revised strategy for decoding as soon as derived and inflected words become common. The strategy that incorporates attention to affixes is shown in Figure 10.1. Please study Figure 10.1 now.

As Figure 10.1 shows, the possibility that an unknown word has a prefix or suffix needs to be considered early in the decoding process. This is the case for two reasons, the first of which is stated below.

> Most prefixes and suffixes are syllables.* For example:
> miscount (mis count)   hopefully (hope ful ly)
> foresee (fore see)   retelling (re tell ing)

The second reason for decoders to look immediately for structural units (prefixes and suffixes) is that they help with meaning. To appreciate this important contribution, compare the following syllabic divisions, the second of which (phonological divisions) ignores the presence of affixes. As a consequence, roots are not kept intact.

Structural Divisions		*Phonological Divisions*	
redraw	disable	redraw	disable
re draw	dis able	red raw	di sa ble

Having seen with examples the significance of structural units for meaning (as well as for pronunciations), you might now wonder why this

---

Contextual cues:
  Looking for syntactic and semantic information.

Structural cues:
  Looking for one or more letters that indicate one or more affixes.

Graphophonic cues:
  Looking at letters and their sequence in a root in order to decode it if it is unfamiliar.

Structural cues:
  Replacing affixes.

Contextual cues:
  Checking to see whether the conclusion about the word is syntactically and semantically acceptable.

Figure 10.1 Sequence for Using Cues

---

* It should be noted that when the suffix *-ion* is added to a root ending in *t*, the letters *tion* form a syllable (*act, ac tion*).

book dealt with phonological units first. The sequence reflects the fact that the majority of words that beginning readers learn are roots. Other words are inflected in simple ways—for example, *girls, talking, rides, played.* At this early stage, words like *girls* and *talking* are taught with whole word methodology; attention does not go to inflections. Later, however, the same words can serve as illustrations when it is time to give explicit attention to the inflections *-s, -ing,* and *-ed.*

More is said in a subsequent section of this chapter about decoding derived and inflected words. Now the question is, What should be the outcomes of instruction with affixes?

OBJECTIVES OF INSTRUCTION

To ensure that students acquire the ability to deal successfully and quickly with derived and inflected words, every lesson for an affix must achieve certain objectives. They can be identified with another reference to the decoder's thoughts about *flawlessly.*

To begin, the letters *-ly* suggested that the pair was an adverbial inflection, which the context reinforced. With that conclusion, the decoder knew the pronunciation immediately. (Earlier, words like *slowly, loudly,* and *weekly* may have been used to teach about *-ly.*)

Next came the recognition that *-less* might be another suffix. The decoder recalled seeing it in *careless.* It is possible that *careless,* along with words like *painless* and *worthless,* were used previously to teach about *-less.* In any case, the decoder knew the pronunciation of *-less* as well as its semantic effect on *flaw.* Such knowledge speeded up the decoding process.

All these details about the decoder's successful efforts indicate that lessons dealing with an affix must aim toward the following outcomes.

Students:

1. Know the spelling and pronunciation of whatever affix is being taught.
2. Understand how that affix affects the meaning of roots.
3. Can transfer all this to a new derived or inflected word.

SCHEDULING INSTRUCTION

The comments about Figure 10.2 that follow begin to answer the question, When should instruction about structural units be offered? Later, when other sections describe lessons, they embellish the answer.

Facilitating Comprehension
Prereading Responsibilities

Teaching new vocabulary
Providing essential background
  information
Establishing purpose(s) for
  reading

Assigned Text:
Independent
Silent Reading

Figure 10.2   Scheduling Instruction

In Connection with Assigned Reading

As Figure 10.2 shows, attending to new vocabulary is one of the things teachers do to enable students to comprehend assigned reading. Of relevance now is that work with vocabulary allows for teaching or reviewing subject matter related to word structure. To illustrate, if one new word is *flawlessly*, it might be used to review the suffixes *-ly* and *-less;* or it might serve to review the strategy for decoding outlined earlier in Figure 10.1. Not to be overlooked is the possibility of a teacher's doing nothing with *flaw-lessly* if students are capable of decoding it themselves. In this case, after the assigned reading is done, the teacher checks to see whether the students succeeded in dealing with the pronunciation and meaning of *flawlessly* and of any other new word that did not receive prereading attention.

At an earlier grade level, a teacher may decide to use the new word *playful* to initiate instruction for *-ful*. This is a wise decision if other new words have the same suffix, or if *-ful* can be affixed to roots the children know—*color, house,* and *care*. Such teaching is desirable, since it makes apparent the usefulness of knowing about the suffix *-ful*.

At Other Times

If all instruction for affixes were offered in conjunction with preparations for assigned reading, the time spent on new words could be sufficiently long as to reduce interest in doing the reading. That is why some instruction for affixes should be offered apart from assigned reading. At such times, it is still important to use derived or inflected words in newspapers, magazines, environmental text, and the like that have the affix being taught. (Should it be the suffix *-y*, a cereal box that displays *crunchy* and *healthy* is excellent instructional material. So, too, is a box of cookies on which *crispy* and *chewy* are printed.) Again, this is done to demonstrate the value of the instruction. Eventually, what is taught apart from assigned reading will come into play when attention goes to new words in selections assigned at some subsequent date.

BEGINNING INSTRUCTION

On the assumption that a framework for thinking about instruction with word structure has been established, it is time to consider how to teach affixes. Because they divide into three kinds (prefixes, derivational suffixes, and inflectional suffixes), it is also time to inquire, Which of the three should be taught first?

To respond, two factors need to be taken into account. The first has to do with difficulty, thus with such questions as, If a child can read *like*, is it easier to deal with *dislike* or *likes*? Because what is familiar (*like*) appears at the beginning of *likes*, learning *likes* is easier. It is also easier because *likes* is a word that young children commonly use in their own speech. These factors suggest that some suffixes ought to be taught before prefixes receive attention. But this leads to another question, Should inflectional or derivational suffixes be introduced first?

The relevant factor here is the kinds of words that beginning readers need to learn. Even a quick look at easy material shows that inflected words like *jumped* and *spots* appear earlier than derived words like *jumper* and *spotless*. A defensible conclusion, then, is that lessons about word structure should be initiated with attention to common inflectional suffixes such as *-s*, *-ing*, and *-ed*.

Instruction with Inflectional Suffixes

Plural nouns occur early in written material; consequently, the first lesson to be described is for the inflection *-s*, also referred to as a *plural marker*. The teacher begins by calling the children's attention to two words they know:

brown cat

After the children read *brown cat* aloud, the teacher says (as she holds up a picture of two brown cats), "If I want to talk about these two brown cats, I can't say 'brown cat.' Instead, what do I need to say so that you'll know I have a picture of more than one brown cat? . . . That's right. I say 'brown cats,' not 'brown cat.' Let me show you what 'brown cats' looks like'':

brown cat
brown cats

"What did I add to 'cat' to make it say 'cats'? . . . Yes, I added *s* at the end. Now let me see if I can fool you. This is the sign you see every day near the box of pencils. (Shows card on which *pencils* is printed.) What is this word? . . . Right. It's 'pencils.' Who can tell me—now think—who can tell me what to do to this word to make it say 'pencil'? . . . Correct. If I take away *s*, it just says 'pencil.' It needs to be 'pencils' on the card because there's more than one pencil in the box. I'll print both words on the board. Look, please, as I write them."

pencil
pencils

"Please read these two words. . . . Good. I'm going to write other words you know, starting with this one."

The teacher quickly prints *pet*, has the children read it, comments about their having two pets in the room, then prints *pets*. After the children read *pets*, other familiar roots are written to which *-s* is added:

pet	top	girl	boy	hat	boat	car	room	dog
pets	tops	girls	boys	hats	boats	cars	rooms	dogs

At the end, the teacher reviews that adding *-s* to the end of words like *cat* and *top* makes them mean more than one.

Eventually, other ways to form plurals are taught when words such as *boxes, ponies,* and *loaves* appear in text. (If children are not ready to learn about the plural form for a word like *pony*, then *ponies* is taught as a whole word.) Meanwhile, the instruction that focused on the plural marker *-s* allows for written practice that attends to both structural and contextual cues. For instance:

1. We have three _____ at home. One is a
pet   pets
_____ , and the other two are _____.
dog   dogs   bird   birds

2. Our _____ is too big. The _____ are hard to
car   cars   door   doors
open and close.

With practice like that shown above, the correct word is written in the blank rather than circled or underlined, because the writing fosters attention to its details.

Other Instruction with Inflectional Suffixes

A lesson for the inflectional suffix *-ed*, which is sometimes referred to as a *past-tense marker*, is described next. The following sentence is on the board:

Today we will play.

Once the instructional group reads the sentence aloud, the teacher inquires, "Did any of you play *yesterday?*" Responses are positive and include descriptions of a variety of activities. The teacher then comments, "I'm going to write a sentence that tells that you played yesterday."

> Today we will play.
> Yesterday we

After printing *we*, the teacher stops to ask, "Should I write 'play' again? Do we say 'Yesterday we play,' or do we say something else? Today we will play. Yesterday we . . . What should I write here?" After the children tell her, the board shows:

> Today we will play.   play
> Yesterday we played too.   played

Once both the sentences and *play* and *played* are read aloud, the teacher suggests, "Please look at this word (pointing to *played*). What did I add to the end of *play* to make it say *played?* . . . Yes, I added *e, d*. When I did that, I showed you played yesterday, not today. I'm going to add *e, d* to other words you know." Eventually, the board displays the following words, each of which is used by a child in a sentence to verify that the past-tense meaning is understood.

play	talk	jump	call	work	walk
played	talked	jumped	called	worked	walked

In the lesson just described, the teacher deliberately avoided using a word taught earlier with whole word methodology (*wanted*). However, children must eventually learn the following generalization for the past-tense marker *-ed*. When they are ready to learn it, the familiar word *wanted* can help illustrate the generalization.

When *-ed* is added to a verb ending in *t* or *d*, it is a syllable (/əd/). Otherwise, *-ed* adds a sound to the verb but not a syllable. For example:

wanted	needed	played	wished
painted	landed	helped	called

In time, students learn about additional ways to indicate past tense (*make, made; say, said; am, was; write, wrote*). But this information is acquired gradually as the need for it arises. Eventually, too, other inflectional suffixes are taught—for instance, small*er*, small*est*, quick*er*, quick*ly*.

Nonstandard Speakers and Inflectional Suffixes

In the lessons described thus far, inflections are linked to oral language ("If we want to tell about something that happened yesterday, what do we have to say? ... Yes, we'd say 'burned,' not 'burn'."). When children's speech is standard English, the connection is helpful; when it is not, references to oral language may cause problems. With that possibility in mind, teachers should adhere to the following guideline: Whereas references to spoken language ought to be made when standard speakers are being instructed, a similar reference may confuse nonstandard speakers who do not always pronounce inflections like -ed when they talk. For such speakers, therefore, instruction ought to be a direct telling process in which it is advisable to make statements like: "When you're reading about something that has already happened—maybe it happened yesterday or last week or even last year—you'll often find the letters e, d at the end of the word. That's why I put e and d at the end of cook. I wanted to show we did that yesterday. We cooked on Thursday. Let's look at some other words that tell about things that have already happened. Please look at these sentences:"

> Last night I burned my finger.
> I walked in the park yesterday.
> This morning I asked my mom for a dime.

Teachers also need to keep in mind that how students respond aloud to an inflected word like *burned* (whether with "burn" or "burned") is less important than is their understanding of the grammatical significance of -ed (or whatever the inflection might be). The fact that understanding is the key issue reflects a point that was underscored very early in this book, namely, that the primary concern of reading instruction lies with comprehension, not with what students say when they read aloud.

Samples of nonstandard deviations that have relevance for instruction with inflections are listed below (2, 8).

Written Language	*Nonstandard Speech*
I dropped it.	"I drop it."
He looks.	"He look."
She is coming.	"She is come."
They let us do it.	"They lets us do it."
He started crying.	"He stard cryin'."
Joe's bike.	"Joe bike."

LATER INSTRUCTION

Very few visits to classrooms are required to learn that derivatives like *unattainable, worthlessness, impracticality,* and *counteraction* present middle- and upper-grade students with a major challenge unless they have a systematic strategy for unraveling pronunciations and meanings (5). Because derived words are composed of a prefix and a root (*miscount*), or a root and a derivational suffix (*spoonful*), or a prefix and a root and a derivational suffix (*preschooler*), this is the time to examine the prefixes and derivational suffixes listed in Table 10.1.

With derived words as the focus, it is also time to ask, Should prefixes or derivational suffixes be taught first? As always, usefulness must be considered. Should it happen that two new words in a selection that will soon be assigned are *disagree* and *disapprove,* it is the perfect time to offer instruction about the prefix *dis-*. Another factor, however, must also be taken into account—one mentioned previously. It is the fact that adding letters to the end of a known root leaves the root more apparent than when letters are affixed to the beginning. Specifically, if students know *act,* they are more likely to see what they know in *actor* than in *react.* That is why the general guideline to follow is to teach some useful derivational suffixes before attention shifts to common prefixes. Such a guideline, it must be emphasized, does nothing to discourage teaching *dis-* when two new words in assigned reading are *disagree* and *disapprove.*

Instruction with Derivational Suffixes

Like all instruction for word structure, known roots are a starting point in lessons for derivational suffixes. Again, three objectives need to be achieved. If the concern is the derivational suffix -*less,* students should end up:

1. Knowing the spelling and pronunciation of -*less.*
2. Understanding its effect on the meaning of roots.
3. Able to deal with -*less* when it appears in a derived word they have not encountered previously.

Let's see how these objectives are achieved in a lesson dealing with -*less.* (Lessons like the one to be described enable students to decode *flawlessly.*) In this case, the proximity of Thanksgiving accounts for a discussion of everyone's blessings, one of which is having a home. This allows for attention to *home* (which is on the board) and to the fact that many more people are without homes than is often realized.

The teacher continues by stating there are a number of different ways to say that many people do not have homes. First she writes:

Many people do not have a home.

Once the students read the sentence together, the teacher says, "The same thing can be said this way," after which she adds to the board:

Many people are without a home.

Table 10.1 Common Prefixes and Derivational Suffixes

Prefix	Meaning	Example	Suffix	Meaning	Example
ir- il- im- in- a- non-	not	irregular illegal impatient inactive atypical nonhuman	-er -or -eer	one who; doer of action	teacher actor auctioneer
un- dis-	opposite of not remove	unlock, unkind disobey disarm	-less	without	spotless
			-able	capable of being	readable
re-	again back	remake recall	-ful -y -ous	full; characterized by	careful oily dangerous
mis-	wrongly	miscount	-ful	amount that fills	cupful
pre-	before	preschool	-ic (ical) -ist	connected with	poetic, historical humorist
fore-	before in front	forewarn foreward	-ness -hood -ship -ance -ence -tion (ation) -ment	state of	softness childhood friendship tolerance dependence action, starvation enjoyment
co-	with	co-author			
counter- anti-	against	counteract antiwar	-ward	in the direction of	homeward
under-	below	underage	-age	act of amount of home of	marriage mileage orphanage
semi-	half partly coming twice	semicircle semitropical semiannual	-ee	object of action	employee

The students read both sentences; the teacher then prints a third, which she herself reads:

> Many people are homeless.

After underlining *home* in *homeless,* the teacher states: "This part of the word is 'home'. When I add *l, e, s, s* to 'home', the word is 'homeless'. It means 'without a home'. 'Homeless' is a short way to say 'without a home'." The teacher then prints:

> homeless = without a home

After rereading *homeless,* the teacher continues, "When I add *l, e, s, s* to the end of a word like 'home', I say it so fast that it sounds like 'lŭss' instead of 'lĕss'. Listen. 'Homeless. Many people are homeless'." (If students know about the schwa sound, this is a time to refer to the occurrence of /ə/ in *less.*)

Before the teacher attends to other roots to which -*less* will be added, she encourages further discussion of homeless people and of how grateful everyone should be to have a home.

Eventually, the group's attention is called back to *homeless*—to how it is pronounced and to what it means. Subsequently, additional known roots are read both alone and with -*less* affixed to them:

mother	tree	shoe	head	tie	spot
motherless	treeless	shoeless	headless	tieless	spotless

For all these words, the semantic effect of -*less* is stressed.

As subsequent lessons concentrate on additional suffixes, they offer students considerable help with word meanings. Soon, for instance, attention to antonyms in a form such as the following is possible:

careless	useless	painless	helpless	colorless	joyless
careful	useful	painful	helpful	colorful	joyful

Systematic and frequent attention to word meanings through the vehicle of derivatives is especially important for the following reason. Although derivatives appear regularly in written material, they are much less common in spoken language. This discrepancy is illustrated below. For each example, the first sentence typifies what might be found in print; the sentence in the parentheses illustrates how the same thought might be expressed in speech.

> The remains of that ship are unsalvageable.
> (They'll never be able to save what's left of that ship.)

Reasonless fear kept her awake.
(She was afraid for no reason, and it kept her awake.)

The handwriting was undecipherable.
(You couldn't even read the handwriting.)

Humorlessness characterizes the man.
(The man has no sense of humor.)

Their tastes are indistinguishable.
(They have the very same tastes.)

He shows unquenchable optimism no matter what happens.
(He's always optimistic no matter what happens.)

The differences illustrated above mean that students can be *expected* to have problems with derivatives. Knowing this, teachers need to make sure that generous amounts of systematic instruction are provided for derived words.

Instruction with Prefixes

Earlier, a recommendation was made to teach derivational suffixes before attending to prefixes. That is not to say, however, that large numbers of suffixes should be introduced before lessons with prefixes are initiated. Why many derivational suffixes are *not* covered first was suggested in the entries in Table 10.1; they show that the meanings of a number of derivational suffixes are abstract, thus difficult to explain and understand (e.g., "state or degree," "act or process"). The difficulty is the reason instruction with some derivatives should soon be followed by instruction with common, easily understood prefixes.

At one time, prefixes stood out in text because hyphens separated them from roots. Because hyphens are much less common now, increased attention must go to prefixes to ensure that students recognize them in unfamiliar derivatives. How a lesson with a prefix might get started is described next.

While discussing the traits of a character in a story, *happy* is mentioned. Afterward, the teacher uses this adjective to teach the prefix *un-* by saying, "The word *happy* reminds me of another word. The word I'm thinking of is interesting because it has *happy* in it, yet it means just the opposite. It means 'not happy.' Can anyone tell me the word I'm thinking of?"*

If nobody can, the teacher answers her own question and then discusses the pronunciation of *un-* and its effect on the meaning of *happy*. Us-

---

* Once, another teacher phrased her comments differently: "I'm thinking of a word that means just the opposite of 'happy.' Can anybody tell me what it might be?" One child responded, "Sad." In this case, the response should—and did—tell the teacher about an important omission in her request. (What was the omission?)

ing other adjectives in the children's reading vocabulary, she provides more illustrations. To highlight relationships, pairs are written as follows:

happy	tidy	hurt	even	fair
unhappy	untidy	unhurt	uneven	unfair

At another time, the same teacher demonstrates that *un-* affixed to verbs means "to do the opposite" (*unbend, unwrap, untie, unlock*). This difference in meaning is important to keep in mind, as commercial materials do not always make the distinction (4). Sometime, too, students need to learn that *un-* at the beginning of a word may be part of another prefix (*underground, underfed*) or an integral part of a root (*uncle, unit*).

One decoder who overgeneralized and reached a wrong conclusion about *u* and *n* in the unfamiliar word *unite* (*The people need to unite if they expect to win*) went through the following trial-and-error process:

> This word tells what the people have to do to win. The *u* and *n* are a prefix, and there's nothing at the end that looks like a suffix. That means *i, t, e* is the root. That would be pronounced "ité." I don't think there is such a word. At least I never heard of a word that sounds like that. Maybe *u* and *n* aren't a prefix. That would make the whole thing the root. If it is, there are two syllables: *u* and *n, i, t, e.* Oh, sure. *Unite.* You have to stick together to win. The people need to unite if they expect to win.

The thoughts of this decoder reemphasize the significance of oral language for decoding, for it was competence in oral language that led to the rejection of *ite* as a root and of *un* as a prefix. The decoder's oral vocabulary also established the correctness of "unite."

To promote equally correct conclusions by other students, teachers should deliberately select words that appear to have prefixes and suffixes but in fact do not and then act out decoding procedures similar to the one just portrayed. (Examples of such words are *presto, remnant, antique,* con-st*able,* *ra*zor, and dig*est.*) By doing this on a number of occasions, teachers provide a model that permits students to apply what they have heard and observed.

SPELLING GENERALIZATIONS
AND WORD STRUCTURE

Identifying structural units in derived and inflected words is not too difficult when the root is unchanged. For instance, even when students cannot read *worth, harm, curb,* and *arch* but have learned about the suffixes *-less, -ful, -s,* and *-es,* identifying the structural units in *worthless, harmful, curbs,* and *arches* is not difficult. However, sorting out the meaningful parts in unknown words like *making, penniless, plentiful,* and *excitable* is more complex because the spelling of the root has been altered. With such words, spelling generalizations can be an important source of help. The recommendation, therefore, is to teach these generalizations not only to help students with spelling but also to provide a strategy for working out the structure of derived and inflected words in which the spelling of the root has been changed. When the generalizations receive attention for the second purpose, the connection between their content and sorting out structural units should be made explicit. Exactly how spelling generalizations help readers is illustrated next.

Using a Spelling Generalization to Decode Unknown Words

One spelling generalization follows: When a root ends in silent *e* (*tape*), the *e* is usually dropped when a suffix beginning with a vowel (*-ed*) is added (*taped*). Even when decoders do not know whether the final *e* in the root is or is not silent, the very common occurrence of silent *e*'s in final position means the generalization just cited will point them in the right direction almost all the time. Consequently, decoders who know about suffixes like *-ing, -ed, -est,* and *-able* should suspect that the roots in unfamiliar words such as *braking, cubed, finest,* and *solvable* are *brake, cube, fine,* and *solve.* Once recognized as roots, all should be easy to decode since they are regularly spelled.

Statements of Spelling Generalizations

The spelling generalization just discussed, plus others, is given in Table 10.2. Any that are unfamiliar should be studied and committed to memory to ensure your readiness to teach them in ways that make apparent their usefulness to readers.

As spelling generalizations are being taught, they should figure in work that concentrates on uncovering roots in derived and inflected words. For example:

merrily	= merry + ly		merriment	= merry + ment
miner	= mine + er		graduation	= graduate + ion
staring	= stare + ing		melodious	= melody + ous
witty	= wit + y		wiry	= wire + y
wisest	= wise + est		enviable	= envy + able

Because the need to sort out roots usually occurs with words in contexts, exercises like the following ought to be common. In this case, students provide what appears in brackets.

Table 10.2 Spelling Generalizations

When a root ends in silent *e*, the *e* is usually dropped when a suffix beginning with a vowel is added. For example:

bake	starve	cube	bride	strange
baker	starvation	cubist	bridal	strangest

When a root ends in a consonant followed by *y*, the *y* is changed to *i* before most suffixes are added. For example:

cry	pony	duty	merry	melody	history
cried	ponies	dutiful	merrily	melodious	historical

When a root ends in a consonant that is preceded by a single vowel, the consonant is usually doubled before a suffix is added.* For example:

rob	mud	chop	run	forget
robbed	muddy	chopping	runner	forgettable

The plural of nouns ending in *f* is formed by changing *f* to *v* and adding *es*. For example:

elf	leaf	calf	loaf	self
elves	leaves	calves	loaves	selves

*The doubled consonant is useful in signaling information about the sound of the previous vowel. Contrasts like the following illustrate the usefulness:

dinner	tapped	hopping	holly
diner	taped	hoping	holy

I work puzzles easily.	[easy + ly]
The kittens ate hungrily from the bowl.	[hungry + ly]
Everyone danced happily around the room.	[happy + ly]
Angrily, the man pounded on the door.	[angry + ly]

Contexts can also be used to review statements of spelling generalizations:

She slammed the door.	I like the coziness of this room.
Don't be so nosy.	He regretted doing that.
He is the tiniest of all.	Their facial expressions were interesting.

SHORT WORDS IN LONGER WORDS

The fact that a few teachers have been heard asking, "Do you see any little word you know in this new word?" combined with the fact that workbook exercises have been known to encourage students to find *at, tent,* and *on* in *attention* (4), underscore the need for teachers to specify the care that must be taken if known words *are* to help with longer unknown words.

To begin, *only roots should be examined to see whether they contain a known word.* Stated differently, the first job (as in decoding) is to consider the possibility that an unknown word may have one or more affixes:

richer   redo   unopened

(rich er)   (re do)   (un open ed)

As the examples show, students who adhere to the guideline stated above avoid the mistake of using *her* to help with *richer,* of using *red* to help with *redo,* and of using *no* to help with *unopened.*

Because a known word assists with an unknown word only when all the letters that compose it are in the same syllable, the second guideline (as in decoding) is to *divide the unknown root into syllables before the search for a known word starts.* This second guideline keeps students from using *cab* for help with *cable* and, for instance, from using *not* for help with *notion.* On the other hand, the same guideline should encourage students to use *fun* to get *fund* decoded correctly *and* quickly. Similarly, known words like *you, raw,* and *war* can help speed up decoding *youth, prawn,* and *dwarf.*

The next two guidelines should come as no surprise because of the significance of vowel letters for pronunciations:

> The shorter word must include all the vowel letters in the syllable. This is why the pronunciation of *eat* helps with *bleat* whereas the pronunciation of *at* does not.
>
> The shorter word must have the same spelling pattern as the syllable in which it occurs. This means that students who use *she* to decode *shed* have problems.

Admittedly, all the precautions that must be taken may lead you to conclude it is easier to tell students, *"Don't* use short words you know to help with longer ones that you don't know!" However, two facts may steer your thoughts in another direction. The first is that none of the guidelines is different from anything already discussed and recommended for decoding. The second fact is the significance of quick decoding for comprehension (7). Given these two facts, the recommended guidelines are summarized in Figure 10.3. As with anything else, they should be taught a little at a time with the help of many examples.

DECODING DERIVED
AND INFLECTED WORDS

Now that sample lessons for affixes have been described, it is time to discuss a strategy for decoding formidable-looking words like *unenviable, fore-*

Precautions	Acceptable	Unacceptable
1. Only roots should be examined to see if they contain shorter known words.	sh<u>rill</u>	<u>non</u>example
2. All letters in the shorter word must be in the same syllable in the longer root.	a<u>muse</u>	<u>amu</u>se
3. The shorter word must include all the vowel letters in a syllable.	h<u>eat</u>	he<u>at</u>
4. The shorter word must have the same spelling pattern as the syllable in which it occurs.	sn<u>ail</u>	<u>met</u>

Figure 10.3 Using Short Known Words with Longer Unknown Words

telling, and *lawlessness*. One reason a strategy needs to be taught was stated effectively as long ago as 1959 by Lee Deighton. He observed that "frequently, polysyllables composed by adding one suffix to another frighten the developing reader out of all proportion to their real difficulty" (1, p. 29).

Directions for systematizing, and thus simplifying, the decoding process for derived and inflected words are given below.

Decoding Derived and Inflected Words

1. Lay aside the prefix first.
2. Lay aside each suffix, one at a time.
3. If the root is unfamiliar, decode it.
4. Put back the suffix immediately next to the root.
5. If there is a second suffix, add that next.
6. Add the prefix last.

Students who have been taught the strategy outlined here are prepared to deal with unfamiliar words like *plentifully, readmit, worthlessness,* and *unenviable* by dismantling and reassembling structural units (initially on paper, later mentally) in the following ways.

plentifully	readmit	worthlessness	unenviable
plentiful	admit	worthless	enviable
plenty	readmit	worth	envy
plentiful		worthless	enviable
plentifully		worthlessness	unenviable

Why prefixes are added last when the structural units of a word are being reassembled (and why they are removed first in the dismantling process) can be explained with the help of words like *unwanted, immeasurable,* and *indefinable.* This is the case because they demonstrate that a prefix is not always attached to roots (*unwant, immeasure, indefine*) even though it is affixed to derived and inflected words containing those roots (*unwanted, immeasurable, indefinable*). Recognition of this fact indicates that the best sequence for all derived and inflected words is to remove prefixes first and add them last.

To see how the strategy that has been outlined functions with unknown words, the thoughts of another decoder are presented. He is having trouble with *unenviable* in the context *They had the unenviable job of having to do it twice.*

> This word says something about the job they had to do two times. The *u* and *n* could be a prefix. I better take a look at the end. If *a, b, l,* and *e* are a suffix, that could mean the *i* is really *y.* If it is, the root is just those four letters: *e, n, v, y.* Oh, sure, *envy.* That means you want something. Maybe somebody has something and you wish you had it. But the prefix makes it mean just the opposite. You don't want it. Let's see. *Unenviable.* That means you don't want their job. That makes sense. Who would want to have to get into that icy water twice? They had the unenviable job of having to do it twice.

Students achieve the competence reflected in the decoding efforts described above when the sequence for using cues shown earlier in Figure 10.1 was taught well and practiced often. The competency just illustrated is also the product of a long series of lessons that achieved the necessary three objectives of every lesson for an affix: (a) knowledge of how the affix is spelled and pronounced, (b) an understanding of its effect on the meaning of roots, and (c) ability to transfer these learnings to unknown words.

APPLYING WHAT HAS BEEN TAUGHT

Students who use what they know about the cueing system of English when they are reading experience the best practice. Such practice is now considered in the framework of a selection in a basal reader. The illustrative selection is the first one in a fourth-grade textbook. It tells about a girl and her grandfather who are riding the Third Avenue El in New York City when the Great Blizzard of 1888 occurs.

New Vocabulary

The words in the story that are said to be new are divided into four categories in Figure 10.4. Please examine the categories and the commentary about Figure 10.4 before proceeding.

As the commentary about Figure 10.4 points out, students who have had consistently effective instruction about contextual, graphophonic, and structural cues should require little help with the new vocabulary. Instead, they can use what they know whenever an unfamiliar word is encountered.

To help teachers decide what needs to be done with new words, guidelines are discussed in the next section. These guidelines were used to establish the four categories of words listed in Figure 10.4.

Guidelines: What to Do with New Vocabulary

Underlying the summary that follows is the importance of students' self-reliance in recognizing new or forgotten words. To foster independence, teachers need to keep certain factors in mind when they decide what to do with new vocabulary, whether it is in a basal selection or in a chapter in something like a science textbook. The five significant factors are listed below.

Factors Affecting Decisions about a New Word

1. Words in students' oral vocabularies.
2. Context in which the new word appears.
3. Spelling and pronunciation of the new word.
4. Students' ability to use contextual, graphophonic, and structural cues.
5. Words in students' reading vocabularies.

By now, the basic significance of oral vocabularies should be so apparent as to make additional comments unnecessary. Even though the relevance of the other factors listed above should also be clear, their significance will be further clarified with illustrations. This seems necessary, given the fact that one pervasive flaw in basal reader programs is the inadequacy of suggestions for new words. In the story about the Great Blizzard of 1888, for instance, six of the thirty-five words listed in Figure 10.4 are supposed to be presented to students in sentences. Teachers adhering to manual recommendations ask volunteers to read the sentences aloud and explain the meaning of the underlined (new) words. Nothing is said in the manual about what to do if problems with either pronunciations or meanings occur except to have the students consult the glossary in the back of the reader. Should any of the remaining twenty-nine words cause problems when the students are reading, they are supposed to use the glossary for them, too.

Context for New Word. As demonstrated many times, it is possible for contexts to be so generous with help that even when students' decoding ability is limited, a new word will not have to be named for them. Inherent in such a statement is that the students can read the words that make up the con-

Figure 10.4   New Vocabulary

Regularly Spelled Roots. The word *zero* (zē' rō) demonstrates that graphophonic
cues often allow only for approximately correct pronunciations. The special
emphasis in the story on cold weather plus the context in which *zero* occurs
initially (*five degrees above zero*) should readily suggest the correct
pronunciation.

Regularly Spelled Compounds. The importance of the elevated train suggests the
need (for some students) for background information that includes attention to
the meaning of *turnstile.*

Regularly Spelled Inflected and Derived Words. Because of contextual help,
meanings should cause no problems except for *indignantly.* Because *indignantly*
appears only once and also because understanding its meaning is unnecessary
for comprehending the story, time limitations may lead to the decision to check
what the students did with *indignantly* after the story is read. This point is made
to reemphasize that excessively extensive preparations for a story can have
negative consequences on students' interest in reading it.

    Some of the inflected words allow for a review of spelling generalizations.
A review of the generalization for the tense marker *-ed* might also be put on the
postreading agenda. (Obviously, nothing should be reviewed unless the need for
it exists.)

Irregularly Spelled Words. Even though *aisle* is irregularly spelled, three factors
indicate it might be possible for students to recognize it: (a) *aisle* is likely to be
in their oral vocabulary; (b) *aisle* appears initially in a helpful context (*The
conductor came up the aisle and stopped at their seat.*); and (c) the content of
the picture on the page duplicates the content communicated in the context.
Because one important goal of an instructional program is independence in
coping with unfamiliar words, a defensible decision is to wait until the story has
been read in order to learn how—or if—students dealt with *aisle.*

    Although *angel* is irregularly spelled, the contextual help available may be
sufficient to allow students to recognize it: *Mr. Smith lay in the snow. His arms
and legs were sprawled out, as if he were trying to make a snow angel.* In this
instance, students' prior experiences have to be considered when instructional
plans are made.

	Regularly Spelled Compounds	Regularly Spelled Derived and Inflected Words	
Regularly Spelled Roots			

Regularly Spelled Roots		**Regularly Spelled Compounds**	**Regularly Spelled Derived and Inflected Words**	
steam	hurricane	turnstile	struggles	remained
chimney	blizzard	pompom	circumstances	sprawled
blast	rung		confused	firmly
zero	rear		checkers	drifts
			conductor	abruptly
			stranded	cautiously
			indignantly	degrees
			huddled	acquainted

Irregularly Spelled Words

aisle	temperature
shield	thermometer
angel	numb
eager	telegraph
flight	

Students for whom ample opportunities have been provided to replace a predicted sound with others should be able to recognize *shield* and *eager*. When words like *night* (or *light*) and *thumb* are known, neither *flight* nor *numb* should be obstacles. Because the basal manual implies that *telephone* is known, *telegraph* is another word that should not require prereading attention. Contextual help is available for the two remaining words, *temperature* and *thermometer*. (*The temperature is dropping fast. The thermometer says five degrees above zero.*)

Needless to say, children who have spent all their lives on a tropical island will have more problems with both the vocabulary and the story itself than will students who have experienced blizzards and have ridden on an elevated train in a big city.

text. Specifically, a kindergarten teacher should not have to use whole word methodology with *Wednesday* if the children's knowledge includes the sequence of the days in a week and, further, if they are able to read *yesterday, was, Tuesday, today,* and *is.* When these conditions exist, the following context should allow kindergartners to reach a correct conclusion about the unfamiliar word *Wednesday:*

<blockquote>
Yesterday was Tuesday.
Today is Wednesday.
</blockquote>

It should be remembered that even though helpful contexts do allow for recognizing words, it is practice that puts them into students' sight vocabularies.

Spelling and Pronunciation of New Word. In theory, students should be able to deal with the pronunciation of regularly spelled roots even when a context reveals nothing more than their grammatical function. Theoretically, too, students should be able to cope with words composed of regularly spelled roots to which one or more affixes are added. Whether practice and theory correspond depends on the students' ability to use graphophonic and structural cues. In turn, that ability reflects the content and quality of decoding instruction.

If it is a teacher's judgment that members of an instructional group can deal with words like *steam, chimney, struggles,* and *circumstances,* four words listed in Figure 10.4, they should not be taught before the selection in which they are found is read. As with all new vocabulary (and any other feature of a selection that could cause problems), some of the time spent with the instructional group after the selection is read should be used to learn whether the words were correctly decoded *and* understood. If the meaning of a word in a particular selection may not be familiar to students and it is important for comprehending the selection, that word should be dealt with during prereading preparations.

Known Words. As mentioned, the words students are able to read account for contexts. Known words also help students to deal with new vocabulary quickly. To return to Figure 10.4, if students who will be reading the story about the Great Blizzard of 1888 know *team, last,* and *ear,* initial consonant additions allow for the efficient decoding of *steam, blast,* and *rear.* In addition, knowing *and* and *raw* should help with *stranded* and *sprawled.* As mentioned in the commentary about Figure 10.4, students who have learned to read *night* or *light* and also *thumb* should have no problems with *flight* and *numb.*

Putting It All Together. Applied to something like a basal reader lesson, all that has now been said about new vocabulary suggests the following two guidelines for teachers:

1. Examine the new words in the selection to be assigned and the contexts in which they occur initially in order to eliminate any that students ought to be able to handle alone because of (a) the words they know, and (b) their ability to use contextual, structural, and graphophonic cues.
2. Use whole word methodology with the remaining words. If any is a derived or an inflected word, present the root first.

SUGGESTIONS FOR PRACTICE

Regardless of when students learn about affixes, either at the time they are being readied for assigned reading or in a separate, special lesson, at least some of the following types of practice might be both appropriate and productive.

■ After comparative and superlative forms of adjectives are taught, students can be asked to illustrate the meanings of descriptions like *rich, richer, richest; busy, busier, busiest; clean, cleaner, cleanest.*
■ Underline the correct answers:

1. Which is the hottest?
     a lighted match   a summer day   a burning building

2. Which is the greenest?
                 a garden   tree leaves   grass

3. Which is the smallest?
                 a puppy   a bird   a kitten

With an assignment like the one just described, questions with indisputably correct answers are unnecessary; their absence, in fact, may lead to interesting discussions.

Responses to the next assignment indicate whether students understand the meaning of *root*. The assignment also allows for practice in following written directions.

■ All of the sentences below include a word ending in er. Some of these words are roots. Others are not. Read each sentence. If the underlined word is a root, write *yes* after the sentence. If the underlined word is not a root, write *no.*

1. I never like to play that game. _____
2. Please pass the butter. _____
3. He is a very fast runner. _____

Similar written assignments can focus on words ending in *or* (e.g., *sailor, color*), and *ing* (e.g., *doing, bring*). Words can be easy or difficult depending on students' ability.

The next suggestion for a written assignment is indirectly concerned with roots and directly with word families.

■ Which are in the same family? Look down each column of words. In each column, underline all the words that belong to the same family as the first word in the column.

read	count	need	roast	skill	each
reader	counter	needy	toast	skillet	teach
ready	countless	needle	coast	skillful	teacher
reading	county	needing	boast	unskilled	teaching

As mentioned earlier, generous amounts of attention should go to derived and inflected words; therefore, written assignments for them are described next.

■ Directions: For each word in the first column, write the root in the second column. Then, in the third column, write a sentence that includes the word in the first column.

	Root	*Sentence*
1. imperfectly	_____	_____
2. unsatisfied	_____	_____
3. recaptured	_____	_____

■ List words in random order, some of which are roots whereas others are derivatives. Selections should ensure that for every root (e.g., *still*) a derivative with a similar meaning (*inactive*) is listed. In a second column on the same sheet, children will write pairs of synonyms selected from the first column—for example: *clean, spotless; loyal, faithful; mad, insane; plain, unadorned.*

Bingo-like cards can be adapted for many different kinds of practice, including some for derivatives:

■ Prepare cards showing such derivatives as *incorrect, uncooked, powerful,* and *unwatered*. Words called out will be roots: *wrong, raw, strong, dry,* and so on. The job is to match synonyms, this time by covering a derivative whenever a root with a similar meaning is called out. At another time, roots are written on cards and derivatives are called out. Now the job is to cover a root if a named derivative includes it.

Other games for word structure are on the next page.

- Make two sets of word cards, one for roots and the other for prefixes and suffixes. As in a card game, deal roots to players. Affix cards are the deck. Students take turns choosing a card. If a selected affix can be added to one of the roots and, second, if students can read and define the meanings of the root and the derivative, they lay that pair of cards down. If the affix is not usable, the card is returned to the bottom of the deck. The first player out of cards is the winner. (In some cases, students will have to consult dictionaries to see whether real words are being formed.)
- Sort derivative cards into "easy," "difficult," and "more difficult" piles, which are placed face down on a table. Cards with the easiest derivatives are marked $1. Difficult ones are printed on $5 bills, and the most difficult of the derivatives go on $10 cards. Players take turns selecting a card from any pile. A correct identification, along with an explanation of the derivative's meaning, allows a player to keep the card. Otherwise it is returned to the bottom of its pile. The winner is the player whose cards add up to the most money.

When reading about these practice activities and, most of all, when decisions are being made about using them with students, it is essential to keep in mind their purpose. To lose sight of the goal—in this case, to increase knowledge of word structure in order to improve decoding ability—is to run the risk of having "fun and games" but not much more. Therefore, as with all other plans for instruction and practice, a teacher needs to ask, "*Why* am I considering doing this?"

SUMMARY

Like the earlier treatment of phonics, the present chapter concentrates on features of words that help readers work out pronunciations. Because, in this instance, the features are affixes (prefixes and suffixes), the cues highlighted in Chapter 10 also help with meaning. Because affixes have to do with the structure of words, they are considered to be structural units.

In order to foster productive instruction with affixes, the essential objectives for lessons are named. All objectives reflect the importance of quick as well as correct decoding for comprehension. In recognition of the fact that affixed words become increasingly common as students advance in their ability to read, a procedure for using a combination of contextual, structural, and graphophonic cues is outlined in Figure 10.1. Subsequently, use of the combination is illustrated. Exactly how to dismantle and reassemble structural units is explained and illustrated, too. Such details are especially important, given the fact that the most frequently used instructional materials fail to give sufficient attention to systematic ways to decode inflected and derived words. This is the case even though such words are common sources of problems for students.

Turning to teachers, Chapter 10 raised and answered two questions. Because affixes consist of prefixes, inflectional suffixes, and derivational suffixes, the first question had to do with a sequence for teaching affixes. Why the following sequence is recommended is explained with examples: (a) common inflectional suffixes, (b) readily understood derivational suffixes, (c) common prefixes, and (d) other prefixes and suffixes. The most common prefixes and derivational suffixes are in Table 10.1.

When to offer instruction about word structure is the second question considered. The importance of allowing students to experience the value of what they are expected to learn and practice accounts for the recommendation to provide some instruction about affixes when time goes to the new vocabulary that appears in text students will be asked to read. The importance of not spending so much time on preparations for assigned reading that students lose all interest in doing it explains why teaching affixes at other times was recommended, too. Regardless of the timing, the need for students to see how lessons contribute to their competence as readers should never be overlooked.

Recognizing the importance of practice, Chapter 10 concludes with a number of examples. Some would be an integral part of lessons. Others can serve well as helpful written assignments.

Generalizations for Decoding: A Summary

Syllabication

Structural Divisions:

Most prefixes and suffixes are syllables (*un lock; care less; play ing*).

When the suffix -*ed* is added to a verb ending in *d* or *t*, it is a syllable (*need ed, dent ed*). Otherwise, it adds a sound to the verb but not a syllable (*marched, pulled*).

When the suffix -*ion* is added to a root ending in *t*, the letters *tion* form a syllable (*act, ac tion*).

Phonological Divisions:

When two consonants are preceded and followed by vowels, a syllabic division usually occurs between the consonants (*win dow*).

When a vowel precedes and follows a consonant, a syllabic division usually occurs after the first vowel (*si lent*).

When *x* is preceded and followed by a vowel, the first vowel and *x* are in the same syllable (*tax i*).

When a root ends in a consonant followed by *le*, the consonant and *le* are the final syllable (*pur ple*).

For purposes of syllabication, consonant digraphs and vowel digraphs function as if they were single letters (*ath lete; au thor*).

Vowel Sounds

When a syllable has one vowel and it is in final position, it commonly stands for its long sound (*silo*).

When a syllable has one vowel and it is not in final position, it commonly stands for its short sound (*album*).

When a syllable has two vowels, the long sound of the first is common (*meet, mete*).

When a syllable has two vowels, one of which is final *e* and the two are separated by two or more consonants, the short sound of the first vowel is common (*pulse*).

Vowel sounds in unstressed syllables are often reduced to the schwa sound (*rándom*).

The digraph *oo* has both a long and a short sound (*cool, cook*).

The digraph *ow* stands for the long *o* sound (*own*), and for the sound in the initial position in *owl*.

When a vowel is followed by *r* in a syllable, three different sounds are possible (*art, her, for*).

When a vowel is followed by *re* in a syllable, five different sounds are possible (*care, mere, hire, bore, pure*).

Y Functioning as a Vowel

When *y* is in medial position in a syllable that has no vowel, it commonly stands for the short *i* sound (*myth*).

When *y* stands for the final sound in a multisyllable word, it usually records the long *e* sound (*fancy*).

Otherwise, *y* is likely to stand for the long *i* sound (*try, style, cycle*).

Consonant Sounds

When *c* and *g* are followed in a syllable by *e*, *i*, or *y*, they commonly stand for their soft sounds (*cell, cigar, cyst; gem, gin, gypsy*). Otherwise, the hard sounds are common (*can, talc, act; glad, pig, wagon*).

The letter *s* stands for either /s/ or /z/ (*see, has*).

The digraph *th* records a voiced and a voiceless sound (*the, thin*).

The digraph *ch* commonly records the sound heard initially in *chop*. It may also stand for the sounds heard initially in *chef* and *chord*.

Together, *q* and *u* stand for either /kw/ or /k/ (*quit, plaque*).

The letter *x* stands for /z/, /ks/ or /gz/ (*xylophone, sox, exact*).

REVIEW

1. Define each term listed below. Include at least two examples in the definitions.

    a. word family   **c.** prefix   **g.** inflectional suffix
    b. root   **d.** derivational suffix   **f.** structural unit

2. From your study of Chapter 10, you should be able to explain the following statement. Support your explanation with examples different from those in the chapter.

    In decoding, structural units are considered first, then phonological divisions. The structural units take precedence over the phonological units because of the fundamental importance of meaning.

3. What are the *structural* divisions in the following words?

    a. imperfectly   **d.** readable   **g.** miscounted
    b. goldfish   **e.** showy   **h.** meaningful
    c. syllable   **f.** reappointment   **i.** fabrics

4. If students have a problem recognizing and/or understanding a derivative, teachers should be prepared to decompose and reassemble the structural parts in a way that helps with both the pronunciation and the meaning. Guidelines for doing that are provided in Chapter 10.

    a. State the sequence for dismantling and synthesizing structural units.
    b. Keeping the sequence in mind, show on paper (as you might list on a chalkboard) the steps in dismantling and reassembling the structural units in the words below.

    resprinkled   unforgettable   momentarily   impersonally

5. Having sorted out the structural units in four words, you should be in a position to comment on the following claim. Referring to spelling generalizations like those listed in Chapter 10, some authors (3) state:

    Although these skills may be useful when composing text, there is little use for such spelling rules when interpreting text. (p. 360)

    Do you agree or disagree with the statement above, and why?

6. The objectives that every lesson dealing with an affix needs to realize are pinpointed in Chapter 10. Keeping them in mind, what should students know and be able to do when a lesson for the prefix *mis-* concludes? Name derivatives that can be used both to help with the instruction and for application.

REFERENCES

1. Deighton, Lee C. *Vocabulary Development in the Classroom.* New York: Teachers College Press, Columbia University, 1959.

2. DeStefano, Johanna S. *Language, Society, and Education: A Profile of Black English.* Worthington, Ohio: Charles A. Jones Publishing Company, 1973.
3. Duffy, Gerald G.; Roehler, Laura R.; and Putnam, Joyce. "Putting the Teacher in Control: Basal Reading Textbooks and Instructional Decision Making." *Elementary School Journal* 87 (January, 1987), 357–366.
4. Durkin, Dolores. "An Attempt to Make Sense Out of a Senseless Basal Reader Lesson." *Illinois Reading Council Journal* 14 (Spring, 1986), 23–31.
5. Durkin, Dolores. *The Decoding Ability of Elementary School Students.* Reading Education Report No. 49. Urbana: University of Illinois, Center for the Study of Reading, May 1984.
6. Durkin, Dolores. *Strategies for Identifying Words.* 2nd ed. Boston: Allyn and Bacon, Inc., 1981.
7. Lesgold, A. M., and Curtis, M. E. "Learning to Read Words Efficiently." In A. M. Lesgold and C. A. Perfetti (Eds.), *Interactive Processes in Reading.* Hillsdale, N.J.: Erlbaum, 1981.
8. Morgan, Argiro L. "A New Orleans Oral Language Study." *Elementary English* 51 (February, 1974), 222–229.
9. Roth, Steven F., and Beck, Isabel L. "Theoretical and Instructional Implications of the Assessment of Two Microcomputer Word Recognition Programs." *Reading Research Quarterly* 22 (Spring, 1987), 197–218.

Chapter 11

Vocabulary Knowledge

PREVIEW

Just as interest in reading comprehension has been increasing, so has interest in vocabulary acquisition. This is natural when it is kept in mind that over several decades, researchers have consistently reported high correlations between knowledge of word meanings and the ability to comprehend connected text.

To the extent that is possible, the treatment of vocabulary knowledge in Chapter 11 takes into account the research that has been reported. That is why this chapter assigns special importance to the reading that students do on their own, as researchers generally agree that this is the richest source for vocabulary acquisition. You might want to take another look, therefore, at ways in which teachers foster reading, which are described in Chapter 6.

Even though it is good to know that what is enjoyable is also productive, it needs to be kept in mind that the students who do most of the independent reading are the better readers. (Or, as has been said, "The rich get richer while the poor get poorer.") This point is made because it reinforces the importance of providing children with the best possible instructional programs year after year.

Features of instruction with vocabulary that make it effective are identified and discussed in Chapter 11. The instruction described is presented in the context of "facilitating comprehension." (See Figure 10.2 in the previous chapter.) The specific context is the prereading preparation made for assigned reading.

Recognizing that much of the assigned reading in classrooms is of basal reader selections, this chapter urges teachers to look in the environment for additional text. Exactly how environmental text is useful for enlarging vocabularies—and for promoting interest in words—is generously illustrated.

Chapter 11 also includes accounts of what has been seen in classrooms when word meanings are the concern. Implications of the observed behavior for work with vocabulary are explained.

As with all the chapters in this book, you are urged to examine the outline and to read the Summary before your study of Chapter 11 begins.

To hear someone say "I know what that word means" is to hear a statement that communicates anything but a single, precise message. For example, having known about cows for a good many years, I feel confident in claiming, "I know the meaning of 'cow'." Nonetheless, my contacts with cows (pictures, movies, quick glances at them from a car) make it unequivocally clear that my understanding of "cow" does not begin to approach the level achieved by children raised on dairy farms. Equally clear is that my understanding of "cow" is superior to that of an individual whose knowledge of "cow" derives solely from the definitions provided by a dictionary found in an elementary school classroom (16): "The full-grown female of any bovine, or oxlike, animal or of certain other animals the male of which is called *bull*, as the elephant, the moose, and the whale" (p. 183). In this instance, persistence is not rewarded, as the second definition in the same dictionary contradicts the first: "A domestic bovine animal without regard to age or sex; as, farmhouses and barns and *cows* in every pasture" (p. 183).

More about dictionaries and glossaries appears later. For now, the significant three points for teachers and prospective teachers are the following:

1. Word meanings are understood at a number of different levels.
2. Which level is sufficient depends on why the meanings need to be known.
3. Means for acquiring word meanings vary greatly in their effectiveness.

LEVELS OF WORD KNOWLEDGE

Isabel Beck and her colleagues at the University of Pittsburgh distinguish among "levels of word knowledge" in a way that emphasizes the importance of rapid lexical access for reading comprehension. ("Lexical access" has to do with the fact that the meaning of a word is stored in a person's memory, which makes the meaning accessible. Rapid lexical access indicates that the meaning can be recalled quickly and effortlessly.) The three levels of word knowledge suggested by Beck et al. (1) are defined here:

Established: Meaning is quickly, even automatically, accessed.

Acquainted: Meaning is known and can be accessed but "only after deliberate attention has been focused on it" (p. 12).

Unknown: Meaning "has not been established in semantic memory" (p. 12).

Why established meanings are significant for reading comprehension is the same reason that correct *and* quick decoding is important: Whenever readers have to attend consciously to individual words, their attention is taken away from the meaning of the whole of the text.

Reading that is not hesitant is now referred to as *fluent*, a term once reserved to describe "smooth" oral reading. The importance of fluency for comprehension has implications for instruction with word meanings: Established meanings are rarely achieved with as few as one or two contacts with a word. Such a contention is especially accurate when the learner must acquire a new label (new name) for a new concept (new referent).

LEVELS OF INSTRUCTIONAL NEEDS

Just as there are levels of word knowledge, so, too, are there levels of instructional needs. Levels of instructional needs refer to the different kinds of tasks teachers face in their efforts to add to students' oral vocabularies. Starting with the easiest, the four tasks are:

1. Teach a label for a familiar referent.
2. Expand the meaning of a familiar referent.
3. Teach an additional label for a familiar referent.
4. Teach a new label for an unfamiliar referent.

Name for Familiar Referent

Teaching a label for a familiar referent is something parents and teachers of young children do with great frequency. Often, one of the first efforts of this kind is getting a child to call his father (familiar referent) "daddy" (label). Helping children learn the names of colors they have experienced is another common example of teaching labels for familiar referents. Later, a child may learn that the very tall buildings he sees whenever he goes downtown are "skyscrapers."

Expanded Meaning for Familiar Referent

Another instructional need, expanding the meaning of a familiar referent, goes on during one's entire life. After all, who really understands the meaning of "death" until a loved one dies? And who truly understands "friendship" until a crisis occurs and it is experienced or sadly missed? Implicit in all this is, first, that the meanings of many words change and grow as people change and grow and, second, that children have not lived long enough to have a full understanding of many words, including fairly common ones.

However, let's take a common word such as *pillow* to trace how its meaning may expand. At first, a child may know a pillow only as something soft that supports his head and makes him generally more comfortable in bed. He may eventually learn that when more than one pillow elevates his head in bed, it reduces the amount of coughing he does. He may also learn that having pillow fights with a sibling is fun but forbidden.

Later, this same individual comes to know that some pillows, such as the ones carefully placed on chairs in the livingroom, serve a decorative function and are not to be touched by head or hand. Still later, when his mother is caring for an ill and elderly grandparent, this person learns that pillows are used to ensure that someone lies in a variety of positions, thus preventing bedsores. Some relatively few children also learn that *pillow* is the name of the structure that supports bowsprits on boats.

Additional Name for Familiar Referent

In the examples just described, the name *pillow* remains unchanged even while its meaning is expanding. A different instructional task is teaching additional names for the same referent. Teachers who use *manuscript writing*, for instance, may not be aware that they are using a new label for the familiar behavior known to children (and parents) as *printing*. Similarly, the furniture salesperson who talks about sofas may not know he is using a new label for what the child accompanying his parents refers to as *couch*. Visits to unfamiliar geographical areas are also common times for acquiring new labels for familiar referents. Even though at home one might carry soft drinks in a bag, elsewhere pop is carried in sacks. All this suggests that even though the classroom is the setting for the treatment of vocabulary knowledge in this chapter, the productivity of nonschool sources of influence should not be underestimated.

Name for Unfamiliar Referent

The influence of all that happens outside the classroom is particularly noticeable when it comes to the fourth and most difficult task in vocabulary instruction: teaching a new label for a new referent. It is now that the value of out-of-school experiences for vocabulary development is so apparent. For example, even while one student is giving a glowing, detailed account of the mountains he and his family saw on their last vacation, other members of the same instructional group may have experienced nothing taller than the pile of dirt hauled to a city park to allow for sledding in the winter.

The difficulty of teaching names for unfamiliar referents was effectively depicted by Edward Dolch as long ago as 1951:

> *The average adult tries again and again to tell children with words what things are. . . . The child asks, "What is a snake?" The adult says, "An animal that crawls along the ground." The child imagines such an animal and asks, "But his legs will be in the way." The adult says, "Oh, he hasn't any legs." So the child takes off the legs and sees a legless body lying there. "But how does he crawl around without legs?" "He wiggles," says the adult. The child tries to make the legless body wiggle. "How does that get him to go forward?" The adult loses his temper. The peculiar way in which part of the snake pushes the other part cannot be described. It has to be seen. Let us go to the zoo. (5, p. 309)*

The essence of Dolch's observations can be summed up as follows:

Experiences   →   Acquisition of → Increase in
(direct or vicarious)   knowledge and   vocabulary
                           concepts

The connections portrayed above are especially relevant for middle- and upper-grade teachers. This is the case because the textbooks they are often expected to use present students with large numbers of words that they have neither seen nor heard before. Of relevance now is that many of these words are in the instructional category, "teaching a new name for a new concept." In spite of this, a traditional practice in the most frequently used materials, namely, basal series, persists: by fourth grade, and sometimes as early as late third grade, meanings are supposed to be clarified by having students look up words in glossaries.

One problem with glossaries and dictionaries is illustrated at the start of the chapter; namely, explanations may be as difficult to understand as the word supposedly being clarified. William Nagy (18), a linguist, specifies this criticism with precise figures. In one basal reader glossary, a word listed is *image*, which is defined as "a likeness." Nagy notes:

> likeness *is a relatively rare word; it occurs less than twice in a million words of text.* Image, *the word it is supposed to be explaining, is far more frequent, occurring 23 times per million words of text. (p. 10)*

With additional examples, Nagy points out another flaw in the glossaries examined: The explanation offered for a word does not fit the context in which the word occurs in the basal selection.

Despite the many problems shared by glossaries and dictionaries, assignments like the following—this was on a chalkboard in a fifth grade—continue to be more common than they ought to be:

1. Write each word three times.
2. Look up the meaning of each word in the dictionary.
3. Write that meaning after each word.
4. Write a sentence using each word.

The fact that many words do not have *a* meaning is discussed next.

POLYSEMOUS WORDS

As Chapter 6 pointed out, and as you know from experience, words often have more than one meaning. The more common a word is, in fact, the more meanings it is apt to have, as shown on the next page.

Don't *run* so fast.
She has a *run* in her stocking.
There will soon be a *run* on the banks.
He batted in a *run* when it counted.
The car will *run* better now.
Everybody wants to *run* for that office.
Would you *run* some errands for me?
They *run* a risk every time they dive.
She really knows how to *run* a business.
Both roads *run* north and south.
I hope I don't *run* into them at the store.
Those trucks seem eager to *run* us down.
The contract will *run* for only one year.
Some children *run* the streets day and night.

A word like *run* is referred to as a *homonym* or a *polysemous* ("many meanings") *word.* Even though the sentences listed above do not exhaust the meanings of *run*, they demonstrate that the common practice of having students look up *the* meaning of a word in a dictionary is not the most realistic or effective way to develop oral vocabularies. Better ways are described here. Before they are, the next section reviews findings and recommendations from research.

RESEARCH: SOME FINDINGS AND RECOMMENDATIONS

Research is not required to inform us of the dependence of reading comprehension on vocabulary knowledge. Have we not all experienced the frustration of not being able to answer a question in an examination—perhaps a very important examination—because the meaning of one key word was unfamiliar? Research data reinforce the significance of vocabulary knowledge. In a study in which sixth graders were the subjects, for example, unfamiliar words in basal reader stories were replaced with familiar ones. As a result, "Comprehension of the stories increased at least 50 percent . . ." (23, p. 604).

Neither experience nor intuition prompt questions about this conclusion; nonetheless, it must be acknowledged that research has also shown that improvement in comprehension is not an inevitable result of preteaching difficult words (17). Some researchers who have wondered why the prereading instruction had little effect on comprehension (1, 18, 25) have pointed out two possible reasons. One was the failure to concentrate on words that were central to the most important content in the text. Dividing available time among all the words whose meanings might not be known is thus questioned. The second reason proposed is related to the first, as it suggests that a superficial understanding of a word's meaning is not likely to contribute to comprehension.

The two reasons suggested for the failure of word instruction to have a positive impact on comprehension are discussed further in the context of guidelines for teaching unfamiliar words.

Because time is not unlimited, the first guideline for teachers to bear in mind is to choose for prereading attention only words that (a) must be understood if the assigned selection is to be comprehended adequately well, and (b) the selection itself does not explain. How this guideline functions is illustrated below.

Swan

For a selection whose purpose is to explain how *swan song* came to mean "a last effort" or "a final piece of work," students should have some idea of what a swan is. However, because two illustrations in the selection show swans, it is only necessary to provide the correct pronunciation for *swan*, because it is irregularly spelled. (*Cygnet* is listed as another new word but is not of major importance. In addition, the selection identifies the referent. Because *cygnet* is regularly spelled, students should be able to reach a correct conclusion about the pronunciation.)

Probe

This regularly spelled word is important to understand in a story about an adolescent who gets into trouble when he tries to keep his best friend out of trouble. In this case, redundancy in the text permits students to infer the meaning, which can be discussed after the selection is read. Whether students reached a correct conclusion about the meaning can also be determined by posing a question about the story that can be answered only if *probe* is understood.

Apprentice

The main character in a story is an apprentice serving under an experienced silversmith. Although *silversmith* is explained in the text, *apprentice* is not. This is a word, therefore, meriting prereading attention.

The first guideline for teachers can now be summarized as follows. Words that are not in students' oral vocabularies should be selected for instruction, not on the basis of their difficulty but in relation to their importance for understanding what the students are expected to read (25). This same point, plus another, was made in the previous chapter in the commentary about Figure 10.4, which lists new vocabulary in a basal selection: "Because of contextual help, meanings should cause no problems except for *indignantly*. Because *indignantly* appears only once and also because understanding its meaning is unnecessary for comprehending the story, time limitations may lead to the decision to check what the students did with *indig-*

nantly after the story is read. This point is made to reemphasize that excessively extensive preparations for a story can have negative consequences on students' interest in reading it."

Once a decision is made that the meaning of a word merits instructional time, the attention it receives should allow for an in-depth as opposed to a superficial understanding. In some instances, in-depth knowledge has already been acquired, as when the instructional task is to teach a name for a familiar concept. (For example, children have seen objects that are either square or rectangular in shape. The task for the teacher, therefore, is to help them learn that one shape is called "rectangle," the other "square.") In-depth knowledge also exists when the need for students is to learn that another name for *scold*—something they have experienced on a number of occasions—is *reprimand*.

A different task faces teachers when the need is to help students understand the meaning of *smoke* used in a selection that tells of various ways in which food is preserved. The same comment applies to *cure*, also in the selection.

A more difficult task is helping students achieve an understanding of such words as *disenchantment*, *awe*, and *wistful*. Unlike other words in which both the referent and the label are also unfamiliar (e.g., *crescent*, *winch*, *dam*, *barge*, *dwarf*, *meadow*), these kinds of words cannot usually be explained with pictures. As a result, the tendency is to try to explain a word such as *awe* with other words, which may be as unfamiliar as *awe*. Some time ago, Albert Harris (9) effectively described the hazards of this all-too-common practice:

> One difficulty with this procedure is the danger of relying on superficial verbalizations. Words that are clear to the teacher may be quite hazy to the child. Many of the classical boners are due to a superficial and inadequate grasp of word meanings. It is not sufficient to tell a child that frantic *means* wild, *or that* athletic *means* strong; *he may try to pick* frantic flowers *or pour* athletic vinegar *into a salad dressing. (p. 409)*

To sum up, then, limited time means that teachers should provide direct instruction only for words that are essential for understanding a given piece of text. The amount of time required for the instruction depends not only on the ability of the students but also on the exact nature of the instructional task. Teachers can define the task for each selected word by considering what it is that is unfamiliar—the label, the referent, or both.

The next sections describe effective ways for adding to students' vocabulary knowledge.

CHARACTERISTICS OF EFFECTIVE INSTRUCTION

Persons who have studied vocabulary instruction agree that effective teaching (a) relates what students know to the word receiving attention, (b) shows the relationship (whenever possible) of the word targeted for instruction to other words, and (c) provides opportunities for students to use the word they are learning in thoughtful ways. Each feature of instruction is now discussed.

Makes Use of What Students Know

Because learning can be viewed as moving from what is known to what is new but related, attempts to instruct about unfamiliar words are improved when students are encouraged to talk about what they know that is relevant to what is to be taught. With this in mind, a teacher might initiate prereading preparations for a selection about *smoking* and *curing* as preservative processes with a comment like, "I don't know why, but twice this week I've had to return milk to the store because it was sour. Has that ever happened in your family?" Guided by the teacher, the ensuing discussion brings out the fact that very cold temperatures help keep certain foods fresh, including dairy products. It is only natural for the teacher to ask next, "Do you know of other ways to keep something like meat and fish from spoiling?" Responses let a teacher know what does or does not need to be done with the words *smoke* and *cure*. In one case, she might end up writing on the board what the students already know about smoking and curing. Now, the overall purpose to establish for the reading that will ensue is to see whether the students learn something new—or contradictory—about the two processes. Consequently, the postreading discussion should concentrate on questions like: What did you read that you already knew? What new information did you pick up? Are there any differences or contradictions between what you told us earlier about smoking and curing and what the author said?

If an instructional group appears to know nothing about smoking and curing as preservative processes, prereading preparations proceed differently. In this case, the teacher asks the students to explain the meaning of *smoke* and *cure* (which are on the board), after which she tells them that both words have different meanings in the selection they will soon read. Because refrigeration has already been discussed as one way to keep foods fresh, the teacher adds that *smoke* and *cure* also have something to do with food preservation. The two processes are clearly explained in the text, and so nothing else is done with the two words at this time. How the meanings of *smoke* and *cure* are extended as a result of the selection will be discussed once the reading is done.

Shows Relationships among Words

In recent years, procedures that use what are called, at various times, *semantic maps, semantic webs,* and *conceptual sets* have been recommended. As stated in Chapter 6, "Whatever the name, attending to an unfamiliar word not in isolation but as a member of a semantically related group of words makes that word more meaningful as well as more memorable." Even though references were made in the earlier chapter to various kinds of meaning-based groups of words, a few additional samples are offered here.

One teacher I'm acquainted with, who recognizes the value of relating one word to others, frequently posts charts showing semantically related words such as the following:

Movement		
walk	dash	scamper
run	stroll	
skip	strut	

As the chart shows, this teacher has a place ready for *stalk* and *swagger*, two words introduced in selections not yet assigned.

Should *gaunt* be a new and important word in a story and the gaunt person is not pictured, its meaning can be clarified with the help of *scaling*. (Use of scaling is appropriate when word meanings differ from each other by degree.) In this instance, the students know *thin, skinny,* and *bony,* which makes the following continuum meaningful:

thin   skinny   bony   gaunt

If the same students have been taught the prefix *mal-*, then the word *malnourished* might be added to the board and discussed in relation to *gaunt*. The fact that words with similar meanings convey different messages might also be considered. Now, words like *skinny, thin, slim,* and *slender* are appropriate, as is the question, "How would you prefer to be described, and why?"

As is seen in these illustrations, discussing words in relation to other words does more than just prepare students to comprehend a particular selection. It also allows for contacts with words that are frequent enough to put their meanings into the category referred to by Beck et al. as "established" (1).

Includes Opportunities to Use Newly Acquired Vocabulary in Thoughtful Ways

Once students seem to understand the words selected for instruction, they should have the opportunity to use them in thoughtful ways. One very meaningful use is provided by reading the selection in which the words appear one or more times. Before or after the selection is read, other contacts should be provided that encourage further thinking about meanings. A few ways in which students can be encouraged to use, rather than just state, meanings are illustrated below.

Questions:
What does it mean when someone says, "The countryside is so gaunt in winter?"

Multiple-choice items:

A hungry squirrel is likely to   stroll
                                  strut   when he sees a nut.
                                  scamper

True-false statements:

He is an ambidextrous talker. _____

Definitions:

Define <u>stock</u>:

a. as a chef might explain it.
b. as a farmer might explain it.
c. as a merchant might explain it.

Completing sentences:

There was a paucity of rain. Therefore,

Analogies:

A _____ is to a cygnet as a horse is to a foal.

Word categories:

Underline all the words below that make you think of your ears rather than your eyes.

bleating   retorted   glared   coastline   stethoscope

Ideally, whenever students are asked to respond to requests like those suggested above, the chance to explain responses should be available. I'm reminded of this need because of what occurred in a first grade in which a group was just completing a page in a workbook. The task was to read the three words listed in each of nine boxes and to cross out the word that did not belong with the other two. One box listed *dog, bird,* and *car.* When one girl was asked why she crossed out *bird*—the "correct" answer is *car*—she explained, "You need a license for a dog and a car but not for a bird."

RESEARCH: OTHER FINDINGS AND RECOMMENDATIONS

Even while some studies are demonstrating the success of vocabulary instruction that adheres to guidelines that have been discussed (1, 3, 25), other researchers are emphasizing that the large number of words that students know cannot be accounted for solely by direct instruction (11, 19, 22). At the center of their portrayal of vocabulary growth is "incidental learning from reading" (11, p. 785). Or as Nagy, Herman, and Anderson put it so well, "our results strongly suggest that the most effective way to produce large-scale vocabulary growth is through an activity that is all too often interrupted in the process of reading instruction: reading" (20, p. 252).

Incidental Learning from Reading

Why regular, extensive reading produces increments in vocabulary reflects the characteristics of effective instruction. To begin, extensive reading promotes the use of what is known to acquire new learnings. Second, reading allows an individual to experience the relationships that exist among words. And, certainly, every instance of reading fosters a meaningful use of words. Finally, by supplying repeated contacts with words over a period of time, extensive, regular reading allows for the fact that the acquisition of meaning is a gradual process that moves from partial knowledge of words to in-depth knowledge.

Based on research, then, recommendations for teachers interested in promoting maximum vocabulary growth are to:

1. Provide as much direct vocabulary instruction of the type described as time permits.
2. Encourage, and allow time for, students to read.
3. Do whatever is possible to increase students' ability to learn words on their own when they do read.

Increasing the independent learning just referred to is covered in Chapter 10, "Structural Analysis," when the value of affixes for ascertaining meaning is discussed. Because the chapter about contexts (Chapter 7) confines the discussion of contextual cues to the help they offer with word recognition, their value for helping with the meaning of words is dealt with now.

Learning from Contexts

Agreement exists about the contributions that contexts make in helping students recognize words that are familiar orally but unfamiliar in their written form. It is also agreed that contexts determine the meaning of a large number of words. That contexts even determine the pronunciation of certain words is referred to earlier when homographs are discussed.

In contrast, whether contexts reveal the meaning of unfamiliar words often enough to allot instructional time to this topic is something still being debated (2, 19, 21, 24). In the midst of the debate, however, certain aspects of the question have sufficient acceptance as to warrant making them explicit here.

One area of agreement is that naturally occurring prose is not nearly as helpful with meanings as some basal reader programs suggest. Another point of agreement—one that is very important for teachers to keep in mind—is that contexts may appear to be more helpful than they actually are. Consider the following context as an example.

Jason and Andrew are brothers. They are siblings.

For those familiar with the word *siblings*, the context seems to help with its meaning. In contrast, for readers who have no idea what *siblings* means, the same context—besides being artificial text—merely indicates that *siblings* is a noun or an adjective that pertains to both Jason and Andrew. Therefore, it could have something to do with their minds (scholars?), with their motor skills (athletes?), with their behavior (delinquents?), or with their occupation (janitors?).

Admittedly, there may appear to be a contradiction between the questions being raised about contextual help for word meanings and the earlier contention that regular, extensive reading is a rich source of vocabulary growth. This is the time, therefore, to point out that extensive reading allows individuals to encounter words over a long period of time and in a wide variety of contexts. Understanding, therefore, may accumulate slowly but steadily. To be remembered, too, is that extensive reading provides contexts that far exceed a sentence or paragraph. Sometimes, in fact, a whole story or article may give precise meaning to such words as *dependent, superstitious, loathe,* and *ambition.*

The question now is, What is the meaning of all this for teachers? It means, first, that students should know that, *at times,* the words they can read will help them with the meaning of unfamiliar words. Within this realistic framework, students can be taught that the assistance may come gradually or, on the other hand, quickly and directly. Students should also be helped to know that when an author explains a word that appears to be important, they should take the time to make sure they understand the meaning, because the word is likely to recur. They should also know that when an author uses a word that seems important, but it is not explained either directly or by other known words, it is time to seek help in a dictionary. Well-taught students are aware that a meaning that fits the context needs to be selected from the dictionary.

Samples of Contextual Help

To help students acquire the understandings just named, their attention should be called to examples of contextual help that are in assigned reading, or whatever else comes to their attention. For teachers who might be helped by knowing how, in fact, contexts do provide help with meanings, the following examples are offered. Space considerations confine the examples to very brief contexts.

To be noted, too, is that what follows are only illustrative examples. More important for your students are examples taken from material they are reading, or are about to read. Keep in mind that collections of these examples may result in classifications different from those named below.

1. ***Definition.*** The most obvious source of help is found in the context that acts like a dictionary and defines a word. This direct assistance characterizes some textbooks because, at least in theory, their function is to ex-

plain and clarify. The following context is used to show that sometimes a definition helps only if other key words are understood:

> The *nucleus* is the center of the atom.

The next context is less like a dictionary than the previous one but is more helpful:

> After they crossed the mountains, they flew over the *desert.* It was very dry because a desert doesn't get much rain. There were no rivers or even creeks, and the soil looked like dry dust and sand.

2. **Synonym.** Providing synonyms is another way contexts help with meanings. The example below reveals the significance of the word *too* for reaching a conclusion about the meaning of *surrendered.*

> When the major *surrendered,* the others gave up too.

3. **Summary.** Sometimes a troublesome word is one an author uses to summarize what preceded it. What comes first, therefore, may help with its meaning:

> When John heard the noise, his knees began to shake. His hands were wet and cold. He felt as if he couldn't move. He was *terrified.*

4. **Simile.** A simile is a figure of speech that compares unlike things. For this discussion, the relevant point is that comparisons may clarify a word's meaning. The following contexts illustrate such clarification:

> The cat's eyes *glowed* in the dark as if they were little lights.
> The sports car *lurched* forward like a dog starting out to chase a cat.
> The speaker's voice *droned* on like the humming of a bee.

At times, neither *as* nor *like* is in a context; however, the comparison is implied with a metaphor:

> He took the money with the *deftness* of a pickpocket.

The illustration just cited reinforces the importance of experiences and world knowledge. Specifically, if a reader knows nothing about the characteristics of successful pickpockets, the context just referred to reveals nothing about *deftness.* In contrast, even a little knowledge of horses makes the following context helpful:

Barry's horse trotted along the path *jouncing* him from side to side.

5. ***Example.*** More prosaic than the simile or metaphor but more explicitly helpful are examples:

Joan is a very *selfish* child. For instance, she never lets any of the other children play with her toys or look at her books.

6. ***Appositive.*** Enclosed with commas, an appositive is another direct source of help:

The *minutes*, a written record of the meeting, were kept by the secretary.

Etymology, a branch of language study dealing with word origins, ought to be viewed as one way to help students expand their vocabularies.

7. ***Antonym.*** As the term *antonym* suggests, this contextual help comes through contrasts, which can be communicated in a variety of ways:

There is a great difference between the *tumult* on the outside and the peace inside.

She always is so disorganized and disorderly. She never does anything in a *methodical* way.

Some parts of the pool are deep but others are *shallow.*

I wonder whether the money will be a blessing or a *bane.*

8. ***Groupings.*** The appearance of a word in a series often assigns it at least a general classification, which may be sufficient for the reader's purpose:

I had to shop for dinner and bought bread, meat, tomatoes, and *yams.*

The wallpaper was so colorful that I can only remember seeing yellow, *aqua*, and black.

Having looked at ways in which contexts assist with word meanings, let's consider what has been learned about students and vocabulary from visiting classrooms.

CLASSROOM OBSERVATIONS: FINDINGS AND RECOMMENDATIONS

Based on frequent visits to classrooms, the need to attend to vocabulary at times other than when students are being prepared for assigned reading has been identified. One time occurs when students appear to be confused about meanings.

Confusion about Meanings

Whenever a class is observed, it seems inevitable that some answers to a teacher's questions about word meanings reveal confusion that reflects disregard for contexts. Instances of observed confusion are described below.

> In one fourth grade, a group of ten was beginning a unit of stories entitled "South of the Border." Asking, "What does *border* mean?" the teacher quickly heard, "It means somebody who lives with you, but he's not in your family." "No," continued the teacher, "it means something else." "I know," volunteered another child. "It means when you feel bored, like you're bored playing the same game."
>
> Elsewhere, the meaning of *bold* (applied to the one who had burglarized a student's home) was getting attention. One child explained its meaning by saying, "It's like when you go bowling." Disagreeing, another proposed, "It's like when a man doesn't have any hair on the top of his head."
>
> In a third grade, the teacher inquired about the meaning of *idle* found in the sentence, *The children were idle.* Almost before the question was completed, one child said, "It means a statue." "No," said the teacher, "That's a different word. Who can tell us the meaning of *this* word?"
>
> In another instance, a class had been studying reptiles in science. To supplement the text, the teacher was showing a film called "Reptiles." Because the narrator used the word "viper" several times, the teacher asked one child in the postviewing discussion, "What *is* a viper?" Without hesitation, the boy answered, "It's what's on a car window to keep it clear when it rains."

The samples of confusion are useful now in making the point that none of the observed teachers wrote anything on the board. Apparently, they had forgotten the importance of *showing* students what is being talked about or said. (One positive by-product of using something like a semantic map is the assurance that words are seen as well as heard.) Applied to the four examples cited above, "showing" means writing the following on the board as the first step in clarifying meanings, which can be done with the help of contexts.

border	bold	idle	viper
boarder	bowled	idol	wiper
bored	bald		

One further example of confusion is cited below. It underscores the need to help students realize that words commonly have more than one meaning and also that contexts must be considered when a selection is made from possible meanings:

> During a discussion of a character in a story, the teacher commented, "She certainly was a patient person, wasn't she?" Everyone agreed. The teacher then asked, "What does *patient* mean?" Immediately one child explained, "It means when you're sick and you go to the doctor and he tells you that you have to go to the hospital."

With this example as an illustration, three guidelines for dealing with confusion about meanings are listed below.

1. To begin, show students the words.
2. Use the words in a sentence or, better yet, in the larger context in which they occurred so the dependence of meaning on context can be underscored (e.g., "But the story wasn't about anyone who was sick. Remember, I used *patient* to describe the kind of person that Melissa was. I said she was patient. What does that say about her?").
3. In addition to reminding students with examples that a word usually has more than a single meaning and that contexts determine meanings, encourage thoughtful responses by not calling on anyone immediately. As another writer has observed, "Students often perceive a discussion as a contest to see who can answer the teacher's question first" (7, p. 145).

By their nature, *homophones* (words with the same pronunciation but different spellings and meanings) absolutely require "chalkboard teachers"; nonetheless, another observation in a classroom revealed the following.

At the time of the visit to this third grade, the teacher was discussing *hole* and *whole* and inquiring about the difference in their meanings. (Neither word had been written. Instead, the teacher simply said there are two different words, both pronounced "hole," and they have different meanings.) The distinction was to be communicated through sentences that the students suggested. The first sentence offered was both interesting and revealing. "Hold your hand up," said one girl. More surprising than her contribution was the teacher's response. "No," she said, "that's the word *hold*, not *hole*." Still, nothing was written.

What should have been done? More specifically, what would the teacher have done if the guidelines referred to earlier were followed? She not only would have written *hole* and *whole* at the start but also would have written contexts like:

> The surprised man fell into the <u>hole</u>.
> That is why his <u>whole</u> body hurts.

Were this done and a student's response still used *hold,* the following contrast is the next *visual* step.

hole
hold

Once the single-letter and single-sound differences are noted, a written sentence adds further help:

The cover over the hole was too heavy to hold.

All this can be summarized with the statement: Reading instruction should give students the chance to see as well as to hear what is being taught and discussed—or confused.

Efforts to help children write also require chalkboard teachers. Not long ago, I arrived in a classroom toward the end of a prewriting discussion. The writing was to be about an ancestor. Nothing was on the board when I arrived, nor was anything written by the time the discussion ended and the writing began. Given the unused chalkboard, the title used by one girl for her composition was particularly interesting: "My Auntsister."

This is an appropriate time to insert an account of one more classroom observation:

Although I did not find a reading lesson *per se* when I arrived, I saw a good example of expanding the world knowledge of first and second graders. The teacher was showing a movie in which Marcel Marceau was demonstrating pantomime. Afterward, the teacher discussed the word *pantomime* and how it is done.

One preplanned activity to give the children a chance to pantomime was called "mirroring." The teacher asked one child to help her demonstrate the activity. Facing the teacher, the student became a mirror. Her job was to copy the slow, steady movements that the teacher made as if she really were a mirror. As the two demonstrated pantomiming, the teacher emphasized that it required concentration. She stressed with the onlookers that they should watch their partner's eyes at all times and that they would be able to see side movements that their partner made because of their peripheral vision. She then explained peripheral vision and gave examples of times when it is used without our even knowing it.

The students then paired up. Everyone seemed to be concentrating as they followed the directions of the teacher. The teacher walked around the room, complimenting certain pairs of students who were working especially well. Eventually, the partners switched roles so that everyone had a turn to be a mirror. At the end, the teacher called the children together to discuss what it was like participating in the act of pantomiming.

Because of all the wonderful things this teacher did, the fact that she never wrote either *pantomime* or *peripheral vision* was unexpected. Writing *mirror* might have added one more word to the children's reading vocabularies. The experience of observing in this room reinforced the fact that even superior teachers need to ask, *"Why* am I doing what I'm doing?"

Unexpected Happenings

As previous chapters point out, highly productive instruction can occur when teachers use unexpected opportunities. How some observed teachers took advantage of the unexpected to add to their students' vocabularies is described next.

Unfortunately, the unexpected opportunity in one case was the result of a badly damaged school building that had been vandalized the previous night. Even though some teachers might have been mentally paralyzed by what was found in the classroom, the observed teacher used the occasion to discuss with her first graders the meanings of *vandal, vandalism,* and *vandalized.* (At first, one child thought Mr. Vandal had done the damage.) Because acoustical tiles had been torn from the ceiling, the meaning of *acoustics* and *acoustical* was not overlooked, nor was the need to write the words for all to see, say, and discuss, even though the teacher had to beat a path to the chalkboard because of the mess.

In another classroom, the Monday following a three-day weekend revealed a half-empty fish tank. "Did the fish drink all the water?" wondered one child. In response, the teacher filled two plates with water; by Wednesday, she was able to use them to explain *evaporate* and *evaporation* in a way that reinforced the fact that vocabulary development has to do with learning concepts, not just words.

Teachers who appreciate the need to narrow the gap between what goes on in school and what happens outside try to realize the potential of current events for expanding vocabularies. Once more, let me illustrate this commendable practice.

Worldwide attention to gasoline shortages prompted one teacher to help students understand *ration, depleted,* and *emergency,* using contexts taken from newspapers. Another teacher used heavy rains and nearby rivers to teach *flood, crest,* and *tributary.* Another teacher, this one of younger children, recognized the forthcoming spring vacation as an opportunity to contrast *solid* and *hollow* as these concepts are realized in chocolate bunnies. One more teacher used an attractive bulletin-board display of Halloween masks made by students to extend the meaning of *mask* by discussing its use in activities like skiing, scuba diving, surgery, and keeping warm.

INSTRUCTIONAL MATERIALS

Thus far, assigned reading (commonly, basal material selections) and free reading have been discussed. However, to overlook the value for vocabulary acquisition of text in the environment would be a serious omission. Such text serves well in promoting not only vocabulary growth but also interest in words. Given the importance of motivation for learning, the appeal of environmental text is of no small importance.

Environmental Text

Available daily are newspaper headlines. Samples of some with obvious potential for vocabulary growth appear in Figure 11.1. (A dependable source of colorful headlines is the sports section of newspapers, because people who compose the headlines go out of their way to avoid using *win, lose,* and *tie.*

Other examples of environmental text are listed in Figure 11.2 in a way that (a) cites the text, (b) tells where it was seen, and (c) points out its instructional potential. Inevitably, whenever teachers bring interesting samples of environmental text to class, students soon bring in more. Often, attention to environmental text can be the beginning of instruction, either planned or unplanned.

Earlier in this chapter, contextual help for word meanings is discussed and illustrated. Environmental text is useful in showing how *nonverbal* contexts may be helpful, too. For instance, the fact that the meaning of the following sentence in a newspaper was immediately apparent had much to do with the proximity of Christmas: *This is the time when we want our pasts forgotten and our presents remembered.* In another case, the smell of paint was the nonverbal context that helped explain the sign shown below.

> Watch it
> or
> Wear it!

To help students appreciate the value of nonverbal contexts for assigning appropriate meanings to words, environmental text like the following can be used. For each example given, notice that where the text was found (situational context) helps explain its meaning.

Text	*Location*
1. New quarters for *your* quarters!	Construction site for new bank building
2. We refuse no refuse.	Garbage truck
3. Eagles Slaughter Hawks!	Sports section in newspaper
4. I hope we don't meet by accident!	Bumper sticker on car
5. Body by Effort	T-shirt on board in gym
6. So glad you could bewitch us	Halloween poster welcoming guests
7. Give us a break.	Sign for glass company

Our chefs have a beef

Records will leave
taxpayers in spin

Humidity puts damper on forest fires

Cases will
house local
memorabilia

Fire sparks
questions

Crafters, florists bloom in spring shows

Stifling voice
of the people

Resource Center
searching for persons in
non-traditional careers

Push on
for arms
accord

Weather service sends
false tornado warning

Overcoming insomnia: Tips from A to Zzzzzz

Foreign films theater's new fare

Age no barrier to beauty

Builders think small
as land prices zoom

Midwest excursions
crowd the calendar

Misplaced loyalty

Door repair can unhinge you

Figure 11.1 Newspaper Headlines for Developing Vocabularies

347

Text	Source	Instructional Value
Don't gamble on quality. See us first.	Advertisement for a new furniture store	Difference in meanings of *quality* and *quantity*. Different uses of *gamble*. (*Don't gamble on quality* versus *Don't gamble on horses*.)
Don't bank it in your sock. Sock it in the bank.	Advertisement for a bank	Multiple meanings of *bank* and *sock*.
Let your fingers do the walking.	Advertisement for Yellow Pages in telephone directory	Figurative use of language.
I'm so poor I can't even pay attention.	Sign in college dormitory	Multiple meanings of *pay*.
Prices do not exceed maximum allowable price.	Sign at gasoline pumps	Meanings of *exceed, maximum,* and *allow*. Effect of suffix *-able* on meaning of root.
No commuter parking.	Sign in lot near train station	Meaning of *commute*. Effect of suffix *-er* on meaning of root.
Completely immersible.	Label on electric skillet	Meaning of *immerse*. Effect of suffixes *-ly* and *-ible* on meaning of root.
Bad news is a depressant.	*Peanuts* cartoon	Meanings of *depress* and *depressant*.
A unique blend of citrus fruits.	Label on bottle of juice	Meanings of *unique, blend,* and *citrus*.

Figure 11.2 Environmental Text

Mythology and Etymology

Anyone acquainted with mythology is aware of its presence in our language. A reason for a teacher to start reading myths to students might originate in product names like Atlas tires, Venus pencils, and Hercules fencing.

Signs in the environment such as "Pedestrian Crossing" provide a starting point for dealing with etymology, another valuable source for learning about the origins and meanings of words. Take *pedestrian* as an example. Its origin is the Latin word *pedalis*, meaning "pertaining to the foot." That origin is reflected in a number of English words:

Word	*Meaning*
pedestrian	One traveling on foot
peddler	One walking about attempting to sell something

Word	*Meaning*
pedal	Part of a bicycle or tricycle where the foot is placed
pedicure	Professional care given the feet
pedestal	Stand on which the feet of a statue are placed
centipede	A hundred-footed insect
biped	A two-footed animal

The content of Table 11.1 explains the origins of other words.

Since the likelihood of attention to origins as a way of expanding vocabularies depends on a teacher's knowledge of etymology, references are listed below. Even though some are fairly old, the information they offer is current. And even though some were prepared for children, the information they provide may be both new and interesting for the adults who read them. Additional helpful sources are referred to elsewhere (10).

Mathews, C. M. *Words, Words, Words.* New York: Charles Scribner's Sons, 1980. Starting out by noting "Human beings are talkative creatures," Mathews goes on to tell in seven chapters how words become available for humans to use. In the telling, the author relates some history of the English language as well as interesting accounts of how certain words made their way into English.

Miller, Casey, and Swift, Kate. *Words and Women.* New York: Anchor Press, 1979. Linguistic sexism is the underlying theme of this book. That it has existed in English for centuries is documented with interesting examples.

McCormack, Jo Ann. *The Story of Our Language.* Columbus, Ohio: Charles E. Merrill Books, 1957. Written for intermediate-grade students, this paperback traces the development of American English. A section in the back lists references that will be useful to anyone who wants to supplement this brief history.

Nelson, Francis W. *The History of English.* New York: W.W. Norton Co., 1963. This is a forty-one-page account of our language by a professor of linguistics. Its straightforward style makes it easy to read.

Kaye, Cathryn B. *Word Works: Why the Alphabet Is a Kid's Best Friend.* Boston: Little, Brown and Company, 1985. As the author explains in the introduction, this is a book about words—why we have them, why we need them, and how we use them.

Funk, Charles E. *Thereby Hangs a Tale.* New York: Harper and Brothers, 1950. This book focuses on words that "acquired their meanings in an unusual manner."

Lambert, Eloise. *Our Language.* New York: Lothrop, Lee and Shepard, 1955. Like so many of the other books that deal with the history of English, this one can be read by middle- and upper-grade students, yet adults will enjoy the interesting content.

Root	Meaning	Example	Prefix	Meaning	Example
audire	to hear	audience	auto	self	autograph
calor	heat	calorie	bi	two	biped
folium	leaf, sheet	folio foliage	bio	life	biography
dicere	to speak, tell	predict	geo	earth	geology
gram	letter	monogram	heter(o)	different, other	heterogeneous
graph	writing	autograph	homo	man	homicide
logos	speech reason study of	monologue logic geology	homos	same, equal	homogeneous
manu-alis	of the hand	manual	hydro	water	hydroelectric
mare	sea	marine	inter	between, among	international
meter	measure	thermome-ter	mal	bad, badly	maladjusted
mimeo	imitate	mimic	micro	small	microfilm
mittere	to send	transmit	mini-mus	little, small	miniskirt
mobilis	movable	mobile	mono	one, alone	monogram
pedis	foot	pedestrian	omni	all, every-where	omnipresent
phobia	fear or hatred of	phobia	photo	light	photograph
phonos	sound	phonics	poly	many	polysyllable
portare	to carry doorway	portable portal	post	after	postscript
scribere	to write	postscript	sub	under further division	submarine subcommittee
sonus	sound	sonorous	super	above, beyond	supersonic
spectare	to see, look at	spectacles	tele	distant	television
tenere	to hold, have	tenacious	therm	heat	thermometer
visio	sight	television	trans	across	transmit

*Suffixes are not included because so many indicate part of speech rather than meaning. Some that do suggest meaning are presented in Table 10.1.

Table 11.1 Latin and Greek Roots and Prefixes: Common Meanings

Laird, Helene, and Laird, Charlton. *The Tree of Language.* New York: World Publishing Company, 1957. This is written for children with middle- and upper-grade reading ability. Some of its most interesting pages tell how individual words came to mean what they do now. Prior to these accounts, other chapters recall some of the early history of English.

Epstein, Sam, and Epstein, Beryl. *The First Book of Words.* New York: Franklin Watts, 1954. The simplicity of this book is disarming, for it offers accurate and interesting information about many aspects of words: prefixes, suffixes, compound words ("struck-together words"), and brand names. Not many adults will read it without learning more about etymology; yet its simple style, combined with illustrations, makes it suitable for middle- and upper-grade students.

Quinn, Jim. *American Tongue and Cheek.* New York: Random House, 1980. A current look at English by a less serious author, this book defends the use of a number of words and phrases that scholars have been "trying to stamp out." In the process, it provides much information about English and its history.

Sperling, Susan K. *Tenderfeet and Ladyfingers.* New York: Viking Press, 1981. This account of the sources of selected words and expressions divides the content on the basis of body parts. Under "finger," for instance, the following expressions are covered: *thumbs down, rule of thumb, keep one's fingers crossed, knuckle down,* and *all thumbs.*

How etymology gets students interested in language, underscores relationships between words, and helps with meanings can be demonstrated by an account of one fifth grade. On the day I was observing, trials in Washington, D.C., were everyone's concern. As a result, the students were discussing *indict.* Questioned about its meaning, they offered wordy definitions, all vague. The teacher, therefore, told of the many languages from which English words have come and explained that *indict* is from the Latin word *dicere,* meaning "to speak," and from the Latin prefix *in,* whose multiple meanings include "against." She then concluded, "The word *indict* means "to speak against someone." The discussion next moved to the connection between that meaning and events in Washington, D.C.

Subsequently, the teacher redirected the students' attention to *indict* (which she had printed on the board), reminded them it had to do with speaking or speech, and asked whether they could think of other words that contained *d, i, c, t.* One child immediately proposed *dictionary,* eventually defined as a book containing words people use when they speak. Another student, whose mother was a secretary, added to the examples by offering *dictate, dictation,* and *dictaphone,* all of whose meanings were clarified. Writing *dictator,* the teacher asked why it was correct to call someone who ruled without asking for advice a "dictator." One student promptly explained, "What he says goes." "Yes," the teacher added, "his word is law."

To show how attention to etymology is possible even at a first-grade level, let me describe what was seen when a small group was being instructed in the use of a typewriter. As the teacher typed, the children watched what appeared on the paper. "What's that?" one child inquired as soon as he saw an asterisk. In response, the teacher typed *asterisk*, pronounced it, and explained that it meant "little star." Directly under *asterisk* she typed *aster*, read that, and explained it was the name of a flower that evidently had reminded someone of a star because that was what *aster* meant. After promising to bring in pictures of asters, the teacher continued with the typing; the children, with their looking.

PRACTICE

How to provide students with thoughtful practice in using newly acquired vocabulary is described under the topic of instruction. A few more possibilities are listed below.

- On tongue depressors, print words whose meanings have been studied. Print synonyms (or antonyms) on other depressors. Put them all in a box. The student's job is to match words by putting appropriate depressors together (back to back) with a clip-type clothespin. Decisions can be checked with a typed list of correct pairs. (For some students, this assignment will teach the referent for "clothespin.")
- Cover two empty juice cans or ice cream containers with gift-wrapping paper. Attach a card to each container, one displaying *fast*, the other *slow*. On other cards print expressions that have been studied (e.g., *like a streak of lightning, at a snail's pace, lagged behind, poked along, make a beeline for*). The goal is to put each expression in the appropriate container.
- Prepare a sheet showing columns of words suitable for the students engaged in the practice. For example:

casing	often	durable	cruise	payment
fence	carefully	rhombus	stroll	fragment
frame	never	oval	silent	check
peak	frequently	crescent	trot	loan

Direct students to read each group of four words, to think about the meaning of each word in a group, and to draw a line through the one that does not belong with the other three. They then tell why they crossed out one word but did not cross out the other three.

- On the back of large, colorful pictures, print descriptive adjectives. Students select a picture and write about the content, using as many of the words as possible. With newly acquired pictures, students should suggest the appropriate descriptions.

■ Practice that attends to both decoding and word meanings is illustrated below.

I love to get up early because it's so _____.

                                     quite   quiet

Jim's pranks _____ his sister.

                   irritate   irrigate

If you're not careful, the cookies will _____.

                                crumble   crumple

The _____ of the error is poor subtraction.

         basic   basis

■ On a chalkboard, list twenty words whose meanings have been studied. Direct students to write the numbers 1 through 10 on their papers in a vertical column. After the numbers, they write any ten of the twenty words. In random order, call out synonyms (or antonyms) for the twenty words. As this is done, students circle a word on their paper whenever a synonym (or antonym) is named. The first to circle all words is the winner.

■ Shuffle a set of word cards and deal them to members of a small group. The deck for the game is other cards on which homophones appear. Students take turns selecting a card from the deck. If they choose one that is a homophone for a card they hold and if they can define the two words, those cards are discarded. If not, the card is placed on the bottom of the deck. The first student out of cards is the winner.

■ Print sentences on cards, each containing a word (underlined) whose meaning is not likely to be known but can be inferred from contextual cues. (Correct definitions are on the backs of cards.) Four students select sentence cards from the deck. Time is allowed for the four to study contexts and decide on meanings. Each student then reads his sentence, explains the meaning of the underlined word, turns the card over, and reads the definition. If the explanation is correct, he advances one space upward on a board like the one shown here.

I am the winner!

(Various markers can be used: paper squares, corn, buttons.) All cards are returned to the deck. The game ends when a player gets to the top of the board.

■ Cover a potato chip can to make it look like a firecracker. Put small cardboard strips in it, each displaying a sentence with an underlined word that was recently taught. On a few cards of similar size, print *Bang!* The game proceeds as players take turns selecting a card from which they read the sentence aloud. The card is kept if they are able to explain the meaning of the underlined word. (Whenever a *Bang* card is selected, it is automatically kept, and the player gets another turn.) The winner is the student with the largest number of cards.

SUMMARY

One summary of Chapter 11 appears in Figure 11.3, which provides a map of the content. A second summary, which follows, refers to the map from time to time.

Because Chapter 11 treated vocabulary instruction as a means for improving reading comprehension, the need for *established* meanings was em-

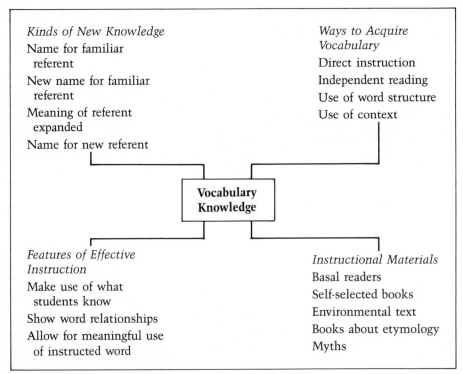

Figure 11.3 Map of Content: Chapter 11

phasized at the start. This is a description that Beck and her colleagues (1) use to refer to words whose meanings are known so well that they can be accessed automatically. The point was made that this level of word knowledge requires much more than one or two contacts with a word. It also calls for something far superior to a definitional approach for teaching vocabulary. This naturally calls into question the traditional practice of basal reader programs that rely on glossaries to explain words.

Because of the connection between vocabulary knowledge and reading comprehension, the amount of research concerned with vocabulary acquisition has been on the rise. Based on data from research, the point was made that two sources for increasing vocabulary are direct instruction and the reading that students do on their own. Features of instruction that make it effective were discussed and are shown in Figure 11.3. Because what needs to be done with any given word is affected by the kind of new knowledge that must be imparted, different types of required learnings were discussed. Again, they appear in Figure 11.3 under the heading "Kinds of New Knowledge."

To maximize the incidental learning that results from students' own reading, some researchers (20, 24) have recommended teaching students how to infer meanings from the structure of words and from contexts. Word structure was discussed in the previous chapter; the present one dealt with contexts. The present chapter also showed with a number of examples how students often explain the meaning of a word without giving any thought to the context in which it occurs. What teachers can do to remedy this omission was illustrated.

Because the importance of motivation should never be minimized, Chapter 11 gave considerable attention to environmental text, because it evokes more interest than textbooks. Using examples from a variety of sources, the chapter pointed out some of the potential of such text for enlarging vocabularies. Keeping student interest in mind, Chapter 11 also urged teachers to get their students involved with mythology and etymology. To help teachers who would like to follow the recommendation but feel unready to do so, books were recommended that are both interesting and informative about our language in general and about certain words and expressions in particular.

REVIEW

1. Explain the content of Figure 11.3 in a way that someone who has not read Chapter 11 will understand.

2. Because the topic of Chapter 11 is word meanings, it seems appropriate to request definitions and examples for each term below.

antonym	homonym	synonym
homograph	homophone	polysemous word

3. **a.** Explain why the two statements below are both correct.

> Pronunciations without meaning are useless for reading.
> Meaning without pronunciation is useful for reading.

b. What is the implication for instructional programs of their both being correct?

4. Having read Chapter 11, you should know the reasons the dictionary assignment seen on a chalkboard in a fifth-grade classroom, which was referred to in the chapter, is of questionable value. What are the reasons?

5. Chapter 11 tells how a group of children responded to their teacher's request to explain the meaning of "border" in the context "South of the Border." Based on the suggestions made in the chapter, explain how you would deal with the children's erroneous explanations.

6. When environmental text is discussed in Chapter 11, examples are cited to make the point that nonverbal contexts sometimes help with word meanings.
   a. What is meant by *nonverbal context?*
   b. For each of the seven examples listed in Chapter 11, point out the value for extending vocabularies.

REFERENCES

1. Beck, Isabel L.; McCaslin, Ellen S.; and McKeown, Margaret G. *The Rationale and Design of a Program to Teach Vocabulary to Fourth-Grade Students.* Pittsburgh: University of Pittsburgh, Learning Research and Development Center, 1980.
2. Beck, Isabel L.; McKeown, Margaret G.; and McCaslin, Ellen S. "Vocabulary Development: All Contexts Are Not Equal." *Elementary School Journal* 83 (January, 1983), 177–186.
3. Beck, Isabel L.; Perfetti, Charles A.; and McKeown, Margaret G. "Effects of Long-Term Vocabulary Instruction on Lexical Access and Reading Comprehension." *Journal of Educational Psychology* 74 (April, 1982), 506–521.
4. Carr, Eileen, and Wixson, Karen K. "Guidelines for Evaluating Vocabulary Instruction." *Journal of Reading* 29 (April, 1986), 588–595.
5. Dolch, Edward W. *Psychology and Teaching of Reading.* Champaign, Ill.: Garrard Press, 1951.
6. Freebody, Peter, and Anderson, Richard C. "Effects on Text Comprehension of Different Proportions and Locations of Difficult Vocabulary." *Journal of Reading Behavior* 15 (Spring, 1983), 19–39.
7. Gambrell, Linda B. "Think-Time: Implications for Reading Instruction." *Reading Teacher* 34 (November, 1980), 143–146.
8. Gipe, Joan. "Investigating Techniques of Teaching Word Meanings." *Reading Research Quarterly* 14 (1978–79, No. 4), 624–644.
9. Harris, Albert J. *How to Increase Reading Ability.* New York: Longmans, Green and Co., 1961.

10. Howell, Helen. "Language, Literature, and Vocabulary Development." *Reading Teacher* 40 (February, 1987), 500–504.
11. Jenkins, Joseph R.; Stein, Marcy L.; and Wysocki, Katherine. "Learning Vocabulary through Reading." *American Educational Research Journal* 21 (Winter, 1984), 767–787.
12. Jiganti, Mary Ann, and Tindall, Mary Anne. "An Interactive Approach to Teaching Vocabulary." *Reading Teacher* 39 (January, 1986), 444–448.
13. McKeown, Margaret G.; Beck, Isabel L.; Omanson, Richard C.; and Pople, Martha T. "Some Effects of the Nature and Frequency of Vocabulary Instruction on the Knowledge and Use of Words." *Reading Research Quarterly* 20 (Fall, 1985), 522–535.
14. McNeil, John D. *Reading Comprehension,* 2nd ed. Glenview, Ill.: Scott, Foresman and Company, 1987.
15. Marzano, Robert J. "A Cluster Approach to Vocabulary Instruction." *Reading Teacher* 38 (November, 1984), 168–173.
16. Merriam-Webster Series. *Webster's School Dictionary.* New York: American Book Company, 1961.
17. Mezynski, Karen. "Issues Concerning the Acquisition of Knowledge: Effect of Vocabulary Training on Reading Comprehension." *Review of Educational Research* 53 (Summer, 1983), 253–279.
18. Nagy, William E. *Teaching Vocabulary to Improve Reading Comprehension.* Urbana, Ill.: National Council of Teachers of English, 1988.
19. Nagy, William E., and Anderson, Richard C. "How Many Words Are There in Printed School English?" *Reading Research Quarterly* 19 (Spring, 1984), 304–330.
20. Nagy, William E.; Herman, Patricia A.; and Anderson, Richard C. "Learning Words from Context." *Reading Research Quarterly* 20 (Winter, 1985), 233–253.
21. Schatz, Elinore K., and Baldwin, R. Scott. "Context Clues Are Unreliable Predictors of Word Meanings." *Reading Research Quarterly* 21 (Fall, 1986), 439–453.
22. Stanovich, Keith E. "Matthew Effects in Reading: Some Consequences of Individual Differences in the Acquisition of Literacy." *Reading Research Quarterly* 21 (Fall, 1986), 360–406.
23. Wittrock, M. C. "Writing and the Teaching of Reading." *Language Arts* 60 (May, 1983), 600–606.
24. Wittrock, M. C.; Mark, Carolyn; and Doctorow, Marleen. "Reading As a Generative Process." *Journal of Educational Psychology* 67 (August, 1975), 484–489.
25. Wixson, Karen K. "Vocabulary Instruction and Children's Comprehension of Basal Stories." *Reading Research Quarterly* 21 (Summer, 1986), 317–329.

Part IV

Instruction: Connected Text

Because existing research provides no reason to question the findings of a study reported in 1975, it is correct to state that almost all of the preceding chapters deal with topics important for comprehending text. The findings, described by Roberta Golinkoff (11), are summarized below.

As compared to good comprehenders, poor comprehenders:

- Make more decoding errors.
- Take more time to decode.
- Ignore contextual cues while decoding.
- Are more concerned with pronunciation than with meaning.
- Read word by word.
- Are less adaptive in the kind of reading they do.
- Are less aware of what it means to comprehend.

The three-chapter treatment of comprehension that makes up the fourth major part of Teaching Them to Read *divides as follows. Chapter 12,*

"Comprehension," looks at comprehension and comprehension instruction somewhat globally in the sense that it provides information that is generally useful for teachers to have. Chapter 13, "Basal Readers and Narrative Text," narrows the focus in order to consider what is important for developing students' abilities to understand stories. Because everything that is known about classrooms makes it clear that most of the narrative text read in school originates in basal readers, Chapter 13 deals for the most part, but not exclusively, with those materials.

Much of the expository text read in school is in content subject textbooks; consequently, how teachers can help students be successful with those books is the dominant theme in Chapter 14, "Content Subjects and Expository Text."

Combined, Chapters 12, 13, and 14 provide an abundance of information about the comprehension process as well as numerous suggestions for instruction and practice.

Chapter 12

Comprehension

PREVIEW

Chapter 12 can be thought of as a continuation of the discussion of comprehension begun in Chapter 1. For that reason, rereading Chapter 1 constitutes preparation for the present chapter.

By the time you finish Chapter 12, you should be able to explain all the terms in the display shown below. In fact, establish that ability as one purpose for reading the chapter.

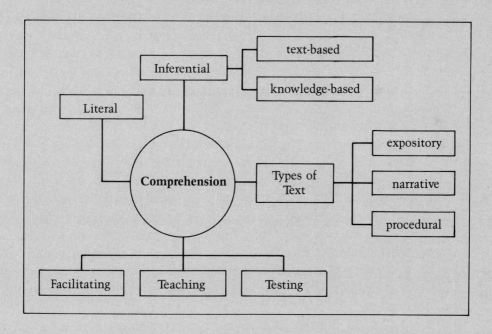

Purposes for reading are discussed frequently in Chapter 12 not only because of their significance for comprehending but also because students often hear directions like the following: "Read the next story and be ready to discuss it tomorrow." Why "Be ready to discuss it tomorrow" is hardly helpful should be clear by the time you finish the chapter.

When teachers do take the time to establish specific goals for students' reading, questions are often used to bring them into existence. This is why questions also receive generous coverage in Chapter 12.

To get a more encompassing picture of all the content of the chapter, you are encouraged to do what teachers should urge *their* students to do whenever expository text is on the reading agenda: Examine both the outline and the summary for Chapter 12 before you start to read it. To establish purposes for the reading, you may also want to examine the questions listed at the end.

Recognizing the importance for reading of activating prior knowledge, this chapter starts with a review of some of the major ideas presented in Chapter 1.

A REVIEW: THE COMPREHENSION PROCESS

Even if you were unfamiliar with Chapter 1, you should not be surprised to learn that it begins with the claim that "reading" and "comprehending" are synonymous. To get you actively and, later, consciously involved with the comprehension process, you are asked in Chapter 1 to draw a picture of the mental image evoked by the sentence *The man is digging a hole for the tree.* Subsequently, the discussion highlights the contributions that knowledge about the world makes to understanding as little as a sentence. You are specifically reminded that it is prior knowledge that allows for some of the inferences that successful reading requires. The dependence of other inferences on an author's words was emphasized, too.

This quick review should now permit you to differentiate among:

1. Literal comprehension
2. Inferential comprehension
   a. Text-based
   b. Knowledge-based

Chapter 1 goes on to explain that it is the active role that readers play in putting together what they finally comprehend that accounts for comprehension being referred to as a *constructive* process in which readers *make meaning* by interacting with the text. The interaction is the reason reading is also viewed not as a passive response to text but as an *interactive* process in which the words on the page *and* the reader's relevant knowledge play key roles.

This leads to a comparison of *external texts* (words on the page) and *internal texts* (words on the page plus inferences). The comparison serves to show why an author's words are said to be merely a *blueprint* for the message that is eventually constructed by the builder, that is, by the successful reader. The significance of the blueprint itself is not minimized, for you are reminded that the constructed message is always constrained by an author's words. The importance of those words is the reason previous chapters explain how and when to use whole word methodology to develop reading vocabularies, how to teach about the cueing system of written English so students can deal independently with words that are visually unfamiliar, and how to extend the number of words whose meanings students know.

Now, having had your own knowledge of comprehension activated, you should be ready to learn still more about the comprehension process.

COMPREHENDING: A PURPOSEFUL PURSUIT

As early as the Preview for Chapter 1, the point is made that little comprehension is likely to result if an individual wanders aimlessly through a piece of text. Instead, adequate comprehension is the product of a journey guided by a prespecified destination.

Like travelers, successful readers sometimes slow down or even stop, perhaps to think about something of interest. Like travelers, too, they may encounter problems that need to be remedied before their reading proceeds. Throughout all of this, however, the destination—that is, the purpose of the reading—is not forgotten.

When discussing the need to have a purpose, the Preview for Chapter 1 lists three questions and suggests you keep them in mind as a way of minimizing the possibility of your reading the chapter without a purpose. Posing prereading questions is something teachers can also do to facilitate comprehension. This is portrayed earlier in Figure 10.2. The point to be made now is that regardless of how purposes *are* established, they should have an effect on the kind and the rate of reading that ensues. The reading done to find a certain date, for instance, ought to be very different from the reading whose purpose is to distinguish between facts about a topic and an author's opinions about it.

Because prereading questions are used so frequently in classrooms to establish purposes for assigned reading and, second, because purpose should determine the kind of reading done, a sequence like the one displayed in Figure 12.1 merits periodic use with students in order to clarify that reading is not static but, instead, encompasses a wide range of behaviors.

From time to time, postreading discussions that center on students' responses to prereading questions should deal explicitly with the fact that

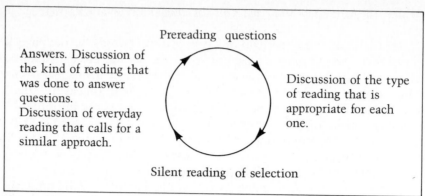

Figure 12.1   Adapting Reading to Suit Purpose

answers to questions have three different origins: (a) the text, (b) inferences derived from the text, and (c) inferences derived from the reader's relevant knowledge. (Instruction designed to teach students about the three origins can have them draw pictures based on the content of sentences in much the same way that you did in the course of reading Chapter 1.) The fact that some questions call for a reader's own opinion should be clarified, too.

Depending on the students, other procedures dealing with questions may be required. With slower children, it might be necessary to explain what it means to answer a question. To achieve that objective, one third-grade teacher who works with poor readers often lists prereading questions in the order in which a selection answers them. Taking one question at a time, she asks the children to stop reading the selection when they think they have the answer. After a child proposes one answer, other probes follow. For instance: What made you think you found the answer? Did you think you found it earlier, then decided you hadn't? Can the answer be shortened and still be correct? Finally the teacher states, "Before you start reading to find the answer to the next question, I'll read this first question again. Then someone can tell us the answer."

Another possibility available to teachers for dealing with questions is to model how to answer them. In this case, a teacher starts with questions that the text answers directly. After posing the question answered first in the text, the teacher reads the material aloud while the children follow it silently. When the answer to the question is offered, the teacher stops, repeats the question, then rereads the answer in the text. The teacher may also choose to act out a time when she thinks she has an answer but learns as she rereads the question that she is mistaken. As mentioned many times, modeling a procedure for students is an effective instructional device. Modeling might even be thought of as a way to ensure that instruction, not just practice, is provided.

PURPOSE AND COMPREHENSION MONITORING

Regardless of how purposes for reading come into existence, they are essential for *comprehension monitoring*. As the name suggests, monitoring is checking up on, or supervising, one's own comprehension. It is an example, therefore, of *metacognition*, which means "thinking about one's own thinking." Peter Johnston effectively portrays the connection between purposes and comprehension monitoring when he states that monitoring requires readers to decide "on the basis of their purpose for reading when to remove their processing from 'automatic pilot,' take conscious control, and instigate the appropriate alternative strategies" (13, p. 27).

Some of the kinds of breakdowns that can occur in the comprehension process are described in Figure 12.2.

The three examples in Figure 12.2 illustrate what Linda Baker and Ann Brown (2) call the *evaluation* side of comprehension monitoring. (The three students evaluated their behavior and identified problems.) The other side of comprehension monitoring is referred to as the *regulation* component. This has to do with the *fix-up strategies* that readers need to use when they realize a problem exists. Fix-up strategies, also called repair or remedial procedures, may involve rereading or, on the other hand, reading ahead to see whether subsequent text provides a solution. Possible fix-up strategies for the three problems just listed follow.

Fix-Up Strategies for Comprehending

Failure to Understand
Not understanding the sentence *Ogden Valley is a large oasis* because the meaning of *oasis* is unknown, the student decides to continue

---

Breakdowns in Comprehending

Failure to understand
   Student encounters the sentence *The Ogden Valley is a large oasis* and realizes he doesn't understand it because he doesn't know what *oasis* means.

Failure to make sense
   While reading *Fran got a sliver in her finger when she was sweeping the kitchen floor,* a student misidentifies *sliver,* calling it "silver." When he reaches the end of the sentence, this student realizes it doesn't make sense.

Failure to realize preestablished purpose
   A student is reading an assigned biography, is enjoying it, and suddenly realizes he has forgotten the assigned reason for the reading: to find those parts of the text that provide evidence that the biography is, at times, fiction rather than fact.

Figure 12.2 Breakdowns in Comprehending

reading on the assumption that subsequent text may clarify the meaning. In this instance, the second sentence following the one causing problems helps by stating: "Unlike the desert that surrounds it, the Valley has many farms with good green pastures for animals." (If the later text had not suggested a meaning clear enough to allow the reader to proceed and *oasis* is a word that seems to be important, an appropriate fix-up strategy is to seek assistance in a dictionary.)

Failure to Make Sense
Realizing that *Fran got a silver in her finger when she was sweeping the kitchen floor* does not make sense, the reader returns to the beginning of the sentence to reread it. The mistake is corrected, and the reader proceeds.

Failure to Realize a Preestablished Purpose
Because enjoyment replaced looking for evidence that a biography is part fact and part fiction, the reader decides, in this case, to go back to the beginning of the biography in order to start again. Fairly quickly, one type of evidence is found, namely, Harriet converses with her brother even though the author could never know exactly what she said. Having noted that piece of evidence, the reader continues with the hope of finding additional kinds of evidence. (Given the importance of fostering an interest in reading, the preestablished purpose was unsuitable for the initial reading of the biography. The evidence sought might have been dealt with during a postreading discussion or could have provided a purpose for a second reading. This is not to suggest the purpose was unimportant but, rather, to question the timing.)

One fix-up strategy not referred to in the three examples described above is adjusting rate of reading. This remedial procedure is important and, apparently, uncommon. Its *infrequent* use is attested to by research data that show that individuals tend to read at a constant rate regardless of what they are reading or why they are reading it (7). With this fact in mind, you might want to reexamine the procedure shown in Figure 12.1.

Having considered the relationship between purpose for reading and comprehension monitoring, let's now look at the connection between purpose and the nature of the text that will be read.

PURPOSE AND TYPE OF TEXT

In our everyday lives, the following sequence is typical:

Need to read → Material selected that → Material read in a way
arises   can fulfill the need   that satisfies the need

Examples of purposes and suitable materials follow.

Purpose	*Type of Text Read*
To learn a person's phone number	Telephone directory
To learn how to dye a white blouse	Directions on box of dye
To relax before going to bed	Novel
To learn the stand a newspaper has taken on a city crisis	Editorial in the newspaper
To learn how the fourth-grade manual in a newly adopted basal series handles comprehension instruction	Fourth-grade manual
To write a paper on the topic "An Uncommon Fruit"	Article in *National Geographic* about kiwis

Adding a third column, "Kind of Reading Done," to the two columns shown above would reinforce the fact that "reading" encompasses a wide range of behaviors that ought to be selected in relation to purpose and the type of text being read.

Of concern now is that purpose and type of text should match. This guideline requires explicit attention because the sequence that usually occurs outside school (purpose → select material) is commonly reversed in classrooms. That is, teachers are expected to have students read certain material—a story in a basal reader, for instance, or part or all of a chapter in a health book—and then establish purposes to guide the students through the text in appropriate ways (material → select purpose). Given this sequence, teachers need to remember that different kinds of text call for different kinds of purposes.

To specify the guideline just stated, two types of text that are commonly read in school are considered, namely, narrative text and expository text. Because each type is discussed in detail in subsequent chapters, the intention now is simply to show that what constitutes an appropriate purpose for reading a story may not be suitable for an article about uncommon fruits.

Narrative Text

Text that tells a story is *narrative* text. Stories come in a variety of forms that include:

realistic fiction	mystery	fable
fanciful fiction	tall tale	legend
historical fiction	fairy tale	myth
science fiction	folktale	epic

Stories, like sentences, have a structure. *Story structure,* sometimes referred to as *story grammar,* is composed of parts that are described in various ways. One very simple portrayal of story structure is shown below:

Setting	Problem(s)	Attempt(s) to Resolve Problem(s)	Resolution of Problem(s)
Central character(s)			
Locale			
Time			

With the help of a basal reader story, which is summarized below, the parts just named are illustrated.

> *Peter, the youngest in his pioneer family, wants more than anything else to be as big as his siblings. Recalling that someone once said that dipping a hand in a certain pool made wishes come true, Peter seeks out the pool, states his wish to grow, dips his hand into the water, and inadvertently falls into it. Lying on the nearby grass to allow his clothes to dry, Peter falls asleep. When he awakes, his clothes, having shrunk considerably from the heat of the sun, make him think his wish came true. Although he is elated at first, the walk home allows for unhappy thoughts about the possibility of being too big—too big to get into his own house, for instance. Once Peter arrives home, he is relieved to find he has not grown. Now he is content just to be able still to curl up in his mother's lap.*

For the story about Peter, the structural parts named earlier need to be expanded slightly:

Setting	Problem	Attempt to Resolve Problem	Resolution of Problem	New Problem	Resolution of Problem
Peter, a pioneer boy, lives in small town.	Wants to be big.	Dips hand in magic pool.	Shrunken clothes suggest growth.	Worry about excessive growth.	Awareness that clothes have shrunk and he has not grown.

When one overall purpose for reading a story is adequate comprehension—another purpose might be to identify the lesson a story teaches—knowing its components is necessary. This is the case because the components define "adequate" comprehension. Indirectly, therefore, they identify unimportant details. This means that if adequate comprehension of a story *is* the intention of a preestablished purpose, that purpose should reflect the structure of the story.

How one teacher used prereading questions to foster adequate comprehension of the tale about Peter is shown in Figure 12.3. The teacher's decision to cover "setting" with a brief, prereading discussion of when the story takes place is also indicated in Figure 12.3. In this case, when the story occurred is important because it accounted for Peter's wearing buckskin clothes and, in turn, for the fact that the sun shrank them when they were wet. (Students brought up in a polyester era might have little knowledge of fabric shrinkage from heat.) Because two illustrations in the basal reader show Peter wearing clothes that are obviously too small, the same teacher decided to save a consideration of why Peter thought he had grown for the postreading discussion.

The four questions listed in Figure 12.3 could be typed, copied, and distributed to members of the instructional group before they start the story. In time, students should understand that they are expected to keep such questions in mind as they read and, further, that if they are unable to answer any, rereading—at least certain parts of the story—is required. This is important, as it moves students toward regulating or monitoring their own comprehension.

It should be noted that, in contrast to the four questions listed in Figure 12.3, twenty-six might be posed by a Teacher B. This is suggested by the fact that the basal manual lists that number of questions. Teachers knowledgeable about story structure either compose their own questions in the way that has been illustrated, or they sort out from all the questions that

Structure	Possible Questions
1. Setting	1. (Cover when background information is provided.)
2. Problem	2. Question: What wish did Peter make?
3. Attempt to resolve problem	3. Question: What did Peter do to get his wish?
4. Resolution of problem	4. (Discuss in postreading discussion, because too-small clothing is clearly portrayed in two illustrations.)
5. New problem	5. Question: Was Peter glad that he got his wish? Why (not)?
6. Resolution of problem	6. Question: How does the story end?

Figure 12.3 Story Structure and Prereading Questions

manuals suggest those that merit being asked because they call attention to the important parts of a story.

As demonstrated in Chapter 13, prereading questions are not the only way to establish purposes for reading stories. The point to keep in mind now is that the structure of narrative text makes some purposes suitable and others unsuitable.

Expository Text

As mentioned, students are commonly asked to read two types of text, one of which is narrative. The second type is *expository.*

Many pages back, the Introduction to *Teaching Them to Read* explains that expository text is informational text. This means that the material of which content subject textbooks is composed consists of expository text. Articles in certain magazines and in encyclopedias are also expository in nature, since their purpose is to provide information.

Unlike narrative text, the structure or composition of expository text usually consists of one or more central ideas that are embellished with related details. This overall structure, referred to as the *macrostructure* of expository text, is reflected in outlines and also in the headings and subheadings that some authors provide.

As the nature of expository discourse suggests, the purposes that teachers (or students) establish for reading informational material should pertain to the major topics covered—assuming they are important enough to warrant reading about them. To illustrate, let's say that an article deals with minerals and provides information about (a) their characteristics, (b) how they differ from plants and animals, (c) where they are found, and (d) their uses. In this case, a teacher may decide to use prereading questions to cover the four major topics; or, before the reading gets started, she might distribute an outline like the following with directions to fill in the missing information either in the course of reading the article or afterward.

I. Characteristics of Minerals
   A. _____
   B. _____
   C. _____
   D. _____
II. Differences between Minerals and Plants and Animals
   A. _____
   B. _____
III. Where Minerals Are Found
   A. _____
   B. _____
IV. How Minerals Are Used
   A. _____
   B. _____
   C. _____

Obviously, the use of an unfinished outline to encourage students to attend to important content is possible only when previous instruction helped them understand the connection between outlines and the composition of informational material. When that *is* the objective of instruction, modeling is an effective procedure to use; brief articles are appropriate material.

The points being emphasized now are, first, that prereading purposes need to be established for expository text and, second, that the purposes should reflect the content of the text.

Procedural Text

Thus far, two kinds of text used in school have been discussed: narrative and expository. The discussion especially highlighted the need for teachers to establish appropriate purposes for each kind. This was done because, unlike life outside the classroom, expectations exist that certain material will be read in school. The expectation creates a sequence *un*like the more natural one that occurs in everyday life:

Real Life   ***School***

Purpose → select material   Material → select purpose

A third type of text is *procedural* in nature. Procedural text is composed of descriptions of procedures for doing something, for making something, or, for example, for getting somewhere. Recipes, therefore, are procedural text, as are directions for assembling a new table. So, too, are the directions on the numerous practice exercises that students are asked to do.

The reason to read procedural text derives directly from the text: to follow the directions or procedures exactly so that the desired goal is realized (e.g., a white blouse is now yellow, or brownies are made, or a vacation resort is reached). Even though purpose is built into procedural text, knowing how to read it in relation to purpose is not something all students automatically know how to do. Given the frequency with which students are expected to deal appropriately with procedural text, explicit instruction for how to read it should be more frequent and regular than it now appears to be.

COMPREHENSION INSTRUCTION

As pointed out earlier, establishing purposes for the reading that teachers expect students to do comes under the heading "Facilitating Comprehension." So, too, does work with new vocabulary and with activating or providing essential background information. (Please review Figure 10.2.)

Two responsibilities other than what is called facilitating comprehension are named in Figure 12.4. The responsibility of concern now is compre-

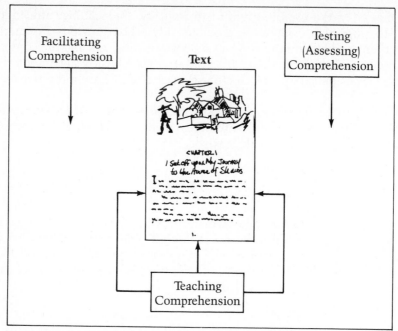

Figure 12.4   Comprehension: A Teacher's Responsibilities

hension instruction: teaching students how to go about processing or understanding connected text.

Delayed Attention to Comprehension Instruction

Anyone who knows the history of reading instruction is aware that widespread interest in comprehension instruction did not surface until the 1970s. To understand the delay, it is necessary to know about certain changes that took place in psychology. This is the case because, just as changes in psychology had clear repercussions on answers to "When are children ready to read?" so, too, did they affect answers to "What can be done to ensure students' abilities to comprehend text?"

As you may recall from Chapter 4, which deals with reading readiness, one major change in psychology occurred during the 1920s. It was then that efforts were made "to elevate psychology to the status of a respected science" (18, p. 390). The effort relevant for the present discussion focused on limiting studies to those that deal with what is observable and testable. According to S. Jay Samuels, this decision moved psychologists as well as educators in the direction of studying "outside-the-head" phenomena, because they could be measured with objectivity and preciseness (18). One consequence for reading was contentment with examining the products of the comprehension process—that is, with assessment. Stated differently, concern continued to be for *what* was comprehended (products), not for *how* it came to be comprehended (process). Such a focus fostered the belief that asking questions about assigned reading is the way to develop students' comprehension abilities. This was clearly the assumption of basal reader manuals over several decades (10).

With the arrival of the 1970s, unprecedented interest in language processing developed. This led to what John Guthrie has called "a veritable explosion" of research to the extent that new journals came into existence to report it—*Cognitive Psychology* and *Discourse Processes,* for example (12). With all the excitement about the possibility of learning what goes on in the head to process language, it was only natural that a parallel interest developed in the processes required for understanding text. One consequence of the interest and the numerous studies that followed was new knowledge and, in many instances, a more precise understanding of existing knowledge, about the comprehension process. Eventually, too, some researchers turned their attention to comprehension instruction.

Nature of Comprehension Instruction

Given the complex, interactive nature of the comprehension process, it is not surprising that total agreement about the nature of comprehension instruction is absent (14). Logically, for example, it seems defensible to claim that whatever is done that helps students understand text is comprehension instruction. Within this very broad framework, instruction concerned with word identification or with cues for recognizing words or with extending oral vocabularies fits under the umbrella called "comprehension instruction." The problem with such an encompassing definition is that it makes comprehension instruction so global and all-inclusive that it no longer is a separate entity. To circumscribe the boundaries sufficiently that its absence from classrooms will be noticeable, this text conceives of comprehension instruction as follows.

If comprehending text is viewed as a collection of mental activities performed during the act of reading, then comprehension instruction can be thought of as something that can have a positive effect on those activities. It is an attempt, therefore, to instruct students about what to do with their minds as they encounter various kinds of text—for instance, dialogues set off by commas and quotation marks; words that signal a consequence (e.g., *therefore*) or a condition (e.g., *if*); and so on.

The conception of comprehension instruction subscribed to in this book also includes attempts by teachers to clarify the need to use what students know to help themselves comprehend. What they know may help them link sentences into a cause-effect relationship (*Ann fell. She hurt her knee.*) or, for example, to identify the referent for a pronoun such as *it (The cat chased the bird. Needless to say, it was not singing.).*

To sum up, teaching comprehension is an attempt to instruct students about what to do with their minds when they encounter various kinds of text or, as the case may be, when they come to a point in a passage that calls on them to use what they know that is relevant. As with other teaching, comprehension instruction is composed of various combinations of imparting information, offering explanations, citing examples and nonexamples, modeling, and asking questions. As with other teaching, too, those persons embarked on offering comprehension instruction should let students know at the outset what it is they are about to teach and, equally important, how what they hope to teach will help the students become better readers.

The emphasis given to "affecting mental activities" in the foregoing discussion of comprehension instruction is the reason modeling has been highlighted in recent years as one effective way to teach students how to comprehend (8). It has received unprecedented attention because it allows teachers to act out what they might do with their own minds when they encounter a simile, an ambiguous pronoun, an inference, or, for instance, words like *first, second,* and *finally* in procedural text.

Even though comprehension instruction as described above is highly recommended, the fact that self-instruction may occur whenever students are engaged in reading should not to be overlooked. Not to be overlooked, either, is the value of those occasions when children learn something about how to comprehend from such sources as other students' comments about how they acquired the answer to a question, or how they went about figuring out the meaning of a puzzling description.

Timing of Comprehension Instruction

One point made earlier is that a match should exist between (a) purpose for reading and (b) type of text read. The same holds true for subject matter for comprehension instruction: The topic selected for instruction should be related to the text students are about to read or have recently read. This means that if the text is a tall tale, a topic like hyperbole—what it is and how and why authors use it—is appropriate.

Whether instruction about hyperbole or any other topic should be provided before or after a given piece of text is read has no single right answer. In the case of hyperbole, one teacher may decide to instruct about it prior to the reading of a tall tale in order to establish a correct mental set for the reading. In contrast, another teacher may delay attending to hyperbole until the tall tale has been read in order to see whether students noticed the exaggerations as well as the functions they served. Now, the exaggerations in the tale serve as examples.

The position taken here is that teachers ought to be the decision-makers about the timing of comprehension instruction (9). Regardless of the decision, no teacher should overlook the need to provide instruction on a topic that is connected with assigned reading. This gives students the opportunity to see the value for reading of what they are expected to learn and remember.

Because of the importance of matching the subject matter of comprehension instruction with the nature of text that students read, the following discussion of sample topics treats one type of subject matter (main idea) that is related to expository text and two topics (referent words and cohesive ties) that are pertinent for all kinds of text.

Sample Topics for Comprehension Instruction

For many years, one of the most frequently covered topics in basal reader manuals and other commercial materials was main idea (and topic sentence). In fact, as early as first grade, teachers have been directed to instruct about main ideas with the help of brief "stories" (10). This was the case even though (a) the concept "main idea" is a difficult one, and (b) it is expository, not narrative, text that may have main ideas, some of which are communicated with topic sentences (4).

To illustrate all this, a slightly revised version of what a basal manual calls a "story," plus the customary multiple-choice format, is shown below.

> Paul asked Betsy to take care of his bird while he was gone. He asked his mother to feed the fish. His father would look after Brownie.
>
> ———   Paul is going away on a vacation.
> ———   Paul is coming home from school.
> ———   All the pets are going away.

According to the Answer Key, the main idea is "Paul is going away on a vacation."

In addition to demonstrating how answers can often be selected through eliminations, the exercise above reflects confusion about "main idea" and "unstated conclusion." (Why the conclusion about a vacation is said to be correct is unclear; Paul's destination could be many different places.) The "story" itself demonstrates that narrative text may have underlying themes—in this instance, "Preparations"—but not main ideas comparable to those sometimes found in expository text.

An example of an expository paragraph—a very dull one—in the same basal program is shown below, also in a somewhat altered form. In this instance, the main idea, which is underscored, is stated explicitly.

> A visit to a large grocery store will show that there are many different kinds of cheese. There are white and yellow cheeses. There are hard and soft cheeses. Some kinds are full of holes.

The text about Paul and the text about cheese have been cited in order to restate the fact that some topics for comprehension instruction are suitable only for certain types of text. In contrast, other topics are relevant for just about everything students read. This is the case for what are sometimes referred to in the literature (5) as *anaphora* or *anaphoric relationships*. Anaphora are what have been called "referent words."

Commonly, referent words are pronouns and adverbs. They may refer to words already mentioned, or to words that appear later:

Park the car in the driveway. It was finally shoveled this morning.

I don't see them. Where did you put the keys?

Play in the backyard. If you stay there, you'll be safe.

Understanding an author's use of referent words requires inferences:

The dog is chasing a cat. He is barking his head off.
   (The inference that he refers to dog is based on the word barking and on the knowledge that dogs, not cats, bark.)

Jeff is learning to be a flutist. He thinks it is a beautiful instrument.
   (The inference that it refers to the unstated word flute is based on the word flutist and on the knowledge that a flutist plays an instrument called a "flute.")

It should be noted that anaphoric relationships like those illustrated above are helpful not only in reducing what could become a monotonous repetition of the same words but also in binding together the content of separate sentences. Serving that function, referent words are *cohesive ties*. How referent words act as cohesive ties, thus allowing for *connected* text, is illustrated below.

Kathy lost her umbrella. This is the second one she lost.

Over the years, the seas changed and the land changed. This happened a very long time ago.

Words other than referent words also function as cohesive ties. Notice in the following illustrations how the underlined words bind together separate sentences:

Rain has been scarce. As a result, my garden is hardly a success.

I know that vase is expensive. Buy it nonetheless.

The water is filtered through many layers of sand. Now the water looks clean.

First, go straight for about two miles. Then turn right at the traffic light.

I'll admit you have been doing your homework. <u>Even so,</u>
couldn't you do it more carefully?

The temperature is on the way to 90 degrees. <u>In addition,</u>
the humidity is high. <u>Together,</u> they create an uncomfortable day.

Even though the primary purpose of this section is to make the point
that comprehension instruction should be related to the type of text students are expected to read, the discussion also identifies some topics for
instruction: main ideas, referent words, and cohesive ties. The following
section names still more topics.

Other Topics for Comprehension Instruction

Because many people still wonder, "But what do you teach when you 'teach
comprehension'?" a number of topics are listed. In addition to clarifying the
nature of comprehension instruction, the topics should be helpful to teachers when they examine a body of text in order to identify the kind of comprehension instruction that is relevant. The additional topics are identified
in the context of what writers do and use in order to communicate.

Typographic Signals. Every author takes advantage of the typographic features of text that help with communication, most of which fall under the
heading "punctuation." This means that readers must be able to respond to
these signals in appropriate ways. Over a period of time, therefore, students
should be taught the following guidelines:

> *Period*
>> signals the end of a thought.
>> indicates an abbreviation.
>
> *Comma*
>> keeps units of meaning together.
>> sets off an appositive.
>> indicates the person being addressed.
>
> *Question Mark*
>> signals a question.
>
> *Exclamation Mark*
>> indicates emotions.
>> suggests emphasis (as do italics and underlining).
>
> *Capitalization*
>> indicates a title, the start of a sentence, or a proper name.
>
> *Semicolon*
>> suggests that what follows is related to what preceded.
>
> *Colon*
>> signals that a series of related items follows.

Paragraph Indentation
   suggests a possible shift in focus.

Descriptions. Describing is something authors often do. Readers need to know, therefore, that descriptions are achieved in a variety of ways. For example:

Adjectives:
   The *cool* weather is *refreshing.*
Adverbs:
   Eventually, the work was done.
Phrases:
   The baby walked *with hesitation.*
Clauses:
   Our house, *which is on a hill,* stayed dry.
Appositives:
   Angela, *the oldest in the family,* has her first job.

To add variety and color to descriptions, authors sometimes use language in nonliteral ways. Consequently, figurative uses of language provide still more topics for comprehension instruction:

Idiom:
   Inferences require reading between the lines.
Hyperbole:
   The tall trees reached to the sky.
Simile:
   He's as thin as a twig.
Metaphor:
   The sun was a gold coin.
Personification:
   As the wind blew, the chimes on the porch sang.

A writer's descriptions may deal with sequence, simultaneous events, or, perhaps, causes and effects. When they do, students profit from knowing that certain words may be available to help clarify these descriptions:

Signal words for sequence:
   first, next, before, later, afterward, earlier, eventually,
   finally, at the end
Signal words for simultaneous events:
   while, meanwhile, at the same time, simultaneously
Signal words for cause-effect relationships:
   because, hence, therefore, as a result, for that reason,
   that is why

Pronoun and Adverb Referents. The frequent use of referent words by writers of narrative, expository, and procedural text is the reason they are discussed earlier. The fact that referent words are a source of problems for students (3, 16) explains why they are renamed now as a possible topic for comprehension instruction:

> We have reading chairs in <u>our</u> room. <u>They</u> are soft.
> The day was wet and cold. <u>It</u> was windy, too. Still, <u>that</u> did not keep <u>him</u> from being outdoors.

Elliptical Sentences. Like referent words, elliptical sentences such as those underlined below allow writers to avoid repeating words. The implied content in elliptical sentences provides more subject matter for comprehension instruction:

> All the children in the family are sick. <u>So is their mother.</u>
> Alan may be late. <u>If so, start the meeting anyway.</u>
> The windows in the garage are dirty. <u>The car is, too.</u>
> "Are you going to the game?" asked Joel. <u>"Yes," answered Beth.</u>

Cohesive Ties. Like referent words and elliptical sentences, cohesive ties appear in both simply written and advanced text. Cohesive ties merit early attention in instruction in order to help children understand that reading is not a matter of processing one word or even one sentence at a time. Attention to intersentence relationships is possible when referent words are considered, since they often function as cohesive ties (e.g., Jim's mom and dad work. *They* are saving to buy a house.). More complex ties are illustrated in the sentences below.

> A [higher animal] has [feelings for other animals of <u>its</u> kind]. <u>It</u> [forms close attachments]. Dogs and chimpanzees <u>do this</u>. Lower animals, like rats, <u>do not</u>. Dolphins also have <u>such</u> feelings.

Complex Sentences. Because long, seemingly complicated sentences often cause breakdowns in comprehending, instruction is required to help children see that what appears to be an incomprehensible sentence may, in fact, be a simple one that is embellished:

> The cat that Teddy got yesterday scratched his mother's best furniture.

Agent	*Action*	*Object*
cat	scratched	furniture

Students also need to be vigilant about the possibility that long sentences may be a combination of several short sentences, each of which is easy to understand. This can be made explicit in a form such as the following:

> Allen heard the bad news, started to cry, and ran home.
> Allen heard the bad news.
> Allen started to cry.
> Allen ran home.

Inferences. The pervasive need for readers to make inferences is clarified with examples in a number of previous chapters as well as in this one. Although it is unnecessary now to add to the examples, it might be necessary to be explicit once more about the importance of assigning instructional time *at all grade levels* to inferences. Calling attention once again to this need stems from the unexpected but fairly common belief that inferential comprehension is required only when difficult material is read.

COMPREHENSION INSTRUCTION: AN EXAMPLE

Having identified topics for comprehension instruction—others are identified in the next two chapters—let me now describe a lesson. The topic is similes signaled by the *as . . . as* construction, because several such similes are in the selection the instructional group will soon read.

Objectives

1. To teach the function of similes.
2. To teach that the construction *as . . . as* may signal a simile.

Instruction. The teacher starts by displaying the following text, which is printed on chart paper. She explains that the words describe someone in

> as white as snow
> as rosy as blood
> as black as ebony

a movie recently shown on television. Since nobody is able to think of the person, the teacher continues, "These words describe 'Snow White.'" Immediately, comments about the movie *Snow White and the Seven Dwarfs* ensue. The teacher then calls the group's attention back to the chart, explaining, "It was said in the film that Snow White's skin is as white as snow. In fact, that's why she's called 'Snow White.' It was also said that her cheeks are as rosy as blood. Of course, we know that her cheeks and blood are different, but comparing the color of her cheeks with the color of blood does help us see what her cheeks are like: very red, indeed. Writers use comparisons like 'as rosy as blood' to help us see in our minds what their words are describing. The author of the story you'll soon be reading uses these kinds of descriptions, too. That's why I wanted to talk to you about them.

"There's one more description of Snow White on the chart that hasn't been read yet. To understand what it tells about Snow White, we need to know what 'ebony' is. Does anyone know? . . . Nobody? . . . Ebony is a very hard and very dark wood. In fact, it's deep black in color. That's why the person who is describing Snow White says that something about her is 'as black as ebony.' Picture Snow White in your mind. What about her is 'as black as ebony'?" Everyone immediately responds, "Her hair!"

The teacher then summarizes: "The person telling us about Snow White describes her by saying that her skin is as white as snow, her cheeks are as rosy as blood, and her hair is as black as ebony. Those words certainly help us see Snow White in our minds. Let's take a look now at descriptions of some other things."

The teacher writes two sentences on the board:

> The boy jumped high.
> The boy jumped very high.

With questions and discussion, the point is made that *very high* indicates a height greater than *high*. Then the following dialogue takes place.

Teacher: I'm going to write some words that mean higher than *very high*. What do you suppose they'll be?

Katrina: Very, very high!

Teacher: No, better than that. [Writes *The boy jumped as high as the sky.*] When I say that the boy jumped as high as the sky, do I mean that he was up in the clouds?

Group: No!

Teacher: No, I'm just trying to impress you with the fact that his jump was *really* high. To do that, I compared it with something that all of us know is about the highest thing around. With the comparison, I hoped you'd get the feeling that this is a person who can *really* jump high. I'll write another sentence that uses a comparison to make a point. This time I want to tell you that somebody came and went very, very quickly. [Writes *They came and went as quick as a wink.*] In this case, why is a wink a good comparison? Chad?

Chad: It's about the fastest thing you do. You do it so fast, you don't even know you do it.

Teacher: Right. I can wink so quickly that it would be hard to know how long it takes. I certainly wouldn't want to have to time it. Here's another good comparison. [Writes *The baby's skin is as soft as silk.*]

After the sentence is read, members of the group get to feel a piece of silk. Then, the teacher summarizes: "Authors use these kinds of comparisons to give you a better feeling for what they're trying to say. They want to make sure you get the point. For the comparisons, they use the word *as* twice—for instance, 'as rosy as blood' or 'as soft as silk.' Now when you see those words, you'll know that the writer is making a comparison. He or she is comparing two very different things, yet the comparison really makes the point. For example, if I wanted to tell you how tough the meat was that we had for dinner last night, I might say something like, 'It was as tough as leather.' When I say that, I don't really mean leather. Meat and leather are different. What I *do* mean is that eating the meat was pretty much like trying to chew leather. In other words, I want to be sure you know just how tough that meat was."

Supervised Practice. Each student receives a paper that lists the following sentences.

> **1.** His booming voice is as loud as thunder.
> **2.** As quickly as a rocket, she took off in her sports car.
> **3.** Today is as windy as a big electric fan.
> **4.** Her dress is as colorful as a spring garden.

Guided by the teacher, the students (a) read each sentence silently, (b) identify the simile and explain why the comparison is a good one, (c) underline the simile, and (d) draw a second line under *as.*

Application. Once the students read the assigned story in their basal reader and respond to four questions posed before the reading began, they will be asked to reread the selection in order to find sentences that have similes with the *as . . . as* construction. The sentences are to be copied and the similes underlined. The page number where each simile was found is to be noted, too.

Subsequent Instruction. Material containing similes signaled by *like* provides another opportunity to deal with comparisons. Now, examples such as the following are useful.

> The visor on his cap is like an awning.
> My little brother keeps following me. He's like my shadow.
> After a week of rain, the sun is like pure gold.

Once the two kinds of similes are taught, "simile" can be used to refer to both. To be emphasized, however, is that it is much more important for students to recognize and comprehend similes than it is to know the name for the comparisons. This point is made because teaching manuals often show more concern for defining terms (e.g., first-person narration and third-person narration) than for explaining to students the significance for reading of what is being defined (10).

As soon as authors of material that students are expected to read use metaphors, they provide other subject matter for instruction. Because metaphors are implied similes *(Our cat is as stubborn as a mule* vs. *Our cat is a stubborn mule.)*, similes and metaphors should be compared at some point. A song known to many children serves well to introduce metaphors:

> Make new friends,
> But keep the old.
> One is silver,
> And the other is gold.

LISTENING COMPREHENSION

Before the chapter ends, one more topic is considered: listening comprehension. It merits attention because of the lingering but mistaken notion that comprehension should begin to be taken seriously at about fourth grade. Contrary to that perception, this and previous chapters demonstrate that teachers of young children also need to provide comprehension instruction.

The purpose of the discussion now is to show with examples that listening activities can be carried out in ways that are likely to contribute to children's ability to comprehend text (15). In this instance, the activities are possible even before children begin to read.

The recommendation to teachers of young children to plan listening activities is not based on the assumption that comprehending spoken language and comprehending written text are identical. In fact, the discussion of listening comprehension starts by pointing out one major similarity and several important differences between listening and reading.

Major Similarity between Listening and Reading

The major similarity between listening and reading is very apparent: The listener and reader both attend to language for the purpose of getting or constructing a message. The two thus display language-processing behavior.

The fact that the basic similarity between listening and reading is obvious often prompts an oversimplified and, therefore, erroneous conclusion:

> listening comprehension ability + decoding ability = reading comprehension ability

Why this equation is an oversimplification is clarified in the following section, which identifies differences between spoken and written language that are relevant for comprehending.

Differences between Spoken and Written Language

Unlike written text, spoken language is fleeting. Unless it is recorded on tape, it is not retrievable. In contrast, written language not only makes words a possible subject for study but also permits behaviors like backward checking and forward scanning. For reasons such as these, the reader is more in charge than is the listener.

Listeners, however, are not totally at the mercy of speakers. Failing to understand, they can express puzzlement with a facial expression or direct question. Because speakers routinely monitor the success of their communication efforts, such responses typically lead to adjustments that may include more careful enunciation, a slower rate of speaking, some repetition, more elaboration, additional illustrations, and so forth.

The nature of spoken language itself offers further assistance to the listener. Features like intonation and stress, for example, are very helpful—much more helpful than their substitutions in print: underlining, italics, bold type, question marks, and exclamation marks. Of even greater significance for communication is the way speakers segment sentences (with pauses) into such meaningful units as a phrase or a clause. Evidently, the commas, semicolons, and periods found in print are not of equal help because research has indicated that instead of processing print into conceptual units, poor comprehenders often read as if a page of text were lines of unrelated words (17, 19).

Even though spoken language does have built-in features for helping with communication, it commonly lacks the elegance of carefully constructed prose. Just how inelegant spoken language can be is made apparent whenever a conversation or even an interview is recorded and then played back. Too obvious to miss are the hesitations, repetitions, corrections, as well as the abandoned and poorly constructed sentences.

Differences in the kinds of sentences that characterize speech and written text have an important implication for any teacher who allots time to listening comprehension as a way of preparing for reading comprehension. The implication is suggested in Figure 12.5. Because written text is not—as is sometimes claimed—"talk written down," the material most suitable for listening comprehension activities is not everyday conversation but, rather, what is referred to in Figure 12.5 as "written text presented orally." This suggests that reading to students is an appropriate topic for illustrating how what is done with listening may contribute to reading comprehension abilities.

Sample Listening Activities

Because reading in school customarily starts with narrative text, some ways to use stories that teachers read to students figure in the examples on p. 385.

Comprehension Requirements	Possible Procedures
Constructing mental images revealed through text	Omit showing illustrations. After the story is read, encourage the children to tell what they think the main character looks like (and *why*). Compare their versions with the author's by showing the illustrations. For another story, the children can draw their own versions.
Following a sequence of events	Stop before the story ends. Ask the children what they think will happen next (and *why*). Afterward, compare their predictions with what did come next. After discussing the order in which events of a story occurred, show children a scroll-like paper with a division for each important event. Help the children decide the kind of picture that can go in each division so that as the paper is unrolled, the plot is revealed. For another story, use similar procedures, this time pulling the paper through a television screen (box with opening on side). As the pictures are displayed, the children retell the story. (The ability to retell what was heard—or read—is reliable evidence of successful comprehension, especially when children do the retelling in their own language. The translation demonstrates that the listener [or reader] has successfully reconstructed the author's message into a form that is personally meaningful.)
Distinguishing between fact and fancy	After reading a fictional account of an animal, read an encyclopedia article about the same animal to allow for a comparison of the two versions. What is factual and what is make-believe in the story should be emphasized through discussion. If the make-believe account deals with an animal that is familiar to the children, draw on their experiences for the comparison.
Evaluating authenticity	Whenever appropriate, encourage children to think critically about characterizations in stories. Pose questions like, "Is that the way children *really* act? If *your* little sister took something of yours, would *you* smile?" A story about a rabbit might make it natural to inquire, "Would a real rabbit feel sorry for a gardener and not eat his plants?"

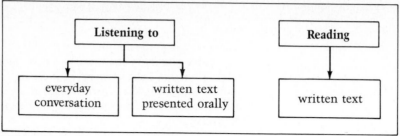

Figure 12.5   Processing Language

Hopefully, a sufficient number of listening activities have now been described to make the point that attention to comprehension need not be delayed until children have acquired reading vocabularies. In fact, the suggestions offered for listening can be followed before reading instruction begins and can be continued while the children's reading ability is just coming into existence. It should also be kept in mind that what is described for listening comprehension can be adapted later to help with comprehending text.

SUMMARY

Chapter 12 begins with a review of what was said about the comprehension process in Chapter 1. The next section, "Comprehending: A Purposeful Pursuit," stresses the need for students to have clearly defined purposes for their reading. Because questions are commonly used in classrooms to bring purposes into existence, this section offers reminders to those posing questions:

1. If necessary, teach students how to answer questions.
2. If necessary, model the process of answering questions.
3. Help students understand that different kinds of questions call for different kinds of reading.
4. Help students understand the three origins of answers to questions.

Continuing the discussion of the importance of purposes for reading, the chapter refers to comprehension monitoring, defined as checking up on, or supervising, one's own comprehension. One point stressed is that the supervision is done in relation to the purposes established for the reading.

The two components of monitoring, evaluating and regulating, are then defined and illustrated. The term *fix-up strategies* is also used; it refers to procedures available to readers when they become cognizant of a breakdown in their efforts to comprehend.

Purpose is central to the discussion again when the different types of text that students read is covered. In this instance, the message is: Just as purpose and the type of reading done must match, so too must purpose and type of text.

Chapter 12 deals next with comprehension instruction. This section begins with a brief explanation (a) of the delayed attention to comprehension instruction, and (b) of why asking assessment questions was once equated with teaching comprehension.

Teaching comprehension, as defined in the chapter, is an attempt to instruct students about what to do with their minds as they encounter various kinds of text. The conception of comprehension instruction subscribed to in the chapter also includes efforts to clarify for students the need to use what they know to help themselves comprehend.

After comprehension instruction is defined, sample topics for instruction are discussed. Even though the selection of a topic should be made by analyzing the text that students are expected to read, it was thought that naming possible topics in the chapter might help not only with the analyses but also in clarifying the meaning of "teaching comprehension." The illustration of comprehension instruction that followed, which focuses on similes, is also intended to clarify the meaning.

Recognizing that responsibility for comprehension has traditionally been delegated to teachers working beyond the early grades, the final section in Chapter 12 attempts to counteract that misguided practice. It also describes listening comprehension activities that should help later with reading comprehension.

REVIEW

1. Because comprehending connected text is the major concern of Chapter 12, it is appropriate to ask, What *is* connected text? (In your description, cite two sentences that illustrate connected text and two that do not.)

2. Explain each statement below.
   a. The message that a reader constructs is constrained by the writer's words.
   b. Prereading purposes allow for comprehension monitoring.
   c. Comprehension monitoring has an evaluation and a regulation component.
   d. Unlike narrative and expository text, the specific reason for reading procedural text derives *directly* from the content of the text.

3. Using examples, differentiate between *activating* and *adding to* relevant background knowledge. (In responding, assume a group of students is about to read an expository selection entitled "Why Does It Rain?") Why is it important for teachers to activate relevant knowledge before students read?

4. Write a piece of text composed of three to five sentences. In any way you choose, show the cohesive texts in your text.

5. Using the outline of Chapter 12 as a prompt, summarize its content.

REFERENCES

1. Alessi, Stephen M.; Anderson, Thomas H.; and Goetz, Ernest T. "An Investigation of Lookbacks during Studying." *Discourse Processes* 2 (July–September, 1979), 197–212.
2. Baker, Linda, and Brown, Ann L. "Metacognitive Skills and Reading." In P. David Pearson et al. (Eds.), *Handbook of Reading Research*. New York: Longman and Co., 1984, 353–394.
3. Barnitz, John G. "Syntactic Effect on the Reading Comprehension of Pronoun-Referent Structures by Children in Grades Two, Four, and Six." *Reading Research Quarterly* 15 (1980, No. 2), 268–289.
4. Baumann, James F. (ed.) *Teaching Main Idea Comprehension*. Newark, Delaware: International Reading Association, 1986.
5. Baumann, James F. "Teaching Third-Grade Students to Comprehend Anaphoric Relationships: The Application of a Direct Instruction Model." *Reading Research Quarterly* 21 (Winter, 1986), 70–90.
6. Baumann, James F., and Schmitt, Maribeth C. "The What, Why, How, and When of Comprehension Instruction." *Reading Teacher* 39 (March, 1986), 640–646.
7. Carver, Ronald P. "Is Reading Rate Constant or Flexible?" *Reading Research Quarterly* 18 (Winter, 1983), 190–215.
8. Davey, Beth. "Think Aloud—Modeling the Cognitive Processes of Reading Comprehension." *Journal of Reading* 27 (October, 1983), 44–47.
9. Duffy, Gerald G.; Roehler, Laura R.; and Putnam, Joyce. "Putting the Teacher in Control: Instructional Decision Making." *Elementary School Journal* 87 (January, 1987), 357–366.
10. Durkin, Dolores. "Reading Comprehension Instruction in Five Basal Reader Series." *Reading Research Quarterly* 16 (1981, No. 4), 515–544.
11. Golinkoff, Roberta M. "A Comparison of Reading Comprehension Processes in Good and Poor Comprehenders." *Reading Research Quarterly* 11 (1975–76, No. 4), 623–659.
12. Guthrie, John T. "Research Views." *Reading Teacher* 33 (April, 1980), 880–882.
13. Johnston, Peter. "Implications of Basic Research for the Assessment of Reading Comprehension." Technical Report No. 206. Urbana: University of Illinois, Center for the Study of Reading, May 1981.
14. Pearson, P. David, and Dole, Janice A. "Explicit Comprehension Instruction: A Review of Research and a New Conceptualization of Instruction." *Elementary School Journal* 88 (November, 1987), 151–165.
15. Pearson, P. David, and Fielding, Linda. "Research Update: Listening Comprehension." *Language Arts* 59 (September, 1982), 617–619.
16. Richek, Margaret Ann. "Reading Comprehension of Anaphoric Forms in Varying Linguistic Contexts." *Reading Research Quarterly* 12 (1976–77, No. 2), 145–165.

17. Rode, Sara S. "Development of Phrase and Clause Boundary Reading in Children." *Reading Research Quarterly* 10 (1974–75, No. 1), 124–142.

18. Samuels, S. Jay. "Resolving Some Theoretical and Instructional Conflicts of the 1980s." *Reading Research Quarterly* 19 (Summer, 1984), 390–392.

19. Steiner, Robert; Wiener, Morton; and Cramer, Ward. "Comprehension Training and Identification for Poor and Good Readers." *Journal of Educational Psychology* 62 (December, 1971), 506–513.

20. Weiss, Maria, and Hagen, Kanae. "A Key to Literacy: Kindergartners' Awareness of the Functions of Print." *Reading Teacher* 41 (February, 1988), 574–578.

21. Yaden, David. "Understanding Stories through Repeated Read-Alouds: How Many Does It Take?" *Reading Teacher* 41 (February, 1988), 556–560.

Chapter 13

Basal Readers
and Narrative Text

PREVIEW

Those of you who have read this book from the beginning are aware of the many references made to basal reader programs. The frequency does not reflect an endorsement but, rather, a recognition of the well-documented fact that basal materials are highly visible in classrooms everywhere.

The whole of basal programs is the initial focus in Chapter 13. This section should be especially helpful to prospective teachers. The inclusion of suggestions for improving basal materials should make the same content helpful to experienced teachers.

In addition to describing the core materials in basal programs, Chapter 13 covers the essential components of basal lessons. Attention thus goes to a teacher's responsibilities for facilitating and assessing comprehension. The main concern of the discussion, however, is comprehension instruction. For that reason, a considerable number of pages show how the narrative text in basal readers suggests subject matter for comprehension instruction. Narrative text is singled out for attention because the following chapter concentrates on expository text.

To make the treatment of teaching comprehension maximally helpful, a number of lessons are included. Each lesson describes assignments as well as instruction, because conscientious teachers are always looking for assignments that students can do alone and that will keep them profitably occupied.

To discourage anyone from concluding that the special attention given basal series implies that they are all that need to be used, the concluding sections in Chapter 13 show how nonbasal stories can add to what is done with the narrative text in basal readers. Again, the objective is to show with specificity how comprehension instruction can be offered, in this case, in conjunction with nonbasal narrative text. That different kinds of stories call for different kinds of instruction is dealt with, too.

The fact that instructional materials known as "basal reader programs" or "basal reader series" exert widespread influence on what is done to teach reading has been underscored in this book a number of times. The influence that the same materials now enjoy in kindergarten was also documented (9).

The earlier attention to basal programs was piecemeal; it is now time to look at these materials as a whole. A single description is adequate because, even though approximately seventeen series are available, the similarity among them is great and obvious.* A number of factors explain the similarity, two of which are identified below.

1. Features of the most successful programs figure prominently in plans made for the next edition of less successful series.
2. In twenty-two states, state-level committees select textbooks. The guidelines they use, in particular those of the largest states, are taken into account by everyone who makes decisions for a series.

BASAL READER SERIES: BASIC COMPONENTS

The materials that make up each basal program are similar. The following sections describe the basic parts.

Pupil Textbooks

The books containing the selections that students read are referred to as the *pupil textbook* or simply "the reader." One or more readers are available for every grade, usually grade one through grade eight.

Three softcovered readers, known as *preprimers* (rhymes with "swimmers"), are characterized as being suitable for most children starting grade one. The first hardcover reader, the *primer*, comes next and is followed by the *first reader*. Combined, all these books are said to constitute first-grade material. For some teachers, and certainly for many administrators, these readers *are* the first-grade reading curriculum.

In all basal programs, two pupil textbooks are prepared for second grade and two for third grade. After that, one is available for each grade.

A relatively new feature of pupil textbooks is pages that provide instruction. (See Figures 13.1, 13.2, and 13.3 for partial examples.) Because research data are not available that either support or question this change, it may be the result of doing what the best sellers do.

---

* "Approximately" is used to describe the number because a few series come and go. Others, in contrast, are routinely on the best-seller list due to effective advertising, large sales forces, and the availability of consultants to help teachers use the programs. The fact that a series has been available for a while engenders confidence among people responsible for selecting a series, which means that "the rich get richer and the poor get poorer" characterizes the basal reader marketplace.

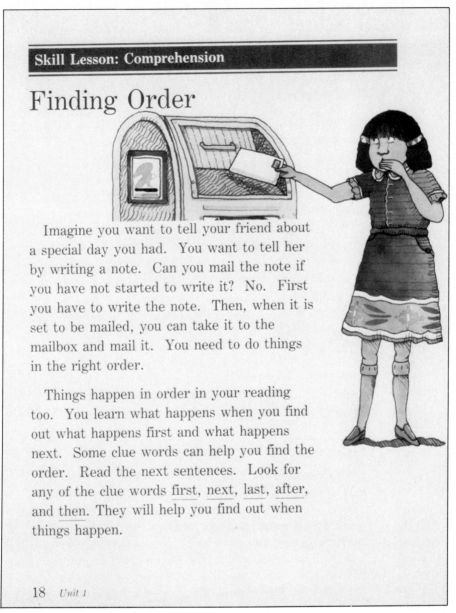

Figure 13.1   Finding Order

Source: Pupil Textbook, *Under the Moon,* Level 5, Grade 2 . Copyright Scott, Foresman and Company, 1987.

Skill

Reading Strategies

Expository and Narrative Writing

All authors have a reason in mind when they write. They may want mostly to give their readers facts, or they may want mostly to tell stories. You can improve your reading by paying attention to the different ways in which authors write.

Expository writing gives readers facts. The author presents a main idea and gives details to support it. You can find this kind of writing in textbooks, magazines, and newspapers.

In **narrative writing** the author tells a story by presenting characters and telling you about their thoughts, words, and actions. You can find this kind of writing in novels and short stories.

If you pay attention to whether the author is mostly giving facts or mostly telling a story, you will know what kind of writing it is — expository or narrative. Knowing the kind of writing will also let you know the kinds of reading skills that you are going to need to use as you read.

Seeing the Differences in Writing

The kind of writing being used affects both your reason for reading and the way you read. Your most important reason for reading an article is to learn the facts the author is telling you. Your most important reason for reading a story is to enjoy the story and to learn something about life from the things that happen to the people in the story. The way authors give facts is very different from the way they write stories. You need to notice and understand those differences in order to read well.

204

Figure 13.2 Reading Strategies

Source: Pupil Textbook, *Explorations,* Level L. Copyright 1987, Houghton Mifflin Company.

Reading Word Problems in Math

To answer a word or story problem, first read the problem carefully. Then several things must be decided before the answer can be found.

What does the problem want the reader to find?

The last sentence usually gives instructions or asks a question. The sentence tells what the reader will need to find as the answer to the problem.

What information does this sentence say to use in solving the problem?

Look for words that are similar to those in the last sentence. For example, the last sentence may ask how many goals four basketball players made. The reader would need to look at the problem to find how many goals each player made.

What information in the problem is not needed?

Decide whether addition, subtraction, multiplication, or division will be used in solving the problem.

If the last sentence asks:

How many are there all together? Use addition or multiplication.

How many are left? Use subtraction.

How many will each one have? Use division.

Add, subtract, multiply, or divide to find the answer to the problem.

92

Figure 13.3 Reading Word Problems in Math

Source: Pupil Textbook, *Copper Sky,* Level N, Grade 6. Economy Reading Series, 1986. Reprinted with permission of McGraw-Hill School Division.

An increased amount of expository text is another change in basal readers. This is the consequence of widespread criticism that questioned the use of almost nothing but stories even though students are expected to learn from expository text when content subjects are taught.

Manuals

However they are described—for instance, as *Teacher's Edition* or *Teacher's Guide*—every series has *manuals*. The most vocal critics of basal materials are likely to describe manuals as scripts for teaching (14). Because manuals do suggest what teachers should say, and even how children will respond, the portrayal is not inaccurate.

The manual format in any series is so similar from one grade to the next that it is possible to identify the name of the publisher by examining a few manual pages at any grade level. Even though publishers say that identical sections for each lesson result in "consistency" and "ease of use," repetitive formats help explain the small amount of change that many students experience during the reading period as they move from one grade to the next.

Because the preparation of basal manuals (and workbooks) is subcontracted to small curriculum-development companies, observations made by an employee of one such company merit attention (23).

> To my mind, the single gravest problem . . . , a weakness that leads to most of the other problems, is the matter of format. . . . Time is money, and formats help publishers make and maintain timetables. . . . The trouble is, very little learning material logically . . . divides into rigid, repeatable forms. But the publishers hold firm, so authors are compelled to twist and bend . . . the material to make it fit the arbitrary, predetermined form. (pp. 44–45)

The fact that form dictates content often accounts for what is referred to in Chapter 5 as "decontextualized instruction." The influence of preestablished formats makes it mandatory for teachers to conceive of manuals as suggestions that can be used, altered, resequenced, or bypassed. Ray Reutzel (24) has even suggested with effective examples that "*Reversing* a basal lesson sequence by beginning at the end and moving backwards (with modifications) . . . shifts the emphasis away from evaluation activities after reading and toward more instructional activities preceding reading" (p. 195). The fact that some teachers spend more time with postreading activities (asking questions and giving assignments) than with prereading responsibilities (new vocabulary, background information, establishing purposes, providing necessary instruction) lies behind Reutzel's recommendation (11).

Whether one moves forward or backward, a very large number of suggestions are in manuals, many of which conclude with references to written exercises. Whenever the large number of suggestions is brought to the attention of individuals responsible for making decisions for a basal series, the common response goes something like, "We assume teachers make selections." Although making selections may seem relatively easy to do, it is a time-consuming activity for two reasons. First, the quality of the suggestions has to be assessed as does their connection with the selection students read. Second, the sequence in which recommendations are made must be considered because the one in manuals rarely allows for a coherent lesson. That is, the suggested parts do not follow each other in a way that adds up to a coherent whole (5, 8, 12).

Workbooks

Originally, basal series had one workbook for every pupil textbook. Now there are at least two. Equally common are various sets of ditto masters. This collection of materials is the origin of many of the written exercises that students do as early as kindergarten (9). The generous amount of material accounts for the widely reported finding that elementary school students spend as much as 70 percent of their time during the reading period doing written exercises (15).

Tests

In recent years, the testing component in basal programs has been noticeably expanded. Currently, end-of-unit tests are supposed to be given intermittently as students read a pupil textbook. When the textbook is completed, an end-of-level test is available.

Even a cursory examination of basal programs shows close correspondence between workbook exercises and test items. As a result of the importance assigned by the public and school administrators to students' performance on standardized tests and mandated competency tests, publishers of basal programs also work hard on matching the practice exercises and tests in their series with these other assessment instruments (10). When it is kept in mind that low scores on highly valued tests are not likely to promote future sales, such efforts are predictable.

A Closing Comment

A segment of an article by three researchers who studied the textbook adoption process provides a suitable conclusion for the description of basal series:

> Basal reader programs, regardless of the publisher, include materials for students from kindergarten through the eighth grade. The materials at each grade include a student book, a teacher's manual, a workbook, a set of ditto masters, and a collection of tests. Some programs sell other supplemental materials. However, unless a program has these basic

materials, it is almost certain to be a commercial failure because of the observed tendency of local districts to avoid the "new," the "unique," or the "experimental" in reading materials. . . . One fundamental aspect of the basal reader marketplace is that less risk results in greater homogeneity. (14, p. 268)

The homogeneity helps explain why classroom observers commonly see almost identical uses made of the time scheduled for reading as they move from building to building and even from one school system to another.

READABILITY

Readability, a term that refers to the difficulty of text, is relevant in any discussion of basal materials. This is the case because readability formulas, which are intended to quantify level of difficulty, are used when pupil textbooks are prepared. The purpose is to produce a series of readers that gradually go from very easy text in preprimers to the much more difficult selections that make up a reader said to be for eighth grade. Why readability formulas are of questionable value is discussed next (29).

Inadequacy of Readability Formulas

Readability formulas—seven have been in general use for some time—are similar in the importance they assign to vocabulary and sentence length as two factors that determine difficulty. The premise of all the formulas is that longer (or uncommon) words and longer sentences make a piece of writing more difficult to comprehend. Calculations based on the formulas result in a number that has been traditionally interpreted as a reading grade-level. Levels range from approximately 1 to 16. (Time-consuming calculations explain the popularity of Edward Fry's graph, which is shown in Figure 13.4.)

At first glance, the assertion that longer sentences and uncommon or polysyllabic words make text difficult seems reasonable. After all, text with just such characteristics has been a burden for us all on occasion. Nonetheless, enough has now been said about the comprehension process to make it clear that a sizable number of factors that enter into comprehension are not incorporated into readability formulas:

Some Missing Variables in Readability Formulas
Text Characteristics:
1. Overall coherence
2. Complexity of ideas and the pace at which they are presented
3. Knowledge that the reader is assumed to have
4. Number of items that must be remembered
5. Availability of help with word meanings
6. Number, complexity, and clarity of cohesive ties
7. Number and complexity of required inferences

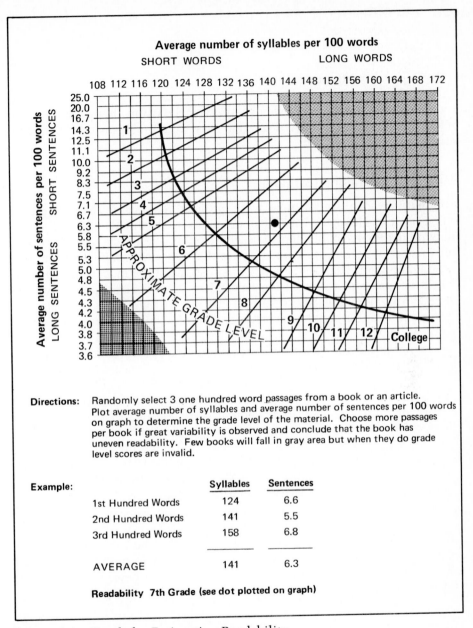

Figure 13.4 Graph for Estimating Readability

Source: From Edward Fry, *Reading Instruction for Classroom and Clinic* (New York: McGraw-Hill Book Company, 1972), p. 232. Copyright © 1972 by McGraw-Hill Book Company and used with their permission.

Reader Characteristics:
1. Prior experiences
2. Relevant world knowledge
3. Interests
4. Cultural background

The variables listed above explain why the claim that a certain basal reader contains selections written, let's say, at a fourth-grade level of difficulty must be questioned.

Misuse of Readability Formulas

Originally, readability formulas were intended to measure the difficulty of a body of text. However, because of the desire to use highly regarded stories in pupil textbooks, publishers of basal programs often use a formula to simplify text. The results are altered stories that contain disconnected text that is less interesting than the original version. One of the most thorough studies of the consequences of using readability formulas to simplify text was done by two linguists, Alice Davison and Robert Kantor (6). The data they report confirm that, used as an adaptation tool, readability formulas do not work.

What does seem to work is demonstrated in a study done by Beck et al. (3). The title of the report of the study pinpoints the concern of the research: "Improving the Comprehensibility of Stories: The Effects of Revisions That Improve Coherence." *Coherence* refers to the degree to which the events in a story are clearly related. In a coherent story, pieces fit together in a way that produces a meaningful whole.

To achieve meaningful wholes, Beck and her colleagues revised two basal stories by clarifying ambiguous referents, rewriting sentences to improve their syntax, replacing implicitly stated relationships with explicit statements, removing excessive irrelevant details, and replacing unclear material with more clearly stated content. While making the revisions, the researchers were careful not to alter plots.

Even though the revisions were longer than the two original stories and had readability levels (according to a readability formula) that exceeded the original versions by two years, subjects in the study were more successful in comprehending the revised stories.

Implications of Readability Research

Knowing about factors that account for well-formed, thus comprehensible stories should help teachers who use a basal program in at least three ways. First, such knowledge identifies topics for comprehension instruction. Second, it provides guidelines for identifying sections of basal stories that may cause problems. And, third, knowledge about factors that affect comprehensibility is helpful when teachers examine recommendations in a basal manual in order to decide what to use, alter and then use, or omit.

BASAL READER LESSONS

To make certain that the referent for "basal reader lesson" is clear, please examine the content of Figure 13.5 with care before proceeding.

You are asked to study Figure 13.5 not because it portrays lessons described in basal manuals but because it provides a model of what basal lessons ought to be. What each lesson ought to be more specifically is a gradual

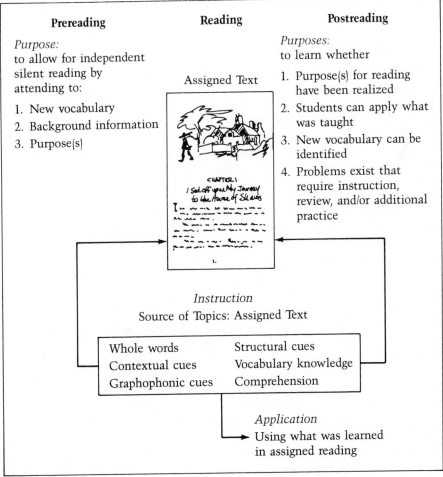

Figure 13.5 Basal Reader Lesson: Essential Components

accumulation of instruction, practice, application, and reflection over the span of several days that results in a successful, well-integrated experience for students. Among other things, coherent lessons show close ties between the text students read and the topics selected for instruction and practice.

How basal programs can be supplemented with other materials is described later. Now, the components of basal lessons are discussed in a way that identifies common flaws in basal manual recommendations as well as ways to remedy them. Underlying the discussion is the assumption that planning for a basal lesson always starts with a teacher's careful reading of the selection that students read later.

PLANNING BASAL READER LESSONS

The comments that follow reflect the content of Figure 13.5.

Prereading Activities

What teachers do before a selection is begun should permit students to read it independently with adequate comprehension. That is why attention to new vocabulary, background information, and purposes for reading is cataloged as "facilitating comprehension."

New Vocabulary. Anyone who examines the most recent editions of basal programs learns that inadequate suggestions for teaching new vocabulary are still characteristic. With that in mind, teachers must accept responsibility for doing much more with new words than any manual now recommends. The inadequacy of their recommendations is the reason detailed attention went to the development of reading vocabularies in earlier chapters.

Background Information. Previous chapters also repeatedly stressed the dependence of successful reading on three interrelated factors: experiences, oral vocabularies, and world knowledge. The attention in recent years to the dependence of comprehension on world knowledge accounts for the increased space allotted to this topic in current basal manuals. In theory, the change is desirable; in practice, problems are noticeable. In one updated series, for example, a story tells how the personal relationship between a boy and his mother improves as they share the enjoyment of riding bicycles. Perhaps because *bicycle* is in the title, whoever prepared the manual recommends a detailed discussion of bicycles to prepare for the story. The suggestion is flawed in two ways. First, the students who will read the story probably have adequate knowledge about bicycles. Second, it is the shared, enjoyable experiences that are important, not the riding of bicycles per se.

In another case, a story in a basal series is about a boy from South America who is made fun of by his new schoolmates because, in his attempts to learn English, he interprets figurative language literally. Instead of proposing a prereading discussion of the problems everyone has in acquiring a new language, the person writing the manual recommends a very detailed discussion of the country from which the boy came.

The point to be emphasized now is that teachers should activate, or add to, students' background knowledge only what is essential for comprehension. To do otherwise is to turn a means into an end in itself.

Purpose for Reading. Much is said in the previous chapter about the need to make reading a purposeful experience for students. There, posing prereading questions to establish purposes is discussed. The focus now is on other ways to make reading a purposeful activity.

You will recall from the previous chapter that a story has a structure with parts that suggest the kinds of questions that call attention to important content. The structure of a story also allows for a *story map*. A story map is a visual representation of the major events in a story and thus is based on its structure. One illustrative map is in Figure 13.6. Because the map portrays a story that is summarized in Chapter 12, please return to that chapter now to reread the section "Narrative Text."

To demonstrate that no one right way exists to construct a story map, another is in Figure 13.7.

Figure 13.8 shows a third map, in this case for a story summarized on the page facing Figure 13.8. It is relevant to note that the basal manual covering the story "Nobody Cares about Me"—its actual title is different—includes thirty-two questions. The number correctly suggests that many are about trivial details. As stressed earlier, asking questions about unimportant content should be avoided because it leads students away from a correct understanding of reading.

Story maps serve a number of functions other than displaying key events and their connections. Initially, a map can be used as a tool for helping students summarize or retell a story. (Sometimes, free recall without a prompt is better, as it allows for learning what students think is important.) Eventually, constructing a map can be a prereading assignment. The need to construct the map establishes a purpose for reading, helps students learn what to attend to as they read, and makes their efforts more fruitful (2, 4, 26). From the teacher's perspective, maps allow for comprehension assessment.*

Teachers who are knowledgeable about mapping are aware that not every selection referred to as a story in basal manuals *is* a story. Especially at the earlier levels, a selection may be nothing more than a series of events. Whenever these selections occur, reduced attention can go to the selection itself while added attention goes to teaching or reviewing a phonics generalization; to teaching or reviewing the precautions to be taken whenever short, known words are used to help with longer, unknown words; to teaching

---

* How teachers use maps to help students compose their own stories is described in two references at the end of the chapter (22, 27).

about or reviewing the use of semantic cues for word recognition; or, for example, to teaching or reviewing the need to know the word or words that pronouns replace. These suggestions underscore the fact that basal lessons should vary much more than is commonly the case.

One variation is called for by a "story" in a basal reader that tells how the deaf mother of two children makes adaptations to compensate for the handicap. Although not a story, the selection is valuable in providing a picture of life from a deaf person's perspective. It also suggests yet another way to establish a purpose for reading. Specifically, the content of the selection makes it an appropriate time to encourage students to consider the problems a deaf person might have—for instance, the inability to hear the telephone and doorbell. Now, learning more about the problems as well as how they are resolved becomes the reason to read the selection. Following the reading, a comparison of the predicted problems, which were written, and the ones that students say the author describes allows for comprehension assessment.

Postreading Activities

Having considered the part of a basal lesson that deals with preparations, let's shift the focus to postreading activities. (Please review Figure 13.5 before proceeding.)

Comprehension Assessment.   Postreading activities are covered now because one of their objectives is to learn whether the purposes established for reading have been realized. Stated differently, comprehension assessment should take a form that reflects why the reading was done. Reflecting the foregoing section, "Purpose for Reading," the following activities exemplify appropriate assessment efforts.

> *Evaluating:*
> Students' responses to questions posed before they began to read.
> Students' efforts to fill in the parts of a story map constructed by the teacher.
> Maps constructed by students after they finish reading a selection.
> Students' descriptions of problems experienced by one who is deaf and of how the person solved them.

Based on classroom observations, two points about comprehension assessment need to be underscored. First, whenever students' answers to questions are the focus for assessment, asking about reasons for responses may provide more pertinent information than the responses themselves. This is not to suggest that students must justify every single answer. After all, too much of a good thing is still too much. Rather, the point is that the routine

(text continues p. 410)

"Peter, the Pioneer Boy"

SETTING

Main Character	Time	Place
Peter	Pioneer days	Rural area

PROBLEM

Peter wants to be bigger than he is.

ACTION TO SOLVE PROBLEM

Peter dips hand into magic pond and wishes to be bigger.

SOLUTION OF PROBLEM

Shrunken clothes suggest to Peter that his wish came true.

NEW PROBLEM

Peter believes himself to be so big he won't be able to get into his own house.

SOLUTION OF PROBLEM

The ability to walk through the doorway of his home and fit on his mother's lap shows Peter he is the same size.

ENDING

Peter is satisfied with his size.

Figure 13.6 A Story Map

THE COCONUT GAME

One day Elephant fell into a pit. "Help!" cried Elephant. The animals ran and looked into the pit. "We can't help you, Elephant," they said. "You are too big. And the pit is too deep." The animals could not help Elephant. One by one they went away.

"Elephant!" called Monkey from the top of the pit. "I'll get you out."

"But how?" asked Elephant. "You are so little."

"Not too little," said Monkey. And away she ran.

Soon Monkey came back. She had a ladder with her. Elephant tried to climb up the ladder. But when he got on it, the ladder broke.

"It's no use," said Elephant. "How will I get out of this pit?"

"You will see," said Monkey. And away she ran.

Soon Monkey came back. She had a rope with her. Elephant took hold of the rope. Then Monkey pulled on it. But Monkey could not pull Elephant out of the pit.

"It's no use," said Elephant. "How will I get out of this pit?"

"You will see," said Monkey. And away she ran.

Soon Monkey came back. Many, many monkeys were with her. Each monkey had a coconut. "Let's play the Coconut Game," said Monkey. Monkey began to roll a coconut into the pit. All the other monkeys began to roll coconuts into the pit.

"Why are you rolling coconuts into this pit?" cried Elephant.

Elephant was very angry. He stomped on the coconuts. He jumped up and down on the coconuts. Elephant grew more and more upset. But still the monkeys rolled coconuts into the pit.

All at once Elephant found himself close to the top of the pit. He walked right out of it! All the monkeys laughed and jumped.

"Didn't you know that someone small can help someone big?" asked Monkey.

"No," said Elephant. "But now I do!"

Source: From *Inside and Out of Pathfinder*—Allyn and Bacon Reading Program by Robert B. Ruddell and others, © Copyright, 1978, by Silver, Burdett & Ginn Inc. Used with permission.

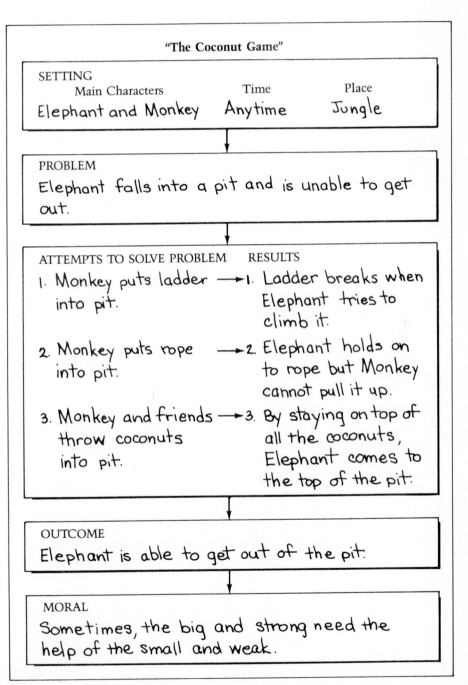

"The Coconut Game"

SETTING
Main Characters	Time	Place
Elephant and Monkey	Anytime	Jungle

PROBLEM
Elephant falls into a pit and is unable to get out.

ATTEMPTS TO SOLVE PROBLEM · RESULTS

1. Monkey puts ladder into pit. → 1. Ladder breaks when Elephant tries to climb it.

2. Monkey puts rope into pit. → 2. Elephant holds on to rope but Monkey cannot pull it up.

3. Monkey and friends throw coconuts into pit. → 3. By staying on top of all the coconuts, Elephant comes to the top of the pit.

OUTCOME
Elephant is able to get out of the pit.

MORAL
Sometimes, the big and strong need the help of the small and weak.

Figure 13.7 A Story Map

"NOBODY CARES ABOUT ME"
SUMMARY

Bonnie is unhappy because she feels nobody pays any attention to her. Recalling that her mother once commented that people who are different get attention, Bonnie puts together The Different Plan. She borrows her mother's fanciest hat, wears it to school, but attracts only the attention of the teacher, who directs Bonnie to take off the hat and put it away.

Bonnie's next plan, The Mysterious Plan, leads her to smile without any apparent cause and then to loud laughter in the presence of her brother. Bonnie asks, "Don't you want to know why I'm laughing?" "No," her brother responds, and leaves the room.

The indifference of her brother leads Bonnie to make one final plan called The Lively Plan. It is prompted by her cousin's observation that lively people get attention. Later, while visiting at the home of her aunt and uncle, Bonnie unexpectedly tap dances, sings, and finally does a cartwheel. By the time she is done, she is alone in the room. Bonnie then resigns herself to the fact that nobody will ever care enough to pay attention to her.

At school the next day, Bonnie's every-growing curiosity about why a classmate, Jack, always has a pickle in his lunch box prompts her to inquire. Surprised that someone noticed and was interested enough to ask, Jack is proud to explain that his dad makes pickles. He then asks Bonnie why she wore such a funny hat to school the previous week. Soon the two childen are enjoying each other's company, telling one another about all the things they like to do.

```
┌─────────────────────────────────────────────────────────────────┐
│                    "Nobody Cares about Me"                        │
│  ┌─────────────────────────────────────────────────────────────┐ │
│  │ SETTING                                                       │ │
│  │ Main Character        Time              Place                 │ │
│  │ Bonnie               Anytime           Anyplace              │ │
│  └─────────────────────────────────────────────────────────────┘ │
│  ┌─────────────────────────────────────────────────────────────┐ │
│  │ PROBLEM                                                       │ │
│  │ Bonnie feels neglected and wants attention.                  │ │
│  └─────────────────────────────────────────────────────────────┘ │
│  ┌─────────────────────────────────────────────────────────────┐ │
│  │ UNSUCCESSFUL EFFORTS TO SOLVE THE PROBLEM                     │ │
│  │ 1. Bonnie wears her mother's fanciest hat to                 │ │
│  │    school.                                                    │ │
│  │ 2. Bonnie smiles and even laughs aloud for                   │ │
│  │    no apparent reason.                                        │ │
│  │ 3. Bonnie dances, sings, and even turns a                    │ │
│  │    cartwheel during a visit to the home of                   │ │
│  │    an aunt and uncle.                                         │ │
│  └─────────────────────────────────────────────────────────────┘ │
│  ┌─────────────────────────────────────────────────────────────┐ │
│  │ SUCCESSFUL EFFORT TO SOLVE THE PROBLEM                        │ │
│  │ Bonnie gives her attention to a classmate, Paul.             │ │
│  └─────────────────────────────────────────────────────────────┘ │
│  ┌─────────────────────────────────────────────────────────────┐ │
│  │ OUTCOME                                                       │ │
│  │ Bonnie receives attention from Paul.                         │ │
│  └─────────────────────────────────────────────────────────────┘ │
│  ┌─────────────────────────────────────────────────────────────┐ │
│  │ MORAL                                                         │ │
│  │ Do unto others as you would have them do                     │ │
│  │ unto you.                                                     │ │
│  └─────────────────────────────────────────────────────────────┘ │
└─────────────────────────────────────────────────────────────────┘
```

Figure 13.8 A Story Map

practice of asking students a question until somebody offers the correct answer and then proceeding to the next question, which is handled the same way, is not likely to improve comprehension abilities (13). Nor is it a way to learn the kind of instruction (or review) from which students will benefit. All this indicates, then, that what a teacher does with answers affects whether questions are or are not instructive for both the students and the teacher.

The second point that may need to be made explicit is that evaluating what has been comprehended in relation to the structure of a story—that is, in relation to the most important parts—is not all that should usually be done. Requesting opinions and encouraging students to talk about possible links between themselves and characters in the story are also important. Such discussions, however, should ordinarily be delayed until it has been confirmed that the story itself was comprehended to the extent that the purposes for reading it require. Beck et al. (4) make the same point this way:

> Enhancing children's comprehension of story content is not the only immediate goal one needs for designing a lesson. Lesson elements that prompt the child to go beyond the story to apply concepts learned in the story to his or her own experiences, or to reflect about the literary forms used are likewise essential. However, ensuring that the child has the best grasp possible of the actual and implied content is the first order goal on which the goals of extending, interpreting, and applying story content are built. (p. 478)

Instruction. As pointed out as early as Chapter 3, "teachable moments" occur whenever it is clear that students have a problem—for example, are getting so caught up with trivial details in a story that they fail to see the critical parts. The identification of this deficiency creates the perfect time to provide instruction about the structure of stories.

To cite another illustration, if a reexamination with students of the selection they just read reveals problems with cohesive ties even though instruction about them was offered earlier, this is an ideal time to provide more instruction that makes use of the cohesive ties in the selection, plus others found elsewhere. (Because connected text inevitably includes cohesive ties, finding them on the spot is no problem.)

Not to be overlooked in this discussion of teachable moments are deficiencies that may be uncovered when new vocabulary is reviewed or when a check is made to see whether decoding abilities were sufficient to deal with the new, regularly spelled words that were omitted when attention went earlier to new vocabulary.

What all these illustrations indicate is that, sometimes, postreading activities include instruction (or review) designed to remedy a problem. If a schedule prohibits a remedy at the time the need is identified, it should be put on the "must be done soon" agenda.

The need for other instruction may be revealed when a teacher reads whatever it is that students will soon read. To discuss this, let's use as an example the basal story referred to earlier in which a South American boy is the subject of ridicule because he assigns a literal meaning to everything said in English. Such a tale obviously suggests the possible need for instruction with literal versus figurative uses of language. The question of concern now is, "Should the instruction be offered before the story is begun or afterward?" The answer is, "It depends." In fact, the best timing for any instruction is always affected by a number of factors that include students' abilities.

A teacher working with poorer readers may give all the time allotted to this group on one particular day to nothing but instruction with new vocabulary and a review of previously taught subject matter that is pertinent for the story about the South American boy. On the second day, this teacher may choose to review the new vocabulary and then offer a lesson on figurative expressions. She may even use for examples some of the expressions in the story itself. The next day, vocabulary and figurative language are reviewed and a purpose is established for reading the story about the South American boy, after which the group reads it silently and independently.

Working with considerably better students, the same teacher may decide not to deal with figurative language ahead of time and, instead, checks the students' ability to interpret the figurative expressions once the story is read. Depending on responses, it is possible that instruction for figurative uses of language—whether recommended in a basal manual or not—will be bypassed.

These points are made because with all the current interest in explicit instruction and, in particular, in comprehension instruction, some teachers may feel compelled to provide lessons whether or not they are needed. Once again, then, the significant question is, *Why* am I doing what I'm doing?

Assignments. The term *assignment* refers to something students are asked and expected to do. An assignment that merits being done is something students *can* do, often alone, from which they acquire greater proficiency (e.g., in scanning to find prespecified information) or better understanding (e.g., the need to read as a unit an appositive enclosed in commas). Ideally, assignments also make clear the value of previous instruction for reading.

Assignments are as appropriate for prereading activities as they are for postreading activities. The reason they are discussed now is that the majority of assignments in basal manuals, most of which are single-page exercises, are postreading assignments. By now, however, it should be clear that one of the things a Teacher A often does is to resequence manual suggestions.

As pointed out earlier, new vocabulary remains one of the most inadequate sections in basal lessons. Part of the inadequacy lies both in the number of assignments and in their quality. The recommendations, therefore, are to use any basal vocabulary assignment that is worth doing before students begin to read the basal selection and, second, to supplement inadequate practice with other assignments focusing on new words—and, perhaps, on words taught earlier that remain a problem. These recommendations are based on the fact that problems with words lead to problems with comprehension.

In the discussion of comprehension instruction that follows, further attention goes to assignments.

NARRATIVE TEXT: SOME TOPICS FOR INSTRUCTION

The previous chapter highlighted the following relationships:

$$\text{Type of text should affect} \quad \rightarrow \quad \begin{cases} 1. \text{ purpose(s) for reading} \\ 2. \text{ kind of reading done} \\ 3. \text{ topics for instruction} \end{cases}$$

The connection between narrative text and topics for instruction is the concern now. To illustrate why certain topics are appropriate for stories, three are considered: flashbacks, cause-effect events, and perspective.

Flashbacks

It was said earlier that teaching comprehension can be conceived of as instructing students about what to do with their minds as they move through text. Moving through narrative text typically requires readers to keep track of, and remember, sequential events. But they also have to be prepared for flashbacks. A *flashback* is an interruption in the narration of chronological events with a reference to the past. Commonly, the earlier event took place before the story itself begins. Although authors sometimes use flashbacks to add variety and interest to their tales, a reference to the past may also be necessary for explaining something occurring in the present.

For many students—again, it is the teacher who must decide—instruction about flashbacks is needed before they read a story in which, for the first time, a flashback occurs. A possible lesson offered before an instructional group begins to read such a story goes as follows. In this case, the teacher elects to use a previously read story to discuss flashbacks.

Teacher: We've read quite a few stories this year and, of course, you've been reading others on your own. In all the stories we've read together, the author tells various things that happen in the order in which they happen. For instance, in the story we just finished, the author writes about two girls who live in a tall apartment building. The interesting part occurs when the girls are in the elevator and can't get to the apartment of one because neither is tall enough to reach the button that has *18* printed on it. How they go about solving that problem is quite clever; but the point I want to make now is that the author of the story tells us what happened in the order in which it happened. She starts at the beginning when one of the girls finally gets permission from her mother to go up to her friend's apartment without having her older sister take her. The writer next describes how the girls go into the elevator only to realize they are unable to reach the right button. The rest of the story tells about the interesting way in which they reach it and finally arrive at their destination.

Displaying a chart, the teacher shows a description of the events she just reviewed, each numbered. This allows her to point out how the events are arranged in chronological order. She continues:

Teacher: Let's pretend *we* are the authors of this story but want to tell it a little differently. To do that, I'll start the story, then you keep it going. In the new version, the beginning tells about the girls sitting in the apartment on the eighteenth floor, resting up a bit from the troubles in the elevator. The older sister of one girl comes in, looks at them, and says, "You look as if you've been into mischief. What did you do now?" That's the beginning of the story. Who wants to tell us what happens next?

Unexpectedly, the group decides unanimously that the best thing is to say nothing. This makes the teacher decide to tell the new version herself, since the reason for all this talk is to deal with flashbacks.

Teacher: I understand why you think silence might be the best thing; however, if the girls say nothing, there is no story. I'm going to suggest something else. I'm going to suggest that the two girls do tell what happened. In my story, the bigger sister is so impressed when she hears what they did that the two little girls feel more convinced than ever that they really are growing up. I know my story isn't very interesting, but I told it the way I did in order to explain that some authors tell a story by going back and forth between the present and the past. This is what I did in my story. On this other chart—please look here—I've written how I told my new version. Please take a look at how I went back and forth from the present to the past and then back to the present again.

The chart being examined displays the following:

Beginning			Return to past	Back to present
Girls are in eighteenth floor apartment.	Sister of one girl arrives.	Sister wants to know what girls have been up to.	Girls tell how they were able to reach the button.	Sister is impressed with how they solved the problem.

After discussing the chart, in particular the sequence of events, the teacher continues:

Teacher: I promise you that the next story in your reader is much more interesting than mine. But the two are alike because, in each case, the characters tell something that happened in the past. In the story I want you to read now, the main character, in this instance a boy named Andy, is lying in a hospital bed so covered with bandages that his own family might not recognize him. As he lies there, Andy thinks of the past, in particular of what caused him to be taken to the hospital in an ambulance. I want you to read only the first two pages. Stop reading when you get to the bottom of page 118. Don't turn the page. Just wait until everyone has finished reading the first two pages.

Once all of the students have finished the two pages, the teacher comments:

Teacher: Before Andy starts thinking about the past—which he does on the next page—let's see what *you* think happened earlier to put Andy into the hospital. Who has an idea?

Carolyn: I think he was swimming, and he went out too far and almost drowned. If it wasn't for the man near him, he'd probably be dead.

Teacher: Carolyn, when a person almost drowns, they might have to go to the hospital, but would they end up being bandaged from head to toe? What did the two pages you just read tell you about how Andy looks?

After it is established that bandages covering one's body are not usually required when a person comes close to drowning, other more plausible notions of earlier events are offered. As the descriptions get more and more violent, the teacher ends the discussion:

Teacher: You certainly thought of a lot of things that might have injured Andy, but now let's see what in fact did happen.

The teacher distributes copies of an assignment sheet, which is shown in Figure 13.9. A volunteer reads each of the three assignments. As everyone appears to understand his or her responsibilities, the teacher suggests that the students return to their places to finish the story about Andy in order to learn, first, why he's in the hospital and, second, what his parents do to cheer him up.

Why this teacher did what she did is explained below.

1. Because the quality of the story about Andy is mediocre at best, the teacher used it primarily as a vehicle for introducing *flashbacks* and also to add to the students' reading vocabularies.

Assignments

1. When you finish reading, you should be able to answer the question, <u>Why is Andy in the hospital?</u>

2. When you know the answer to this question, <u>do page 43 in your workbook</u>. If necessary, you can look at the story about Andy. Be sure to read the directions at the top of the workbook page before starting.

3. The next job is to answer another question, this one asked of a girl named Nell. <u>Read what follows. Then write how Nell answers.</u> When we meet again, you can read to the others the words you put in Nell's mouth, <u>Write what she said below.</u>

Nell felt tired and grouchy. Seeing how tired she looked, Fran inquired, "How come you're so tired, and it's only 11 o'clock in the morning?"
Nell explained, "

Figure 13.9   An Assignment Sheet

2. A basal workbook page was assigned because it deals with both the story about Andy and flashbacks. Specifically, it requires students to arrange eight sentences describing events in the story in the order in which they actually occurred. The students then check any statement that tells about an event revealed with a flashback. Directions for both tasks are clearly stated at the top of the page.

3. The assignment to put words into Nell's mouth was given for several reasons. Checking this assignment later will allow for further attention to flashbacks. (At that time, the teacher will introduce the term

flashback.) Second, because the group learned about figurative expressions earlier, "putting words into Nell's mouth" permits a review of literal versus figurative uses of language. Earlier, too, attention was called to authors' uses of synonyms for words like *said* and *asked* in conversations (e.g., *stated, uttered, inquired, wondered*). This topic will also be reviewed.

4. Having students consider possible reasons for Andy's trip to the hospital creates interest in finding out what did occur. It thus provides a reason for continuing beyond the first two pages of the story.
5. All the assignments were stated in writing to ensure that none is forgotten. Using an assignment sheet also demonstrates one reason for learning to read: to be able to follow written directions.

Cause-and-Effect Events

Although it is sometimes said that a story is a series of cause-effect events, that is an oversimplification. Some events, after all, are merely sequential; others occur simultaneously. It is three types of events, therefore, that provide additional subject matter for comprehension instruction. Even though the focus now is cause-effect events, students should eventually be able to distinguish among the three types just named.

Cause-and-effect events that are often central to the plots of stories divide into three categories: physical, psychological, and a combination of the physical and psychological (18). All three categories are illustrated in Figure 13.10. Please examine that material now.

Physical causality is easiest for children to understand because whether occurring in stories or real life, the connection between the effect and what brought it about is commonly overt. For instance:

Person wearing muddy shoes walks on clean floor → floor is dirty.
Person exerts downward pressure on pedals → wheels of bicycle turn → bicycle moves.

All basal manuals cover cause-effect relationships; however, the recommendations often show greater concern for definitions of *cause* and *effect* than for how cause-effect relationships play a key role in the development of stories (11). Teachers, therefore, need to remember, first, that terminology should never become an end in itself and, second, that when a topic like cause-effect relationships is covered, the connection between knowing about such relationships and understanding the events in a story should be made clear. The work of one teacher who kept these guidelines in mind is described next.

The instruction is part of the preparations being made for reading a selection in a basal reader. Thus far, the new vocabulary has been taught. In addition, two basal workbook pages providing for word practice have been

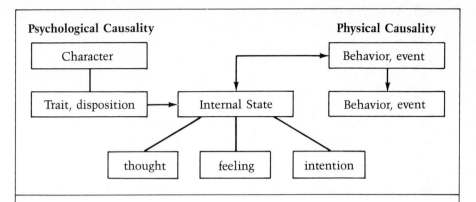

Physical Causality

Protagonist throws snowball. It strikes the head of another boy, knocking him to the ground.

Psychological Causality

Embarrassed by the fall and with his head throbbing with pain, the boy resolves to seek revenge.

Psychological-Physical Causality

Protagonist is insecure, leading her to believe that people do not pay any attention to her. Feeling ignored, she does a series of unusual things. Thinking her to be peculiar, individuals in her environment ignore the protagonist in obvious ways. Later, curious about a boy's having pickles in his lunch box every day, the protagonist asks him why he always has pickles. This leads to the child's showing interest in the protagonist.

Figure 13.10 Examples of Causality in Narrative Text

assigned along with another teacher-made practice sheet. The final work for this first day is to call the students' attention to cause-effect relationships in a way that shows their relevance for reading stories. Because this is the first time anything explicit has been done with cause and effect, more will be done the next day. At that time, the topic will be reviewed, then extended in a way that relates it directly to the basal selection that the students read next.

On this first day, the teacher introduces cause-effect events as follows.

Teacher: Before you go back to your places to practice reading the words you learned today, I want to talk about one more thing because it will help you understand stories better. To get started, I'll use the story I read to the class yesterday. Does anyone remember what I read yesterday?

Jeanne: I do. The story was about a baby hippopotamus named Herbie. He wanted to be a bird because birds can fly.

Teacher: What happened to Herbie? Carol?

Carol: Nothing very good, that's for sure. But it was just a dream.

Teacher: Who wants to tell us about Herbie's dream?

Jon: I will. He dreamt he was a bird. His size didn't change, but he had wings. I think the first thing he did was use his wings to reach a telephone wire. Naturally it broke.

Teacher: Then what, Jon?

Jon: I've kind of forgotten, but I think the next thing he did was to sit on a bird's nest and, of course, he was so big the nest fell apart. I've forgotten the other things but, in any case, having wings didn't work out very well for him.

Teacher: That's for sure. Like us all, Herbie wanted to be something other than what he was. However, by the time the story ends, he is very happy to wake up and learn he is still a hippopotamus. I'll put some of the things you've been saying about Herbie on the board. In one column I'll write what he did. In the next, I'll write what happened when he did that.

The teacher asks Jon to repeat what he said earlier. As he does this, the teacher fills in the columns:

What Herbie Did	*What Happened*
1. Sat on telephone wire.	1. Wire broke.
2. Sat on nest.	2. Nest fell apart.

The instruction continues:

Teacher: This first column shows two things Herbie did once he had wings and thought he was a bird. The second column shows what happened, first when he sat on the wire and then when he decided to take a rest. So one thing caused something else to happen. The fact that something causes something else to happen goes on all the time and not just in stories. In our own lives, too, one thing might cause another thing to happen. I'll show that on the board, too, once I erase what happened to Herbie.

After writing the following, the teacher asks a member of the group to read both columns aloud:

Cause	*What Happened*
Patty fell.	Her knee is bleeding.

Then the teacher says:

Teacher: Falling is something all of us have done at one time or another, so we know that falling can cause bloody knees. That's why I wrote "Patty fell" under the word "cause." It caused the bleeding. Gene?

Gene: The fall didn't cause the cut. You get a sore knee when it hits the sidewalk. In gym, we have thick mats. If you fell on one of them, you wouldn't have a bloody knee.

Teacher: That's a good point, Gene. I wasn't careful enough. Let me try again.

The teacher alters what she originally wrote:

	Cause	*What Happened*
Patty fell.	She scraped her knee on the sidewalk.	The scraping made the skin on her knee bleed.

Gene is asked to read the three columns, after which the teacher says:

Teacher: Gene, is this better?

Gene: Yes. For a different example, you could say that she fell on the ice and then her knee got pounded, and she ended up with a broken bone.

Teacher: Correct. And if she fell on that gym pad you talked about before, nothing might happen. Very good, Gene. You're really thinking. Your head is working better than mine today. Let's all try to think of times in our own lives when something caused something else to happen.

Eric: I can think of something right away because it happened yesterday. I was late for dinner, so my dad said I couldn't watch TV.

Teacher: Good example, Eric. That will only take two columns. In the first, I'll write *Eric was late for dinner.* In the second, I'll write *Cannot watch television.*

Gene: I know what you could write in another column.

Teacher: Eric was sad? Is that right, Eric? When you couldn't watch television, did you feel sad?

Eric: Not exactly sad, but I wasn't happy either.

Teacher: So Gene is correct. Not being able to watch TV did cause something else to happen. It made Eric feel less than happy. For now, I think we have enough examples of how one thing often causes something else. When you start the story in your reader tomorrow, you'll want to be looking for things that cause other things to happen. But that's for tomorrow. To help you get ready, I want you to do something today. Please open your workbook to page 91.

The rest of the time is spent reviewing the purpose of the workbook page (connecting statements listed in two columns, the first describing something that happens, the second telling what resulted). The previously assigned work for vocabulary is reviewed before the students leave the reading area.

Let's shift now from cause-effect relationships to another topic that is relevant for understanding stories, namely, perspective.

Perspective

All of us have heard, said, and experienced, "Every story has at least two sides." As with life, so it is with narrative text. How a story unfolds depends at least in part on who is doing the telling. Perspective (and its effect on stories), then, is yet another suitable topic for instruction designed to help students understand narrative text.

The subsequent discussion of perspective starts with text found in beginning basal readers, then moves to consider more difficult text.

Beginning Text. The problems that perspective can cause are not always appreciated by those who make decisions for the beginning pupil textbooks in basal programs (20). If they were, the "stories" that make up the bulk of preprimers and primers might be replaced with easy expository text about familiar topics of interest to young children. (Such a change is unlikely as long as marketing data indicate that the consumer wants stories in beginning readers.) Exactly how perspective may make life difficult for readers of "easy" stories can be illustrated with as few as two sentences:

1. "June," said Patty, "get the dime in my jacket."
2. June said, "Patty, get the dime in my jacket."

As can be seen, reading the first sentence must be done from Patty's perspective. That is, Patty is doing the talking, is making the request, and is the one with a jacket. In contrast, comprehending the second sentence requires understanding that June is central, since she directs Patty to get the dime.*

One more example of dialogue, which seems simple on the surface, suggests other problems related to perspective:

"Don't tease my dog," Al said. "If you don't stop, I'll tell your dad when he gets home tonight."

In this instance, the reader must view life from the perspective of someone named Al. It is unclear whether Al is talking to one or more persons; more clear is that the other person is neither his sibling nor an adult.

To comprehend this "simple" text, the reader must further conclude that *my* refers to Al, and that *you* and *your* refer to the person(s) to whom Al is giving a direction and then a warning. Also necessary is the understanding that "tonight" refers to a time period in Al's life, not the reader's.

If nothing else, all this should clarify for teachers of beginners that whenever dialogues in stories are something children are expected to understand, they provide ample subject matter for instruction. Stated more broadly, the message is that many of the topics that have been discussed— for instance, world knowledge and comprehension, inferences, referent words, cohesive ties, cause-effect relationships, and now perspective—may be essential topics for instruction. This should help dispel the myth that comprehension instruction can be delayed until about third or fourth grade.

---

* You may recall the recommendation in Chapter 2 to have dialogues like these read aloud in order to clarify any misunderstanding they may generate.

More Difficult Text. Commonly, stories are told from a third-person perspective. In such cases, it is as if the teller of the tale is able not only to look down at the characters to describe their activities and relationships to others but also to get inside their heads so that thoughts and feelings can be described, too.

Eventually, students are expected to deal with a mix of third-person and first-person narration. Depending on the story, the initial contact with first-person narration may be an appropriate time (a) to compare first-person stories with the third-person perspective, and (b) to discuss words that signal a first-person perspective—*I, my, we,* and so forth. Later, the need to read another first-person narrative allows for the opportunity to pinpoint possible effects on a story when it is told from one person's point of view.

To get a discussion of such effects under way, students can be asked to read a paragraph like the following.

> *How I Got a Ticket*
> I was driving on the highway. I made sure I didn't go faster than 65 miles an hour, because that is the limit. Even so, I was soon stopped by a police officer in an unmarked car. He said his radar showed I was going 72 miles an hour. I explained I was on my way to see my mother, who is ill, but was careful not to speed. I still got a ticket.

Once members of the instructional group read the paragraph, a line of questioning might go as follows, given the fact that the teacher's intention is to deal with possible effects on content when it is written from one person's perspective.

1. To what kind of a ticket does the title refer?
2. Who is telling about the driver who got the ticket?
3. How do you *know* that the person who got the ticket is the one who is telling how he or she got it?
4. Why do you think the driver mentioned to the police officer that he or she was driving to see a sick person?
5. Why do you suppose the driver mentions that the police officer was in an unmarked car? By the way, what *is* an unmarked car? . . . I'll repeat the question I asked earlier. Why do you think the driver referred to the fact that the police car was unmarked?

At the end, the teacher asks, "Do you think this incident about getting a ticket would be described the same way if the police officer were telling what happened?" Immediately, the group responds, "No!" This is a perfect time, therefore, to distribute the assignment sheet shown in Figure 13.11.

The assignment to tell how the officer explains why he gave a speeding ticket is part of the preparations being made for the story referred to earlier called "Nobody Cares about Me." (The story, which is told by Bonnie herself, is summarized on the page facing Figure 13.8.) When the group meets the next day, some of the time with the teacher will be spent on having

---

Assignment

Now that you have read the driver's side of the story, pretend you are the officer who gave the ticket. Use the space below to tell *his* side of the story. To get you started, what he says at first is *typed* below. The title is there, too.

Why My Job Is Tough

I'm a police officer. This morning

Figure 13.11 Perspective: An Assignment

volunteers read their accounts of how the officer did the telling. The point the teacher plans to emphasize is the significance of the storyteller on content. This provides a suitable introduction to the basal story about Bonnie. (A suitable postreading assignment is to have the students retell the same story, this time from the perspective of Bonnie's brother.)

NARRATIVE TEXT: NONBASAL STORIES

To ensure that nobody reading the chapter concludes that a professional use of basal readers is sufficient for developing superior instructional programs, this final section deals with nonbasal narrative text. One assumption of the discussion is that narrative trade books are among the materials teachers read to students.* A second assumption is that trade books selected by students themselves constitute part of the independent reading that contributes so much to vocabulary knowledge, to comprehension abilities, and, no less important, to an interest in reading. One further assumption is that nonbasal stories can supplement the narrative selections in basal programs. This last assumption is addressed first.

---

* A *trade book* is written for the library and bookstore market rather than for schools. The abundance of paperbacks makes such books much more affordable than was once the case.

Independent-Level Books

If narrative trade books are to function both in supplementing basal selections and in providing profitable assignments, their readability levels need to be such that students can comprehend them without help. To review the value of reading independent-level material, benefits identified in Chapter 6 are repeated below.

Reading independent-level material:

1. Promotes self-confidence and, with it, a greater interest in reading.
2. Shifts attention from individual words to the meaning of connected text.
3. Allows for the consolidation and realistic use of what has been taught.
4. Adds to the reader's world knowledge.

The ensuing discussion assumes that the nonbasal stories referred to can be read independently.

Perspective

The pervasiveness of different perspectives in narrative text, plus the problems they often create, warrant another look at that topic. Now the question is, How can nonbasal stories help not only with perspective but also in keeping some students profitably occupied so that a teacher is free to work with others?

Earlier, when the story about Bonnie, the girl seeking attention, was the focus, the point was made that the underlying theme might be very different had Bonnie's brother been the author. If the brother's version was written by students using either a first-person or third-person perspective, at least some of the new stories would probably have a theme like "Sisters are self-centered." The shift provides evidence that who is doing the telling makes a difference. That makes it important for readers to know who, in fact, *is* telling the stories they read.

Once some of the students' new accounts of Bonnie are read aloud and the effects of perspective discussed, a teacher may choose to do something else with perspective. Appreciating the value of models for clarifying an assignment, the teacher has already rewritten "Little Red Riding Hood" from a unique perspective:

> *Little Red Riding Hood*
> *by*
> *The Wolf*
>
> Life is hard for a wolf like myself. I get into trouble because I have a very big appetite. I'm always hungry.
> Last week I met a cute little girl in the woods. She was taking some food to her grandmother, which smelled very good. Do you think she'd give me some? Not on your life.

Some kids are really selfish. I ran off to the grandmother's house. I thought she might share some food with me, once her granddaughter went back home. I made the mistake, though, of peeking in her window. As soon the grandmother saw me, she hid in a closet.

By then I was ready for a little fun. I found some clothes in another closet and dressed up to look like a grandmother. I was sure I could fool the little girl into giving me the food. But, again, I had problems. She screamed as loud as she could the minute she saw me. Soon, a nasty-looking man holding an axe appeared. That was enough for me. I yanked off the clothes and ran for my life.

Now I'm really hungry. In fact, I'm thinking right now of how to get some food. Maybe I can find a few tasty pigs somewhere.

Before distributing copies of the revised tale, the teacher reads the original version to the group. After the revision written by the teacher is distributed and read silently, a comparison is made between the two versions. Again, why there are differences is emphasized. The teacher then gives each member of the group a different story. The assignment is to read the story in order to rewrite it from the viewpoint of the character named on a piece of paper inserted into the book.

Types of Fiction

As the previous chapter pointed out, fiction divides into a number of different types:

realistic fiction	mystery	fable
fanciful fiction	tall tale	legend
historical fiction	fairy tale	myth
science fiction	folktale	epic

Knowing the genre they are about to read is helpful to students in a number of ways.

To illustrate, because the story about Peter, a pioneer boy referred to in the previous chapter, is realistic fiction, knowledgeable students can conclude that dipping his hand into a pond will not cause Peter to grow. Were it a fairy tale, on the other hand, dipping a hand into a pond might cause much more spectacular phenomena than just growing taller.* When a piece of text *is* a fairy tale, readers should expect not only human characters but also giants, ogres, witches, and, of course, a fairy or two. All this means that one way to help students develop into successful comprehenders of

---

* As you can see, the characteristics of different kinds of fiction have implications for what is taught about cause-effect relationships.

narratives is to teach them about the different kinds that are available and the characteristics of each.

To specify what can be done to establish appropriate mental sets for different kinds of fiction, fables are used. They are chosen because they have readily recognizable features: First, animals are usually the protagonists and, second, a lesson or moral lies beneath the surface of the tale.

The best known fables are those supposedly written centuries ago by a man named Aesop. Using Aesop's fables at the start is recommended for several reasons. First, they are found in every library. Second, they are sufficiently popular that slightly different versions of the same tale are usually available. This allows for attention to differences, in particular to those that *make* a difference—that is, to those that have to do with important parts of the story's structure. Not to be overlooked, either, is that many of the Aesop fables are available in easy-to-read text, often supplemented with excellent illustrations.

Because many fables are short, some teachers choose to introduce children to this genre by reading fables to them. After a sufficient number have been read, children readily pick out the unique features. In the case of those by Aesop, students also learn that the three most popular animals in his fables are the fox, the wolf, and the lion, all of whom display predictable traits.

Preparing children for fables by reading some to them helps when this genre appears in a basal textbook. I was recently reminded of the help during a classroom observation. In this case, the teacher was preparing an instructional group for a legend. Because it was the students' first encounter with legends, the teacher spent considerable time on certain of their features. As a result, insufficient time was given to the many words described as being new—even to those that were central to the important parts of the legend. The consequences were clear—and predictable: As soon as the students took turns reading the legend aloud, many words could not be identified.

The point to be stressed, then, is that the kinds of fiction that are in basal textbooks should, at times, affect what teachers elect to read to students. Basal selections should also help teachers decide what to do with what they read. One further recommendation has been made by Ira Aaron:

> Basal reader series are usually used in a school or school system for at least five years. Therefore, when a series is adopted, teachers and librarians should determine which children's books to order in quantity to use as follow up to selections in the pupil texts.* (1, p. 127)

Character Traits

Prominent in narrative text are the traits of the key players—human, animal, or otherwise. How an author reveals the traits—with direct descriptions or, for instance, indirectly through behavior—provides further subject

---

* This suggestion is in one of the fourteen chapters that make up *Children's Literature in the Reading Program*, which offers helpful suggestions to teachers eager to extend or improve what they do with literature.

matter for comprehension instruction. Before such instruction is offered, it is helpful to deal with the traits themselves. Again, fables are highly appropriate when that is the concern.

As an example, take the fable referred to earlier in which a monkey is able to help an elephant. Children reading the tale readily see the traits of each animal, in particular, those of the monkey. Attention to her behavior can be the start of a list of character traits that grows as more stories are read. The beginning of such a list is shown below. The traits named are suggested by the behavior of the monkey in "The Coconut Game."

	very	*some-what*		*some-what*	*very*	
			Character Traits			
kind	____	____		____	____	unkind
smart	____	____		____	____	dumb
patient	____	____		____	____	impatient
calm	____	____		____	____	excitable

Lists like the one illustrated above can be used in many ways. As suggested, it will be lengthened as stories are read and new traits identified. Once a sufficiently large number of traits are listed, those on the left-hand side can be arranged in alphabetical order to facilitate use of the chart. By this time, the chart will make an attractive addition to a bulletin board to be consulted whenever the traits of characters in stories are worth discussing.

Obvious, too, is the value of such a chart for helping explain antonyms, for dealing with prefixes, and for adding to students' knowledge of word meanings. Better descriptions of the characters in the stories that students themselves write might be another by-product. Like the best of instructional materials, then, such a list serves a variety of useful purposes.

A Final Comment

Even though the "usefulness" of narrative trade books should not be underestimated or bypassed, their value in helping students acquire an interest in reading must not be forgotten. All this is to say that students should never become so occupied with learning about reading that no time is left to read. It is taken for granted, therefore, that every classroom is a literate environment in which the books that students can elect to read are placed in a prominent, attractive area that is readily accessible to all.

SUMMARY

Unlike the references to parts of basal series that are in earlier chapters, the whole of basal programs is one major focus of Chapter 13. The chapter begins, in fact, by describing materials found in every basal series now available. That each series uses one format for every lesson was mentioned, because this practice accounts for some of the flaws in basal programs. Chapter 13 reemphasizes that these flaws make it mandatory for teachers to examine manual recommendations carefully, once they have read the selection that students will be expected to comprehend. Reading the selection is necessary, as it provides guidelines for deciding which manual recommendations to use, alter, resequence, or omit. It is this discriminant use of manuals that allows for the development of coherent basal lessons in which all the parts add up to a meaningful whole.

Readability is the next topic covered, since consideration of readability formulas by publishers of basal programs accounts for additional flaws. The flaw highlighted in the chapter pertains to adaptations of stories. The specific flaw is that many of the adapted stories turn out to be more, not less, difficult than the original versions. They also are less interesting.

The description of the inadequacy of readability formulas allowed for a listing of variables that affect the comprehensibility of text. In addition to underscoring the inadequacy of the formulas, the list identifies factors that teachers need to consider, and some of the things they need to do, in order to help students make their way successfully through assigned reading.

To show with specificity how teachers can use but also improve basal materials, considerable attention is given to the essential components of a basal lesson. The components divide into facilitating, teaching, and assessing comprehension. The major concern of Chapter 13, however, is comprehension instruction. The more circumscribed concern is instruction that helps students comprehend narrative text.

With that as the goal, specific basal stories are used to show how their content suggests topics for comprehension instruction. To make sure that basal stories are correctly seen as constituting merely one type of material, the chapter includes a section on nonbasal narrative text. Together, the two allow for identifying topics that are suitable for comprehension instruction. They include flashbacks, cause-effect events, perspective, and character traits. The fact that different kinds of fiction call for different kinds of instruction is illustrated, too.

Chapter 13 closes with the reminder that students should never be kept so occupied with learning about reading that too little time is left to read. Nor should reading instruction ever become so standardized and routine that it diminishes the desire to read. Stated differently, teachers need to keep in mind that students who cannot read are far outnumbered by students who can read but don't.

REVIEW

1. It is often helpful to deal with an overview of the content of expository text before the parts are considered. For that reason, the first request is to explain the content of Figure 13.5.

2. Although Figure 13.5 does not make this point directly, it implies that the text to be assigned should be read by a teacher before plans are made for a basal lesson. Explain with specific examples why this is an essential first step.

3. Chapter 13 states that manuals and practice exercises in basal programs are routinely written by employees of small curriculum-development companies. Review Chapter 13 now in order to cite examples of problems that are probably the result of this practice.

4. Read a randomly selected story in a basal reader. (Be sure it really is a story.)
   a. Based on the text used to relate the tale, name topics for comprehension instruction that ought to help students who will be asked to read the story. (Omit topics named in the chapter even if they are pertinent. On the other hand, include evidence for your decision about certain topics being helpful.)
   b. For the same story, construct a map. Describe how you went about constructing it. Finally, how might the map be used with children either before they start the story or after they have read it?

REFERENCES

1. Aaron, Ira E. "Enriching the Basal Reading Program with Literature." In Bernice E. Cullinan (Ed.), *Children's Literature in the Reading Program*. Newark, Del.: International Reading Association, 1987.
2. Beck, Isabel L., and McKeown, Margaret G. "Developing Questions That Promote Comprehension: The Story Map." *Language Arts* 58 (November/December, 1981), 913–918.
3. Beck, Isabel L.; McKeown, Margaret G.; Omanson, Richard C.; and Pople, Martha T. "Improving the Comprehensibility of Stories: The Effects of Revisions That Improve Coherence." *Reading Research Quarterly* 19 (Spring, 1984), 263–277.
4. Beck, Isabel L.; Omanson, Richard C.; and McKeown, Margaret G. "An Instructional Redesign of Reading Lessons: Effects on Comprehension." *Reading Research Quarterly* 17 (1982, No. 4), 462–481.
5. Daines, Delva, and Reutzel, D. Ray. "The Instructional Coherence of Reading Lessons in Seven Basal Reading Series." *Reading Psychology* 8 (1987, No. 1), 33–44.
6. Davison, Alice, and Kantor, Robert N. "On the Failure of Readability Formulas to Define Readable Texts: A Case Study from Adaptations." *Reading Research Quarterly* 17 (1982, No. 2), 187–209.
7. Duffy, Gerald. "From Turn-Taking to Sense-Making: Toward a Broader Definition of Reading Teacher Effectiveness." *Journal of Educational Research* 76 (January-February, 1983), 134–139.
8. Durkin, Dolores. "An Attempt to Make Sense Out of a Senseless Basal Reader Lesson." *Illinois Reading Council Journal* 14 (Spring, 1986), 23–31.
9. Durkin, Dolores. "A Classroom-Observation Study of Reading Instruction in

Kindergarten." *Early Childhood Research Quarterly* 2 (September, 1987), 275–300.

10. Durkin, Dolores. "Influences on Basal Reader Programs." *Elementary School Journal* 87 (January, 1987), 330–341.

11. Durkin, Dolores. "Is There a Match between What Elementary Teachers Do and What Basal Reader Manuals Recommend?" *Reading Teacher* 37 (April, 1984), 734–745.

12. Durkin, Dolores. "Reading Comprehension Instruction in Five Basal Reader Series." *Reading Research Quarterly* 16 (1981, No. 4), 515–544.

13. Durkin, Dolores. "What Classroom Observations Reveal about Reading Comprehension Instruction." *Reading Research Quarterly* 14 (1978–79, No. 4), 481–533.

14. Farr, Roger; Tulley, Michael A.; and Powell, Deborah. "The Evaluation and Selection of Basal Readers." *Elementary School Journal* 87 (January, 1987), 267–281.

15. Fisher, C.; Berliner, D.; Filby, N.; Marliave, R.; Cohen, L.; Dishaw, M.; and Moore, J. *Teaching and Learning in Elementary Schools.* San Francisco: Far West Laboratory for Educational Research and Development, 1978.

16. Goodman, Kenneth S. "Basal Readers: A Call for Action." *Language Arts* 63 (April, 1986), 358–363.

17. Lehr, Fran. "Story Grammar." *Reading Teacher* 40 (February, 1987), 550–552.

18. McConaughy, Stephanie H. "Developmental Changes in Story Comprehension and Levels of Questioning." *Language Arts* 59 (September, 1982), 580–589.

19. Moss, Joy. "The Fable and Critical Thinking." *Language Arts* 57 (January, 1980), 21–29.

20. Murphy, Sandra. "Children's Comprehension of Deictic Categories in Oral and Written Language." *Reading Research Quarterly* 21 (Spring, 1986), 118–134.

21. Nessel, Denise. "The New Face of Comprehension Instruction: A Closer Look at Questions." *Reading Teacher* 40 (March, 1987), 604–606.

22. Piccolo, Jo Anne. "Writing a No-Fault Narrative: Every Teacher's Dream." *Reading Teacher* 40 (November, 1986), 136–142.

23. Pseudonymous, Scriptor. "The Ghost Behind the Classroom Door." *Today's Education* 67 (April-May, 1978), 41–45.

24. Reutzel, D. Ray. "Reconciling Schema Theory and the Basal Reading Lesson." *Reading Teacher* 39 (November, 1985), 194–197.

25. Shannon, Patrick. "A Retrospective Look at Teachers' Reliance on Commercial Reading Materials." *Language Arts* 59 (November/December, 1982), 844–853.

26. Spiegel, Dixie Lee, and Fitzgerald, Jill. "Improving Reading Comprehension through Instruction about Story Parts." *Reading Teacher* 39 (March, 1986), 676–682.

27. Stark, Constance G. "A Story Writing Map." *Reading Teacher* 40 (May, 1987), 926–927.

28. Wixson, Karen K. "Questions about a Text: What You Ask about Is What Children Learn." *Reading Teacher* 37 (December, 1983), 287–293.

29. Zakaluk, Beverley L., and Samuels, S. Jay (Eds.). *Readability: Its Past, Present, and Future.* Newark, Del.: International Reading Association, 1988.

Chapter 14

Content Subjects
and Expository Text

PREVIEW

Two facts that are familiar to teachers were kept in mind as this chapter was being written. One is that subject-matter textbooks are not made up of consistently well written, interesting prose. Actually, some content is so irrelevant for elementary school students as to require asking why an author ever decided to include it. The second fact is that some of the students who are expected to acquire information from these textbooks do not even come close to having the reading ability or the experiences that the expectation assumes.

These two facts create problems for teachers and students alike. They also cause problems for authors writing about the topic that is the title of Chapter 14. To alleviate some of the problems for the present author, two decisions were made. One was to use social studies textbooks to exemplify expository text. This decision is justified by the fact that most of the points made can be applied to all kinds of informational texts. The circumscribed focus also keeps Chapter 14 from covering so much that nothing is covered well.

The second decision was to confine the chapter to recommendations that are reasonable—that is, that can be followed by teachers who, first, do not spend all their waking hours either teaching or preparing to teach and, second, have students who cannot read textbooks without help.

Even if Chapter 14 were addressed to teachers who work only with extremely proficient readers, two assumptions would remain the same:

1. It is impossible to find a textbook that deals with nothing but well-written, highly important content that is relevant for elementary school students. In part, this reflects the fact that easy reading is hard writing.
2. At the elementary school level, it is more important to teach students how to acquire information from text than it is to cover all the content in a textbook.

These two assumptions are not meant to suggest that teachers should take lightly their responsibility to teach *important* content.

After all, its acquisition increases students' knowledge about the world. Rather, the assumptions stated above are intended to make the point that selections from all the content in a textbook need to be made and, second, that both the selected content and how it is written provide subject matter for instruction.

Chapter 14, then, has two main purposes. First, it is meant to help teachers and prospective teachers instruct about social studies content thought to be important. Second, it is intended to show how the text that conveys the content can be a vehicle for helping students learn how to learn from expository discourse.

Before starting the chapter, *please read the summary section at the end.*

What is seen when middle- and upper-grade classrooms are observed during social studies accounts for some of the content in the present chapter (8, 20). Research dealing with the comprehension of expository text, and with the nature of expository text itself, explains the inclusion of other content. To get the chapter under way, findings from the observations are summarized.

SOCIAL STUDIES: CLASSROOM PRACTICES

Data from the classroom observations that had the greatest impact on the development of the chapter describe practices that have been common for a long time. It is unlikely, therefore, that any will be surprising.

To begin, some students in all the classrooms were unable to read the assigned textbook. Nonetheless, nothing was seen that could be called comprehension instruction. Instead, the concern was to cover content, even when the content was unimportant or, on a few occasions, out-of-date.

Because covering content *was* the goal, teachers often relied on procedures that "told" the content to the poorest readers. A round robin reading of a chapter or of part of a chapter by the best students was not uncommon, for example. In such cases, the oral reading was stopped intermittently to allow for a question or an explanation from the teacher.

In other classrooms, all the students were asked to read a specified section of a chapter silently, after which a discussion took place. Only certain students participated because, presumably, others were unable to understand the text. In a few classrooms, students were expected to respond in writing to questions about a chapter; however, because some could not do the reading, they could not do the writing.

Elsewhere, teachers had taken the time to rewrite a chapter in a simplified form; in other instances, substantial amounts of material supplemented textbooks. Even in these classrooms, however, the focus was still on learning content.

Having reviewed classroom practices, it is now time to repeat a point made in the Preview: The philosophy underlying this chapter is that teachers have two responsibilities when subject matter areas are the concern. The first is to teach important content; the second is to teach students how to go about comprehending expository discourse. Put differently, if elementary and high school teachers continue to give all their attention to content, when will students learn how to learn from text?

CONSEQUENCES OF CLASSROOM PRACTICES

One consequence when students have not learned how to learn from expository material is effectively portrayed in tongue-in-cheek observations by Robert Ireland:

> Often, the child who tries the hardest suffers most in reading textbooks. He thinks he must read carefully and remember all the information. He starts a textbook chapter on the Plains Indians. The first paragraph names nine different tribes. He rereads and "studies," trying to memorize all nine. The second paragraph names five rivers and two mountain ranges. Again, "study," memorize. By this time, he's getting pretty well fed up with the book and with reading in general. The next paragraph describes the buffalo. It is high shouldered, shaggy. He thinks it looks like his brother and then goes on. The buffalo has hair like a lion and a hump like a camel. Picture that! By this time, he has been reading for fifteen minutes and has covered three paragraphs. (15, p. 586)

That the passing of time does not bring improvement is supported in a portrayal of the reading habits of older students enrolled in a highly regarded university. Although the following comments appeared several decades ago in an article by William Perry, a researcher, nothing currently known about the study procedures of college students questions the accuracy of the characterization:

> The typical approach of 90 percent of these students was to start at the beginning of the chapter and read straight ahead. No attempt was made to survey the chapter, note marginal headings, or first read the recapitulation paragraph in which the whole structure and summary of the chapter was given. Thus, none of the clues and signals provided as a basis for raising questions were used to identify specific purposes for reading. (21, p. 196)

COMPREHENSIBILITY OF EXPOSITORY TEXT

Implied in the observation just quoted is that textbooks are considerate in the help provided for understanding content. The opposite conclusion, however, has been reached in more recent analyses of text. In fact, one result of this body of research is the description "inconsiderate text" (1).

The factors that make text "inconsiderate," and thus difficult to comprehend and remember, are discussed next. The discussion proceeds, not by noting what makes text inconsiderate but, to the contrary, by focusing on factors that facilitate understanding. This perspective is taken because it allows for attention to features of text that teachers should encourage students to use to help themselves understand. Attending to the positive should also help teachers choose more wisely if they find themselves on a committee responsible for selecting new textbooks.

Although the following discussion features the positive aspects of helpful text, it shows indirectly that the problems some students have in understanding textbooks are not necessarily the result of deficiencies in reading.

Considerate Expository Text

To begin, the overall structure (macrostructure) of considerate text makes it easy for readers to understand how all the topics fit together. Or, as Bonnie Armbruster and Thomas Anderson have stated, in coherent text, "central ideas across the entire discourse are woven together in such a way as to make relationships among the ideas clear and logical" (1, p. 5). A student's ability to see how the content of a chapter is organized and fits together promotes both understanding and retention.

Of importance, too, is that authors of considerate text omit irrelevant content, because it distracts a reader's attention from central ideas. On the other hand, the same writers include graphic aids such as tables and maps whenever they will serve to explain or, perhaps, summarize. Once the decision is made to use these aids, the text informs readers not only about their function but also about when to examine them.

In the most considerate of text, readers are further helped by introductory sections that orient them to the whole of the chapter, review previous content that is relevant, or raise questions that arouse curiosity about the text to be read. Still more assistance is in summaries that underscore key ideas and their interrelationships. Questions are also likely to be available in considerate text in order to highlight important content in yet another way. Between all this are headings and subheadings that accurately preannounce forthcoming topics.

Looked at in smaller segments (microstructure), considerate text shows not only clear, well-constructed sentences but also a use of cohesive ties that makes apparent intersentence and interparagraph connections. The content of one sentence or paragraph thus flows smoothly into the content of an adjacent sentence or paragraph. Easy-to-understand definitions of terms that are both important and likely to be unfamiliar are additional sources of help in considerate text.

Interest Value of Expository Text

Not to be overlooked is that the very best organization and writing cannot compensate for dull content. I make this point because my own review of social studies textbooks has left the impression that a sizable amount of the material is deficient in comprehensibility not only because of such factors as poor organization and excessive detail but also because many topics are uninteresting. These topics, plus others that are far removed from the lives of students, often keep the best readers in a class from deriving either new knowledge or enjoyment from their textbooks (10).

The type of information often found in textbooks makes it difficult to understand the persistence of some teachers to give almost all their time to content and practically none to instruction for understanding expository discourse. After all, it is the latter instruction that will allow students to learn from, *and* enjoy, all the interesting expository material that sits on the shelves of libraries everywhere. When it is kept in mind that a "major impediment to effective learning is a deficient knowledge base" (5, p. 19), the need to help students acquire information on their own cannot be disregarded.

Content and Reading Instruction

Admittedly, it is easier in theory than in practice to distinguish between content instruction and reading instruction. This is particularly true when procedures for teaching about content aim, not toward rote learning and memorization, but toward understanding. To be specific, should help with how to understand graphs and tables be cataloged as instruction about content or about how to understand common features of expository text? To cite another example of the same quandary, take the case of helping students see how a particular chapter often defines terms with appositives (e.g., *Climate, the weather an area has over a long period of time, varies from one part of the country to another.*). Should this help be placed under the heading "Teaching Content" or "Teaching How to Learn from Text"?

The position taken here is that making distinctions in a book like this one is much less important than is the inclusion of material—no matter how it is characterized—that helps teachers use textbooks to increase both the world knowledge of students and their ability to acquire information from text. Therefore, statements like "This is content instruction" and "This is reading instruction" will not be found. It is taken for granted, nonetheless, that the many topics for reading instruction identified and discussed in Chapters 6 through 13—including decoding—enter into a teacher's efforts to improve students' abilities to comprehend textbooks (14). The topics covered earlier receive almost no attention in the present chapter only because space limitations prohibit unnecessary repetition.

STRUCTURE OF EXPOSITORY TEXT

Chapter 12 points out that a global view of stories reveals a structure. In the simplest of tales, the four main components are (a) setting, (b) problem, (c) attempt(s) to resolve the problem, and (d) resolution.

A global view of expository material reveals much greater variety in structure, both within a single body of text and when two or more are compared. Sometimes, as in stories, expository text follows the pattern in which a problem or goal is presented, after which both the efforts to deal with it and the outcome are told. Like stories, chronology may also be significant, or cause-and-effect relationships might be the concern. At still other times, important information is about one or more processes; in other cases, comparisons and contrasts constitute one obvious pattern. Still other authors choose a plan in which question-followed-by-answer is used until all the intended information is communicated. Less often than is commonly believed—certainly less often than basal manuals suggest—expository text is composed of main ideas embellished with related or supportive details (3).

Over the years, the fact that expository and narrative text have different structures and purposes has caused questions to be raised about the likelihood that having students read nothing but stories in the early grades is the best way to prepare them to learn from expository material later. As mentioned previously, the concern and complaints account for the presence now of expository selections in all the basal readers, starting at the early levels. Whether children's experiences with these short expository selections will help with the more difficult and longer material in content subject textbooks awaits investigation. Whether ability to deal with expository text will accrue from the instruction now found in basal manuals as well as in the readers themselves (see Figures 13.1, 13.2, and 13.3) lacks an answer, too. Clearly, both answers are likely to be positive only if teachers make apparent to students the connection between what is taught and read during the "reading period" and what needs to be done in order to comprehend content textbooks.

Meanwhile, the following sections may offer help that can improve instruction for both content and comprehension.

SOCIAL STUDIES TEXTBOOKS

Although some school systems choose to use two rather than one basal series, purchasing a single series is the routine procedure for social studies. Like basal programs, a social studies series is composed of textbooks (and teachers' manuals) sequenced by grade level. Typically, the range spans kindergarten through grade eight. Each level deals with a theme; in grade five, for example, social studies series prepared for use in the United States focus on its history and geography.

Currently, all the social studies series have workbooks and tests. Like basal programs, other materials can be purchased—for instance, exercise sheets, outline maps, atlases, posters, and even letters to send to parents.

It is generally true that starting at about third or fourth grade, teachers are expected to use the textbook said to be for their grade level. On the other hand, I have never heard nor read anything anywhere that required teaching all its content. Consequently, selecting content that merits attention is a responsibility that a Teacher A accepts.

TEACHERS' PLANS: SOME ASSUMPTIONS

The following discussion of how teachers might go about planning for instruction assumes that textbooks are covered one chapter at a time. In no way, however, does this suggest that a chapter is always the best unit to use. What *is* best is something each teacher must decide after taking into account factors like students' abilities and the nature of the text.

A second assumption is that teachers are the ones who must also decide how much time to spend on a chapter, should that be the unit selected to study. In this case, importance of content ought to be the primary consideration.

The content of social studies textbooks accounts for a third assumption, namely, that teaching procedures that are suitable for one chapter may be totally or partially inappropriate for another. Nobody should conclude, therefore, that the suggestions made here are equally suitable for every chapter—or for every group of students. Instead, the suggestions serve the more modest function of providing illustrations.

The fourth assumption concerns the timing of activities. Specifically, just because the present chapter deals with "Vocabulary" before it discusses "Previewing a Chapter" is no reason for teachers to adhere to the same sequence. That a preview, for example, might provoke curiosity about terms in a caption for an effective photograph is a very real possibility and suggests the wisdom—at least some of the time—of rearranging the order in which the two topics receive attention. It also suggests that, at times, attention to important terms will be part of a preview.

All that the present chapter does, then, is cover topics that ought to be considered when plans are made for content areas. In no way is the order in which they are covered indicative of the sequence that should be followed in classrooms. Stated differently, it is not accidental that as early as Chapter 3 in this book, the ability to make prudent decisions is cited as one characteristic that separates superior teachers from their colleagues.

With all these assumptions in the background, let's now consider the planning that all teachers need to do to achieve effective work with content subject textbooks.

READING A CHAPTER: A NECESSITY FOR TEACHERS

To select the important content is one reason teachers should always read carefully the material from which they expect students to learn. The selected content, in turn, identifies important concepts and vocabulary.

A second reason for the reading is to find out what the author of the chapter assumed students know. When the assumptions exceed what students actually know, teachers must compensate for any deficiency when students are being prepared for reading the chapter.

The third reason for teachers to read the chapter is to learn whether the text has features that make it considerate or inconsiderate. How knowing about the features of the text to be read may affect teachers' plans is illustrated below.

Considerate Text: Appositives Define Terms

1. Before students start to read a chapter, let them know with one or two examples that terms will often be explained with appositives. (This assumes that earlier instruction about appositives was offered.)
2. Encourage students to use this source of help with unfamiliar terms.
3. Postreading activities will include a check to see whether students used the appositives and whether the appositives were sufficiently helpful.

Inconsiderate Text: Ambiguous Pronouns Stand for Chunks of Text

1. Before students do any reading, review the use of a pronoun to replace another word.
2. Using examples taken from the chapter, provide instruction about pronouns that replace chunks of previous text.
3. Postreading activities will include returning to parts of the chapter in order to learn whether students were successful with the more advanced use of pronouns, in particular with those for which referents are ambiguous.

It should be noted that when parts of a chapter are inconsiderate because the content is irrelevant or unimportant, the solution is simple: Either tell students to omit those parts from their reading, or withhold assigning them significance by excluding the content they cover from the objectives established for reading the chapter.*

To sum up, then, a teacher's plans begin with a thoughtful reading of the material students will soon study. The goals for this reading are three:

1. To identify important content, which, in turn, suggests important concepts and vocabulary.
2. To see what the author assumes students already know. (Any error in the assumptions points out what teachers need to attend to when they are readying students for a chapter.)
3. To identify features of the text that are considerate or inconsiderate. (How this enters into a teacher's plans was just illustrated.)

PREPARING STUDENTS FOR A CHAPTER

One question that must be addressed in a teacher's plans is what will be done to ready students for reading a chapter. As in basal lessons, means for facilitating comprehension include attention to the new concepts and vocabulary judged to be important; to the background knowledge that comprehending the content requires; and to the purposes that, first, guide students' reading and, later, serve as a basis for learning whether objectives for the chapter were realized.

As the ensuing discussion shows, efforts to teach vocabulary are often closely tied to, or even overlap with, efforts to add to students' relevant knowledge. This is expected, since it is difficult to separate "teaching vocabulary" from "imparting information" when vocabulary is used to provide the information. Even so, vocabulary and background information are treated separately.

Key Vocabulary

In order to stress immediately that there is no one best way to teach vocabulary, two chapters, each of which is the initial chapter in social studies textbooks that cover the geography and history of the United States, serve as illustrations. Both chapters introduce terms important for geography.

The first of the two chapters exemplifies considerate text. Covering the bottom portion of two successive pages is a colorful graphic display that

---

* A recent examination of a chapter about Egypt revealed a section dealing with differences in how flat maps as opposed to global maps portray the world. No reference is made to Egypt. Given the fact that the chapter is difficult because of the author's decision to dwell on uninteresting features of Egypt, this section ought to be omitted from consideration. However, because the segment on maps includes important information, it should be dealt with at another time.

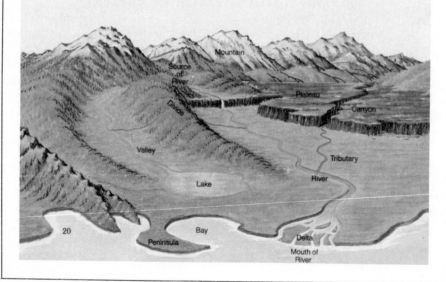

Words for Land and Water

basin the land drained by a river and the streams that flow into it; land surrounded by higher land

bay part of a larger body of water that extends into land

canyon a narrow valley with high, steep sides

cape a point of land that extends into water

coast land along the ocean

delta land built up by deposits of soil which collect at the mouth of a river

divide the highest ridge of land that separates two regions drained by different river systems

gulf part of a body of water that extends into land, often larger than a bay

harbor an area of deep water that is protected from winds and ocean currents, forming a place of shelter for ships

hill a raised part of Earth's surface, smaller than a mountain

inlet a narrow body of water, smaller than a bay, that extends into land

island a body of land surrounded by water, smaller than a continent

Figure 14.1

Source: Karen McAuley and Richard Hall Wilson, *The United States Past to Present* (Lexington, Mass.: D. C. Heath & Co., 1987), p. 20. Reprinted by permission of D. C. Heath & Co. from *Heath Social Studies,* Copyright © 1987.

clarifies the terms students are expected to learn. Above the display are fairly good definitions. (Figure 14.1 shows the first of the two pages. The bottom of the page is in color, which helps clarify the definitions.)

As with all vocabulary instruction, terms in the first chapter that are likely to be familiar are covered first. This guideline reflects the importance of helping students realize what they already know about what they need to know. Further clarification of the terms might come from the students themselves with specific examples—Lake Tahoe and the Adirondack Mountains, for instance, when the words *lake* and *mountain* receive attention. Subsequent pages in the same chapter provide still more examples, some of which are supplemented with photographs.

Because the vocabulary in the chapter lends itself to topically related sets of words, graphic displays can serve as summaries. *Semantic webs*, which are illustrated in Figure 14.2, help to develop what researchers refer to as a *schema* (skē´-mə). A schema is "an organized network of concepts embodying some aspect of knowledge" (12, p. 266). In the case of the semantic webs in Figure 14.2, the knowledge pertains to water and land.

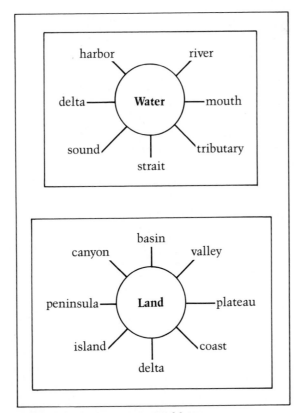

Figure 14.2   Semantic Webbing

Scaling, referred to in Chapter 11, can be used with some of the terms discussed, as their meanings differ from each other by degree. This is illustrated in Figure 14.3.

Having looked at a considerate chapter, let's switch the focus to a chapter in another book. It, too, introduces terms needed for geography. In this case, however, students are expected to read the pages that explain the terms at the same time that they are supposed to refer to an assortment of maps found on later pages. Used as is, this poorly organized chapter is likely to result in little learning and much frustration.

For teachers, an alternative procedure is to list on the board any term likely to be familiar. How many *are* familiar determines how many new terms to teach. (The words not dealt with can be taught in subsequent chapters as the need for them arises.) Explanations for the new terms can be supplemented with maps and photographs scattered throughout the textbook. Again, specific examples from students should be elicited. Again, too, graphic displays like those in Figures 14.2 and 14.3 can function in interrelating and summarizing the terms covered.

To conclude this discussion of work with key vocabulary, some points made in earlier chapters are reviewed below.

Guidelines for Teachers: Work with New Words

1. Whenever possible, relate new terms to words already understood. If students know about mountains, discuss the new word *plateau* in relation to mountains.
2. Rapid lexical access (meaning is recalled promptly and effortlessly) is essential for comprehension. For that reason, time spent on vocabulary should concentrate on words connected with important content in order to make sure that they receive ample attention.
3. Extra attention is required for unknown words whose referents are also unknown. This means that teaching *harbor* to students who have no idea what a harbor might be is more difficult and time-consuming than is teaching *harbor* to other students who are familiar with the referent but do not know the label. Whenever possible, pictures should be used when both the label and referent are unknown. (Fortunately, one prominent part of current subject matter textbooks is highly effective photographs, many of which are in color.)

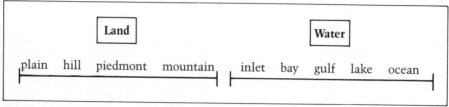

Figure 14.3   Scaling

4. Key terms should be in students' sight vocabularies before a chapter is begun.

Background Knowledge

Because what is known affects what is comprehensible, making sure that students have the prerequisite knowledge for understanding a chapter is an important responsibility. Usually, at least part of what students know or, as the case may be, misunderstand, surfaces when new vocabulary is discussed. Attending to vocabulary typically allows, too, for activating, or adding to, world knowledge.

All this is illustrated with a chapter about Canada, in which some of the vocabulary expected to get attention is *Parliament, Senate, House of Commons, prime minister, Supreme Court,* and *province.* With students living in the United States, who, if they are using this textbook, have just finished an extensive treatment of their own country, promoting comprehension with analogy can be accomplished by discussing the words just named in relation to others the students should know: *Congress, Senate, House of Representatives, president, Supreme Court,* and *state.*

Because the same students should also be familiar with the geography of the United States, attending to a large wall map of North America or to the smaller one in the textbook might be the next step in developing background information for the chapter about Canada. The fact that the two countries share more than an extensive border should be emphasized. Specifically, how the two share the Great Lakes, Niagara Falls, the St. Lawrence River, the Rocky and the Appalachian mountains, and the Great Plains can be shown.

The fact that some students have visited Canada or learned about it from books or television provides additional sources of information that should always be used.

Because the first part of the chapter highlights differences as well as similarities between Canada and the United States, activating previously acquired information can be accomplished with questions about the topics covered in the chapter as they pertain to the United States—for instance, "The First Settlers," "The First European Settlers," and "Effects of the American Revolutionary War."

Purposes for the Reading

Because the first major section of the chapter deals with similarities and differences between the United States and Canada, purposes established for that section should have the same two-sided focus. One possible prereading assignment, therefore, might use teacher-made ditto sheets on which the topics covered appear as headings. The first topic is listed at the top of a sheet as shown on the next page.

Similarities and Differences
between the United States and Canada

The <u>First</u> <u>Settlers</u>

As the first section of the chapter about Canada is read, students write under each heading how the United States and Canada are alike or different. Enough blank space separates headings to allow for the writing. Responses will be discussed during postreading activities.

The second major section of the chapter covers Canadian provinces. As is often the case with textbooks, the attention is needlessly detailed. One defensible plan, therefore, is to deal with the second section as follows. Only the fifth graders capable of comprehending the second part without help will be asked to read it. (The whole class heard the names of the provinces earlier when *province* was contrasted with *state*.) Directions to the better students are to skim two worksheets provided by the publisher of the textbook before the second section is begun. Completing the exercises requires matching the names of the provinces, first, with described characteristics and, second, with the occupations of the inhabitants. These responses will also be considered during postreading activities in order to make one important generalization: Where people live affects how they live.

Extra Help for Poor Readers

The decision to assign the second part of the chapter only to students who can read it independently allows a teacher to work with the others on the first part, which is judged to be more important. Depending both on their reading ability and on the composition and content of the text, help that enables these students to comprehend the first part of the chapter, taking one topic at a time, might include (a) a review of one or more terms discussed earlier with the entire class; (b) further attention to a map or graph that helps clarify content; (c) explanations of such descriptions as *mouth of the river, bed of rock, school of fish, farming the seas;* and (d) instruction that focuses on any part of the text that may be problematic. Help with ambiguous pronouns illustrates such instruction.

Following the extra assistance, the poorer readers will be asked to read silently about the initial topic covered—in this case, "The First Settlers." A volunteer then reviews the content orally. Anything that impeded comprehension is discussed or explained. Finally, the students write their own responses on the assignment sheet under the appropriate heading. Adhering to this procedure, a teacher has time in between topics to help the better readers with whatever problems or questions they may have.

RATIONALE FOR THE PROCEDURES USED

When the fifth-grade teacher read the chapter about Canada, she reached three conclusions. First, certain children will not be able to comprehend the material without assistance. Second, the initial part of the chapter is useful because it allows for a review of information acquired earlier about the United States and, further, for a comparison of the United States with a close, important neighbor. The third conclusion is one this teacher often reaches about chapters in social studies textbooks: The detailed account of each Canadian province in the second part of the chapter is excessive and likely to be of little interest to fifth graders in the United States. Therefore, in addition to making sure that all the students understand *province* and can pronounce the names of the Canadian provinces, all she wants to stress with the detailed descriptions is the interrelationship between where people live and how they live.

The conclusions just described account for the teacher's decision to (a) have all the students read the first part of the chapter, (b) help the poorest readers in ways that make it possible for them to understand the first part, and (c) assign the second part only to students who can read it independently.

It should go without saying that if the teacher in question had access to large, colorful pictures of various parts of Canada, or to something like a slide collection, they would be used to add both information and interest to the textbook's bland content. Current news about Canada that might be of interest would be discussed, too.

ADDITIONAL WAYS
TO ENHANCE COMPREHENSION

Improved comprehension is the goal of the preparations that teachers make for assigned reading. Other ways to achieve the same objective are described next. When or whether to use what is described is a decision each teacher has to make.

Previewing a Chapter

As explained as early as the Introduction to this book, helping students examine the overall organization of a chapter before they read it fosters information acquisition and retention. Having made these claims, it might be necessary to explain why the fifth-grade teacher just referred to omitted a preview of the chapter about Canada. The explanation lies in the fact that all the preparations that the teacher did provide, starting with new vocabulary and ending with assignments, stressed comparisons and contrasts. Because the structure of that part of the chapter judged to merit careful attention is based on comparisons and contrasts, a formal preview was bypassed. The message inherent in this teacher's decision is an important one: Do not preview a chapter just for the sake of previewing it.

For times when a preview is considered necessary, or when students are just beginning to learn about previewing, the following brief summary should be helpful. As you read it, please keep three points in mind. First, the reason for previewing chapters should be explained to students. Second, the exact nature of a preview is affected by the nature of a chapter. And, third, teaching students about the structure of a chapter is less helpful than explaining how they should use the structure to help themselves understand.

Possible Procedures
for Previewing a Chapter

STEP ONE: *Title and Introductory Paragraph*

Direct students to read the title silently. The introductory paragraph might then be read aloud either by you or an able student. Even this brief contact with the chapter might elicit responses, especially if you probe a bit: Does anyone know something about this already? Does it remind you of anything we talked about earlier?

Having students think and talk about a topic, often referred to as *brainstorming,* is important because, first, it activates prior knowledge and, second, it helps students see the connection between what they already know and what they will be learning. The discussion might also reveal misunderstandings.

STEP TWO: *Structure of Chapter*

To help students see how the chapter has been assembled, have them look at headings and subheadings. If either includes words in need of clarification, take the time to discuss them. Should one or more footnotes be used, their purpose ought to be clarified.

STEP THREE: *Graphics*

Students might next be asked to leaf through the chapter to find graphic material. Again, questions should provide a focus so that the students do not view what is being done as aimless browsing. Questions about pictures, for instance, can call attention to details that might be overlooked or, perhaps, assist in estimating the actual size of what is pictured. Queries about other graphics might lead to responses that suggest students need help. For example: How are the lines and arrows to be interpreted in a diagram? If the chapter introduces a new type of graphic aid—let's say a time line—more careful attention is necessary.

STEP FOUR: *Summary*

To wrap up the overview, the summary at the end of the chapter should be read. If questions are included, either at the end or intermittently throughout the chapter, they should be examined, too. If, for the first time, students are using a textbook in which questions are interspersed throughout a chapter, they should be shown how to use the questions.

Afterward, students can be asked if *they* have questions they hope the chapter answers. Their questions can be either incorporated into purposes established for reading the chapter or discussed later during postreading activities.

Graphic Representations of Content

As mentioned, the purpose of a preview is to make apparent both the topics covered and their interrelationships. Sometimes, other means for reaching this goal can replace a preview. The outline of a chapter in which headings and subheadings are listed is one possibility, because it highlights a hierarchy of topics or ideas as well as the order in which they are covered. Other possibilities, referred to at various times as graphic organizers, semantic mapping, idea mapping, and concept clusters, are illustrated in Figure 14.4. As the content of Figure 14.4 suggests, graphic displays of content, initially prepared by a teacher and—with practice—eventually constructed by students, can also serve as summaries, once a given piece of text has been read. Not to be overlooked is that they provide opportunities for a teacher to assess what was learned or, perhaps, misunderstood.

Teaching Students How to Study

Used before a chapter is begun, previews and the various graphic organizers just referred to promote comprehension in two ways. They reveal how the content is organized and what the content covers. All these procedures, therefore, can be thought of as ways to promote cognitive readiness for a chapter.

Learning the content is something else. A procedure long recommended for helping students learn how to learn content is referred to as SQ3R (survey, question, read, recite, review). In spite of the recommendations and the fact that SQ3R receives attention in almost all the basal reader programs, it is not a procedure that is allotted much time in classrooms. This is the case even though very few students—including those in college—use a systematic plan for studying.

On the assumption that the need to teach students how to acquire information from text is more widely accepted now than it once was, SQ3R is described next. It is likely that the description will bring to mind two topics discussed earlier in Chapter 12: comprehension monitoring and fix-up strategies. You will also see that the *survey* part of SQ3R is an abbreviated version of what is referred to in the present chapter as a preview.

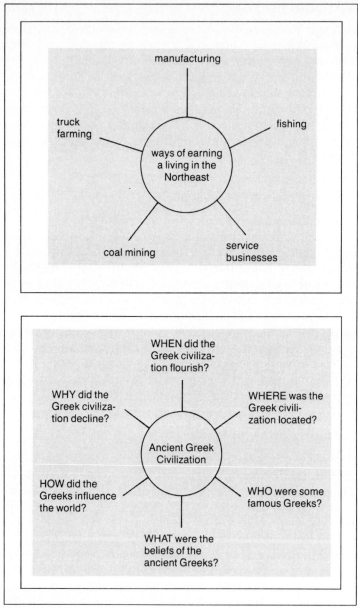

Figure 14.4   Graphic Organizers

Source: From *Using Graphic Organizers in Social Studies* by Bonnie B. Armbruster, Number 22 of the Ginn Occasional Papers, © Copyright, 1985, by Silver, Burdett & Ginn Inc. Used with permission.

Even though the outline of studying presented below focuses on a chapter, early use by students of SQ3R under a teacher's guidance ought to deal with something shorter than that—with a magazine article, for example. Participants in the initial uses of SQ3R ought to be as few in number as is possible.

Procedures for Studying Expository Text: SQ3R

Survey: Skim through the chapter to get the general gist of both the organization and the content. Attend only to headings and subheadings, captions, graphics, and summaries.

Question: Return to the start of the chapter. Taking one section at a time, turn the heading or subheading into a question. "How do people use magnets?" is the question to pose if the heading or subheading is "Use of Magnets." To keep the question in mind, write it.

Read: Read the section to answer the question.

Recite: Looking away from the book, recite the answer to yourself. If this is difficult or even impossible, reread the section, keeping the question in mind.

Review: After using the above procedures with each section, review all the questions to see whether they can still be answered. If any cannot, reread the section that is causing problems.

Having looked at the use of SQ3R from a student's perspective, let me conclude with reminders for teachers who may be working for the first time with this systematic way to study.

Reminders to Teachers: SQ3R

Survey: To foster the type of reading that a survey warrants, only a prescribed amount of time should be allowed. Otherwise, students are likely to read too slowly for the stated purpose. (This allows for giving explicit attention to the need for flexible reading that takes into account the relationship between [a] purpose for reading and [b] kind of reading done. To review what was said earlier about flexibility, see Figure 12.1.)

Question: Typically, students require help when headings are first turned into questions. Provide examples to specify transformations. For instance:

Heading	*Question*
Provinces	What is a province?
Prairie Provinces	What are prairie provinces?
Problems of Rapid City Growth	What are the problems when a city grows fast?

Recite: When a group is involved, the recitation is done aloud by individuals. When students use SQ3R themselves, it is done silently.

Review: Comments about the recitation part of the pattern apply to the review as well.

Once students can use SQ3R on their own, the teacher-guided previews of chapters referred to earlier are unnecessary. What remains essential, however, are periodic references to the use of SQ3R. This contrasts with basal reader programs: They deal with SQ3R once or twice, then rarely refer to it again.

Reciprocal Teaching

Before discussing another way to help students comprehend, namely, through *reciprocal teaching,* it should be pointed out that as long ago as 1969, Anthony Manzo recommended the use of what he called the "Re-Quest Procedure" (16). Following Manzo's recommendations, a teacher and a group of students read a passage silently, then take turns asking questions of each other. "The teacher," Manzo writes, "should be actively attempting to serve as a model of good questioning behavior" (p. 125).

During the 1980s, the ReQuest Procedure was expanded considerably by Annemarie Palincsar and Ann Brown (19). The expansion, referred to as *reciprocal teaching,* is a procedure in which a teacher and a group of students take turns leading a discussion whose purpose is to reveal the meaning of a segment of text that all have just read. At the start, the teacher models the procedure as often as seems necessary. Eventually, whoever (teacher or student) has the turn:

1. *Asks a question* about the content of the segment just read.
2. *Clarifies* misunderstandings.
3. *Summarizes* the content.
4. *Predicts* the content, if this is possible, of the next segment.

Comments by Palincsar and Brown about the clarification component of reciprocal teaching are worth quoting:

> *Clarification is particularly important with students who have a history of comprehension difficulty. . . . These students very likely believe that the purpose of reading is saying the words correctly; they may not be uncomfortable with the fact that . . . the passage is not making much sense. When students are asked to clarify, their attention is called to . . . reasons why text is difficult to understand, e.g., unfamiliar vocabulary, unclear referent words, new and perhaps complicated concepts. They are taught to be alert to the effects of such impediments . . . and to take the necessary measures to restore meaning, e.g., reread, ask for help. (18, pp. 772–773)*

A number of sources are available that assist in initiating and progressing with reciprocal teaching, some of which are in the references listed at the end of the chapter (6, 18, 19). All provide detailed suggestions.

SUPPLEMENTARY MATERIALS

Because the treatment of topics in social studies textbooks often has little appeal for elementary school students, every effort should be made to have additional material available. Material (and experiences) chosen to supplement a chapter in a textbook ought to serve one or more of the following functions:

1. They should add to, or elaborate on, the important content.
2. They should provide reading experiences suitable for highly proficient readers.
3. They should allow for independent reading by poorer students. Each of the three functions is discussed in the following sections.

Extending Content

Ways to supplement important content come in many forms. Depending on both the content and where students live, trips to museums and historical sites are one possibility. Using the specialized knowledge or experiences of individuals in the community is another way to extend information. Other means available to all teachers were seen recently in a classroom occupied by third graders. They were studying Native Americans. The observation reinforced the fact that what teachers do with supplementary materials determines their value.

In this instance, the teacher showed a fairly lengthy filmstrip, presumably to extend content in the textbook. (The purpose is conjectured, since the teacher never explained to the students why they were to watch the filmstrip. The only preparation was, "When everyone is quiet, I'll show a filmstrip about Indians.") As it turned out, the content was both important and interesting for anyone able to comprehend the narration, which was advanced for third graders. Listening to the narrator made it clear that, if nothing else, preparations should have attended to vocabulary. This conclusion stems from the fact that the narrator used words like *primitive, mound, artifact, festival, community, effigy, incorporate, theocracy, cremation, cult,* B.C., A.D., *ancestor,* and *ceremony.* (Other difficult terms were used, but the rapidity of the narration allowed for recording only the ones listed.)

Immediately following the filmstrip, the teacher announced her intention to read two Indian legends. The third graders listened to the two with more than adequate attention. When the second legend was concluded, so, too, was the social studies period.

The lessons that teachers and prospective teachers can learn from this classroom observation are numerous and important. Although much that needs to be said has been said before, the following points still merit attention.

As with written material, teachers should familiarize themselves with the content of a filmstrip (or a movie or a videotape) before plans are made for its use. Had the observed teacher previewed the filmstrip—the assumption is that she had not—it is likely she would have reached two conclusions: (a) The content is important and interesting, but (b) something needs to be done to help the children acquire the information provided.

Even when filmstrips are easy to comprehend, helping students establish a mental set for the content is essential. What a filmstrip covers, for example, can be described in broad, general terms; or, perhaps, questions can be posed to students to get them thinking about the topic. Any way it is done, something should be planned to provide for an introduction.

In the case of the filmstrip about Native Americans, it probably would have been wise to show it in two or three parts, each preceded by attention to difficult terms. Each part could then be followed by discussion and opportunities for both the teacher and the students to raise questions. Because the content was informative and interesting, the teacher might have even elected to show the filmstrip again, this time in its entirety.

What about the two Indian legends? Again, preparations should have been made. Were it the first time the teacher had read legends, this genre should have been discussed. The fact that legends are stories, for example, should have been clarified in order to allow for a distinction between the factual information in the filmstrip and the fictional nature of legends. That many North American legends originated with Indians and Eskimos could have been explained, too.

All these recommendations can be summarized by saying that the third-grade observation revealed a number of missed opportunities to be instructive about a number of important matters. The same observation reinforced again the fundamental importance of teachers' asking themselves, *Why* am I doing what I'm doing?

Providing for Additional Reading

While observing this classroom, a recurring thought was the ease with which the filmstrip and legends suggested topics for supplementary reading. With the help of a librarian, both informational material and legends, written at various levels of difficulty, could be made available in an attractive display. The collection would provide another means for supplementing the content of the textbook and for promoting independent reading.

The third-grade teacher might also have chosen to ask the best readers to research a limited number of topics, using sources like an encyclopedia or magazines such as *National Geographic.* Meanwhile, she and the poorest readers could spend time together with some of the easiest trade books, alternating between the content of pictures and the content of the text.

Using Reference Materials. Even though certain students *are* highly proficient readers, it should not be assumed that they know intuitively how to find material in something like an encyclopedia, or that they know how to take notes on the information about which they will write or report orally. Time spent with these students, guided by steps like the following, will be fruitful for promoting an efficient use of reference material.

Helping Students Find Pertinent Material in Encyclopedias

1. Pose a question—for example, Were the first legends in books like those I read to you? To help students remember the question, write it.
2. Guide a discussion whose purpose is to decide under what topic the answer to the question is likely to be found in an encyclopedia.
3. When the article is located, have the students read it silently, paragraph by paragraph. After each paragraph ask, "Does this deal with the question? . . . Why (not)? If it does not, move to the next paragraph.
4. At the end, repeat the question. Ask students to answer, using their own words.

Taking Notes. Help with how to take notes for a written or an oral report is another common requirement even when students are quite able. Under a teacher's supervision, the following procedures should be productive.

Helping Students Take Notes

1. Once pertinent material is found, ask the group to read silently until a shift in focus occurs.
2. Have volunteers retell what they learned.
3. Ask each member of the group to write a few sentences about the content.
4. Ask some volunteers to read their written accounts so that they can be checked for accuracy and attention to the most important content.
5. Have the group continue with the silent reading until the next shift in focus occurs. Reuse the procedures described above.
6. At the end, have one or more students retell what they learned with the help of their notes.

Reporting Orally. Oral reports by students often figure in a teacher's plans for synthesizing and summarizing what a class learned from both a textbook and supplementary sources. Therefore, help with oral presentations is important, too. In fact, oral reports should not be requested until there has been an opportunity to discuss with students those factors that make an oral report informative and interesting.

One type of summary that might result from such discussions is shown next. It should be displayed for all students to see and, at appropriate times, to reread.

Reminders for Oral Reports
1. Stick to the topic
2. If necessary, use brief notes or an outline but do not read a report.
3. If possible, illustrate material by using pictures, objects, diagrams, and so forth.
4. Don't talk too long.
5. Try to be interesting.

Material appropriate for oral reporting is illustrated below.

■ Interest in people can be used to advantage by having able readers tell what they learned in a biography or an autobiography. If biographies of the same person by different authors were read, oral reports might stress similarities and differences in the two accounts. What the textbook told about the person also needs to be considered.

■ The histories of certain words are sufficiently interesting that brief oral reports about them can be both appealing and informative.

■ If a display table includes realia or pictures, plus cards that ask questions about them, oral reports can provide answers.

■ Interesting newspaper or magazine articles might deal with topics relevant to a chapter's content, and able readers can report on them. Later, others should be encouraged to read the articles themselves.

■ If able readers are asked to study textbooks chosen because of old copyright dates (with the help of guideline questions), they can prepare oral reports featuring differences or even contradictions in what the older publications said as compared to what the students' own textbook related about a given topic. In this case, the oral report functions in pointing out the significance of copyright dates.

Having considered a wide variety of procedures for dealing with the content of subject matter textbooks, let's now look at ways of concluding the work done with a chapter.

POSTREADING ACTIVITIES

As explained earlier, the objectives established for a chapter point directly toward the objectives of postreading activities. Because prereading objectives should divide between some that pertain to the content of the chapter (e.g., similarities and differences between the United States and Canada) and some that are intended to improve students' abilities to acquire information from text (e.g., understanding that a pronoun can refer to a chunk of text), postreading activities should be planned so as to cover the two kinds of objectives. The reading side of the picture has been dealt with extensively in previous chapters; the focus now is on objectives having to do with content selected as being sufficiently important to merit serious attention.

Two points need to be made about such objectives. The first is that postreading activities should deal with important content in ways that synthesize any bits and pieces of information that have been acquired. As stressed earlier in the chapter, if all or certain students are asked to read about the characteristics of Canadian provinces, time spent on each province during postreading activities should not obscure the main reason for the reading: to help students understand that the geography of an area has a direct effect on how people live, earn a living, and spend their leisure time. If some able readers were asked to do additional research on the Eskimos living in Canada because the chapter said little about them, their reports could highlight the same cause-effect relationship. The relationship will assume even greater meaning by having the students discuss how where they live affects their lives.

To cite another illustration, if certain students were asked to prepare picture dictionaries for the geographical terms introduced in a chapter, having the opportunity to examine this material allows for bringing together the individual terms through comparisons and contrasts, plus specific examples supplied by students. At other times—depending on the nature of the chapter, in particular on the nature of the important content—materials like semantic maps, displays of captioned pictures, a filmstrip or film, an outline, or a time line may also serve to synthesize what has been learned.

The second major point to be made about postreading activities has to do with assessment. As is true of any assessment worthy of a teacher's time, what is learned during postreading activities should be used to make informed decisions for the next chapter to be studied. What were various students able or unable to do and learn? What do the students seem to enjoy? On the other hand, what is tedious? What could I as a teacher have done to facilitate even more the students' ability to comprehend important content? These are just some of the questions that ought to be on the minds of teachers as they execute plans for postreading activities.

To sum up, then, postreading activities should function in (a) integrating for students the various kinds of information they have acquired, and (b) allowing a teacher to see what might be done to make the study of the next chapter more productive and interesting. It should go without saying that postreading activities should also allow for clarifying any misunderstandings that students may have.

SUMMARY

Chapter 14 begins with a brief account of what was seen in grades three through six when social studies was being taught. Findings are reported because they verify that covering content is the major concern even when it is unimportant or out-of-date. The findings made it necessary to ask, If teachers only attend to content, when will students ever learn how to learn from expository text?

Chapter 14 proceeds to describe ways for dealing with social studies textbooks that attend both to content and to the text that communicates it. First, though, the point is made that teachers are not in a position to know what to do with a chapter until they have read it carefully. Purposes for the reading include:

1. To identify the important content.
2. To identify the concepts and vocabulary that students must know if the important content is to be understood and retained.
3. To learn what the author assumed students already know about the topics covered in the chapter.
4. To identify features of the text that might be confusing (e.g., figurative uses of language) or that might be a roadblock to comprehension (e.g., pronouns with ambiguous referents).
5. To see whether any graphic aid (e.g., map, diagram, graph) is included that students may not be able to interpret.

Once teachers read a chapter, they are in a position to establish objectives that pertain both to content and to ways of learning how to acquire information from text.

Because the structure of expository text is less familiar and more complex than that of narrative discourse, Chapter 14 recommends previewing chapters. The recommendation stems from the fact that a preview gives students a bird's eye view of a chapter that allows them to see not only its parts but also how the parts fit together. The chapter notes that teacher-guided previews also prepare students to learn how to study on their own with the help of a technique like SQ3R, which is described.

Other preparations recommended for a chapter are hardly new: attending to key vocabulary, providing essential background information, and establishing purposes for the reading. Because the vocabulary in social studies often includes semantically related words, ways to highlight the relationships are illustrated.

Chapter 14 acknowledges that one major problem that teachers face when working with content textbooks is the limited reading ability of some students. That is why Chapter 14 attends to ways of helping poorer readers obtain information from textbooks. The procedures referred to include modeling and reciprocal teaching. Both aim toward helping students to increase the information they comprehend and, in the process, to learn how to go about deriving information. As Chapter 14 points out, helping poorer students understand that the essence of reading is deriving meaning, not naming words, is a major accomplishment. The chapter also suggests that limiting the amount of text that poorer readers are assigned may be necessary. As with all students, only important content should be the concern.

Important content can often be expanded and made more interesting with supplementary materials. Therefore, Chapter 14 reminds its readers that just as students need to be prepared for reading a chapter, so, too, do they need to be readied for seeing something like a filmstrip whose content is related to a chapter.

The availability of additional information in books was not overlooked, since they allow not only for adding to students' knowledge but also for meaningful reading practice. Such practice is possible only when a classroom collection of books (and magazines and newspapers) is written at various levels of difficulty. The variety ensures that poor readers will not be frustrated and that the best readers will be challenged.

Even though the students who cannot read the textbook often are a teacher's greatest concern, the responsibility to provide suitable assignments for superior readers is recognized. In their case, independent research on topics related to a chapter is possible. Such research is maximally productive only when students are given help in finding relevant material and in taking notes. Procedures for providing assistance with both are outlined in the chapter. Because oral reporting is often the means chosen to communicate what researchers learn, reminders for effective oral reports are listed, too.

Chapter 14 ends by emphasizing the four major objectives of postreading activities: (a) to learn whether the comprehension instruction offered was effective, (b) to synthesize the content learned from various sources, (c) to identify and clear up any misunderstandings, and (d) to learn from what was done with the chapter what might be done with the next one.

REVIEW

1. Using examples, distinguish between (a) learning the content in a social studies textbook and (b) learning how to learn the content.

2. How does Chapter 14 justify the firm recommendation that teachers should always read carefully any chapter they intend assigning to students?

3. Explain with examples the meaning of this statement: The objectives established for a chapter define what requires attention during postreading activities.

4. A previous chapter dealt with the structure of narrative text. What did Chapter 14 say about the structure of expository material?

5. In the discussion of considerate and inconsiderate text, the point was made that an examination of subject matter textbooks often shows that the problems children have understanding them is not necessarily evidence of deficiencies in their reading ability. What does this mean?

6. Chapter 14 reemphasized points made in previous chapters:
   a. *Modeling* is often more instructive than explanations. (Exactly how can a teacher's modeling help students learn how to learn from text?)
   b. Unknown words whose referents are also unknown are the most difficult words to teach. (What are examples of such words that are likely to be in social studies textbooks?)
   c. A question teachers must ask if instruction is to be improved is, *Why* am I doing what I'm doing? (Why was there the need in Chapter 14 to make the same point one more time?)

7. It has been said that the only preparation some students make for reading a chapter is to count the pages. Chapter 14 described preparations likely to be more helpful. What are they?

8. Contrast how you usually study with recommendations made in Chapter 14.

REFERENCES

1. Armbruster, Bonnie B., and Anderson, Thomas H. *Producing Considerate Expository Text* (Reading Education Report No. 46). Urbana: University of Illinois, Center for the Study of Reading, January 1984.
2. Armbruster, Bonnie B., and Gudbrandsen, Beth. "Reading Comprehension Instruction in Social Studies Programs." *Reading Research Quarterly* 21 (Winter, 1986), 36–48.
3. Baumann, James F. "The Frequency and Placement of Main Ideas in Children's Social Studies Textbooks: A Modified Replication of Braddock's Research on Topic Sentences." *Journal of Reading Behavior* 16 (1984, No. 1), 27–40.
4. Berkowitz, Sandra J. "Effects of Instruction in Text Organization on Sixth-Grade Students' Memory for Expository Reading." *Reading Research Quarterly* 21 (Spring, 1986), 161–178.
5. Brown, Ann L.; Campione, Joseph C.; and Day, Jeanne D. "Learning to Learn: On Training Students to Learn from Texts." *Educational Researcher* 10 (February, 1981), 14–21.
6. Brown, Ann L., and Palincsar, Annemarie S. *Reciprocal Teaching of Comprehension Strategies: A Natural History of One Program for Enhancing Learning* (Technical Report No. 334). Urbana: University of Illinois, Center for the Study of Reading, April 1985.
7. Davey, Beth. "Think Aloud—Modeling the Cognitive Processes of Reading Comprehension." *Journal of Reading* 27 (October, 1983), 44–47.
8. Durkin, Dolores. "What Classroom Observations Reveal about Reading Comprehension Instruction." *Reading Research Quarterly* 14 (1978–79, No. 4), 481–533.
9. Gaskins, Irene W. "Reading for Learning: Going beyond Basals in the Elementary Grades." *Reading Teacher* 34 (December, 1981), 323–328.
10. Guzzetti, Barbara J. "The Reading Process in Content Fields: A Psycholinguistic Investigation." *American Educational Research Journal* 21 (Fall, 1984), 659–668.

11. Heimlich, Joan E., and Pittelman, Susan D. *Semantic Mapping: Classroom Applications.* Newark, Del.: International Reading Association, 1986.

12. Herman, Patricia A.; Anderson, Richard C.; Pearson, P. David; and Nagy, William E. "Incidental Acquisition of Word Meaning from Expositions with Varied Text Features." *Reading Research Quarterly* 22 (Summer, 1987), 263–284.

13. Holmes, Betty C., and Roser, Nancy L. "Five Ways to Assess Readers' Prior Knowledge." *Reading Teacher* 40 (March, 1987), 646–649.

14. Horowitz, Rosalind, and Samuels, S. Jay. "Reading and Listening to Expository Text." *Journal of Reading Behavior* 17 (1985, No. 3), 185–197.

15. Ireland, Robert J. "Let's Throw Out Reading!" *Reading Teacher* 26 (March, 1973), 584–588.

16. Manzo, Anthony V. "The ReQuest Procedure," *Journal of Reading* 13 (November, 1969), 123–126.

17. Niles, Olive. "Integration of Content and Reading Instruction." In Theodore L. Harris and Eric J. Cooper, (Eds.), *Reading, Thinking, and Concept Development.* New York: The College Board, 1985, 177–194.

18. Palincsar, Annemarie S., and Brown, Ann L. "Interactive Teaching to Promote Independent Learning from Text." *Reading Teacher* 39 (April, 1986), 771–777.

19. Palincsar, Annemarie S., and Brown, Ann L. *Reciprocal Teaching of Comprehension-Monitoring Activities* (Technical Report No. 269), January, 1983. Urbana: University of Illinois, Center for the Study of Reading.

20. Pearson, P. David, and Gallagher, Margaret C. *The Instruction of Reading Comprehension* (Technical Report No. 297). Urbana: University of Illinois, Center for the Study of Reading, 1983.

21. Perry, William G. "Students' Use and Misuse of Reading Skills: A Report to the Faculty." *Harvard Educational Review* 29 (Summer, 1959), 193–200.

22. Piccolo, Jo Anne. "Expository Text Structure." *Reading Teacher* 40 (May, 1987), 838–847.

23. Ratekin, Ned; Simpson, Michele L.; Alvermann, Donna E.; and Dishner, Ernest K. "Why Teachers Resist Content Reading Instruction." *Journal of Reading* 28 (February, 1985), 432–437.

24. Santa, Carol M.; Isaacson, Leanna; and Manning, Gary. "Changing Content Instruction through Action Research." *Reading Teacher* 40 (January, 1987), 434–438.

25. Stahl, Steven A., and Jencil, Sandra J. "Discussion Is What Makes Semantic Maps Work in Vocabulary Instruction." *Reading Teacher* 40 (October, 1986), 62–67.

26. Uttero, Debbra A. "Activating Comprehension through Cooperative Learning." *Reading Teacher* 41 (January, 1988), 390–395.

Part V

Reading and Writing

It was not too long ago that a reviewer of a manuscript for an earlier edition of Teaching Them to Read questioned the attention that writing received. After all, this person said, the book is supposed to be about reading. Rereading that review was an interesting experience, given all the attention that has gone in the meantime to interrelationships between the reading and the writing processes.

Just as it is natural in the present to connect the two processes, so too was it natural in the past to keep the two apart; each was conceived as being essentially different. As the two went their separate ways, reading was viewed as a fairly passive response to print in which the main obstacle to receiving an author's message was unfamiliar words. Reading text that was written in one's own native language, therefore, was a matter of naming words correctly. Doing that as quickly as possible was the key to comprehending (11). Explicit instruction in how to comprehend was not thought to be necessary; instead, the important responsibility of a teacher was to learn whether comprehension had been achieved (7, 8). The classroom focus, then, was on assessing the products of reading, not on the process itself.

End products were also the concern when students wrote. In this case, sentence structure, punctuation, spelling, handwriting, and neatness were of central importance when compositions were evaluated. Whereas reading was pretty much confined to the category "communication," writing in the classroom was also used for chastisement. Writing done as punishment sometimes took the form of repeating a specified number of times sentences like "I must not be late for school." Words missed on a spelling test might also result in repetitious writing.

In the late 1950s and throughout the 1960s, so-called creative writing became popular. I recall being in one classroom during that period in which a bulletin board displayed pictures. Children were to take one down when they finished an assignment so that they could begin the next assignment: Write something about the selected picture. When I asked one girl why she chose a butterfly, she explained, "Because I want to fly." "Why didn't you choose the airplaine?" I asked. "This is creative writing," she said. "You choose something silly, like flying a butterfly."

If nothing else, the current interest in writing has shifted the focus from contrived assignments and questionable interpretations of "creativity" to opportunities for students to write about what they know and feel. Whether the newer conception of writing will allow for improvement not only in students' ability to write but also in their ability to read is a question yet to be answered by reliable, extensive, and long-term research.

Chapter 15

Reading-Writing Connections

PREVIEW

Chapter 15 opens with a review of classroom practices that were common when attention routinely went to the end products of reading and writing rather than to the processes of which each is composed. It is noted that some of the practices still persist both in classrooms and in commercially prepared instructional materials.

The chapter continues by drawing a parallel between certain aspects of reading and certain aspects of writing. It does this by attending, first, to the preparations that effective readers and authors make; by next describing common elements that underly the reading and writing processes; and, finally, by portraying what successful individuals do when they finish their reading and writing in order to add, in one case, to their comprehension and, in the other, to the clarity and appropriateness of their composition.

As is always the case when something new, or something perceived to be new, appears on the scene, reactions to the growing awareness of similarities in the reading and writing processes include both misunderstandings and unfounded enthusiasm (22). Consequences of these two responses are also discussed. Why the enthusiasm requires discipline is explained with a reference to the paucity of long-term studies that allow for generalizations.

After that, Chapter 15 enumerates possible effects of writing on reading and of reading on writing, *if* instruction in both is process-oriented. It proceeds by describing how reading and writing activities can be combined in ways that are likely to enhance reading comprehension.

The chapter concludes with another reminder of the need for teachers to ask, *"Why* am I doing what I'm doing?"* whenever they consider possible ways to give increased attention to writing. Without the introspection that such a question is meant to promote, students can end up doing so much routine and even meaningless writing that it will soon be on their list of "least favorite subjects in school."

If you have not already done so, please examine the outline of Chapter 15, which offers another overview of the topics covered.

The active role that successful readers play as they process text is emphasized as early as Chapter 1. The nature of that role is pinpointed in such statements as "Readers construct meaning." You may in fact recall from the first chapter how you as a reader constructed the meaning of *The man is digging a hole for the tree* in order to arrive at the details of a mental image—or an actual picture—based on the sentence. You will probably recall, too, how you built the meaning of the sentence by using the nine words and the order in which they occurred in combination with inferences derived both from the text and from your own relevant knowledge. Descriptions like "construct," "build," and "make" meaning suggest why readers are now seen as having much in common with writers. What they share accounts for the use of such expressions as "reading and writing connections" (20, 22, 23, 29, 30).

EARLIER CONCEPTIONS OF READING AND WRITING

As mentioned in the Introduction to the chapter, viewing readers and writers as sharing a number of tasks and behaviors is not a perception that has always existed (6). In past decades, clear distinctions were made between reading and writing that, in a sense, kept them apart. This is reflected in the assignment of reading to "receptive process" and of writing to "productive process." How all four of the language arts have traditionally been divided and contrasted is shown below.

Productive	Receptive
speaking	listening
writing	reading

Characterizing reading as a receptive process is not so much incorrect as it is incomplete. After all, the words on a page must be "received" before an author's intended message can be constructed. The importance of "receiving" the author's words, however, in no way diminishes the accuracy of the contention that reading and writing have certain key components in common.

Even when reading and writing were thought to be significantly different, and thus were contrasted rather than linked, they often received similar treatment in classrooms. For example, students usually both read and wrote to satisfy an external demand—commonly, to carry out an assignment. As a consequence, neither the reader nor the writer had any real purpose except to comply with the assignment. Nor was there any genuine audience except the teacher. The teacher, in turn, typically looked at both reading and writing not as processes that she might help to improve but as something having products that required evaluation. In the case of reading, evaluation was usually attempted with numerous assessment questions. For writing, assessment concentrated on spelling, punctuation, and sentence structure as well as on handwriting and neatness.

Even though, at one level, interest in reading and writing has shifted to the processes that occur in each, at another level, interest persists in the end products of both. With reading, concern for products continues to be reflected in the numerous assessment questions still found in the most influential of materials, basal series. If anything, in fact, the unusual amount of interest in writing has increased the number of assessment questions listed in the basal readers themselves, for which written answers are often expected. In this case, two facts need to be kept in mind. First, the best of questions commonly require long answers—often, too long to write. And, second, when students are required to write answers, they respond as briefly as possible.

Judith Langer adds other important reminders for teachers as she contrasts oral and written responses:

> Most often, class discussions tend to elicit freer thinking than written assignments in that students are more likely to venture unorthodox opinions, to explain their thoughts, and to respond more personally, more creatively, and more experimentally than when they write. It seems the moment youngsters are asked to write their reactions to what they have read, the situation becomes more test-like, with student and teachers focusing on language and forms which have been taught and need to be learned. (16, p. 340)

MORE RECENT CONCEPTIONS OF READING AND WRITING

Whereas "making meaning" has always been considered a writer's responsibility, the need for successful readers to assume the same posture came to be appreciated much later. The difference explains why it is only in relatively recent years that widespread attention has gone to reading and writing connections.

Similarities other than the one of making meaning have been highlighted (10, 23, 29). Because the concern of this book is reading, the ensuing discussion of similarities that are frequently discussed looks first at reading and then at parallel components of writing. The similarities themselves pertain to (a) prereading and prewriting planning, (b) the two processes themselves, and (c) postreading and postwriting activities.

Readers' Plans

As is underscored in previous chapters, what individuals do—or are helped by teachers to do—before reading begins should have a positive impact on comprehension. Emphasized on a number of earlier pages is the reader's need not only to have the background knowledge that comprehending a particular piece of text requires but also an awareness of having it. Conscious awareness is important, as it fosters use of relevant knowledge during the reading process. Activating prior knowledge (and, in some cases, adding to what is known) thus constitutes one component of "making plans to read." The hope for what teachers do to help students plan for their reading is that transfer will occur when students are reading on their own. To cite one specific example, the hope is that when they are about to read a magazine article entitled "The Exquisite Beauty of Australian Rainforests," students will give some thought to Australia and to rainforests. Examining the photographs in the article is one way to provoke prereading thoughts.

Awareness of the type of genre to be read is another important part of planning for reading, as the nature of the text suggests the type of structure that the author probably used. As the previous chapter stresses, knowing about, and using, the author's structure helps not only with comprehending but also with remembering what was comprehended (1, 17, 25, 26, 27). In the case of the article about rainforests in Australia, the titles of the sections into which the article is divided offer cues about the structure.

Knowing the genre that is about to be read also helps readers select purposes for reading, as certain genre and certain types of purposes go hand-in-hand. As has been stressed, having purposes in mind before reading commences keeps a person from wandering aimlessly through a piece of text not knowing for sure what is most important, what is fairly important, or, as the case may be, what can be skipped.

All this is to say that reading is a purposeful pursuit that is most likely to succeed when prereading planning occurs. Such planning correctly provides different mental sets for reading a factual description of the bluebonnets in Texas and, on the other hand, an Indian legend that accounts for the abundance of these flowers in that state.

Having considered readers' preplanning, let's shift the focus to the prewriting plans made by successful authors.

Writers' Plans

Admittedly, many people seem to believe that one can just sit down and promptly produce a superb piece of text. At least that is what students often seem to think. Successful authors, on the other hand, know from experience that the omission of adequate planning often leads to well-filled wastebaskets. To be sure, prewriting preparations are no guarantee that what is eventually written will be spared that fate. Nonetheless, it is difficult to dispute the contention that making plans for writing is as necessary to achieve clarity as is making plans for reading to achieve comprehension.

Writers' plans involve many of the components of planning for reading. To start, writers must have adequate knowledge of the topic about which they have chosen to write. Because activating and organizing what is known commonly reveals what is unknown but essential, it is not unusual for a writer's early plans to include attempts to learn more. Often, in fact, authors are as much researchers as they are writers.

As is true of reading, having a purpose for writing is also essential. Even though a writer's original purpose may be altered in the process of writing—this is also true of readers—having a goal at the outset helps establish a hierarchy for what is important. In turn, that helps the writer select and organize anticipated content.

In the case of the writer, selecting the topic as well as a purpose are decisions that are directly related to the intended audience. The audience also figures in the writer's choice of genre. A story, for instance, may be a more effective medium for conveying a certain message to a certain audience than is something like an essay.

The various points that have now been made can be summarized by saying that prewriting decisions about topic, audience, purpose, and genre are interrelated, and also essential, if the writing that is produced is worth reading.

Readers in Action

As has been stressed so many times before, the behavior of the successful, strategic reader is characterized by active efforts to understand, which are guided by preestablished purposes. Some of this mental activity is required by the need not only to link one segment of text to one or more other segments but also to recall the parts in order to construct the whole. Meanwhile, the proficient reader's prior knowledge is being accessed at appropriate times. This may help with integrating parts into wholes; it may also raise questions about the accuracy of the message being constructed. Questions about the adequacy of what is being built in the reader's head may also be prompted by the purposes guiding the processing.

At times, questions about adequacy or correctness may be sufficiently frequent or important that the reader feels the need to slow down or even stop. Stopping allows for employing remedial strategies—rereading a sentence, a paragraph, or more, or, perhaps, using a dictionary to look up the meaning of a word that seems to be of key importance. Based on what is done or learned from fix-up strategies, a revision of the constructed message may follow. On the other hand, the extra steps taken may reconfirm both the adequacy and the accuracy of the message being assembled. And so the process proceeds for actively engaged readers until the end of the text is reached.

As the next section makes clear, what authors often do in the act of composing corresponds in many ways to the reading behaviors just described.

Writers in Action

As we know from our own experiences, some of the mental activity that goes into composing occurs at a very conscious—even a very stressful—level. This is most likely to be the case when what is being attempted is difficult to achieve to the writer's satisfaction. Trying to link together many different kinds of content in a way that produces a well-integrated whole illustrates one occasion when the writing process may be very consciously experienced; and this is the case even when the whole is no more than a paragraph. Building smooth transitions from one paragraph to the next are other times when the mental activity required by composing becomes apparent. Now, the first sentence written for a paragraph may be rewritten (or discarded) more than once.

Like readers, writers may also find it necessary to step back from their efforts in order to adopt the perspective of another person so that the meaning that has been constructed can be examined somewhat objectively. Now, decisions to revise may be made for the purpose of improving organization, incorporating unplanned content, deleting what was originally thought essential, elaborating ideas, or connecting separate ideas. Audience-minded writers are especially prone to stop and ponder; they are anxious to make sure that both the message they are building and the way they are constructing it are clear and appropriate.

Postreading Activities

One of the most desirable features of postreading discussions is the opportunity they give readers to learn whether they succeeded in constructing an author's intended message. Admittedly, the objectivity of authors' messages varies greatly; nevertheless, limits do exist even with text that allows for—even encourages—great divergence in interpretations. No matter what was read, therefore, one reason for postreading discussions in classrooms is to give students the chance to see in what ways their reading did or did not succeed, and why. A second important reason is the opportunity discussions provide to hear the messages constructed by others and, at times, to learn how they went about constructing them.

Whether postreading reflection is carried on in a group or alone, it may identify the need to reread. Sometimes, rereading the entire text may be required—for example, when so much effort went into constructing the meaning of parts that too little was left to reassemble them into a whole. At other times, rereading one or more segments may be necessary because, in this case, the original processing was so taken up with the whole that certain important details were missed or forgotten. Either way, rereading may lead to revisions of both literal and inferred meanings.

For teachers working in classrooms, this suggests that if a text is worth reading, rereading all or parts of it for specific reasons that are clear to students should not be uncommon. Nor should purposeful rereading be viewed as a necessity only for low achievers.

Postwriting Activities

As has been suggested, authors are usually much more conscious of their behavior than are readers. Certainly that is the case when it comes to revising. For writers, the revising, or self-editing, that makes a difference usually starts with a reconsideration of why the writing was done in the first place.

Different kinds of purposes—to inform, to express feelings or opinions, to persuade, to entertain—provide different mindsets for a reviser. Equally important for the revising process is the ability of authors to step outside themselves, as it were, in order to evaluate what they have written from the perspective of the intended audience. From this vantage point, content that seemed clear when the draft was prepared may now be embarrassingly muddled. At such times, fix-up strategies may include reorganization of the content, additions in the form of examples, or deletions. Eventually, self-editing may concentrate on individual sentences or, on the other hand, on improving how sentences fit—or do not fit—together.

In the end, the effective writer—now essentially a reader—goes over the whole of the text as objectively as possible in order to see if the preestablished purpose has been achieved in a way that is appropriate for the prospective audience.

A Summary

One way to synthesize as well as to extend the points made about the common processes underlying reading and writing is to quote Alan Purves (19). The introduction to his written reaction to a paper dealing with reading and writing connections follows.

> *Reading this paper as a commentator forced me to write as I read. Since I am a self-conscious sort, I found myself at certain times wanting to edit, to revise, and to plan my response. As I read, then, I was acting as a writer, but I was not writing as one normally thinks of writing; I was reading. That I put pen to paper does not make me a writer in the sense of an individual who purposively sets out to produce a text. I was, rather, using some acts that writers use in order to formulate my understanding of, and response to, the text. Similarly, as I write this commentary I do perform certain acts of reading, such as going to the authors' text, looking at my notes, or looking at my own drafts. Yet I am essentially composing a text, not reading one. Neither reading nor writing as purposive activities with their own integrity should be confused although there may be individual acts in each that come from the other. Reading and writing have parallels, true, but they are not identical. (pp. 1–2)*

Having quoted someone else's thoughts about connections between the reading and writing processes, let me now add some of my own.

TWO REACTIONS
TO READING-WRITING CONNECTIONS

Whenever something new, or something perceived as being new, makes its way into the domain of education, predictable responses include misinterpretations as well as an enthusiasm that is so great as to foster unfounded claims. References to these problems were made, you recall, when Chapter 4 covered the history of the reading readiness concept. The reading-writing connections reviewed in this chapter have prompted the same two reactions, in particular to the writing side of the coin.

Misinterpretations

To illustrate, the increased interest in children's composition has, in some instances, fostered much more classroom attention to writing than was once typical. Unfortunately, the focus often continues to be on products rather than on the ways in which students arrive at them. The fact that the new interest lies in the processes of which writing is comprised seems to have been lost or, perhaps, was never really understood. This means that writing assignments are still given, then forgotten until it is time to grade the papers.

Evidence that the prewriting planning that was discussed earlier is usually omitted is accumulating. In one report (13), the following conclusion was reached: "After careful observation of teaching practices in 57 classrooms, we have determined that prewriting experiences are absent in most writing instruction" (p. 7). The point being made is that directives like "Write at least two pages about the concert we just heard" have not gone out of existence in spite of the tall pile of articles now available that stress the need, first, to help students plan for their writing and, second, to provide guidance during the writing itself.

All the points made in this section are summed up effectively in an article by Leland Jacobs, in which he responds to the question, "Is it wrong to assign writing?" Jacobs says:

> If "assigning" means prescribing topics, dictating page arrangements and specific lengths to what is written, or using the writing experience merely to practice skills that have just been taught, then the assignment will have been unproductive. Such practices curb children's imagination and their unique writing styles. On the other hand, if "assigning" means providing time and opportunities for discussing ideas, for thinking through what the young writer wants to say, for drafting the composition, and for seeing the writing process through to its finished product, then the children will be on their way to becoming writers. (14, p. 44)

Unfounded Enthusiasm

Responses to the widespread interest in writing that take the form of exaggerated enthusiasm can be summed up by saying that some individuals have come close to proposing that the best way to teach children how to read is to concentrate on the process of writing. As it happens, however, the kind of research that can inform us with assurance about the long-term effects of writing instruction on reading ability, or about the effects of reading instruction on writing, has yet to be done (24). The most popular type of reporting has produced insightful, interesting information about individual children; however, even though anecdotal accounts of small numbers of students are often useful in generating hypotheses to be tested, they do not provide data from which reliable generalizations can be made. It should be noted that one extensive analysis of the data that are available, done by Timothy Shanahan (21), found reading and writing abilities to be more independent than is generally assumed.

After reviewing the literature, another author, Sandra Stotsky, writes:

> *While a large body of research has been devoted to conceptualizing the reading process and to exploring alternative approaches to the development of reading skills, very little research in reading has examined the influence of writing instruction or writing activity on the development of reading comprehension. Similarly, while a large body of theoretical and experimental research in writing has focused on methodological issues, very little research in writing has examined the influence of reading instruction or reading experience on the development of writing ability. Moreover, studies correlating measures of reading ability or reading experience with measures of writing ability have appeared only sporadically through the years and at widely varying developmental levels. (24, p. 627)*

Why too little knowledge about interactions between reading and writing instruction exists is explained somewhat differently in an article by Angela Jagger and others (15). These authors believe that insufficient information about what actually takes place in classrooms has been a major impediment to our knowing more than we do about reading-writing connections. They claim:

> *Among educators it is generally accepted that there is a relationship between reading and writing. However, . . . the nature of this relationship is still unclear. Why? Most research on the reading-writing relationship has been correlational and experimental in nature and has ignored the instructional context. As a result, it provides little information about what children learn from their reading that influences their writing and what they learn from their writing that influences their reading. Clearly, we need to know a great deal about the instructional context if we are going to understand how the amount and type of reading children do in school influences their knowledge of written discourse, how their writing experiences affect that knowledge, and how instruction in reading and writing can facilitate this learning. (p. 298)*

POSSIBLE EFFECTS OF WRITING ON READING

Lacking a body of reliable research data, even cautious individuals who are knowledgeable about the reading-writing connections enumerated earlier in the chapter are likely to agree that process-oriented writing instruction should make some contributions to reading ability if only by encouraging students "to read like a writer" (28). Adopting such a posture, students are more likely when they are reading:

- To use the structure of the text and such details as explanatory examples to help themselves understand;

- To be conscious of the need to know to what it is that referent words refer;
- To be watching for signal words that point to cause-effect relationships, sequence, probability, opinions, and enumeration;
- To be more aware of the possibility that the message they are constructing may have to be altered if it does not match existing knowledge or, for instance, if the message constructed from one section of the text contradicts the meaning derived from another.

Also kept in the foreground when an individual reads with the eye of a writer is the possibility that the composition of the text may be sufficiently poor that extra effort and close monitoring are both essential if the intended meaning is ever to be achieved. On the other hand, reading like a writer may also result in a very conscious appreciation of how well the author achieved his or her goals.

Now, what about reading instruction and its possible effects on students' writing ability?

POSSIBLE EFFECTS OF READING ON WRITING

The components that the reading and writing processes share make it seem logical to conclude that when instruction helps students become consciously aware of the reading process, the same instruction should have a positive effect on the ability of students to write. However, as is pointed out earlier, research has yet to identify the exact effects of reading instruction on writing.

Meanwhile, individuals interested in the writing process have suggested that the act of reading itself contributes to writing ability. Lucy Calkins, for example, reports that some young writers learn how to punctuate from their experiences with reading (3). Linda Flower and John Hayes (10) maintain that extensive reading is likely to affect an individual's writing because "a well-read person simply has a much larger and richer set of images of what a text can look like" (p. 28). A small body of research supports the contention of Flower and Hayes by showing that children's writing reflects the structure of the text found in basal readers (5, 9). For example, using two groups of second graders as subjects, Barbara Eckhoff (9) found direct and obvious connections between the two basal series that the children used and the kinds of writing they produced. Finally—and this point has been made before—what is too apparent to have to document is that the information students acquire from their reading allows for possible content for their own writing.

Until research of the future does or does not identify with substantial, reliable data the impact of reading instruction on students' writing, probably the safest conclusion is one suggested as long ago as 1975 by Marie Clay: Reading and writing are mutually helpful to the extent that instruction in both emphasizes meaning (4).

To conclude, descriptions are provided of how writing can be joined with reading in a way that makes it likely that the writing will enhance the success of the reading.

READING AND WRITING COMBINED IN CLASSROOM ACTIVITIES

Recognizing the variety of times when writing may help with reading, the subsequent sections illustrate when writing might take place prior to reading; when it might be useful to have students stop their reading in order to write; and when writing might be productive after something has been read.

Writing: Before Reading

Anyone who engages in writing learns fairly quickly that it is a highly effective means for illuminating the unknown. In fact, attempts to write often send novelists back to the library—or to a primary source of information—to learn more about the setting chosen for their tales. With equal frequency, authors whose intent is to inform are humbled by the awareness of not knowing nearly as much as they assumed they knew at the time they began to write.

Keeping all this in mind, some teachers elect to have students write what they know about a topic before they start to read what an author has to say about it. Such writing need not be more than a list of sentences, or less, dealing with major ideas; for, in this instance, writing is serving the purpose of activating what is known or is thought to be known. Later, hearing others read what they know may add to a student's existing knowledge. On the other hand, it may raise questions about conflicting information and, perhaps, about gaps in what the group as a whole seems to know. Such conclusions provide a genuine purpose for the reading.

Examples of other prereading writing done to achieve the goals just described follow.

- Before an instructional group reads a story whose central theme is jealousy, a teacher can prepare the students to write about jealousy by having them discuss it—what *jealousy* means, whether they themselves have experienced it, whether they have ever seen jealous behavior in pets, and what the common causes of jealousy are. Next comes the writing, which is followed by an exchange of thoughts as volunteers read what they wrote. Once the story itself is read, a discussion can focus on a comparison of the students' ideas about jealousy with what the story had to say about it.
- In one classroom, a teacher asked students to recall in writing where they were and what they experienced the previous evening when an unexpected earthquake occurred in the community. The original plan was to have all read a brief, factual account of earthquakes, once some of the students read their recollections aloud. Interestingly, what was

read in almost every instance revealed major confusion between the nature of an earthquake and that of a tornado. Some students even wrote about seeing an "equator watch" move across the bottom of their television screens. Needless to say, the unexpected confusion altered considerably what the teacher discussed, and had students read, about earthquakes.

■ Preparations for an expository selection about the importance of conserving energy might include an assignment to list observed examples of wasted energy at home. The next day's discussion may refer to a light left on in a closet, a fan running in an empty room, an unwatched television program, and a partial load of clothes in the washing machine. Such a discussion gives students reasons to learn why one author thinks it is important to conserve energy, not waste it. They are thus ready to read.

The important point for teachers to remember is that students cannot be expected to write when they know practically nothing about a topic. For some groups, therefore, prereading writing about bird migration, dams, erosion, or, perhaps, a day spent in a desert is meaningless. Recognizing that students can hardly write about what is unknown, Irene Gaskins, director of a school for poor readers, suggests that one phase of prewriting done to prepare for reading is the collection of facts. She further suggests that "the search for facts should take students to numerous sources to gather information. In addition to exploring easy reference materials for information, the students may interview an expert or examine newspapers" (12, p. 857).

Writing: During Reading

The decision to have students stop reading in order to write should be made with care, for this is just as likely to result in interference with comprehension as it is to facilitate it. With stories, for example, there may or may not be natural stopping places that allow for written predictions of how the story is likely to end or, for instance, for students to compose their own endings. If there *are* such places and the writing is done, some of it should be shared, after which the reading continues. In this case, postreading discussions ought to allow for comparisons of what the author and the students wrote, or for responses to questions like, "Whose ending did you like best, and why?" Students' endings that hardly match what was read beforehand provide evidence of the need to use future reading to demonstrate that the ending for a story is a natural consequence both of the characters and of what occurred earlier in the story.

In the case of a good story, it is important to distinguish between having children read to a certain point, after which they (a) predict what is likely to happen next, or (b) write their own ending. Encouraging new endings has been criticized by Leland Jacobs for the following reasons:

> It is unfair to the author because it destroys the wholeness of the literary creation, since the ending is interrelated with, and dependent upon, all

that has preceded it. Having children write their own endings isn't fair to the children, either, because it gives them the impression that the story isn't important for its own sake, and it takes away from the possible enjoyment of the selection. Moreover, it gives children a false notion of what story writing is. (14, p. 38)

Unlike most of the narrative text that is read in school, expository text may require a teacher to follow the dictum, "Divide and conquer." As the previous chapter indicates, poorer readers often have to deal with chapters in content subject textbooks section by section. If the segments are chosen with care, the meaning of the whole will not be lost.

Whenever students do require stopping points along the way to the end of a chapter, they can be asked to summarize either orally or in writing what they have learned up to a certain point. As with all summaries, this is a time for teachers to make sure that students are comprehending the most important content and, further, that they are seeing correctly any relationships that are developed in the text.

Writing: After Reading

Once something has been read, many opportunities are available to use writing in ways that can be fruitful for the reading. Possibilities are described next:

- Subsequent to a group critique of how well an author described and illustrated the process of making an assortment of puppets, students who did the reading can be asked to write directions for making something else—a kite, a cover for a book, a pinwheel, a paper box, and so on. In this case, materials necessary for doing the constructing need to be available so that other students can read the directions and make what the writers described. Later, the students responsible for the construction can show what they made, read the directions they used, and comment about how easy or difficult it was to follow the directions. Constructive suggestions for making the directions clearer, should this be necessary, conclude the discussion.
- As students make their way through workbooks, they inevitably encounter unclear directions, which can be copied until a sufficient number are found to warrant a letter to the publisher complaining about the lack of clarity with very specific criticisms. Better directions written by the students accompany the complaints.
- After students discuss the cause-effect events described in a chapter in their social studies textbook, they can be asked to write about cause-effect events in their own lives, starting with sentences like *The wind blew so hard last night that the leaves still on our tree were gone by this morning.* Later, reading about other cause-and-effect relationships can be followed by more embellished descriptions of cause-effect connections—in the form of a paragraph, for instance—again taken from the students' own lives.

- Topics studied in science provide many opportunities for students to learn to write and, at the same time, to write to learn. Depending on the topics, questions such as the following can be both provocative and productive:

  > Pretend you are a raindrop falling to the ground. Describe where you have been.

  > Pretend you are the moon. Tell why you are important to the earth.

  > Select one organ in your body. Explain why you think this is *the* most important organ.

- After students have read and discussed a story told from a first-person perspective, they can be asked to rewrite the tale, now told from the point of view of another character. This might change a story that tells about a girl who feels other children pick on her to one that describes the same girl, now depicted as a person who gets what she gives. As mentioned in Chapter 13, written assignments like this are helpful in illustrating that how a story is told depends to some extent on who is doing the telling.

- If the plot of a story continuously shifts from the present to the past and back to the present again, a postreading assignment can be the preparation of a time line that shows the sequence of events in the story, each event described with nothing longer than a sentence.

ONE FINAL COMMENT

Recent visits to classrooms at a variety of grade levels highlight the need for a word of caution as this chapter on the connections between reading and writing comes to a close. The need exists because, in some instances, teachers' determined efforts to include increased amounts of writing is resulting not only in compositions of questionable quality but also in contrived kinds of writing—writing for the sake of writing, if you will. These teachers need to be reminded of what James Britton said as long ago as 1970:

> *There is a whole world of experience to be interpreted, and writing is a major means of interpreting it. Why, therefore, do we go around looking for practice jobs, dummy runs, rigged or stage-managed situations, when in fact the whole of what requires to be worked upon is there waiting to be worked upon? Every time a child succeeds in writing about something that has happened to him or something he has been thinking, two things are likely to have occurred. First, he has improved his chances of doing well the next time he tries; in other words, his piece of writing has given him practice. And secondly, he has interpreted, shaped, and coped with some bit of experience. (2, p. 37)*

The classroom observations referred to at the start of this section indicate that in many instances, the overuse or poor use of writing is occurring in the classroom of a Teacher B. This is so because numerous suggestions for clarity constitute one of the appropriate changes in basal series. Some publishers are now even selling separate workbooks for writing.

Keeping all these developments in mind, it seems entirely appropriate to end this chapter with one more reminder of the need for teachers to ask themselves continually, "*Why* am I doing what I'm doing?" To have students write because it is the "in" thing to do, or because a manual recommends it, can hardly be justified. Given the enormous number of objectives that need to be realized if everyone is to acquire the highest level of literacy that each is capable of achieving, it behooves teachers to make decisions that allot time only to meaningful, productive activities.

SUMMARY

The chapter briefly reviews older conceptions of reading and writing, which assigned the role of "receiving communication" to reading and "producing communication" to writing. Chapter 15 also points out how the earlier notions about literacy fostered classroom attention to the end products of reading and writing rather than to efforts to improve the processes that make up each ability.

How the newer process-oriented views of reading and writing have made explicit the various ways in which the two abilities interface is considered next. The fact that both reading and writing are meaning-making processes requiring similar kinds of preparations, similar kinds of active participation, and similar reactions to constructed meanings was then developed.

In spite of similarities in reading and writing, the need to take a somewhat wait-and-see attitude regarding the benefits that readers may derive from writing instruction and, in addition, the benefits that writers may derive from reading instruction, is underscored. Caution is recommended because of the lack of studies that are capable of yielding data that can support or, as the case may be, deny the existence of such benefits. Until long-term studies are done, it seems logical to agree with Marie Clay (4) that reading and writing will both improve from literacy instruction that assigns primary importance to meaning.

The chapter concludes with illustrations of writing activities that might enhance reading comprehension. The examples start with prereading writing, then shift to during-reading writing activities, and conclude with illustrations of writing that might be done after a piece of text is read.

REVIEW

1. Chapter 15 refers several times to process-oriented and product-oriented views of reading and writing.
   a. Distinguish between the two views of reading.
   b. Describe consequences of each of the two views of reading for classroom practices.

2. How does the process-oriented view of writing portrayed in the chapter compare with how you yourself go about writing expository text? Divide your response, as does Chapter 15, into prewriting, during-writing, and postwriting behaviors.

3. James Squire states that "our failure to teach composing and comprehending as process impedes our efforts not only to teach children to read and write, but our efforts to teach them how to think" (22). What do *you* think about this contention, and why?

4. As Chapter 15 points out, some individuals believe that comprehension will be improved if readers learn to read like a writer.
   a. Exactly what does it mean to "read like a writer"?
   b. Is it possible that reading like a writer may actually impede comprehension by fostering attention to an author's craft rather than to his or her intended message?

5. Chapter 15 describes ways in which writing activities might serve to help with reading comprehension. The samples are divided into pre-reading, during-reading, and postreading possibilities. Describe one additional writing activity for each of the three time periods. Explain why you think each of your suggestions might enhance reading comprehension.

REFERENCES

1. Berkowitz, Sandra J. "Effects of Instruction in Text Organization on Sixth-Grade Students' Memory for Expository Reading." *Reading Research Quarterly* 21 (Spring, 1986), 161–178.

2. Britton, James. "The Student's Writing." In E. Evertts (Ed.), *Explorations in Children's Writing*. Urbana, Ill.: National Council of Teachers of English, 1970.

3. Calkins, Lucy M. "When Children Want to Punctuate." *Language Arts* 57 (May, 1980), 567–573.

4. Clay, Marie. *What Did I Write?* London, England: Heinemann Educational Books, 1975.

5. DeFord, Diane. "Literacy: Reading, Writing, and Other Essentials." *Language Arts* 58 (September, 1981), 652–658.

6. Duin, Ann Hill, and Graves, Michael F. "Intensive Vocabulary Instruction As a Prewriting Technique." *Reading Research Quarterly* 22 (Summer, 1987), 311–330.

7. Durkin, Dolores. "Reading Comprehension Instruction in Five Basal Reader Series." *Reading Research Quarterly* 16 (1981, No. 4), 515–544.

8. Durkin, Dolores. "What Classroom Observations Reveal about Comprehension Instruction." *Reading Research Quarterly* 14 (1978–79, No. 4), 481–533.

9. Eckhoff, Barbara, "How Reading Affects Children's Writing." *Language Arts* 60 (May, 1983), 607–616.

10. Flower, Linda, and Hayes, John. "The Cognition of Discovery: Defining a Rhetorical Problem." *College Composition and Communication* 31 (February, 1980), 21–32.

11. Fries, Charles C. *Linguistics and Reading.* New York: Holt, Rinehart and Winston, 1962.
12. Gaskins, Irene W. "A Writing Program for Poor Readers and Writers and the Rest of the Class, Too." *Language Arts* (November/December, 1982), 854–861.
13. Gonzales, Phillip C., and Grubb, Melvin H. *Composing Writing Prompts.* Ginn Occasional Paper No. 19. Lexington, Mass.: Ginn and Company, 1985.
14. Jacobs, Leland B. "The Child Writer." *Teaching K–8* 18 (August/September, 1987), 38–44.
15. Jagger, Angela M.; Carrara, Donna H.; and Weiss, Sara E. "Research Currents: The Influence of Reading on Children's Narrative Writing (and Vice Versa)." *Language Arts* 63 (March, 1986), 292–300.
16. Langer, Judith A. "Reading, Thinking, Writing . . . and Teaching." *Language Arts* 59 (April, 1982), 336–341.
17. McGee, Lea M. "Awareness of Text Structure: Effects on Children's Recall of Expository Text." *Reading Research Quarterly* 17 (1982, No. 4), 581–590.
18. McNeil, John D. "Writing to Comprehend." In *Reading Comprehension*, 2nd ed. Glenview, Ill.: Scott, Foresman and Company, 1987, 163–177.
19. Purves, Alan. *Commentary* (Reading Education Report No. 55). Urbana: University of Illinois, Center for the Study of Reading, December 1984.
20. Rubin, Andee, and Hansen, Jane. "Reading and Writing: How Are the First Two R's Related?" Reading Education Report No. 51. Urbana: University of Illinois, Center for the Study of Reading, August 1984.
21. Shanahan, Timothy. "The Nature of the Reading-Writing Relation: An Exploratory Multivariate Analysis." *Journal of Educational Psychology* 76 (June, 1984), 466–477.
22. Shanahan, Timothy. "The Reading-Writing Relationship: Seven Instructional Principles." *Reading Teacher* 41 (March, 1988), 636–647.
23. Squire, James R. "Composing and Comprehending: Two Sides of the Same Basic Process." *Language Arts* 60 (May, 1983), 581–589.
24. Stotsky, Sandra. "Research on Reading/Writing Relationships: A Synthesis and Suggested Directions." *Language Arts* 60 (May, 1983), 627–642.
25. Taylor, Barbara M. "Children's Memory for Expository Text after Reading." *Reading Research Quarterly* 15 (1980, No. 3), 399–401.
26. Taylor, Barbara M., and Beach, Richard W. "The Effects of Text Structure Instruction on Middle-Grade Students' Comprehension and Production of Expository Text." *Reading Research Quarterly* 19 (Winter, 1984), 134–146.
27. Taylor, Karl K. "Summary Writing by Young Children." *Reading Research Quarterly* 21 (Spring, 1986), 193–208.
28. Tierney, Robert J., and Leys, Margie. "What Is the Value of Connecting Reading and Writing?" In Bruce T. Peterson (Ed.), *Convergences: Transactions in Reading and Writing.* Urbana, Ill.: National Council of Teachers of English, 1986, 15–29.
29. Tierney, Robert J., and Pearson, P. David. "Toward a Composing Model of Reading." *Language Arts* 60 (May, 1983), 568–580.
30. Wittrock, M. C. "Writing and the Teaching of Reading." *Language Arts* 60 (May, 1983), 600–606.

Part VI

Students'
Instructional Needs

The frequent references that have been made to the need for introspective teachers who routinely ask themselves, Why am I doing what I'm doing? reflect the fact that diagnostic teaching is the central concern of Teaching Them to Read. *"Diagnostic" describes the work of teachers who, even while offering individualized instruction, routinely look for evidence of what still needs to be taught to whom or, as the case may be, retaught or at least reviewed.*

Although "diagnostic" does have to do with an attitude toward teachers' responsibilities, diagnostic teaching is always grounded in a knowledge of what can be taught to initiate or advance students' reading abilities. The dependence on that knowledge explains why Chapters 6 through 14 deal with subject matter for instruction and, in particular, why an explicit, concentrated look at diagnostic teaching was postponed until now.

As suggested, teachers with a diagnostic outlook accept responsibility for deciding who needs to learn what. Given the fact that a class is usually composed of students who vary in their ability to read, these same teachers must also decide how to organize their classes in ways that facilitate offering individualized instruction. It is to these two areas of decision making that the final two chapters in Teaching Them to Read are directed. Chaper 16 describes means by which teachers can uncover what needs to be taught to whom. After that, Chapter 17 discusses how students can be organized or grouped so as to make it easier to provide suitable instruction. What helps teachers manage as well as organize a class is considered, too.

Even as these last two chapters were being written, the fact that some teachers are content to be a Teacher B was not forgotten. Nor were all the other teachers who are doing their best to become a Teacher A. It is to individuals in the second category that Chapters 16 and 17 are addressed. Without them, in fact, it would be pointless to write a book like Teaching Them to Read.

Chapter 16

Assessing Instructional Needs

PREVIEW

Because increasing individualized instruction in classrooms is the central concern of the forthcoming chapter, this is an appropriate time to review its details.

Individualized instruction:

Deals with what the students being taught have not yet learned but are ready to learn.

Is directed toward an objective that, if attained, will advance existing reading abilities.

Proceeds at a pace that is suitable for the students.

Chapter 16 is intended to show how teachers can learn which of the many objectives that are relevant for reading have not yet been realized by their students. Because classroom teachers are the audience, the described means for assessing instructional needs are confined to those that are possible to use when the responsibility is for a sizable number of students.

Even though the underlying theme of Chapter 16 is *the only reason for assessment is to improve instruction,* it still starts with a description of two kinds of evaluation instruments that make few if any contributions to that goal. The two are *standardized* tests and *competency* tests. They are discussed because, like it or not, teachers often have to administer them. Their inclusion in the chapter, then, is explained by the need to recognize reality.

Once these two kinds of commercially prepared tests are described and critiqued, Chapter 16 proceeds to discuss how classroom teachers can acquire information about students that does have direct implications for instruction. This discussion divides into (a) teacher-devised tests, (b) assessment that is an integral part of lessons, and (c) naturalistic assessment.

The discussion of naturalistic assessment allows for underscoring two important points. First, assessing students' instructional needs should not be thought of as a "special occasion" but, rather, as a daily practice. Second, knowledgeable and secure teachers are as interested in identifying flaws in their instruction as they are in learning about shortcomings in students' reading ability.

If assessment is equated with administering commercially prepared achievement tests, then the only conclusion possible is that much assessment goes on in schools. A different conclusion must be drawn, however, when assessment is equated with efforts to learn about students' abilities and shortcomings so that appropriate instruction can be offered. As is pointed out in Chapter 5, the two conclusions are correct even for kindergarten (4, 6).

The conclusions prompt a number of questions: Why are commercial tests administered? What is the nature of these tests? Do any provide information that does identify instructional needs?

The following sections cover these questions as briefly as possible, since the main purpose of Chapter 16 is to describe how classroom teachers can obtain information that tells them what needs to be taught to whom.

REASONS FOR THE USE
OF COMMERCIAL TESTS

Why the administration of commercially prepared achievement tests has become a taken-for-granted practice can be explained with a number of facts. One that must be acknowledged immediately is the persistent—sometimes highly vocal—contention by the public and the politicians that schools are not sufficiently successful in teaching reading. This fact contributes to the popularity of tests because of the belief by many people that success or the lack of it can be identified with scores from commercial achievement tests.

One of the most extreme responses to the criticism (as well as a willingness to go along with the questionable notion that test scores accurately describe reading ability) is merit pay. This is the practice of paying teachers according to their instructional effectiveness, which is "tied to instructional output in the form of achievement test scores" (17, p. 21). Data are not available that tell either the number of school systems that have a merit pay program or how long such programs are kept. Nonetheless, the effects of merit pay on a school system, reported by Patrick Shannon (17), merit attention because they dramatize possible consequences when unwarranted importance is assigned to scores achieved on a commercial test. One teacher in the school system that Shannon studied referred to the adoption of a merit pay program this way:

> The district was under so much criticism for falling short of certain nationwide standards in reading. They had so much bad press. This was simply a method to inspire teachers to achieve better on standardized tests. . . . The five step procedure, the commercial materials, and the stipend are all ways to raise the scores. (p. 29)

Another teacher in the same school system had this to say:

> I'm pushed harder to get my kids through commercial materials. I have to be at a certain point in the commercial materials by the end of the year. Otherwise I'm in trouble. I have to make my lessons quicker. I'm pushed so I push. . . . That sounds terrible I know . . . but what else can I do? (pp. 30–31)

Admittedly, the quoted responses exaggerate the importance that most school systems assign to tests. Nonetheless, the teachers' comments reflect some facts:

1. Schools administer annually at least one reading achievement test. In some instances, scores are merely noted on the children's records. In other instances, scores are used to form instructional groups, or to decide which students require remedial instruction, or to report students' progress to parents. Less frequently, test scores figure in judgments about faculty members' ability to teach.
2. As mentioned in Chapter 13, those in the publishing business who are responsible for what is covered and how it is tested in commercial reading programs take into account in systematic ways the content as well as the format of the most frequently used achievement tests. This is done to maximize the likelihood that students using their programs perform satisfactorily on the tests. To increase even more the likelihood of adequately high scores, basal programs now include manual segments and worksheets that deal with teaching students how to take tests.
3. For a variety of reasons, some teachers do teach to whatever tests they are expected to give. As just pointed out, other teachers allow assessment to drive instruction in a way that is portrayed below (5):

Achievement tests ⟶ basal reader tests ⟶ basal reader
               affect   affect
workbooks and ditto masters ⟶ how time is spent in classrooms.
               affect

Some would say a more realistic portrayal shows two-way connections:

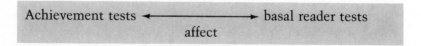

Achievement tests ←————————→ basal reader tests
affect

The two-way link portrayed above is suggested by the fact that just as those who are responsible for basal series keep track of the most frequently used assessment instruments, so, too, do those who prepare the achievement tests monitor the content of basal reader manuals and tests. The fact that some publishers now produce both tests and basal programs facilitates the two-way communication.

NATURE OF COMMERCIAL ACHIEVEMENT TESTS

No matter how current practices are portrayed or are interrelated, the influence of commercially prepared tests on what occurs in classrooms, starting as early as kindergarten and first grade (6, 12), can hardly be denied. That being the case, this section deals with the tests and the reasons they are commonly the subject of criticism. The coverage is brief, as the central theme of the chapter is increasing individualized instruction.

Two types of tests are described, *standardized* tests and *competency* tests. The selected focus is not intended to deny or underestimate the frequent use of end-of-unit, end-of-level basal reader tests. Instead, the omission of basal tests from the discussion is explained by the fact that many comments made about standardized and competency tests apply equally to basal tests. In addition, what is said in previous chapters about basal workbooks and ditto sheets applies to the basal tests, because all these materials are more similar than different.

Standardized Tests

Commonly, standardized tests evaluate word recognition, vocabulary knowledge, and comprehension. As the common meaning of *standardized* suggests, procedures for administering the tests are described in detail in the manuals and are assumed to be followed by whoever gives the tests. Usually, this is a classroom teacher. Often, procedures include stipulated time restrictions.

Standardized tests are also referred to as being *norm-referenced*, because they allow for comparisons of achieved scores with the distribution of scores attained by a large sample of students elsewhere. These students are called the *norming population.*

Because the scoring is done by computers, it, too, is highly standardized. Computer scoring is less useful to teachers, however, who, when they scored the tests themselves, had the opportunity to acquire information that, at times, offered help in selecting instructional objectives.

Because of computer scoring, schools can request from the publisher multiple kinds of scores—for instance, raw scores, percentile ranks, stanines, and grade equivalents, all of which are defined in the test manuals. Here, only grade-equivalent scores are discussed.

Grade-equivalent scores merit attention because they are sufficiently misleading that the International Reading Association passed a resolution in 1981 urging publishers to eliminate them (8). The resolution resulted from the widespread misconception that when a raw score is converted to a grade equivalent by using tables provided in test manuals, the converted score describes a student's ability in relation to materials. Stated specifically, the concern that prompted the resolution just referred to is rooted in the fact that a grade-equivalent score such as 5.2 does *not* signify that students achieving that score are necessarily able to read fifth-grade material.

More recent complaints about standardized reading tests are directed to their assessment of comprehension. Typically, comprehension abilities are evaluated by having students read short passages, after which they select answers to questions about the content from a list of possible answers.

Multiple-choice formats have always spawned criticism, as they allow for lucky guesses; they also reward students who have developed a high level of so-called test wiseness. In addition, a multiple-choice format makes it impossible to know when a correct answer was chosen for the wrong reason and when a wrong answer was selected for a defensible reason.

Criticisms of standardized tests that are confined specifically to comprehension are listed below. They are divided between those that have been heard for some time and others that reflect more current understandings of the comprehension process.

Comprehension Tests: Traditional Concerns

Test passages are prepared and their difficulty assessed with readability formulas. (Why these uses of readability formulas are questionable is discussed in Chapter 13.)

Questions about some passages can be answered without reading the passages.

Scores are difficult to interpret when a test includes difficult questions for easy passages and easy questions for difficult passages.

Comprehension Tests: More Recent Concerns

Some of what is important to teach is not tested. Bypassed, for instance, are comprehension-monitoring abilities and the selection of appropriate fix-up strategies. (What is not tested is an important issue, because what is omitted may not be allotted instructional time.)

The pervasive influence of prior world knowledge on comprehension is not taken into account. (To avoid problems created by differences in world knowledge, authors of tests commonly rely on questions that are answered directly in a passage. Whenever this occurs, only literal comprehension abilities are evaluated. Test authors also use brief passages that cover a variety of topics on the erroneous assumption that the variety neutralizes the influence of differences in students' background information.)

Comprehension scores reveal little about the reasons for a student's poor performance. (Whether comprehension broke down at the word, sentence, or passage level is unknown. Nor can anything be determined about students' uses of text structure to help themselves understand, as the brevity of many passages precludes their having much of a structure. It should be noted that high scores present the same problem: They reveal little about the exact reasons for the success.)

Even though school administrators and other individuals defend the administration of standardized reading achievement tests as a means for making comparisons or for tracing growth or the lack of it in large groups of students, nobody can claim that the results of these tests offer teachers help with decisions about appropriate instruction. Authors of the tests, in fact, might be the first to say this is not their purpose. In fairness to the authors, it must also be emphasized that they cannot be blamed for the misuse or overuse of their tests.

Competency Tests

Originally, competency tests were proposed as a means for bringing together, rather than keeping apart, testing and teaching. This was to be accomplished by evaluating reading ability not in relation to a norming population as do standardized tests, but in relation to specifically defined behavioral objectives (e.g., Can sort out the roots in twenty inflected words in which the spelling of the roots is altered). Competency tests are also described as being *criterion-referenced*, because arbitrary criteria are established to define what is called "mastery." To illustrate, a student who is able to sort out a minimum of sixteen roots with altered spellings in a list of twenty derived words might be said (according to one test) to have achieved mastery on that particular ability.

Not unexpectedly, interest in this way of evaluating reading resulted in a number of commercial programs in the 1970s that came to be called "management systems." *Wisconsin Design* (11), one of the best known of these commercial programs, assessed 309 different skills. It goes without saying that basal series also began to resemble management systems in the 1970s; this is reflected in advertisements for basal programs that made such boasts as, "We cover more than 300 subskills!" (5).

At first, certain features of criterion-referenced tests made them appear to be a major improvement over the norm-referenced standardized test. Comparing students' scores with curriculum objectives, rather than with scores of a norming population, made good educational sense. From a different perspective, it was thought that the specification of objectives would keep teachers on track—that is, would clarify exactly what it was they were attempting to teach. Other people approved of competency tests because they could be used to satisfy the public's demand to hold schools and teachers accountable for student achievement.

Because competency tests soon became one part of instructional packages that included large numbers of workbooks, exercise sheets, and elaborate devices for recording test scores, the consequence for classrooms was nothing like what had been predicted by enthusiastic supporters of competency tests. For example, passing tests that evaluated very circumscribed skills seemed to be the goal. To reach it, exercise sheets bearing close resemblance to the tests were routinely assigned. The fact that reading has to do with such abilities as comprehending a story, acquiring information from a magazine article, and understanding written directions in order to reach a certain destination was put on the back burner. Clearly in the foreground, on the other hand, was a sequence for teachers that went something like this: administer pretests, record results, assign worksheets, administer posttest, record results.

Because of the importance assigned to mastery, the time that remained after all the required testing and record-keeping were done commonly went to helping the lowest achievers increase their scores. As Hoffman and Rutherford observed, "There is no incentive or motivation to work with students who have already mastered the objective" (7, pp. 89–90).

It was not surprising that the highly mechanistic, atomistic view of reading that competency tests fostered soon brought out the critics. Their main complaint was that mastering literally hundreds of discrete subskills apart from their use in authentic text did not automatically result in reading ability. This criticism was reinforced in the latter part of the 1970s by the growing awareness that comprehension is a holistic process that requires the integrated use of much more than what the competency tests evaluated piece by piece.

Even though it is accurate to say that the critics helped reduce the influence of competency testing, the amount of money that school systems continue to spend on both competency and standardized tests is clear evidence that interest in—even demands for—such testing has not diminished (15). The strong likelihood that externally mandated assessment will continue makes any attempt to improve reading achievement tests very important (19, 21). One small step taken in that direction is the inclusion of pre-reading purpose-setting questions in the comprehension part of a frequently used standardized test (14). This was done with the expectation that prereading questions activate relevant knowledge and, in addition, encourage a reader to attend to those parts of a passage that are related to the preestablished purpose.

Meanwhile, teachers still need to collect information that can help them make decisions about day-by-day instructional needs.

DETERMINING INSTRUCTIONAL NEEDS

Three ways for learning what needs to be taught (or reviewed or retaught) are considered. The three reflect the fact that instructionally relevant information can come (a) from teacher-devised tests, (b) from the assessment that is a part of instruction, and (c) from observing and listening to students as they work their way through each school day.

Teacher-Devised Tests

As has been acknowledged, externally mandated tests do influence to various degrees what teachers teach and, therefore, what students have an opportunity to learn. This is referred to as early as Chapter 5, when the influence of both tests and workbooks on instruction in kindergarten is described. Nonetheless, the influence of commercial materials is never so great that it excludes from the agenda of conscientious teachers their own efforts to assess. Whenever teacher-devised assessment is planned, two guidelines need to be kept in mind:

1. Restrict the focus of the assessment to something specific. A suitable concern is students' ability to understand similes that are signaled by the *as . . . as* construction. A focus that is unsuitable because of its scope and nonspecificity is students' ability to understand figurative language.
2. Restrict the focus of assessment to something that can be taught fairly soon. Having information about many topics is not the objective of assessment that is relevant for instruction. A little assessment followed by teaching, followed by more assessment followed by teaching—this is the sequence that allows assessment to have a positive impact on an instructional program.

Examples of teachers' efforts to acquire information about instructional needs are presented next.

Illustrations of Teacher-Devised Tests

As you read the descriptions of the instruction-oriented assessment that follow, note the close connection between the objective of the testing and how the testing is done. The connection suggests that "Why am I doing what I'm doing?" is as important to ask when assessment is planned as it is when instructional decisions are made. Notice, too, how the teachers' concern is to learn not only about shortcomings but also about abilities. The two-sided concern is necessary, since information about both is needed for planning suitable instruction.

Ms. White. Over a period of five years, Ms. White taught both third and fourth grades. Even though she always believed that the basal materials prescribed for those grades give excessive, even tedious, attention to dictionary skills, it was only now that she felt sufficiently confident to omit nonessentials. To pinpoint what was unnecessary, she conducted brief, individual tests close to the start of the year—she was now teaching third grade—in which the objective was to learn who was unable to use a dictionary sufficiently quickly. Five words made up the test. Results indicated that only two children had trouble; consequently, they became a special-needs group, and it was only to them that instruction and assignments with location skills would be given. Meanwhile, the whole class worked on using a pronunciation key in dictionaries and on choosing meanings that fit particular contexts. Sentences taken from science and social studies textbooks were used.

Approximately one month later, another test was given. This time the purpose was, first, to see whether the students could pronounce unfamiliar words with the help of diacritical marks and, second, to learn whether additional help with selecting appropriate meanings was needed. For this test, words were presented in sentences. One result of the testing was the establishment of a special-needs group composed of thirteen students to whom further help with choosing relevant definitions would be given. The other sixteen would get no further dictionary assignments even though the assigned basal reader workbook continues to offer dictionary exercises for what seems like an endless amount of time.

Ms. Paul. This teacher has twenty-six bright second graders, all of whom read well. Like other teachers in her building, Ms. Paul is obliged to use basal readers and workbooks written for the grade she teaches. Once children complete these materials, anything else is permissible.

To make the best of what she believes is an indefensible policy—at least insofar as her present class is concerned—Ms. Paul started the year determined to eliminate any manual segment, workbook page, or ditto sheet that dealt with what her students know or with what is not essential for reading. Falling into the latter category is what is sometimes done with contractions, specifically, having children write the words for which contractions substitute and having them note the letters that the apostrophe replaces. Aware that all that is required for reading is the ability to identify contractions and to understand their meanings, Ms. Paul decided to begin by eliminating nonessentials insofar as contractions are concerned.

She first listed all the contractions that were reviewed or introduced in the basal series she has to use and then composed sentences that included them all. For the testing, each child read the sentences aloud, which permitted Ms. Paul to learn whether they were pronouncing the contractions correctly. Following that, the children told in their own words what each sentence meant. This procedure was used because the meaning of the sentence depended on knowing the meaning of the contraction. In the end, the test confirmed what had been suspected: Time did not have to go to contractions because the children knew them as well as their teacher.

Mr. Oliver. This teacher has a third-grade class in which eleven students are mature in their behavior and proficient in their reading. The two characteristics encouraged Mr. Oliver to give them numerous written assignments at the start of the year. In fact, their reading program was composed of reading basal selections, completing workbook pages and worksheets, and doing written reports. Recognizing both the shortcomings and monotony of the combination, Mr. Oliver decided in November to collect diagnostic information so that suitable instruction could begin.

He started by meeting with each of the eleven students to learn what they do with unknown words. Because the specific goal was to learn what is done when only spellings are available to help, he compiled a list of twenty words, some likely to cause problems. That was mentioned at the start of each session, as was the reason for having it: to learn whether further help with decoding is necessary.

In the initial conferences, only root words were used; for the second, derived and inflected words were listed. By asking the students to think out loud whenever they came to a word they were unable to identify immediately, Mr. Oliver ended up with a number of notations that pinpointed what still needed to be taught about decoding.

In the end, only one child in the group was so proficient as to require no further help. Mr. Oliver offered her the chance to read self-selected trade books while the others had advanced decoding instruction; however, she preferred to stay with the group. As it turned out, her observations about difficult words (especially derived and inflected words) made a useful contribution to the fast-paced work of these advanced students.

Ms. Antley. This second-grade teacher is just starting the second month of a new year. Earlier, while listening to certain children read selected passages in order to organize instructional groups, she noticed that two boys, both spending a second year in second grade, seemed content to say anything whenever they encountered a word they were unable to identify. It was as if they did not realize that reading is a sense-making process. To learn more about them, Ms. Antley met with each separately to see what he knew about contextual cues. With this objective in mind, she had the boys read aloud fifteen sentences with deleted words—for instance, "When you come in, _____ the door." Any word was accepted for a blank as long as it made sense.

Results of the brief conferences showed need for attention to the semantic aspects of reading as well as to the use of contextual cues for help with word recognition. Therefore, Ms. Antley plans to concentrate at first on material that she will read to the boys, much like the kindergarten teachers did who are referred to in Chapter 7. Later, written sentences similar to the ones that figured in the original diagnosis will be used. Still later, Ms. Antley plans to learn how the two boys use contextual cues plus minimal graphophonic cues, because they know most letter-sound relationships. In a subsequent diagnostic session, therefore, she will use sentences like *When you come in, cl____ the door.*

The teacher-devised testing just described allows for attention to the fact that all teachers need to know how students respond to words—in particular, what strategies they use with unknown words. To acquire this information, oral reading of unfamiliar material is called for.

To make sure that what is heard when a student reads aloud has significance for instructional decisions, a teacher must look, not for "mistakes" per se, but for possible patterns in the student's responses. Stated differently, *how many* misidentifications occur is less important than is the *nature* of the misidentifications. Questions like the following, therefore, should guide the listening. Answers may suggest what needs to be taught or retaught.*

> ### *Monitoring Oral Reading to Establish Instructional Needs*
>
> Are high-frequency words automatically identified?
>
> Are all available cues being used with unfamiliar words?
>
> Do misidentifications follow any pattern? For instance, are contextual cues overused or, to the contrary, does the use of spellings dominate?
>
> Exactly how are graphophonic cues used? For example, is the sequence of sounds commonly rearranged (*felt* read as "left")? Are sounds added (*pet* read as "pest")? Are sounds commonly omitted (*cart* read as "car")? Is equal attention given to initial, medial, and final sounds?
>
> What is the student's strategy for working out long, seemingly complicated words? Or does a strategy even exist?
>
> What is done with unknown inflected and derived words? Is any attempt made to sort out the root? Do altered spellings of roots cause problems? Are prefixes and suffixes recognized as such?
>
> Are unfamiliar words worked on aggressively and persistently, or is there a tendency either to omit them or to depend on outside help?

Recording Results of Teacher-Devised Tests

If the results of teacher-devised tests are to influence instructional decisions, they have to be remembered; consequently, recording the results is recommended. To prevent record-keeping from becoming an end in itself,

---

* Monitoring oral reading in the way suggested by many of the listed questions is related to the section in Chapter 7 entitled "Miscue Analysis." This is an appropriate time, then, to reread that material.

however, whatever is written should be as brief as possible. Keeping both brevity and simplicity in mind, teachers find it useful to have on hand copies of a sheet like the following:

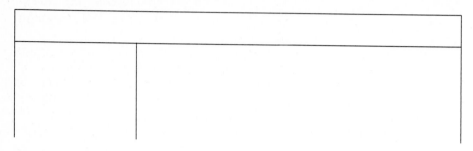

The sheet shown above allows for both flexible and instantaneous use. To illustrate, if a teacher decides to learn whether each member of an instructional group is able to identify twenty-five high-frequency words that have been taught over several weeks' time, she can write the students' names in the left-hand column; which words were tested at the top; and which were missed after each student's name.

Records for oral reading done to uncover how students cope with unknown words embedded in text require somewhat detailed information. In this case, teachers often choose to record the oral reading so it can be analyzed later. Having a copy of the text that a student reads allows for a marking system that is illustrated below.

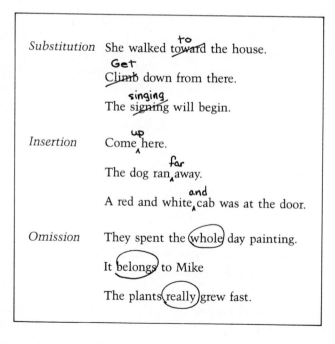

Now that examples of teacher-devised tests and ways to record results have been given, let's move on to take another look at the assessment that is an integral part of lessons.

Assessing Instructional Outcomes

In Chapter 3, instruction is categorized as (a) planned, intentional instruction; (b) unplanned, intentional instruction; and (c) unplanned, unintentional instruction. The point to be emphasized now is also made in the earlier chapter, namely, planned lessons should always include opportunities to learn whether the objectives were realized. The recommended cycle for planned instruction is portrayed below.

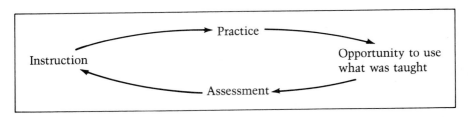

As has been stressed many times, the most meaningful assessment allows for information about students' ability to use (apply) what was taught in authentic text. Such information can then direct a teacher in deciding what should be taught next or, as the case may be, what needs to be retaught.

Teachers who adhere to the instructional cycle shown above would have no difficulty were they required on a daily basis to complete a questionnaire like the one in Figure 16.1.

Because ways for learning whether the objectives of instruction were realized are described in previous chapters, another source of instructionally relevant information that is available all the time is discussed next.

Naturalistic Assessment

Defining *naturalistic assessment* as "diagnosing by observing" should allow you to see that support for such assessment is pervasive in *Teaching Them to Read*. The definition should also suggest that naturalistic assessment occurs—or should occur—daily. Its ongoing nature is recognized in the Introduction to this section of the book when it is said that teachers with a diagnostic orientation "routinely look for evidence of what still needs to be taught to whom or, as the case may be, retaught or at least reviewed."

Illustrations of Naturalistic Assessment

Even though numerous examples of naturalistic assessment are in previous chapters, three more follow. The first example describes what was seen in a kindergarten.

1. List below what you attempted to teach today, and to whom.

    Instructional objectives   Students

2. Why did you select those objectives for those individuals?

3. Did the students learn what you planned for them to learn?

    ——— yes   ——— no

4. If yes, why do you think they did?

    If no, why do you think they did not?

    If no, what is the next step?

Figure 16.1 Diagnostic Teaching: Reading

The teacher was working with a group of eight. Her objective was to help the children understand that words that are the same when spoken look the same when written. To help realize the objective, each child was given a copy of "Hickory, Dickory, Dock," a nursery rhyme familiar to all. When the teacher asked the children to put a finger under the first word in the first line, none understood the request. Because it was clear that the preestablished objective was too advanced, the teacher used the time instead to help the group understand the meaning of "word" and how empty space shows where one word ends and the next begins.

The second example of naturalistic assessment was seen when a teacher was working on syllabication.

Before providing practice in segmenting into syllables unknown roots that have a VCV spelling pattern, the observed teacher reviewed the generalization for such words with the help of known words that were on the board (e.g., *pilot, elect*). The teacher then wrote *unite*. Because nobody could read it, the teacher asked for a suggestion about where to divide the word into syllables so that it could be decoded. The student who responded said to divide it between *n* and *i*. Asked why he thought that was the place for a break, the child explained that *u* and *n* are a prefix. With the help of *untie* and *unlock* and of *under* and *uncle,* all of which were printed on the board, the teacher reviewed that prefixes like *un-* are attached to real words only; and that since *ite* is not a word, the *u* and *n* are not a prefix.

The third example also has to do with decoding.

The goal of the lesson was to teach the generalization: When there is one vowel in a word and it is not the last letter, it usually stands for its short sound. Correctly, the teacher used familiar words to help explain the new generalization:

> and
> ask
> bad
> can

Later, to summarize the lesson, the teacher inquired, "Can someone say what you learned today?" Someone did, observing, "When a word has one vowel, it'll be an *a*." Recognizing the problem was with the illustrative words, the teacher started the lesson again, this time using *at, end, big, not, cub,* and *ten* for examples. Now the objective of the instruction was realized without any difficulty.

The lesson about a vowel sound was deliberately listed at the end of the illustrations of naturalistic assessment because it makes an important point: Naturalistic assessment should serve as a means for improving teaching as well as for evaluating learning.

To provide a contrast for the professional behavior of the teacher just described who was working with short vowel sounds, a dialogue heard in another classroom is repeated below. It took place after a basal story had been read in round robin reading fashion. The teacher seemed highly dependent on a manual.

Teacher: Why would a good title for this story be "One Good Turn Deserves Another"?

Students: [No response]

Teacher: You're not listening. I said [this is repeated in a louder voice] why would a good title be "One Good Turn Deserves Another"?

Students: [No response]

Following the brief interchange—or lack of interchange—the teacher told the group that if they didn't listen, they wouldn't be able to learn anything. She then proceeded to ask some of the literal questions about the story that were in the manual.

Because there was no evidence that a failure to listen accounted for the lack of a response to the teacher's first question, other problems were likely to be the cause. If a diagnostically oriented teacher chose to ask the question, reasons for the failure to get an answer would be considered. For instance:

1. Because the question pertained to the underlying theme, was the problem rooted in the students' inability to infer the theme?
2. Because the question was phrased in nonliteral terms, might the wording have been the problem?

Diagnostically oriented teachers do not abandon unanswered or incorrectly answered questions. Instead, they try to *understand* the reasons for the problem, in particular, what they suggest for necessary instruction.

SUMMARY

Chapter 16 begins with a description and critique of two kinds of tests that classroom teachers are often required to administer. The two are standardized tests and competency tests. The critiques are required by the fact that the concern of the chapter is assessment that yields information that can increase individualized instruction. Why neither standardized nor competency tests meet that criterion is explained. Some of the reasons have to do with the failure of the tests to evaluate comprehension in ways that reflect the nature of the comprehension process.

Chapter 16 then considers three means by which classroom teachers can collect information that is relevant for decisions about instruction. This discussion starts with tests that teachers themselves can devise. Guidelines for such testing include the following:

- A specific objective needs to be identified before thoughts go to constructing a test.
- What is tested should not exceed what can be taught in the near future. Unused information helps nobody.
- How the test is carried out should reflect the objective.
- What students know and can do is just as important to identify as are their shortcomings, as both have implications for instruction.
- What is learned from the testing should be recorded in the simplest and briefest way possible.

The second means for assessing instructional needs occurs as an integral part of preplanned lessons. This type of assessment is illustrated in

Chapter 3 as well as in other chapters whenever lessons are described. In some cases, the lessons were circumscribed; at other times, they were as encompassing as a basal reader lesson.

The third means for learning about instructional needs discussed in Chapter 16, naturalistic assessment, is available all the time to teachers with a diagnostic orientation. Exactly what some teachers learned about instructional needs and what they did about them are described in the chapter. To provide a contrast, a reference is also made to one teacher who did not appear to be diagnostically oriented; she tended to blame rather than to try to understand.

REVIEW

1. Describe the essential features of standardized tests and competency tests. Next, explain why neither is helpful in promoting an instructional program that accurately reflects the nature of the comprehension process.

2. Of fundamental importance to both teaching and assessment is the question, "*Why* am I doing what I'm doing?" With examples, explain the significance for both.

3. Reread the guidelines for teacher-devised tests that are in the Summary section of Chapter 16. Next, reread the descriptions of teacher-devised testing that are in the chapter. Explain how each example reflects the guidelines.

4. The following notations were made to show how a child read the paragraph. (Correct responses were supplied whenever a word was misread in a way that destroyed meaning.)

Every year, Susan's teacher takes her class on a trip. This year they are going to a museum [music]. The museum (they are going to) has stuffed animals. Some animals are dinosaurs [dying]. The children like dinosaurs, (so) they are eager [eagle] to go to the museum. Right now, they are reading about dinosaurs so (that) they will know what [that] they are seeing when they arrive [get to] at the museum.

---

   a. Based on the notations, demonstrate what the child said at the time he read the paragraph aloud.
   b. Which of the unexpected responses are the most serious, and why?

5. Uncovering problems is pointless unless remedies follow. What might an exercise that begins like the following help to remedy?

I'd like to _____ them for their work.

         price   praise

It was _____ a beautiful day.

     quite   quiet

The _____ is round.

   word   world

6. Chapter 16 states that readability formulas are used by authors of standardized tests to write test passages and to assess their difficulty. Reread the section "Readability" in Chapter 13 in order to state why these uses of the formulas must be questioned.

REFERENCES

1. Bussis, Anne M., and Chittenden, Edward A. "Research Currents: What the Reading Tests Neglect." *Language Arts* 64 (March, 1987), 302–308.
2. Calfee, Robert C. "The School As a Context for Assessment of Literacy." *Reading Teacher* 40 (April, 1987), 738–743.
3. Duffy, Gerald G.; Roehler, Laura R.; and Putnam, Joyce. "Putting the Teachers in Control: Basal Reading Textbooks and Instructional Decision Making." *Elementary School Journal* 3 (January, 1987), 357–366.
4. Durkin, Dolores. "A Classroom-Observation Study of Reading Instruction in Kindergarten." *Early Childhood Research Quarterly* 2 (September, 1987), 275–300.
5. Durkin, Dolores. "Influences on Basal Reader Programs." *Elementary School Journal* 87 (January, 1987), 331–341.
6. Durkin, Dolores. "Testing in the Kindergarten." *Reading Teacher* 40 (April, 1987), 766–770.
7. Hoffman, James V., and Rutherford, William L. "Effective Reading Programs: A Critical Review of Outlier Studies." *Reading Research Quarterly* 20 (Fall, 1984), 79–92.
8. International Reading Association. "Misuse of Grade Equivalents." *Reading Teacher* 35 (January, 1982), 464.
9. Johnston, Peter. *Implications of Basic Research for the Assessment of Reading Comprehension* (Tech. Rep. No. 206). Urbana: University of Illinois, Center for the Study of Reading, May, 1981.
10. Moore, David W. "A Case for Naturalistic Assessment of Reading Comprehension." *Language Arts* 60 (November/December, 1983), 957–969.
11. Otto, Wayne, et al. *Wisconsin Design for Reading Skill Development.* Minneapolis: National Computer Systems, 1977.
12. Rasinski, Timothy V. "The Role of Interest, Purpose, and Choice in Early Literacy." *Reading Teacher* 41 (January, 1988), 396–400.
13. Resnick, Daniel P., and Resnick, Lauren B. "Standards, Curriculum, and Performance: A Historical and Comparative Perspective." *Educational Researcher* 14 (April, 1985), 5–20.
14. Rowe, Deborah W., and Rayford, Lawrence. "Activating Background Knowledge in Reading Comprehension Assessment." *Reading Research Quarterly* 22 (Spring, 1987), 160–176.

15. Ruddell, Robert B. "Knowledge and Attitudes toward Testing." *Reading Teacher* 38 (February, 1985), 538–543.
16. Shannon, Patrick. "Mastery Learning in Reading and the Control of Teachers and Students." *Language Arts* 61 (September, 1984), 484–493.
17. Shannon, Patrick. "Teachers' and Administrators' Thoughts on Changes in Reading Instruction within a Merit Pay Program." *Reading Research Quarterly* 21 (Winter, 1986), 20–35.
18. Tuinman, J. Jaap. "Determining the Passage-Dependency of Comprehension Questions in Five Major Tests." *Reading Research Quarterly* 9 (1973–74, No. 2), 206–223.
19. Valencia, Sheila, and Pearson, P. David. "Reading Assessment: Time for a Change." *Reading Teacher* 40 (April, 1987), 726–732.
20. Winograd, Peter, and Smith, Lynne A. "Improving the Climate for Reading Comprehension Instruction." *Reading Teacher* 41 (December, 1987), 304–310.
21. Wixson, Karen K.; Peters, Charles W.; Weber, Elaine M.; and Roeber, Edward D. "New Directions in Statewide Reading Assessment." *Reading Teacher* 40 (April, 1987), 749–754.

Chapter 17

Organizing for Instructional Needs

PREVIEW

Rereading Chapter 13, "Basal Readers and Narrative Text," is one way to prepare for Chapter 17. The rereading should help because, like the earlier chapter, Chapter 17 is based on certain assumptions:

1. Almost all teachers use basal materials to some extent.
2. The time in a daily schedule set aside for reading includes the use of these materials.
3. Even when a basal series is viewed as the core of an instructional program, it needs to be supplemented with other materials.
4. The assignments that students are asked to do should not be confined to workbooks and ditto sheets.

Whereas Chapter 13 focuses on a professional use of basal materials, the concern of Chapter 17 is for the ways in which classrooms can be organized to expedite that use. The two main questions addressed, therefore, are, first, how can a class be organized to allow for the fact that differences in reading ability call for different instruction and, second, what can teachers do to ensure that the plans they make for instruction and practice are executed without too many distractions or interruptions?

Even though schools employ both intraclass and interclass types of organizations, only the former is considered. The focus of the chapter, then, is the self-contained classroom in which a teacher is responsible for providing reading instruction for the members of her own class. What is said about these classrooms applies equally to an interclass organization—that is, to situations in which students from more than one classroom are grouped for instruction on the basis of ability. This is the case because "homogeneous" grouping reduces but never eliminates differences. To think that it does create a group of students who are the same in ability is a reflection more of wishful thinking than of a realistic understanding of reading and children.

If a knowledgeable, caring teacher had no more than about eight students who were similar in their ability to read, providing appropriate and successful instruction would be fairly easy. Differences in interests could also be accommodated without too much trouble. As it is, the larger number of students who make up a class, coupled with what may be great variation in reading ability, make individualized instruction difficult but, as superior teachers demonstrate, not impossible to achieve. It seems appropriate to compare these successful teachers to a symphony orchestra conductor who is able to synthesize into a meaningful, harmonious whole a large number of different musicians and instruments.

Admittedly, I know nothing about the intricacies of successful orchestration; but I do understand from experience that organizing students in ways that facilitate offering appropriate instruction to everyone is no small feat. A speaker at a conference once expressed my own feelings when he said, "effective organization is the end product of trial and error." Inherent in his observation is that getting students, materials, and time organized in a way that allows a teacher to be effective is an evolutionary process that gradually progresses as decisions are made and remade throughout the whole of a year.

DIFFERENCES IN TEACHERS

The decision that has an impact on many others is not always made consciously, which means it often escapes reexamination. I refer to the perception a teacher has of her responsibilities as a reading instructor. Why this affects other decisions can be explained by contrasting two teachers.

The first views her responsibilities as moving students through a basal reader, the workbook that goes with it, and whatever exercise sheets the representative of the basal publisher succeeded in selling. With such a perception, this teacher uses the time assigned to reading in a way that differs markedly from the second teacher, whose priorities are identified in the following statement:

> The major goal of my instructional program is to develop each child's potential for comprehending print via silent reading. To attain it, instruction and practice must focus on whatever it is that will advance each child's abilities. To keep children involved and trying, every effort must be made to help them see the relevance of reading in their own lives. The importance of motivation for learning also makes it necessary to have materials that match not only their abilities but also their interests. In the end, I evaluate myself not just on the basis of how well the children read but also by the frequency with which they *do* read.

Just as teachers' priorities are undeniably significant for the way class-rooms are run, so too are their personalities. On this point, Carl Wallen offers sound advice to teachers:

> *You should be frank about the fact that the best degree of structure is largely how* you *define it. Some teachers cannot tolerate much movement in the classroom. They feel distinctly uncomfortable when a child moves around the room in an apparent search for adventure. On the other hand, some teachers feel the same degree of discomfort if children are too quiet and too still. They enjoy movement and the ambiguity that characterizes it. Because you must live comfortably in the classroom, you should . . . allow for as much structure as you and the children find comfortable. (21, p. 475)*

The differences in teachers that have been referred to, joined with other differences of equal significance (e.g., knowledge of subject matter for instruction, industry, motivation), make it impossible to offer recommenda-tions for organizing a class that are acceptable to all. A suggestion that would be viewed by some teachers as beyond their reach or even unrealistic might be scorned by others as being excessively modest or too conservative. In spite of the complexity caused by differences, it is still hoped that the present chapter will be helpful to a number of teachers and prospective teachers either immediately or eventually.

DIFFERENCES IN STUDENTS

Just as differences in teachers affect how instructional programs are orga-nized and executed, so too should differences in students' abilities affect the content of programs. Ways to learn about differences is the subject of Chap-ter 16. How to organize both time and students in ways that take the differ-ences into account is the concern now.

Ordinarily, differences in how well members of the same class can read require working with less than the entire group. Not to be minimized, either, is the difficulty of getting and maintaining the attention of large numbers of students. In spite of this, there *are* times when teachers can work profitably with a whole class. To support the contention, the first sec-tion that follows describes circumstances that make it appropriate to in-volve everyone in an activity. After that, working with individuals is consid-ered, but only briefly because it is difficult for classroom teachers to find time to tutor students. In contrast, the treatment of subgroups, which comes next, is much longer. The length reflects the fact that teaching sub-groups is generally the most effective and efficient way to provide instruc-tion that reflects abilities.

It should also be pointed out that even though working with the whole class, with individuals, and with subgroups are discussed separately, spending time in all three ways is usually characteristic of successful teachers.

WORKING WITH THE WHOLE CLASS

When the way a classroom is organized is viewed as a means for facilitating individualized instruction, it is natural to wonder, Should teachers ever work with an entire class? Both the means-end framework and the need for efficiency suggest an answer: Whenever an entire class has need for the same instruction or practice, it makes very good sense—in theory—to work with everyone together. To illustrate, if just about everyone in a third grade reads aloud in a way that lacks luster and sparkle, the teacher might have the whole class participate in choral reading, using material that everyone can read. (Samples of material suitable for choral reading are in Figures 2.2 and 2.3.) This means that selections might be fairly easy for some; however, because the purpose of the activity is to improve oral reading done to communicate, it is unnecessary—even undesirable—to have students read the most difficult material they are capable of handling. About once each month, then, time will go to choral reading as a way of fostering appropriate expression, plus enjoyment for all and helpful word practice for some.

Whole-class instruction is something I myself used recently. In order to provide one-on-one reading to two groups of kindergartners, arrangements were made with two fifth-grade teachers for each of their students to read to a kindergartner weekly. The original plan was to have the teachers provide instruction (or review) about story grammar as a way of helping the fifth graders, first, to know what is important to discuss with the kindergartners and, second, to choose good stories. (The school librarian agreed to help with selections and to model how to read to young children.) After learning that neither fifth-grade teacher was familiar with story grammar, I did the teaching myself with the help of "The Coconut Game," a story map (see Figure 13.7), and a chalkboard. To provide a nonexample of a story, I also read aloud a selection from a basal reader. From what I could tell, all thirty-nine fifth-graders were attentive and certainly eager to begin reading to the younger children. They may have also learned something about stories that will help with the more advanced narrative text that they read in their own classrooms.

Another reference is made to whole-class instruction in Chapter 3. In this case, the teacher read a book about whales and dolphins to her class for the purpose of clarifying the differences between mammals and fish. Given the significance of world knowledge for comprehension, this kind of reading ought to be more common than it now is.

What may be *too* common can be explained with a reference to an observation in a second grade. At the time of the visit, the teacher was introducing new vocabulary to everyone. Later, as she explained why she taught the words to the whole class, the teacher said it saved time. She added that she was "a strict disciplinarian," "ran a tight ship," and thus was able to get sustained attention from everybody. This contrasted with the fact that a sizable amount of off-task behavior was observed from the back of the room while the words were being named and discussed at the front.

Coupled with many other visits to classrooms, the second-grade observation provides evidence that even when an entire class stands to profit from a given piece of instruction, some members may learn very little because of inattentiveness. This suggests that only when what is being done is likely to capture everyone's attention should whole-class instruction be scheduled.

WORKING WITH INDIVIDUALS

Working with one student seems so inherently valuable that neither an explanation nor a defense of this use of a teacher's time seems necessary. What should not escape attention, however, are the reasons that motivate individual assistance. This point needs to be made because classroom observations indicate that some teachers are required to help individuals as a consequence of giving the same assignments to the whole class even when the ability of its members to do them is clearly unequal (7). The moral of the story? "Private lessons" are desirable when the instruction that a student requires deviates substantially from what others need. Commonly, the requirement will be easier instruction.

Usually, teachers in federally and state-funded programs are available to provide easier instruction. Whenever these programs are scrutinized, however, they are often criticized (4). A common concern is the lack of communication between the classroom and the "special" teacher. For instance, one survey concluded that

> a large proportion of teachers in the survey, 70 percent, reported that a specialist instructed students in their classes. However, less than half of these teachers reported ever receiving suggestions from the specialist. In other words, the addition of a specialist to a school staff typically means that selected children are taken out of the classroom on what is often called a "pull-out" basis. It is not typical for the specialist to give suggestions to the teacher or provide diagnostic feedback or materials. (7, p. 286)

The conclusions of a more recent study in which forty observations of remedial instruction settings provided the data are hardly more encouraging (3). They reinforce the conclusion just quoted and also provide others that question the kind of instruction provided students in need of extra help. Because the same questions have been raised about the classroom instruction that groups of poor readers often receive, the criticisms are dealt with later.

With a student whose "problem" is advanced ability, extra teachers are not usually available to help. Classroom teachers, therefore, must do whatever they can to effect further progress. Some meet this need with the help of an advanced basal reader from a series different from the one a school is currently using. Intermittent instruction focusing on topics suggested by the basal selections, plus independent reading of books that are related in some way to a basal selection, plus workbook assignments worth doing, can combine into instruction and challenge from which a particularly able student profits. Other ways to accommodate advanced readers are described in subsequent sections of the chapter.

WORKING WITH SUBGROUPS

As mentioned, the differences in reading ability that are apparent in every classroom make it impossible to offer a maximum of individualized instruction if nothing but whole-class teaching is used. This is not to say that organizing the members of a class on the basis of ability results in homogeneous groups; students and reading are both too complex to expect such a consequence. Nevertheless, smaller groups do give knowledgeable, conscientious teachers many more opportunities to provide appropriately differentiated instruction. Because of that potential, much of this chapter deals with classroom organization in the context of "teachable groups."

GENERAL-ACHIEVEMENT SUBGROUPS

Because differentiated instruction ought to get under way as soon as possible, the traditional practice is to organize subgroups at first on the basis of general achievement. (Comments like "He's reading at a second-grade level" and "She's pretty much a fifth-grade reader" refer to general achievement.) One justification for using general achievement for initial grouping is that it is easier to identify than are special instructional needs—for instance, needs to learn to use graphophonic and contextual cues in a more balanced way, or needs to learn to select meanings offered in a dictionary that fit specified contexts, or needs to adapt rate of reading to suit the purpose of the reading. What must be recognized, too, is that basal reader programs foster the use of general-achievement levels to organize groups, as the textbooks in all such programs are organized on the same basis.

Because general-achievement subgroups *are* so common, they receive a generous amount of attention in the sections that follow. The generosity reflects the belief that what is done often should be done well.

IDENTIFYING GENERAL-ACHIEVEMENT LEVELS

If general-achievement subgroups are formed to make it easier to offer individualized instruction, decisions about the membership of each group should be made with care. However, the decisions should not consume so much time that the temptation exists to keep all the groups intact until the school year ends. The recommendation, therefore, is to be careful about decisions but not compulsively so.

Information about students that is relevant for (a) organizing general-achievement subgroups and (b) selecting the basal reader that each is ready to use comes from cumulative records, standardized tests, and oral reading tests. Each source of information is discussed.

Cumulative Records

Once children enroll in school, information about them begins to accumulate. The cards on which it is kept are usually called *cumulative records.* These records are linked to decisions about general-achievement subgroups because they include information about reading. For general-achievement estimates, the most helpful information identifies the materials that a student completed the previous year. This allows a teacher to know at a glance something about the general achievement of everyone in the room. If certain students, for instance, completed but did not go beyond a certain basal reader in second grade, their third-grade teacher has some idea not only of their general ability but also of a suitable textbook. Most often, cumulative records can be examined before a school year begins.

Standardized Achievement Tests

Standardized tests, you recall, are discussed in Chapter 16. Because the concern of that chapter was identifying instructional needs, the usefulness of standardized test scores had to be questioned. Viewed in the framework of identifying general-achievement levels, however, raw scores derived from these tests enable a teacher to rank order students. When the list of scores is compared with whatever information is on the cumulative records, teachers can often get a fairly good picture of the range of abilities in their class and of the textbooks likely to be at the students' instructional levels. If a sizable discrepancy exists between the two sources of data, it is time to look at a student's ability more carefully. This calls for a discussion of oral reading tests.

Teacher-Devised Oral Reading Tests

Teacher-devised oral tests were also discussed in the previous chapter. There, they are recommended as a means for learning exactly how students cope with unfamiliar or forgotten words embedded in connected text. Given that objective, the number of misidentified words is said to be less significant than the nature of the misidentifications.

When the reason for an oral test is to identify both general-achievement levels and suitable textbooks, other features of the oral reading assume importance. Before they are described, three terms that pertain to the difficulty of text in relation to a student's reading ability need to be defined:

> *Independent level.* Material written at a level of difficulty that allows a person to comprehend it without help.
>
> *Instructional level.* Material that is difficult enough that it can add to a student's abilities if it is used with an effective instructor.
>
> *Frustration level.* Material that is so difficult that it cannot be understood even if help and instruction are available.

Because the purpose of the oral test now being proposed is to learn which textbook in a given basal reader series is at a student's instructional level, word identification and comprehension abilities are taken into account in the testing in ways outlined below.

Level	Unidentified or Misidentified Words	Unanswered or Incorrectly Answered Questions
Independent	One (or fewer) words per 100	10 percent
Instructional	Five (or fewer) words per 100	25 percent
Frustration	Ten (or more) words per 100	50 percent

As you can see, the criteria leave some gray areas open to question. Along with a teacher's own judgment, however, they provide helpful guidelines (not rules) when an oral reading test is used to choose textbooks suitable for instruction.

Procedures for preparing and administering such a test follow.

Passages for an Oral Test. Basal reader passages of about 100 to 300 words need to be chosen. Ideally, understanding the content should not be dependent on knowing what was said prior to each selected passage. If it is, the earlier content must be summarized before the test begins.

To make the test useful for more than one student, the difficulty of selected passages should range from about two grade-levels below the classroom in question to about two grade-levels above it. Following this guideline makes the test available for use whenever the need arises to learn about a student's ability. The enrollment of a child after the school year has begun is one occasion when such a test is useful.

Questions for an Oral Test. Because the testing takes into account comprehension abilities, questions are required for each passage. Even though the number and kind of questions are determined by the passage, they should vary whenever possible. Ideally, questions focus on both stated and implied content.*

Administering an Oral Test. "Trying a book on for size" is an apt description of the teacher-prepared basal reader test being discussed. To make sure that the first one is comfortable, a passage thought to be at a student's independent level starts the test. A request to read the passage orally, accompanied by a brief explanation for the reading and how it will be conducted ("When you finish reading this, I'll ask you a few questions.") gets things started. Sometimes, so much competence is displayed immediately as to make completing the passage unnecessary. A comment like, "This is too easy for you, isn't it?" allows for a shift to more difficult text. It may also become clear very quickly that a passage is at a student's frustration level. Again, a quick change is necessary.

Whenever a student is reading a passage that appears to be at his instructional level, the number of misidentified words should be monitored. (The inability to pronounce a difficult proper name should not be counted as an error, nor should a mistake that is corrected by the reader.) If a student is reading from one copy of a passage and the teacher has another, misidentifications can be noted on the second copy. Because comprehension is of concern, too, each oral reading of a passage is followed by the preselected questions.

Shortcomings of an Oral Test. Flaws inherent in the teacher-devised test under consideration should be obvious to anyone who read previous chapters. William Henk has specified some of the shortcomings:

> Children are . . . classified as reading on a certain level with limited regard to external factors such as type of text, its structure, style, and topic, or internal variables such as readers' prior knowledge, interest, or purpose. (13, p. 861)

On the assumption that the results of a teacher-prepared oral basal test are interpreted as being nothing more than a rough estimate of a student's instructional level, its use should be considered in spite of the flaws, especially when little or nothing is known about a particular student.

---

* Asking comprehension questions about orally read material is defensible when the purpose is to learn as quickly as possible about appropriate material and subgroup placement. In contrast, when the goal is to learn about particular comprehension abilities, silent reading is preferred.

A Summary

The discussion thus far has been concerned with means for dividing a class into groups, each composed of students whose general achievement in reading is similar. In the process of learning about general-achievement levels, a teacher also learns which textbook in a basal series constitutes instructional-level material for each group.

Three ways to acquire information about abilities and their range were recommended. The first is to examine cumulative records, which typically indicate the basal materials that have been completed. The second way is to rank order members of a class on the basis of raw scores achieved on the last commercial test administered, which is often a standardized test. Combined, these two sources of information allow a teacher to see the range of abilities in her class as well as clusters of students whose ability seems similar. Should the two sources of information be at odds for any child, he or she should be given an oral test. When it is kept in mind that one objective of the test is to learn which basal reader approximates a student's instructional level, test passages will be taken from whatever basal series is used.

Because none of the three ways to acquire information is infallible and, further, because students' abilities can be expected to change in a variety of ways not always predictable, the most basic recommendation is to view general-achievement groups not as something having memberships that never change but, instead, as a temporary means for offering suitable instruction at the start of a new school year. As reading abilities change, so too should the makeup of groups.

ESTABLISHING GENERAL-ACHIEVEMENT SUBGROUPS

In theory, the range of differences in students' abilities determines how many subgroups to establish. Practical considerations cannot be ignored, however. More specifically, if a teacher is unwilling or unable to spend the time required to plan for a large number, fewer subgroups than what the differences suggest should be used. This guideline applies to a recently observed third grade in which there were five general-achievement subgroups. Meeting with one of them, the teacher's initial question was, "Did I assign you a story to read over the weekend?" Meeting with another group later, she started by inquiring, "What book are we reading in?" Although one visit is hardly sufficient to reach reliable conclusions, it is possible that fewer subgroups would have allowed for more effective teaching in this particular room.

The obvious lesson to be learned from an incident like the one just described is that having many groups is neither desirable nor undesirable. What counts is whether subgroups allow for as close a match as is possible between students' needs and what is taught. Within that framework, compromise may be necessary. Descriptions of defensible compromises follow.

Ms. Greyson is starting her first year of teaching. The approximate general-achievement levels of the twenty-seven third graders in her class are distributed as follows:

Grade III: *Reading Levels*

	I	II	III	IV
Number of students	2	9	14	2

Ms. Greyson wants very much to match instruction with needs but, as a new teacher, is insecure about her ability to manage everything and everyone. To start, therefore, she has two groups. Eleven students are in one, sixteen in the other. Her goal is to make adjustments as the school year progresses and her self-confidence increases.

Another teacher, Mr. Poli, makes compromises for different reasons. He feels sufficiently competent to work with subgroups; however, he has just transferred to a school in which whole-class instruction is all that is used in both fourth and fifth grade. One consequence is that his sixth graders are unaccustomed to working on their own and need experience in doing assignments while he works with others. That is why Mr. Poli begins with two subgroups even though the following general-achievement range exists:

Grade VI: *Reading Levels*

	III	IV	V	VI
Number of students	2	9	10	9

Mr. Poli plans to change gradually either to three or four groups, but he correctly believes that the first job is to help students establish work habits that allow for uninterrupted instruction.

In another school, Ms. Thorpe has twenty-five students reading at the following general-achievement levels:

Grade II: *Reading Levels*

	I	II	III	IV	V
Number of students	1	10	6	5	3

Of the ten students reading at a second-grade level, three are very sure of themselves and seven are not. With that in mind, Ms. Thorpe begins the year with the subgroups shown on the next page.

Group 1	*Group 2*	*Group 3*
8	9	8

The three teaching situations described illustrate that a variety of factors affect decisions about the number and the membership of instructional groups. Even though all these decisions should be made carefully, in no sense should they be thought of as final and unchangeable. As mentioned, an essential feature of productive subgrouping is that it remains flexible throughout the year, allowing for the peaks, valleys, and plateaus that characterize learning.

STUDIES OF GENERAL-ACHIEVEMENT SUBGROUPS

Concern about the negative effects on students of being placed in lower achieving groups is common, and rightly so. Pessimistic expectations that are hardly kept hidden are not likely to promote progress, nor will low self-esteem (14). What cannot be overlooked, however, is the frustration of being "over one's head," which is common among low achievers when nothing but whole-class instruction is offered.

In need of emphasis here are findings from classroom studies that started being reported in the late 1970s (1, 2, 6, 17, 19). They are of considerable significance as they indicate that the work done with low-achieving groups often contributes to, rather than alleviates, their problems with reading. "Once a bluebird always a bluebird," therefore, may be the result of well-intentioned but misguided instruction.

One of the first to call attention to the differential treatment of reading groups was Richard Allington. In a report called "If They Don't Read Much, How They Ever Gonna Get Good?" (1), Allington documented the fact that students in higher groups read about three times as many words per day as do poorer readers. One reason for the difference is the common use of overly difficult material with low achievers, which is generally read aloud. Some of the consequences of the mismatch have been summarized by Shannon:

> Students in high groups are often asked to read texts which are easy for them; however, students in low groups are often placed in materials in which they misread at least one in every ten words. This difficulty inhibits low group students' use of context, forces them to read word by word, and makes them rely on phonic characteristics of unknown words. Their frequent mistakes trigger student and teacher interruptions, and the unfortunate cycle begins anew. (17, p. 608)

Allington sums up the cycle of unfortunate events when he says that "those who need the most and best get the least and worst." Previous chapters should have clarified not only why the practices referred to by Shannon are "the worst" but also what needs to be done to achieve "the best."

One contributor to the achievement of the best is special-needs subgroups, which are discussed next.

SPECIAL-NEEDS SUBGROUPS

Observant teachers learn fairly quickly that the members of a general-achievement subgroup are not identical in their ability either to read or to profit from instruction. At times, the nature of the differences is such as to warrant shifts to different groups. At other times, differences may suggest the need for a temporary *special-needs subgroup* to remedy a problem or, as the case may be, to allow for suitable challenge.

To illustrate the two reasons for forming special-needs groups, let's look in on a fourth grade. The month is February, and the day is Wednesday. The week's schedule for the reading period (9–10:15 A.M.) is in Figure 17.1. So, too, is a description of how time is scheduled to be used on Wednesday.

In the following description of this fourth grade, the references to a boy named Tom are meant to illustrate what can be done to accommodate a need for extra instruction. A girl named Susan figures in the description of a way to provide suitable challenge.

Accommodating Poorer Readers

The time is now 9:25 on Wednesday. Tom is in Group 1 (see Figure 17.1) and has just finished working with the teacher. His group discussed a story in a basal reader and was assigned three pages in the basal workbook, all dealing with material that extends the story. Tom and the others were asked to complete the assignment before doing anything else because the workbooks will be collected at 10:15, corrected, and returned Friday.

The second job for Tom originated in his special-needs group, which met the day before (see Figure 17.1). Composed of students from two general-achievement subgroups, its members are excessively slow in finding alphabetically organized material. On Tuesday, therefore, the teacher discussed and demonstrated procedures to make such a search easier. She then gave the following assignments:

1. Spend time Tuesday acquiring information about a bird in an encyclopedia. (Each student is assigned a different one so that different volumes can be used. The birds selected are some likely to be unfamiliar.) Whatever seems important or is of interest about the bird is to be written in a form that will allow for a brief discussion on Thursday. Once sufficient notes are taken, a telephone directory for any ten students in the room is to be made. (A model of a directory is shown; attention is called to the alphabetical listing as well as to the attractive cover.) Because the town in which the school is located has a small population, each child receives a copy of the current directory.

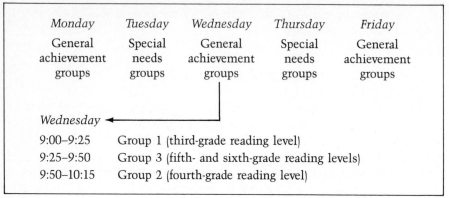

Figure 17.1 Distribution of Time in a Fourth-Grade Classroom

2. Spend time Wednesday finding in a dictionary appropriate meanings for ten words, each embedded in a sentence listed on a sheet. Under each sentence, the meaning will be written. Under that, a sentence is to be added that uses the word in question. (To clarify the task and to serve as a reminder of what it is, the sheet starts with one sentence for which the requested work is done.)

The teacher's plans for Thursday, another special-needs day, is to have Tom and the members of his group (a) review the use of alphabetical order to find something, (b) discuss what each learned about a bird, (c) go over the assignment sheet dealing with appropriate meanings, and (d) look at all the telephone directories with special attention going to the use of alphabetical order to arrange the ten names and numbers. Finally, each student will have the chance to discuss any problem encountered in doing the various assignments. If no major difficulty is identified insofar as use of alphabetical order is concerned, this special-needs group will be disbanded.

What has now been said about accommodations made for Tom can be summarized by looking at life in the classroom from his perspective:

Tuesday: Special-Needs Group

Tom's teacher discussed and demonstrated how to find alphabetically arranged material.

Tom looked up "cockatoo" in an encyclopedia in order to write whatever seemed important or interesting about this bird.

Tom made a telephone directory and designed a cover.

Wednesday: General-Achievement Group

The teacher and Tom's group discussed a recently read story.

Tom worked on three pages in a basal workbook.

Tom did the dictionary assignment.

Thursday: Special-Needs Subgroup

See the previous page.

Accommodating Better Readers

To show how the same fourth-grade teacher accommodated Susan in her instructional plans, other activities occurring during the same week are described. Susan is a member of Group 3, composed of the eight best readers in the class (see Figure 17.1).

Members of Group 3 are studying words and their histories. (Uncertain about the group's reactions to her plans, the teacher is taking just one week at a time.) When general-achievement subgroups met on Monday, the teacher introduced Group 3 to the idea that words have histories and that studying them can be very interesting. To support her statement, she related how certain words and expressions came into our language and how their meanings took shape over time. (Books that provide information about words and their origin are in Chapter 11 in the section "Mythology and Etymology.") Having already been introduced to the dictionary, these students were also told about Noah Webster, of his special interest in words, and of the work of lexicographers.

The introductory discussion on Monday set the stage for three assignments to be completed by Friday:

1. The two most advanced readers, one of whom is Susan, were told about unabridged dictionaries and the attention they give to word histories. They were asked to go to the school library, where the librarian will be waiting to show them a copy of a dictionary. Their job for Friday is to bring in and discuss an unabridged dictionary (with the approval and help of the librarian), to show its content, and to tell the history of a few particularly interesting words.
2. The next two most advanced children in Group 3 were asked to read *Noah Webster, Boy of Words*. The objective is an oral report of the book, also to be ready by Friday. (The teacher would have liked to assigned the biography to all eight students, but only two copies are available.)
3. Books dealing with the history of American English were distributed to the remaining four children. Their job is to select words from the books whose histories they will relate on Friday.

Ordinarily, Tuesday is for special-needs groups. This week, however, the Group 3 general-achievement subgroup is a special-needs (or special-opportunity) group; consequently, plans for these students proceed differently. The two dictionary children worked in the library on Tuesday while the two who are reading about Noah Webster continued with that. The teacher was thus free to give time on Tuesday to the four children who are reading about words from a variety of books. They talked about some and began to make decisions about the words to discuss Friday. In certain instances, word families will be referred to (e.g., *port, porter, portable, transport*), so plans were made to construct charts showing word relationships.

From 9:25 until 9:50 on Wednesday, the teacher divides her time between the two children who are working with the dictionary and the two who are reading about Noah Webster. With both pairs, her aims are to identify what these students have been learning, to provide suggestions about what might have been overlooked or underplayed, and to make plans for Friday's oral presentations.

On Thursday, usually a special-needs day, the eight children in general-achievement Group 3 will meet with the teacher to coordinate plans for Friday. Having concluded that they will be presenting highly interesting material, the teacher plans to allot part of the reading period on Friday for the students to discuss with the rest of the class what they have done and learned. Following the presentation, she herself will show easier books that also deal with word histories. They will become part of the classroom collection and, it is hoped, some of what students select during free-reading periods. The attention to word histories might eventually result in a focus for a subgroup brought together because of a mutual interest in this kind of study.

Other Special-Needs Groups

How one fourth-grade teacher went about accommodating special needs during one particular week was just described. To supplement the description, please reread the section in Chapter 16 called "Illustrations of Teacher-Devised Tests." That section explains how other teachers identified, and then responded to, special needs.

One other description of a teacher's efforts to accommodate differences is described. What is done, in this case to deal with a chapter in a science textbook concerned with magnetism, starts with whole-class instruction that originates in a film. In interesting ways, the film tells about magnetism, emphasizing the meanings of words that include *magnet, magnetism, field, pole, attract, repel,* and *metal.* Afterward, this third-grade class discusses the content. The teacher then reads a brief book that describes how magnets function in our everyday lives. Students add to the information with references to the use of magnets in can openers and in attaching notes to refrigerators.

The next day, the science period starts with different students doing different things. The seven lowest achievers meet with the teacher who, first, reviews the most important content communicated in the film and, second, guides the students through the chapter in the textbook for the purpose of examining the most important content, some of which is revealed with the help of pictures. This is done because none of the seven has sufficient ability to comprehend the textbook alone.

Six students who *are* able to read the textbook are now doing that, guided by a list of questions that focus on key ideas. Six more are reading about, and planning for, the experiments they have been asked to demonstrate to the class. While all this takes place, another able student is reading a brief but interesting book about magnets that she will read to, and discuss with, the seven lowest achievers when they finish working with the teacher. At that time, the teacher will divide her attention between the students reading the textbook and those preparing experiments.

On the third day, members of the class meet together to observe the experiments and, with the help of the teacher's probing, to review and synthesize what they learned about magnetism from the various sources. It should be noted that, in this case, the teacher's commendable plans were fostered by the fact that she has only fifteen copies of the prescribed science textbook even though she has twenty-one students.

What this teacher allowed for is what is sometimes referred to as *cooperative learning* (18, 20). Rather than promote competition among the students, she arranged for ways in which all were able to contribute to what the class as a whole learned about magnetism.

MANAGING A CLASSROOM

It would be difficult to argue with the contention that the most carefully devised plans for individualized instruction cannot be executed in the midst of interruptions and distractions. Given that fact, classroom management is a relevant topic for a chapter focusing on ways in which classrooms can be organized to accommodate general and specific differences in reading ability.

What is clear to anyone who visits schools on a regular basis is that well-run classrooms are not born. Instead, they are made by teachers who carry in their heads a model of the kind of classroom and behavior they want. Even though the characteristics of certain classes may, at times, make it virtually impossible to achieve the ideal, it is nonetheless used as a standard against which the teacher measures both herself and her students.

As the comments of Carl Wallen (21) pointed out earlier, different teachers can be expected to want different kinds of classrooms. Research has shown that the formulation of whatever *is* wanted must get started immediately. In a report of their study of classroom management, Carolyn Evertson and Linda Anderson state that the most effective teachers "begin at the moment of the first day of school to establish themselves as leaders of their classrooms" (9, p. 165). These teachers know—probably from experience—that students' initial contacts with a classroom and a teacher constitute a very important event. "Effective managers," according to Evertson and Anderson, "prepared [for the first day] a careful introduction to the room, explaining to their students what each area was and how it would be used . . . " (p. 165). Gradually, procedural details are explained—when and where to sharpen pencils, where to put finished work, how to check out a book or magazine from the classroom library, and so forth. Students who follow the stipulated procedures are praised; others are reminded kindly but firmly about infractions of rules. In the end—and this is hardly surprising—one of the most apparent characteristics of effective managers is consistency in enforcing rules.

What should not be lost sight of in this discussion is the interdependent relationships between effective management and effective instruction. The link is reflected in a number of the recommendations made throughout *Teaching Them to Read*. For instance:

Some Reminders to Teachers

Do not begin instruction until it appears that everyone is attentive.

Do not call on the first student to raise his hand. Allow for "think time."

Do not distribute materials until it is time to use them.

Do have all essential materials available.

Do explain to students the connection between what is about to be taught and how to be a better reader.

Do allow students the opportunity to experience the usefulness of what they are learning through application in authentic text.

Do make sure that students understand and are able to do whatever assignments are given.

Do put assignments in writing so students will remember them.

One way to summarize the connection between effective teaching and effective classroom management is to say that a maximum of individualized instruction contributes as much to students' desirable behavior as it does to their advancement in reading.

SUMMARY

Organizing a class in ways that facilitate offering individualized instruction is the central concern of Chapter 17. The fact that members of a class vary in their ability to read—even in so-called homogeneous classes—means that an organization that allows only for whole-class teaching must be questioned. Although Chapter 17 does describe circumstances that justify working with an entire class, such work ought to be rarer than it sometimes is. This is so not only because of differences in ability but also because of the difficulty of getting and keeping everyone's attention when the group being instructed is large.

One of the most common ways to cope with differences in reading ability is to organize a class into teachable groups. Generally, the first groups organized are based on differences in general achievement, since they are easier to identify than are specific differences. Three sources for learning about general achievement are considered in Chapter 17: (a) information on cumulative records, (b) raw scores from commercial tests, and (c) oral basal reader tests prepared by teachers. Information from these sources allows not only for group placement but also for the selection of material written at the students' instructional levels.

What is meant by instructional-level, independent-level, and frustration-level material is explained. The values to be derived from reading independent-level material are discussed in two earlier chapters. The problems that result from the use of frustration-level material are described in the present one. The basic problem is that overly difficult material fosters attention to words, not meaning. (That the use of excessively difficult material hardly cultivates a love for reading should be too obvious to mention.) Because classroom research shows that frustration-level material is often used with the poorest readers in a class, Chapter 17 suggests that what is sometimes done with these children may contribute not to the solution of their problems but to their continued existence.

Although the use of instructional-level material with general-achievement subgroups is much more effective than is whole-class teaching, the eventual combination of general-achievement and special-needs groups is even better. How teachers have been seen to organize schedules in ways that accommodate both types of groups are described.

Recognizing that children will be children, Chapter 17 closes with a brief discussion of classroom management viewed as one of the variables that make individualized instruction possible. The basic points made have to do with the need, first, for teachers to have a mental model of the classroom they want and, second, to begin working to achieve that model no later than the first day of school.

REVIEW

1. Why is it correct to say that individualized instruction contributes as much to minimizing discipline problems as it does to maximizing reading ability?

2. Summarize what Chapter 17 says about attaining effective classroom management.

3. When teachers use general-achievement subgroups, they often end up with three. Why do you think this is the case? Are the three groups desirable or undesirable?

4. When variables other than general achievement are used to group students for instruction, the stigma of being a low achiever may not be quite so apparent. With that in mind:
   a. Describe two ways to group children that are not based on differences in general achievement.

b. Why might the variety reduce the stigma of being in "the low group"?

5. Chapter 17 refers to research that explains why some students remain in the lowest achieving group year after year. First, specify results of these studies and, second, explain why what is sometimes done with poor readers is not likely to improve their ability to read.

6. On the surface, helping individual students seems very praiseworthy. Nonetheless, cite the example of individual help referred to in Chapter 17 that points to the need to know *why* individual help is necessary before a meaningful judgment can be made about it.

7. This is an appropriate time to return to Figure 3.3 and to reread what is said about it. Once that is done, redraw Figure 3.3 to portray what *ought* to be characteristic of reading instruction.

REFERENCES

1. Allington, Richard L. "If They Don't Read Much, How They Ever Gonna Get Good?" *Journal of Reading* 21 (October, 1977), 57–61.
2. Allington, Richard L. "The Reading Instruction Provided Readers of Differing Reading Abilities." *Elementary School Journal* 83 (May, 1983), 548–559.
3. Allington, Richard; Stuetzel, Helen; Shake, Mary; and Lamarche, Sharron. "What Is Remedial Reading? A Descriptive Study." *Reading Research and Instruction* 26 (Fall, 1986), 15–30.
4. Allington, Richard L., and Broikou, Kathleen A. "Development of Shared Knowledge: A New Role for Classroom and Specialist Teachers." *Reading Teacher* 41 (April, 1988), 806–811.
5. Borko, Hilda; Shavelson, Richard J.; and Stern, Paula. "Teachers' Decisions in the Planning of Reading Instruction." *Reading Research Quarterly* 16 (1981, No. 3), 449–466.
6. Bristow, Page S. "Are Poor Readers Passive Readers? Some Evidence, Possible Explanations, and Potential Solutions." *Reading Teacher* 39 (December, 1985), 318–325.
7. Cohen, Elizabeth G.; Intili, Jo-Ann K.; and Robbins, Susan H. "Teachers and Reading Specialist: Cooperation or Isolation?" *Reading Teacher* 32 (December, 1978), 281–287.
8. Durkin, Dolores. "What Classroom Observations Reveal about Reading Comprehension Instruction." *Reading Research Quarterly* 14 (1978–79, No. 4), 481–533.
9. Evertson, Carolyn M., and Anderson, Linda M. "Beginning School." *Educational Horizons* 57 (Summer, 1979), 164–168.
10. Fuchs, Lynn S.; Fuchs, Douglas; and Deno, Stanley L. "Reliability and Validity of Curriculum-Based Informal Reading Inventories." *Reading Research Quarterly* 18 (1982, No. 1), 6–25.
11. Haller, Emil J., and Waterman, Margaret. "The Criteria of Reading Group Assignments." *Reading Teacher* 38 (April, 1985), 772–781.
12. Harris, Larry A., and Lalik, Rosary M. "Teachers' Use of Informal Reading In-

ventories: An Example of School Constraints." *Reading Teacher* 40 (March, 1987), 624–630.

13. Henk, William A. "Reading Assessments of the Future: Toward Precision Diagnosis." *Reading Teacher* 40 (May, 1987), 860–870.

14. Higgins, Helen B. *Noah Webster, Boy of Words.* Indianapolis, Ind.: Bobbs-Merrill, 1961.

15. Johnston, Peter H. "Understanding Reading Disability: A Case Study Approach." *Harvard Educational Review* 55 (May, 1985), 153–177.

16. Mayher, John S., and Brause, Rita S. "Learning through Teaching: Is Your Classroom Like Your Grandmother's?" *Language Arts* 63 (October, 1986), 617–620.

17. Shannon, Patrick. "Reading Instruction and Social Class." *Language Arts* 62 (October, 1985), 604–613.

18. Slavin, Robert E. "Cooperative Learning: Where Behavioral and Humanistic Approaches to Classroom Motivation Meet." *Elementary School Journal* 88 (September, 1987).

19. Stanovich, Keith E. "Mathew Effects in Reading: Some Consequences of Individual Differences in the Acquisition of Literacy." *Reading Research Quarterly* 21 (Fall, 1986), 360–406.

20. Talmage, Harriet; Pascarella, Ernest T.; and Ford, Sue. "The Influence of Cooperative Learning Strategies on Teacher Practices, Student Perceptions of the Learning Environment, and Academic Achievement." *American Educational Research Journal* 21 (Spring, 1984), 163–179.

21. Wallen, Carl J. *Competency in Teaching Reading.* Chicago: Science Research Associates, 1972.

Index